Cam
Cara

Great Britain & Ireland 1998

Top: Conwy Touring Park,
Conwy

Right: Morriscastle Strand Caravan
Park, Kilmuckridge

Below: Stanmore Hall Touring Park,
Bridgnorth

© West One (Trade) Publishing Ltd. 1997

The establishments in this guide have been selected from our Camping & Caravanning Site database and are included on the basis of a 'paid-for' listing; and have not been inspected.

ISBN 1-900327-16-3 paperback

A CIP catalogue record for this book is available from the British Library.

Cartography: The Map Room, London

Printed and bound in China

Published by West One (Trade) Publishing Ltd, Portland House, 4 Great Portland Street, London, W1N 5AA. Tel: 0171 580 6886

Publisher	Alan Wakeford
Managing Editor	Stan Dover
Production Manager	Ted Timberlake
Production Team	Tim Price
	John Jones
	Peter Drew
	Matthias Thaler
	Elaine Pate
	Tim Wheatley
	Louise Coleman
Advertising Sales Director	Marcia Smythe
Sales Executives	Yeside Akiwowo
	Virginie Bellivier
	David Kemp
	Robert Case
Finance Director	Kevin Fitzgerald
Finance and Administration Team	
	Sarah Browne
	Freddie Brexendorff
	Katya Skaff
	Eddie Malone
	Margarita Guerra
Chief Executive Officer	Martin Coleman
P.A. to C.E.O.	Jan Gale

Contents

Directory of Sites

How to use the guide

A typical entry from the guide.

COCKERMOUTH Cumbria   **10A1**

Wyndham Hall Caravan Park
Old Keswick Road, Cockermouth CA13 9SF
📞 **01900-822571**
Open 1 March-15 November 🚐 🚍

A family site. Short walk into the market town (Cockermouth), and quarter of an hour drive to Keswick.

Size 12½ acres, 42 touring pitches, 24 with electric hookup, 42 level pitches, 105 static caravans, 9 🚿, 21 WCs, 2 CWPs

🧺 ✕ ♿ 📞 🎏 GR 🔲 ⚠ 🎏 🔌 Calor Gaz WS
➡ Off the A66 on the Old Keswick Road.

This book is divided into clear sections: useful information, directory of sites and maps. The 19-page map section at the back of the book plots the locations of sites. The front section of the guide provides essential information for campers, including guidelines for towing a caravan, and security tips, in addition to an explanation of how to use the directory. For easy reference, the guide is arranged in alphabetical order by town.

Choosing your site
The type of site you choose to visit will depend on the holiday you have in mind. For those who want peace and quiet, to get away from the crowds and noise of everyday life, there are sites with only the most basic facilities, where a friendly nod to a fellow camper may be all the human contact you have. Others may prefer somewhere more lively, with every modern facility, play areas for children, and evening entertainment laid on. We hope we have provided all the information you need to choose your site, but if you are unsure about anything at all, check with the site before you book.

Size
The total area of the site is given in acres; not all this area may be used for touring pitches. We give the number of pitches for touring visitors in caravans, motor caravans and tents, and how many of these pitches are level, and how many have electric hook-ups. We also give the number of static caravans on the site.

Please note that these are not necessarily for hire. Where caravans and chalets are available for hire, it is shown under rental. We next list the number of hot showers, WCs and chemical waste disposal points (CWPs) on the site.

Disabled facilities
Sites shown with this symbol have some facilities for the disabled, but it is essential to ask the site in advance whether they cater for your personal requirements.

Dogs
Most sites accept dogs, but owners are expected to keep their pets under control (often on a lead while on the site) and to exercise them with consideration for other campers. Some sites will permit only one dog per camping unit, while others will not accommodate certain breeds – it is advisable to check when booking.

Prices
The prices are those quoted to us by the site management and show the price for two people plus car/caravan, car tent or motorhome. It is always advisable to confirm charges before your arrival at a site.

Prices quoted for Camping & Caravanning Club Sites are for non-members only. Members will pay a different rate.

Booking
As a general rule, it is necessary to book at peak periods for all sites. Out of high season, it is advisable to book if you want to stay at one specific site, or in an area with few sites. Even in low season, it is sensible to telephone ahead to check on the space available and to time your arrival so that if a site is full you have time to find space on another site.

Symbols & abbreviations

⊟	Licensed bar
⊡	Cold storage
⊡	Launderette
☎	Telephone on site or within ¼ mile
🐕	Dogs allowed
♿	Suitable for disabled
✗	Restaurant on site
✗¼	Restaurant within ¼ mile
⚏	Shop on site
⚏¼	Shop within ¼ mile
☕	Snacks on site
☕¼	Snacks within ¼ mile
🚐	Motorhome
🚍	Caravan
⚑	Tent
ℂℂ	Credit cards
🎠	Childrens playground
🏊	Indoor swimming pool
🏊	Outdoor swimming pool
▣	Table tennis
▣	Snooker/billiards
▣	Horse riding
▣	Gym
▣	Fishing
▶	Golf
▣	Sauna
⚲	Tennis
▣	Squash
TV	TV room
GR	Games room

Complaints

Should you have any cause for complaint at any site featured in this guide, speak to the site owners as soon as the problem arises. This gives them a opportunity to put it right and you the chance to enjoy your stay.

Credit cards

Where a site accepts credit cards, the cards accepted are shown after the price information.

Description and directions

The short description of the site gives an idea of what sort of site it is, what amenities it has and what the surroundings are like. The directions should enable you to locate the site from the nearest main road.

Caravan storage

'WS' shows a site which has winter storage for caravans. Please contact the site direct (not the RAC) if you wish to store a caravan.

Caravan Security

Good security is absolutely essential if you want to protect your caravan from theft. Much of the advice given below applies to trailer tents and motor caravans as well as to caravans. It will show you:

♦ how to deter theft by using security devices and by taking sensible precautions
♦ how to make it less likely that your caravan will be broken into and
♦ what you can do to get your caravan back if it's been stolen.

Finally, do remember that caravan theft is relatively rare. By taking sensible precautions you can make sure that it doesn't happen to you.

SECURITY DEVICES

Some of the many security devices you can buy are better than others. None will prevent the your caravan from being stolen but all will make it less likely. Devices vary in quality so you should buy the best you can afford. Make sure the thief knows it's there so use bright paint on wheel clamps and display the security stickers that manufacturers usually supply with their equipment.

Don't assume that your caravan is safe if it's parked on your driveway or in your garden. After storage compounds, private driveways are the most popular target area for theft.

Security systems

A reliable alarm, properly fitted, can deter thieves but don't forget that an alarm that goes off when there is no security risk can make you the most unpopular person in the road or on the campsite and may deter neighbours from raising the alarm if there is a real emergency.

If you keep your van at home, you may want to consider linking it into your home security system, if you have one. Talk to your security consultants ... it may be a simple task.

Hitch locks

Hitch locks provide a reasonable degree of protection. A good lock is necessary so buy the best you can afford (preferably in heavy gauge steel) and ensure it covers the tow socket fixing bolts. Some hitch locks will lock

CARAVAN WATCH

Early in 1995 Essex Police launched a crime prevention initiative called Caravan Watch with a view to raising public awareness of caravan theft in the Essex area. The aim of the scheme is to encourage owners to make their caravans as secure as possible, more identifiable and therefore less attractive to a thief.

The scheme has generated wide interest already and has spread to other areas of the country such as Lincolnshire, Yorkshire, Cheshire, and Sussex. You can register all the details of your caravan with the scheme. The more details a caravanner can supply, the better the chance of recovering a stolen vehicle. If you change your vehicle the Essex police will supply a new sticker for free.

A sticker displayed on the caravan identifies the make and registration number of the usual towing vehicle. With the sticker displayed, a thief risks either a caravan with an unmatched tow vehicle, or breaking into the caravan to try and remove the sticker.

For more information on Essex Police Caravan Watch Scheme, please contact Wickford police station tel: 01268 561312.

the caravan to the car so you need to ensure it is unlocked before you commence towing. Hitch locks are useful on site or for short stays but do not generally offer adequate security when the caravan is in storage.

Wheel clamps

As a rule, the easier a wheel clamp is to put on, the easier it will be for the thief to remove it. Remember that some wheel clamps can be bypassed if they allow the thief to remove the entire wheel. Buy a good one and check that it fits your caravan before you do.

Wheel stands

Putting your caravan on wheel stands can be a useful deterrent but removing the wheels won't stop the tenacious thief. You should

check with your insurer before fitting wheel stands as some policies require that wheel clamps are fitted at all times. Check your handbook too: some manufacturers recommend wheel stands for winter storage.

Security posts

Security posts cemented into a drive or hard surface will physically prevent your van from being moved off site. Lockable, some are detachable or fold down to allow access. Others have a towball fitted to the top of the post so that your caravan can be fitted to it with a hitch lock.

SECURITY PRECAUTIONS

If you follow the advice below in addition to using security devices, it is even less likely that your caravan will be stolen and more likely that it will be recovered if it is. Act now.

Records

Take photographs of your caravan showing distinctive features, including scratches and dents, if any. Keep a note of your chassis number. If your van has been CRIS registered, do not keep those documents, or any others that the thief may find useful, in it.

CRIS

Under the Caravan Registration and Identification Scheme, almost all caravans (there are some exceptions) should since 1992 have a 17 digit number stamped into their A frame and etched into at least three windows. The owner is issued with a registration document like a car log book. If you are buying a CRIS registered van, you can phone CRIS with the 17 digit number and the name and address of the owner and they will be able to tell you if it has been lost or stolen or if there is outstanding finance on it. Ring 01722 411430 between 8.00 am and 8.00 pm Monday to Saturday and from 10.00 am to 5.00 pm on Sunday.

Vehicle Watch

Vehicle Watch is a scheme designed to significantly increase the chances of a stolen vehicle being spotted by the police. Register and you will be issued with a sticker. The police regularly stop vans displaying this sticker, particularly between midnight and 5.00 am when there is a greater chance of the van being a stolen vehicle. So if you belong to the scheme, it's a good idea to carry proof of ownership with you in case you are stopped.

Etching

Etch your caravan chassis number or postcode on all windows and mark them in hidden places inside the van, such as inside a cupboard or under a bed. Ultra violet pens are useful for this as the results are very difficult to detect in non-UV light. A simple spirit-based felt-tip pen used on raw plywood is almost impossible to remove.

Roof marking

Many police forces recommend marking the roof of your van with (for example) a number of your choice in large stick-on letters which can be recognised by a police helicopter. You can do it yourself or use a commercially available kit.

Microchip

Several companies will embed into your caravan structure a microchip that can be detected by a scanner. Be warned that there is as yet no central network of scanners for tracing stolen vans. From 1998 all new caravans will have a microchip inserted into their structure at the time of manufacture. This chip will carry the 17 digit number referred to under CRIS above.

Tracker

Under this scheme, Tracker will fit a hidden transmitter into your van. If your caravan is reported stolen, the transmitter may be activated to emit a signal which can be picked up by a homing device, allowing the police to locate it. Tracker has scored some notable successes but be aware that it is a battery operated system that's only activated when your van is reported stolen. This can be a problem if your van is in long-term storage and is checked only occasionally.

Storage

If you can't store your van at home, local planning officers may supply details of landowners who have areas where planning permission for caravan storage has been granted. Don't choose a storage area on price alone. Storage areas are particularly popular with thieves: there's plenty of choice and sometimes little chance of being disturbed. Some are high security sites with security guards, floodlighting and sophisticated security systems. Others are not. If you take seat cushions home when your van is in winter storage, you will make it a less attractive prospect for the casual thief.

Similarly, removing all personal items and leaving the curtains open and cupboard doors open will encourage the opportunist thief to look elsewhere.

Holidays

Don't relax your guard when you're on holiday. Remember: thieves will steal caravans from picnic sites, motorway service areas and laybys and at times of the year when both demand and supply may be high.

Buying a caravan

Don't buy caravans in the dark, in pub car parks or motorway service areas. Always try to visit a seller's home. Make sure it is the seller's home. Unscrupulous sellers have been known to use the drive of an empty house.

Check that the number plate is the same on the van as on the tow car. Temporary and handwritten number plates should be regarded with suspicion.

If you contact a seller and are asked to ring only at certain times, make sure you aren't ringing a public phone box ... a sure sign that something is adrift. Ring 100 and ask the operator to check the status of a line.

Check the caravan chassis number. Has it been removed or altered? If so, contact the police.

Both the major caravan organisations keep lists of members. Check with them to see if the van you are interested in has been listed as stolen. Camping and Caravanning Club 01203 694995, Caravan Club 01342 327433.

Selling a caravan

Never part with your caravan until the buyer's cheque has been cleared. This includes building society cheques and bankers drafts. They could be forgeries or stolen.

Crime prevention

If you have any information about caravan theft or disposal of stolen caravans, use the confidential free phone Crime Stopper line 0800 555111. You don't have to give your name if you don't want to and you may be entitled to a reward.

This section has been written with the kind assistance of the Camping and Caravanning Club.

HINTS & TIPS

Don't neglect the servicing of your caravan. An on-the-spot police caravan check at the M5 service area in Exeter, reported in *Practical Caravan*, revealed more faults than expected. Out of 118 caravans inspected, only 33 were in a satisfactory condition, so make sure your caravan is in good repair and working order before setting out on a journey. The survey revealed that:

◆ 32 tyres in the spot check were perished while two caravans had already.

◆ The brakes of many of the caravans had been neglected.

◆ 15 caravans had defective lighting.

◆ 37 vans had too much downward pressure exerted on the towbar - in some cases by more than 100 per cent above the factory recommendations - and most vans had at least 80 kg on the hitch.

◆ You should also make sure the van has registration plates on the back, and that the jockey wheel braces are not worn.

FROM ONLY £6.50 PER PITCH PER NIGHT

SO MANY EXTRAS FOR NOTHING EXTRA? IT MUST BE HAVEN.

With 27 scenic locations for 1998 in England and Wales, no one but Haven offers you so much for so little.

FREE family daytime activities. **FREE** Fun Pools. **FREE** Tiger Club for 5-11 year olds and **FREE** sparkling evening entertainment.

Many special offers, including 2 free nights.

Plus excellent touring facilities, including showers, washing-up sinks, shaver and hairdryer points, disposal points and electrical hook-ups.

That's why, for great value, great fun Tenting and Touring holidays, it must be Haven.

Caravan Safety

Safety on the road is vital so you should ensure that your caravan or trailer is serviced and maintained by a skilled professional at regular intervals. You will also need to make sure that you carry out key checks before every trip. Some of these checks are simple and you may feel you can carry them out yourself, many are best left to the professionals. Caravan accidents are extremely rare and their number has decreased in recent years but make sure you take all necessary precautions before you set out. Above all, drive safely.

Tow bar

A well-fitted and maintained tow bar is vital for safety as it is the means by which car and trailer are connected. Make sure all bolts are tightened to the recommended torque figure and that there is no cracking or rusting around the mounting points.

Tyres

Your tyres are all that's between you and the road, so look after them: proper maintenance will improve performance and road safety. Never mix radial and cross-ply tyres. Before every trip, check the pressure and condition of your tyres and make sure that your caravan wheel nuts are tight and that wheel trims are securely attached. Always carry a spare wheel.

Brakes

Good brakes can save lives so brake maintenance is best left to qualified professionals. But do keep an eye on brake cables and mechanisms: get them checked if you have any doubts. Always connect the breakaway cable or secondary coupling to a separate mounting point and not to the tow ball. Its purpose is not to keep caravan and car together in the event of a tow bar failure.

Electrics

Road lights on your caravan or trailer are operated from the tow vehicle through a 12N socket and plug. Check indicators and lights are in working order before setting off. A visual or audible device must be fitted inside the car to show that the traffic indicators are working.

Suspension

Check the condition of both car and trailer suspension regularly. It's important for safety as well as comfort. When your caravan is attached to its vehicle, it should tow level or slightly nose down, never nose up. If you find that the rear of your car sags, you may need to review your suspension arrangements. Get advice from your dealer or a specialist.

Mirrors

An adequate rear view mirror that gives a good view of the road, both behind and along both sides of your caravan, is essential. Generally, this means that you will need special towing mirrors as well as making sure those you already have are properly adjusted.

Coupling

Before every journey, make sure that the jockey wheel and all steadies are raised and secured and that the coupling head on the trailer is fully engaged with the tow bar of the towing vehicle.

Trailer weight

Responsible bodies recommend that the loaded weight of your caravan should not exceed 85% of the kerb weight of your car. Experienced towers may sometimes exceed this recommended limit but the loaded weight of your trailer should never exceed the kerb weight of the towing vehicle, or the car manufacturer's towing limit.

Nose weight

This is the weight you put on the tow ball of your vehicle and is typically between 50 kg and 100 kg. For best stability, the nose weight should not exceed 7% of the actual laden weight of the caravan. Adjust the loading around the caravan's axle as necessary to ensure that your trailer's nose weight does not exceed this limit.

Payload

Also known as the gross weight, this is the weight of the items that you are allowed to carry in your van for personal use. You will find this figure in the manufacturer's handbook. Check before every trip to make sure you don't exceed the total weight allowed. It is important when loading your van to keep weight low down and over its axle.

Corners

Remember when negotiating roundabouts and corners that your van will not follow exactly the same path as its towing vehicle. To avoid hitting the kerb, you will need to take a wider path so that the rear of your trailer clears the kerb line. Remember too, that when turning right at junctions, you will have to turn later and then more sharply than if you were driving solo.

Reversing round corners can be difficult and needs practice. Always use a helper to keep an eye on the back of the van if you can. Unhitching and manhandling the van may sometimes be necessary.

Hill starts

With a trailer in tow, you need more throttle to get you going on a hill start. Delicate clutch avoids stalling.

Speed and overtaking

Watch your speed. Exceeding legal speed limits for caravans is dangerous and may cause you to lose control. Remember that your van/car combination is heavier and wider than a solo vehicle and you will therefore need to allow yourself plenty of time and space for overtaking.
If traffic builds up behind you, pull over at a convenient spot to allow other vehicles to pass.

Braking

When towing, it will take you an average of 20% more distance to stop. ABS systems may improve braking performance but they are no substitute for proper anticipation, so remember to leave more space between you and the car in front and to allow plenty of time for braking.

Instability

Lateral instability (snaking) is the most common form and is usually the result of bad loading, excessive speed, or both. But it can be caused by air displaced as heavy vehicles pass you. Vertical instability (pitching) can occur if you hit a pothole. In neither case should you apply your brakes hard as you may make matters worse. Instead, slow down gradually by easing off the accelerator. A stabiliser will help but proper weight distribution and a good car/van match is essential.

Tiredness

Tiredness can kill, so if you're planning a long journey make sure you allow enough time for breaks.

This section has been written with the kind assistance of the Camping and Caravanning Club.

Caravans, trailers and the Law

This is a brief summary of some of the more important things you should know.

- Caravans and their towing vehicles should be in such a condition that they cause no danger to other road users.

- You are allowed to drive up to 60 mph on motorways and dual carriageways. On all other roads, the speed limit is 50 mph unless lower limits are in force.

- Normally, cars can tow a trailer up to a maximum of 7 metres long, excluding the A frame. Trailers should usually be no more than 2.3 metres wide.

- No special driving licence is needed to tow a caravan. If they have passed their car test after 1st January 1997, some new drivers may need to take an additional test if they want to tow a very large caravan.

- Your trailer must carry a number plate displaying the number of the tow vehicle and red reflecting triangles.

- Passengers are not allowed to travel in any trailer while it is being towed.

- You must have a full driving licence before you attempt to tow.

- Towing vehicles must not use the outside lane of a three (or more) lane motorway, even when overtaking.

- Trailer tyres must be capable of carrying the gross load of the trailer and have a tread depth of no less than 1.6 mm across the central three-quarters of the breadth of the tyre and around the entire circumference.

- Trailer caravan outfits must not park at parking meters.

- Stopping in a lay-by is considered an obstruction. You may be moved on.

- If you park your caravan in the street overnight you must display lights all round.

- Make sure your motor insurance policy covers you for towing.

The Caravan Towing Code

Reproduced by kind permission of the National Caravan Council.

Reproduced by kind permission of the National Caravan Council.

SCOPE OF THE CODE

The Code applies to all trailer caravans of maximum laden weight not exceeding 2,030kg (4,475 lbs), overall width not exceeding 2.3m (approx 7'6") and overall length not exceeding 7m (approx 23'), excluding the drawbar and coupling. This is legally the maximum size of trailer that can be towed by a motor car.

Objectives
✔ To provide simple, easily understood advice on the safe matching of towing vehicles to caravans;

✔ To make recommendations on the selection of the ratio of caravan weight to towing vehicle weight so that safe towing may be achieved under the varying conditions which may be met on the road;

✔ To give advice on the engine size and power required for satisfactory towing both for the ability to restart on a gradient and to maintain a reasonable speed relative to the traffic flow on various types of road;

✔ To set out the factors the caravan user needs to take into account before towing a caravan.

DEFINITIONS OF TERMS USED

The caravan
EX WORKS WEIGHT
The maximum weight of the caravan as stated by the caravan manufacturer, as new with standard fixtures and fittings. (Note: because of the differences in the weight of materials supplied for the construction of caravans, variations of + or -5% of the manufacturer's stated ex works weight can be expected.)

ACTUAL LADEN WEIGHT
The total weight of the caravan and its contents when being towed.

MAXIMUM LADEN WEIGHT
The maximum weight for which the caravan is designed for normal use when being towed on a road, laden.

NOSEWEIGHT
That part of the weight of the caravan supported by the rear of the towing vehicle.

The towing vehicle
KERB WEIGHT
The weight of the towing vehicle as defined by the vehicle manufacturer.
This is normally:

✔ with a full tank of fuel;

✔ with an adequate supply of other liquids incidental to the vehicle's propulsion;

✔ without driver or passengers;

✔ without any load except loose tools and equipment with which the vehicle is normally provided;

✔ without any towing bracket.

The Caravan/Towing Vehicle Combination
CARAVAN/TOWING VEHICLE WEIGHT RATIO
The actual laden weight of the caravan expressed as a percentage of the kerb weight of the towing vehicle, ie:

$$\frac{\textit{actual laden weight of caravan}}{\textit{kerb weight of towing vehicle}} \times 100 = \_\_\%$$

How to estimate the actual laden weight:
The basic items required for two people to go caravanning will weigh a minimum of 100kg in total. These will include food, crockery, cutlery, cooking utensils, clothing, bedding, gas bottles and water carrier. The weight of any additional items required (eg battery, awning, portable toilet, spare wheel, TV, etc) must be added to the basic total.

A further 25kg for each additional person should be allowed for basic items.
   Having established the total weight of items to be carried by the caravan this must be added to the ex works weight to obtain the estimated actual laden weight.
   If in doubt this can be done on a public weighbridge.
   The address of the nearest public weigh bridge in a locality may be obtained from the area Trading Standards Department (Weights and Measures).
   The Department's telephone number will be found under: County Council; Metropolitan Council, London Borough Council or Regional Council (for Scotland). Please note weighbridges have varying weight tolerance levels.

FACTORS WHICH MUST BE CONSIDERED FOR SAFE TOWING

Driver's towing experience

Experience of towing is not essential for taking up caravanning but drivers without experience should take greater care when manoeuvring. Speed should be built up gradually in order to get used to the handling and braking characteristics.

For those who would like training, there are courses available and details may be obtained from the specialist clubs. Further experience should be gained before tackling the more difficult elements of towing (higher weight ratios, mountain passes, difficult terrain, etc).

Caravan/towing vehicle weight ratio

This ratio has a major influence on stability. It is recommended that:

a) the actual laden weight of the caravan should always be kept as low as possible. The lower it is when the caravan is being towed on a road, the safer the caravan/towing vehicle combination will be.

b) as a general rule, the actual laden weight of a caravan should not exceed the kerb weight of the towing vehicle, particularly if the latter is a conventional car (saloon, coupé, hatchback, estate, convertible, etc).

c) the greater the actual laden weight of the caravan is in relation to the kerb weight of the towing vehicle, the more careful and experienced the driver needs to be.

d) care must always be taken not to exceed the towing vehicle's loading and towing limits.

The law requires that caravans and their towing vehicle and the loads that they carry must all be in such a condition that no danger or nuisance of any kind is caused.

Power-to-weight ratio of towing vehicle to caravan

The performace of the towing vehicle has an important bearing on its suitability for towing and, therefore, on the selection of the caravan to match the towing vehicle. There are many factors involved, which are often contradictory, such as brake horsepower, gearing, torque characteristics, turbo-charging and fuel injection.

No hard and fast rules can be stated but, as a general guide, conventional petrol engines with a capacity up to approximately 1500cc should be adequate for towing a caravan weighing around 85% of the kerb weight of the towing vehicle. Above 1500cc such engines should manage a caravan weighing up to 100% of the kerb weight of the towing vehicle and still give adequate performace but it should be noted that the towing vehicle manfacturer's limit is, in some cases, less than the kerb weight.

While the towing vehicle may manage 100%, attention is again drawn to the recommendation under the previous heading. 'Caravan/towing vehicle weight ratio', that a weight ratio of 85% is an ideal starting point.

Diesel engines of whatever size have a lower performance for a given cubic capacity compared to petrol engines.

When climbing, a 10% loss of power with a petrol engine and slightly less with a diesel engine should be expected for every 1,000 metres gain in height. A good reserve of power is, therefore, very necessary for towing up gradients at altitude. Vehicles with automatic transmission may need additional cooling for the gearbox when towing. The advice of the manufacturer should be sought.

WHEELS

Caravan wheelnuts should be tightened to the setting stated by the caravan manufacturer (user instructions) and should be checked with the use of a torque wrench regularly. If a spare wheel and tyre is carried it must be suitable for use on that caravan.

Types of tyre fitted

The tyres specified by the caravan manufacturer should be satisfactory for towing in the United Kingdom of speeds up to 62mph (100kph) at the maximum laden weight of the caravan. In certain countries overseas, it is legal to tow at higher speeds. If it is intended to visit such countries and tow up to the higher speed limits then it is important that the suitability of the tyres is first checked with a caravan dealer.

Tyre pressures

Caravan and towing vehicle tyres must be at the pressures recommended for towing or heavy loading. Towing stability may otherwise be affected. The pressures should be given in the towing vehicle and caravan handbooks.

DISTRIBUTION OF WEIGHT IN THE CARAVAN AND CAR

Equipment and effects should be loaded in the caravan so that any heavy items are low down near the floor and mainly over or in from the axle(s). The remainder should be distributed to give a suitable noseweight at the towing coupling.

Incorrect caravan loading will result in poor towing stability. Overloading of the towing vehicle's rear suspension will also result in poor towing stability.

The weight should be distributed so that each caravan wheel carries approximately the same load.

Noseweight

It is recommended that the noseweight should be varied to find the optimum for towing, dependent upon the actual laden weight of the caravan. Experience has shown that the noseweight should be approximately 7% of the actual laden weight (i.e. between 50 and 90kg).

Measurement of Noseweight

The noseweight may be measured using a proprietary brand of noseweight indicator. Such equipment is obtainable from caravan dealers.

Another simple method is to use bathroom scales under the coupling head with a piece of wood fitted between the coupling head and the scales, of such length that the caravan floor is horizontal with the jockey wheel raised.

STABILISERS

A stabiliser should never be used to try to improve a caravan/towing vehicle combination which has poor stability, because instability will reappear at a higher speed. However, a good stabiliser can make an acceptable caravan/towing vehicle combination more stable and safer to handle.

TOWING VEHICLE'S REAR SUSPENSION

It is important that the towing vehicle's rear suspension is not deflected excessively by the noseweight on the tow ball. If it is, the steering and stability will be affected. The greater the towing vehicle's rail overhang (the distance between rear axle and towing ball) the greater the effect the noseweight will have on the towing vehicle's suspension.

After trying out the caravan it may be found that stiffening of the rear suspension is necessary, but note that this may give the towing vehicle a firmer ride when not towing.

There are a number of suspension aids available and advice should be sought on which to use and how to fit them. It is important to ensure that the caravan is towed either level or slightly nose down.

Servicing

A caravan is a road vehicle and, therefore, requires regular servicing, with particular attention to the braking system, wheels and tyres, and road lighting. These items are fully covered in the standard servicing schedule of the Caravan Service Centre Scheme run by the NCC. There are over 150 RAC inspected workshops in the Scheme, which is operated in conjunction with both RAC and the Caravan Club.

MIRRORS

The driver of the towing vehicle must have an adequate view to the rear. If there is no rear view through the caravan windows it is essential that additional exterior towing mirrors are fitted to provide a view along both sides of the caravan.

Any rear view mirror must not project more than 200mm beyond:
a) the width of the caravan when being towed.
b) the width of the towing vehicle when driven solo.
Note: Any rear view mirror fitted shall be 'e' marked and cover the field of view as stipulated by type approval requirements.

ROADLIGHTING

Make sure:
a) all cable connections are of correct length to avoid disconnection or trailing of the cable on the ground.
b) all road lights and indicators are working correctly before setting off.

Conventional connection of 12N and 12S seven pin sockets

Power for the caravan's roadlights and electrical equipment is transferred from the towcar by means of a pair of seven pin plugs (on the caravan) and sockets (on the car). Though these look similar at first glance they are not interchangeable because they have different arrangements of pins and contact tubes.

The roadlight plug/socket is known as type 12N (normal) and is usually coloured black. The second plug/socket is known as 12S (supplementary) and is conventionally coloured grey.

An arrangement whereby the car's rear foglights are extinguished when the caravan roadlights are connected (to prevent glare from light reflected off the caravan's front wall) is permissable. All other lights on the rear of the car must work when the caravan is being towed

Connections for the caravan battery charging and refrigerator circuits should be controlled by relays. These ensure that the caravan battery is never recharged at the expense of the car battery; and that power is transmitted to the fridge only when the car engine is running to avoid the risk of flattening the car battery.

BRAKES

For caravans exceeding a maximum weight of 1500kg the braking device must be such that the caravan is stopped automatically if the coupling breaks.

For caravans below 1500kg a breakaway cable is required. If there is not an automatic stopping device always ensure that the breakaway cable, when fitted, is secured to the towing vehicle.

VEHICLE CARAVAN CONNECTION

Always ensure that the towing hitch is correctly locked to the ball prior to setting off.

SPEED LIMITS AND MOTORWAY DRIVING

Reduce speed
a) in high or cross winds
b) downhill
c) in poor visibility

HIGH SIDED VEHICLES

Extra care should be taken when passing or being passed by high sided vehicles. As much space as possible should be given between vehicles to avoid air buffeting.

Remember, courtesy and safety.

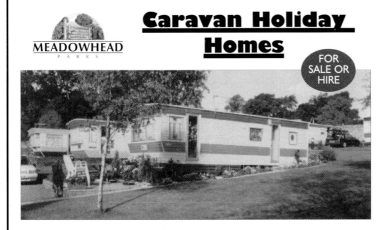

Useful Addresses

British Holiday & Home Parks Association
Chichester House, 6 Pullman Court, Great
Western Road, Gloucester GL1 3ND
Tel: 01452 526911/411574

The Camping and Caravanning Club
Greenfields House, Westwood Way, Coventry,
West Midlands CV4 8JH
Tel: 01203 694995

The Caravan Club
East Grinstead House, East Grinstead,
West Sussex RH19 1UA
Tel: 01342 326944

The Motor Caravanners' Club
22 Evelyn Close, Twickenham, Middlesex
TW2 7BN   Tel: 0181 893 3883

National Caravan Council Limited
Catherine House, Victoria Road, Aldershot,
Hampshire GU11 1SS   Tel: 01252 318251
(comprehensive list of members includes
manufacturers, dealers, parks and traders).

**Society of Motor Manufacturers &
Traders Ltd,**
Motor Caravan Section
Forbes House, Halkin Street, London
SW1X 7DS
Tel: 0171 235 7000
(listing of members available)

UK TOWING BRACKET SUPPLIERS
Towing brackets should be made to British
Standard BSAU 114b or the 28th July 1993
equivalent international standard ISO 3853.

Anchor Towbars Ltd
Orchard House, Appleby Hill, Austrey,
Atherstone, Warwicks CV9 3ER
Tel: 01827 830039

Bumper to Bumper Ltd
38 Melford Court, Hardwick Grange, Woolston,
Warrington, Cheshire WA1 4SD
Tel: 01925 815661

B. Dixon-Bate Ltd
Unit 45, First Avenue, Deeside Industrial Park,
Deeside, Flintshire CH5 2LG
Tel: 01244-288925

Exhaust Ejector Co
11 Wade House Road, Shelf, Halifax, West
Yorkshire HX3 7PE
Tel: 01274 679524/5/6

PCT Leisure Ltd
Holbrook Industrial Estate, New Street,
Holbrook, Sheffield S20 3GH
Tel: 0114 2510210

Peter J. Lea Co Ltd
Shaw Road South, off Shaw Heath, Stockport,
Cheshire SK3 8JG
Tel: 0161 480 2377

Tanfield Ltd
Blatchford Road, Roffey, Horsham, West Sussex
RH13 5QR
Tel: 01403 269100

Towsure Products Ltd
151-183 Holme Lane, Sheffield S6 4JR
Tel: 0114 2340542

Watling Engineers Ltd
88 Parkstreet Village, St. Albans, Hertfordshire
AL2 2LR
Tel: 01727 873661

Witter Towbars Ltd
18 Canal Side, Chester CH1 3LL
Tel: 01244 341166

BRITISH TOURIST AUTHORITY
Tourist Information Centres are located in
cities and towns throughout Great Britain with
information on places of interest for tourists.
These Information Centres are indicated by
distinctive 'i' signs placed in their vicinity. The
addresses of the National and Regional Tourist
Boards are as follows.

English Tourist Board
Head Office: Thames Tower, Black's Road,
Hammersmith, London W6 9EL
(written enquiries only)

Scottish Tourist Board
Head Office: 23 Ravelston Terrace, Edinburgh
EH4 3EU
Tel: 0131 332 2433
(written and telephone enquiries only)

Wales Tourist Board
Head Office: Brunel House, 2 Fitzalan Road,
Cardiff CF2 1UY   Tel: 01222 499909

Northern Ireland Tourist Board
Head Office: St Anne's Court, 59 North Street,
Belfast BT1 1NB
Tel: 01232 231221

LONDON OFFICE: 11 Berkeley Street, London
W1X 5AD   Tel: 0171 355 5040

Useful Addresses

Irish Tourist Board (Bord Failte)
Head Office: Baggot St. Bridge, Dublin 2
Tel (00 3531) 2844768

LONDON OFFICE: 150 New Bond Street, London
W1Y 0AQ
Tel: 0171 493 3201

Channel Islands
GUERNSEY TOURIST BOARD
PO Box 23, North Plantation, St Peter Port,
Guernsey GY1 3AN
Tel: 01481 723552

JERSEY TOURIST BOARD
Liberation Square, St Helier, Jersey
Tel: 01534 78000

NATIONAL PARKS
The most beautiful, spectacular and dramatic
expanses of country in England and Wales have
been given the status of National Parks under
the National Parks and Access to the
Countryside Act, 1949, in recognition of their
national importance. ten *National Parks* were
established during the 1950s: *Brecon Beacons,
Exmoor, Dartmoor, Lake District,
Northumberland, North York Moors, Peak
District, Pembrokeshire Coast, Snowdonia and
the Yorkshire Dales.* In addition, the Norfolk and
Suffolk Broads *The Broads,* were established in
1989, although not a National Park by name, it
has equal status to the Parks. *The New Forest* is
also considered by many to be of comparable
quality to a National Park and legislation that
will provide it with similar protection is currently
being drafted.

The essence of each of these areas is in the
striking quality and remoteness of much of their
scenery, the harmony between activity and
nature that they display and the opportunities
they offer for suitable forms of recreation.
National Parks are 'national' in the vital sense
that they are of special value to the whole
nation. But designation of an area as a National
Park does not affect the ownership of the land.
It does not remove from local communities the
right to live their own lives, nor does it give the
public any right of access.

The 1949 Act also created *Areas of
Outstanding Natural Beauty.* The landscape in
these areas is no less beautiful but the
opportunities for extensive outdoor recreation
are lacking. The following 39 Areas of
Outstanding Natural Beauty have been
designated:
*Anglesey; Arnside and Silverdale; Blackdown
Hills; Cannock Chase; Chichester Harbour;
Chilterns; Clwydian Range; Cornwall; Cotswolds;*
*Cranborne Chase & West Wiltshire Downs;
Dedham Vale; Dorset; East Devon; East
Hampshire; Forest of Bowland; Gower Peninsula;
High Weald; Howardian Hills; Isles of Scilly; Isle
of Wight; Kent Downs; Lincolnshire Wolds; Lleyn;
Malvern Hills; Mendip Hills; Norfolk Coast; North
Devon; North Pennines; Northumberland Coast;
North Wessex Downs; Quantock Hills; Shropshire
Hills; South Devon; South Hampshire Coast;
Suffolk Coast and Heaths; Surrey Hills; Sussex
Hills; Sussex Downs; Solway Coast, Wye Valley.*

Although there are no National Parks or
Areas of outstanding Natural Beauty in Scotland,
there are 40 National Scenic Areas (NSAs),
designated in 1980 under the 1972 Town and
Country Planning (Scotland) Act, which are
given a measure of protection through special
development control procedures. Protection of
the NSAs is the duty of Scottish Natural Heritage
(formed from the merger of the Countryside
Commission for Scotland and the Nature
Conservancy Council for Scotland in 1992).

Countryside Commission
John Dower House, Crescent Place, Cheltenham,
Gloucestershire GL50 3RA
Tel: 01242 521381

The Countryside Council for Wales
Plas Penrhos, Penrhos Road, Bangor, Gwynedd,
LL57 2LQ
Tel: 01248 370444

FOREST PARKS
The Forestry Commission
231 Corstorphine Road, Edinburgh, EH12 7AT
Tel: 0131 344 3303

The Forestry Commission is one of Britain's
largest providers of tourist and recreation
facilities, attracting over 50 million day-visitors
every year and encouraging the public to enjoy
the publicly-owned forests in its care through its
freedom to roam policy. It also provides for
many activities including walking, picnics,
mountain biking, orienteering, skiing, field
sports, water sports and nature study.

THE NATIONAL TRUST
The National Trust is an independent charity
responsible for the preservation of many historic
houses, industrial monuments, formal and
romantic gardens, nature reserves, open
countryside and hundred of miles of Britain's
coastline. Details of the various National Trust
activities can be obtained from:

The National Trust
36 Queen Anne's Gate, London SW1H 9AS
Tel: 0171 222 9251

The National Trust, North Wales Office
Trinity Square, Llandudno, Gwynedd LL30 2DE
Tel: 01492 860123

The National Trust, South Wales Office
The King's Head, Bridge Street, Llandeilo,
Carmarthenshire SA19 6BB
Tel: 01558 822800

The National Trust, Northern Ireland
Rowallane House, Saintfield, Ballynahinch, Co.
Down BT24 7LH
Tel: 01238 510721

The National Trust for Scotland
5 Charlotte Square, Edinburgh, EH2 4DU
Tel: 0131 226 5922

ENGLISH HERITAGE

Over 350 ancient monuments, buildings and
other sites are looked after by English Heritage
(formerly known as the Historic Buildings and
Monuments Commission). Further details can be
obtained from:

English Heritage
23 Savile Row, London
W1X 1AB   Tel: 0171 973 3000

General Advice

ROADSIDE CAMPING
Camping or siting a caravan on verges or laybys is not allowed. However, permission to
camp on land near by can often be obtained
from the farmer or landowner.

If an outbreak of foot and mouth or swine
vesicular disease occurs, campers must be very
careful to follow all necessary precautions.

LONDON
If you are visiting London with a caravan on tow,
try to avoid travelling across the centre of
London, particularly during the rush hours
Monday to Friday 0800-1000 and 1600-1800
hours, and if you are unfamiliar with the route.
Parking of car/caravan outfits at meter bays is
not permitted. It is best to leave a caravan at the
site and visit central London solo, or by public
transport. If it is essential to park an outfit in
London, find a suitable car park. Underground
and multi-storey carparks often have a height
limit which will not permit access for caravans or
motor caravans.

MOTORWAY SERVICE AREAS
Caravans are permitted to park at motorway
service areas for the purpose of utilizing the
facilities. Parking for the purpose of cooking
meals etc., is not usually permitted, and at some
service areas it is forbidden to lower the corner
legs of a caravan for any reason. Charges for
overnight stops are available on application to
the individual service areas.

RAC MOTORING SERVICES - USEFUL NUMBERS

Breakdown	0800 82 82 82
in the Republic of Ireland	1800 555 005
Minicom Supertel	0800 626 389
Customer Assistance	0990 722 722
Travel Information	0990 275 600
Legal Services	0990 533 533
Holiday Reservations	0161 480 4810
Hotel Reservations	0870 603 9109
Insurance Direct	0345 121 345
Publishing Services	01304 204 256
Travel Sales	0800 550 055
Technical Advice	0990 333 660
Vehicle Examinations	0990 333 660
Signs Service	0800 234 810

To join the RAC, telephone   0800 550 550

0800 numbers are free
0345 numbers are charged at the local rate
0990 numbers are charged at the national rate

Essential site seeing!

Here's your chance to focus in on some 200 of the loveliest sites in Britain. Our Club sites offer you the opportunity to enjoy the friendliest of atmospheres and to experience the very high calibre of facilities for which 'the caravanners favourite' is renowned. Many of our Club sites are open to non-members.

So why not send off for our 1998 Sites of Discovery brochure today - and see for yourselves!

THE CARAVAN CLUB

So much more to enjoy

England

*Top: Blackland Lakes Holiday
& Leisure Centre, Calne*

*Right: Southern Leisure Centre,
Chichester*

*Below: Little Switzerland Caravan
Site, Folkestone*

RaC

ABINGDON Oxfordshire   4B2

Thames Bridge House Caravan Site
Clifton, Abingdon OX14 3EH
📞 01865-407725
Open April-October ▲ ⊕ ⊞
Size 12 touring pitches, 12 with electric hookup, 6 static caravans, 3 🏠, 6 WCs, 1 CWP
£ car/tent £5-£8, car/caravan £8-£10, motorhome £8, motorbike/tent £5-£8
Rental ⊕ £95-£135
⬛¼ ✗¼ ◗¼ ⬛ ⬛ ☑ Calor Gaz ✝
Last arrival time: 9:00
➡ Off A415, signposted to site. Four miles N from Abingdon and four miles from Wallingford.

ACLE Norfolk   9F3

Reedham Ferry Camping & Caravan Park
Ferry Road, Reedham, Acle NR13 3HA
📞 01493-700429 **Fax** 01493-700999
Open March-end October ▲ ⊕ ⊞
Size 4 acres, 20 touring pitches, 20 with electric hookup, 20 level pitches, 4 🏠, 4 WCs
£ car/tent £6.50-£14, car/caravan £6.50-£14, motorhome £6.50-£14
⒞ Visa
✗ ◗ ☑ ⅙ ✝
Last arrival time: 10:00
➡ 7 miles S of Acle on B1140, situated on the N bank of River Yare.

ALNWICK Northumberland   13F3

Camping & Caravanning Club Site
Dunstan Hill, Dunstan, Alnwick NE66 3TQ
📞 01665-576310
Open end March-start November ▲ ⊕ ⊞
Size 12 acres, 150 touring pitches, 66 with electric hookup, 12 🏠, 18 WCs, 1 CWP
£ car/tent £5.60-£8.60, car/caravan £5.60-£8.60, motorhome £5.60-£8.60, motorbike/tent £5.60-£8.60, children £1.50
⒞ MasterCard Visa
⬛ ⬛ ⚲ ⅙ ✝
Last arrival time: 11:00
➡ Travelling N on A1 turn right for Seahouses on B1340. Site is ¾ mile S of Embleton, follow signs for Craster.

Don't forget to mention the guide
When booking, please remember to tell the site that you chose it from
RAC Camping & Caravanning 1998

Proctors Steads Caravan & Camping Park
Procters Steads, Craster, Alnwick NE66 3TF
📞 01665-576613
Open March-October ▲ ⊕ ⊞

A good sheltered, level site covering 3½ acres one mile from the sea, Dunstanburgh Castle and Craster. Excellent for beaches, golf courses and coastal walks.

Size 3½ acres, 70 touring pitches, 40 with electric hookup, 70 level pitches, 20 static caravans, 8 🏠, 10 WCs, 1 CWP
£ car/tent £8, car/caravan £8, motorhome £8, motorbike/tent £8, children £1
Rental ⊕ Chalet. From £150
⬛ ✗ ◗ ⬛ ⬛ ⬛ Calor Gaz ⅙ ✝ WS
Last arrival time: 10:00
➡ From A1 take B1340 for 2 miles. Follow signs.

ALWINTON Northumberland   13F3

Clennell Hall
Alwinton NE65 7BG
📞 01669-650341
Open all year ▲ ⊕ ⊞

A caravan site situated in the Border country of the Cheviot Hills and set in the grounds of Clennell Hall, a 16th century, Grade II Listed building. The caravan site provides an ideal base for many outdoor pursuits, which are available within a short distance, such as: fishing, bird watching, orienteering, mountain biking, walking, trail riding, golf and pony trekking.

Size 14½ acres, 50 touring pitches, 44 with electric hookup, 50 level pitches, 18 static caravans, 8 showers, 20 WCs, 1 CWP
£ car/tent £6-£8.50, car/caravan £8.50-£11, motorhome £8.50-£11, motorbike/tent £6
Rental £85-£225 (cabins & caravans)
GR TV Calor Gaz WS
Last arrival time: 11:00
➜ From Rothbury follow the B6341 for 4 miles, turn right signed Harbottle and Alwinton. Go through Harbottle village and follow the sign for Alwinton, continue for 2 miles and after second bridge turn right signed Clennell Hall. From Otterburn take the B6341. Turn left 5 miles beyond Elsdon and turn left again ½ mile beyond Holystone, onto road to Harbottle.

AMBLESIDE Cumbria 10B2

Camping & Caravanning Club Site
Grizedale Hall, Grizedale, Ambleside LA22 0GL
01229-860257
Open end March-end September
Size 4 acres, 60 touring pitches, 10 with electric hookup, 2 showers, 5 WCs
£ car/tent £4.60-£6.80, motorhome £4.60-£6.80, motorbike/tent £4.60-£6.80, children £1.40
CC MasterCard Visa
GR
Last arrival time: 11:00
➜ From A5092 take road signed Colton, Oxen Park for 5 miles to site on right.

ANDOVER Hampshire 4B3

Wyke Down Caravan & Camping Park
Picket Piece, Andover SP11 6LX
01264-352048 Fax 01264-324661
Open all year

A family-owned park with country pub and golf driving range. Ample space for caravans and tents. A relaxing, peaceful setting with scenic views.

Size 7 acres, 150 touring pitches, 31 with electric hookup, 150 level pitches, 4 showers, 14 WCs, 1 CWP
£ car/tent £8, car/caravan £8, motorhome £8, motorbike/tent £7, children £1
CC MasterCard Visa
GR TV Gaz
➜ Follow International Camping signs from A303, Andover Ring Road, then through village. Picket Piece signposted two miles ahead.

APPLEBY-IN-WESTMORLAND Cumbria 10B2

Wild Rose Park

Ormside, Appleby-in-Westmorland CA16 6EJ

☎ **017683-51077 Fax 017683-52551**

Open all year А 🚐 🚐

Beautifully landscaped park in quiet countryside, with superb views across the Eden Valley to the Pennines. Level or gently sloping hardstanding and grass pitches.

Size 40 acres, 240 touring pitches, 200 with electric hookup, 110 level pitches, 240 static caravans, 20 ℝ, 60 WCs, 3 CWPs

£ car/tent £7.30-£11.60, car/caravan £7.30-£11.60, motorhome £7.30-£11.60, motorbike/tent £3, children £1.50

ℂℂ MasterCard Visa

🛒 ✕ 🍴 🗑 🗎 🗠 🗟 GR 🔌 📺 ⚠   Calor Gaz ♿ 🐾 WS

Last arrival time: 10:00

➡ From B6260 take road marked to Ormside and Souloy at village of Burrells. After 1½ miles take left turn to Ormside. Take first right and right again into park.

See advert on previous page

ARUNDEL West Sussex   4C4

Camping & Caravanning Club Site

Slindon Park, Slindon, Arundel BN18 0RG

☎ **01243-814387**

Open late March-late September А 🚐 🚐

Size 2 acres, 46 touring pitches, 12 with electric hookup, 1 CWP

£ car/tent £3.20-£4.80, car/caravan £3.20-£4.80, motorhome £3.20-£4.80, motorbike/tent £3.20-£4.80, children £1

ℂℂ MasterCard Visa

🛒 🐾

Last arrival time: 11:00

➡ From A27 turn towards Eartham, then towards Slindon. Site on right.

Maynard's Caravan & Camping Park

Crossbush, Arundel BN18 9PQ

☎ **01903-882075**

Open all year А 🚐 🚐

Size 2½ acres, 70 touring pitches, 62 with electric hookup, 70 level pitches, 4 ℝ, 9 WCs, 1 CWP

£ car/tent £7.50, car/caravan £7.50, motorhome £7.50, motorbike/tent £7.50, children £0.50-£1

🛒 ✕ 🍴 🗑 🗎 🗟 ⚠   Calor Gaz ♿ 🐾 WS

➡ From Arundel ¾ miles on A27 to Worthing. Turn left into car park at Beefeater pub.

ASHBOURNE Derbyshire   8A2

Callow Top Holiday Park

Buxton Road, Ashbourne DE6 2AQ

☎ **01335-344020 Fax 01335-343726**

Open March-November А 🚐 🚐

Select holiday park situated in beautiful Derbyshire countryside. Ideal base for Alton Towers, Tissington Trail cycle path and Carsington Reservoir.

Size 9 acres, 160 touring pitches, 80 with electric hookup, 160 level pitches, 17 static caravans, 6 ℝ, 16 WCs, 1 CWP

£ car/tent £8, car/caravan £8, motorhome £8, motorbike/tent £8, children £0.75

🛒 ✕ 🍴 🗑 🗎 🗠 🗟 GR 🔌 ⚠   🍴 ♿ 🐾

Last arrival time: 10:00

➡ ½ mile from Ashbourne on the A515 Buxton Road. The entrance is opposite Sandybrook Garage. Follow the private road for ½ mile (past Haywood Farm); reception is located in the Callow Inn.

ASHBURTON Devon   3D3

Ashburton Caravan Park

Waterleat, Ashburton TQ13 7HU

☎ **01364-652552**

Open Easter-September А 🚐

Secluded, south-facing wooded river valley within Dartmoor National Park. A haven of peace, centrally located for easy access to the moors, coast or the historic cities of Exeter and Plymouth.

Size 4 acres, 35 touring pitches, 4 with electric hookup, 35 level pitches, 9 static caravans, 6 🚿, 7 WCs, 1 CWP
£ car/tent £7-£9, motorhome £7-£9, motorbike/tent £7-£9, children £1.50-£2.25
Rental 🚐 £100-£280
🔲 📞 🔲 Calor Gaz ⚙ ⛟
Last arrival time: 10:30

Parkers Farm Holiday Park
Ashburton TQ13 7LJ
📞 **01364-652598 Fax 01364-654004**
Open Easter-October ▲ 🚐 🚍

A large working farm with beautifully terraced marked pitches overlooking Dartmoor. 12 miles from Torbay. Family run, very clean and friendly. Free showers. Children's and pets paradise. 1996 prices. Also cottages and caravans.

Size 10 acres, 80 touring pitches, 80 with electric hookup, 80 level pitches, 25 static caravans, 10 🚿, 12 WCs, 3 CWPs
£ car/tent £4.50-£8.50, car/caravan £4.50-£8.50, motorhome £4.50-£8.50, motorbike/tent £4.50-£8.50, children £1
Rental 🚐 Chalet. £90-£400
℀ MasterCard Visa
⚑ ✖ 🍴 🔲 📞 🔲 🔲 🅖🆁 🔲 ⚠   ⚙ Calor Gaz ⚙ ⛟ WS
➡ Take A38 Exeter to Plymouth. When you see sign 26 miles to Plymouth, take second left at Alston Cross, marked Woodland and Denburt. 400 yards down road.

PARKERS FARM HOLIDAY PARK

Site situated on a 300 acre working farm, lots of animals. Beautifully terraced level campsite, large pitches, overlooks Dartmoor, 12 miles Torbay. Very clean, fully tiled shower block and new block for 1997 – also cottages and caravans, some new.

HIGHER MEAD FARM, ASHBURTON, NEWTON ABBOT, SOUTH DEVON TQ13 7LJ
Tel: 01364-652598 Fax: 01364-654004

River Dart Country Park
Holne Park, Ashburton TQ13 7NP
📞 **01364-652511 Fax 01364-652020**
Open 1 April-mid September ▲ 🚐 🚍

Magnificent 90 acre park once part of a Victorian country estate. The camping area is set along the fringes of woodland in gently sloping parkland. An ideal site for exploring Dartmoor and the South Devon coast.

Size 90 acres, 120 touring pitches, 80 with electric hookup, 120 level pitches, 16 🚿, 16 WCs, 1 CWP
£ car/tent £9.20-£12.20, car/caravan £9.20-£12.20, motorhome £9.20-£12.20, motorbike/tent £9.20-£12.20, children £3.75-£4.80
℀ MasterCard Visa
⚑ ✖ 🍴 🔲 📞 🔲 🔲 🔲 🔲 🔲 📺 ⚠   ⚙ Calor Gaz ⚙ ⛟
Last arrival time: 10:00
➡ M5 Motorway at Exeter, take A38 Expressway towards Plymouth. Exit at Peartree Cross junction. Follow brown signs.

ASHFORD Kent 5E3

Broad Hembury Farm Caravan & Camping

Steeds Lane, Kingsnorth, Ashford TN26 1NQ

☎ 01233-620859 Fax 01233-620859

Open all year ▲ 🚐 🏕

Surrounded by quiet Kentish countryside. Park graded 'excellent' by E.T.B, offering every modern facility. Convenient for channel crossings and hundreds of interesting places to visit.

Size 5 acres, 60 touring pitches, 48 with electric hookup, 60 level pitches, 25 static caravans, 6 🚿, 16 WCs, 1 CWP

£ car/tent £9-£12, car/caravan £9-£12, motorhome £9-£12, motorbike/tent £9-£11, children £1.50

Rental 🚐

CC MasterCard Visa

🛒 ✕¼ 🍴¼ ⊟ 🛒 🖥 GR 🔍 TV /ʌ Calor Gaz 🐕

Last arrival time: 8:00

➡ From J10 on M20 take A2070 for 2 miles, then continue on A2042 following signs for Kingsnorth. Left at second cross roads in village.

ASHINGTON Northumberland 13F3

Wansbeck Riverside Park

Green Lane, Ashington NE63 8TX

☎ 01670-812323

Open all year ▲ 🚐 🏕

Size 75 touring pitches, 25 with electric hookup, 10 level pitches, 8 🚿, 10 WCs, 1 CWP

£ car/tent £6.70-£7.75, car/caravan £7.35-£10, motorhome £7.35-£10, motorbike/tent £7.75

🛒 🍴 🚿 🛒 ⊟ 🖥 /ʌ Calor Gaz � 🐕

Last arrival time: 10:00

➡ Just off A1068 between Guideport and Ashington. Only 4 miles from Morpeth and A1.

AXMINSTER Devon 3E3

Andrewshayes Caravan Park

Dalwood, Axminster EX13 7DY

☎ 01404-831225 Fax 01404-831225

Open 1 March-31 January ▲ 🚐 🏕

A family park overlooking the Axe Valley. Luxury 'Rose Award' caravans set amongst maturing trees. Excellent facilities for touring/camping. Heated outdoor pool.

Size 12 acres, 90 touring pitches, 80 with electric hookup, 40 level pitches, 80 static caravans, 12 🚿, 18 WCs, 2 CWPs

£ car/tent £8, car/caravan £8-£9.50, motorhome £8-£9.50, motorbike/tent £5, children £1

Rental 🚐 £85-£360

CC MasterCard Visa

🛒 ✕ ✕¼ 🍴 🍴¼ ⊟ 🛒 🖥 GR /ʌ Calor Gaz 💺 🐕 WS

Last arrival time: 10:00

➡ Turn N at Taunton Cross on A35, 3 miles from Axminster, 6 miles from Honiton, signposted to Dalwood and Stockland.

AYSGARTH North Yorkshire   10C2

Westholme Caravan Park
Aysgarth DL8 3SP
☎ 01969-663268
Open 1 March-31 October ▲ 🚐 🚛

Set in the Yorkshire Dales National Park, enjoying striking views amidst splendid walking and touring country.

Size 22 acres, 69 touring pitches, 44 with electric hookup, 69 level pitches, 42 static caravans, 8 🚿, 16 WCs, 2 CWPs
£ car/tent £6.50-£9, car/caravan £6.50-£9, motorhome £6.50-£9, motorbike/tent £5.90-£7, children £1
🛒 ✕ 🍽 🗑 🔌 🗄 🧺 GR TV 🏧   🔥 Calor Gaz 🐕
➡ 7 miles W of Leyburn turn left off A684, ¾ mile after junction with B6160. 1 mile E of Aysgarth.

BAKEWELL Derbyshire   8A2

Camping & Caravanning Club Site
Hopping Farm, Youlgreave, Bakewell DE45 1NA
☎ 01629-636555
Open end March-end September ▲ 🚐 🚛
Size 11.9 acres, 100 touring pitches, 60 with electric hookup, 1 CWP
£ car/tent £3.20-£4.80, car/caravan £3.20-£4.80, motorhome £3.20-£4.80, motorbike/tent £3.20-£4.80, children £1
🎫 MasterCard Visa
🔌 🏧   🐕
Last arrival time: 11:00
➡ Take A515 from Buxton (not A6), signposted 'Monyask Youlgreave Arbor Low', turn left, head for Youlgreave then turn right down lane by church wall. Over bridge, then turn right up farm track for ½ mile.

Greenhills Caravan Park
Crow Hill Lane, Nr Ashford-in-the-Water, Bakewell DE4 1PX
☎ 01629-813467 Fax 01629-815131
Open all year ▲ 🚐 🚛
Size 8 acres, 100 touring pitches, 46 with electric hookup, 37 level pitches, 65 static caravans, 8 🚿, 17 WCs, 1 CWP

£ car/tent £9-£10, car/caravan £9-£10, motorhome £9-£10, children £1
🛒 🗑 🔌 🏧   🔥 Calor Gaz 🐕
Last arrival time: 10:00
➡ One mile NW of Bakewell on A6, turn S signed Over Haddon to site on right.

BAMBURGH Northumberland   13F3

Waren Caravan Park
Waren Mill, Bamburgh NE70 7EE
☎ 01668-214366 Fax 01668-214224
Open 27 March-31 October 🚐 🚛
Size 99 acres, 200 touring pitches, 57 with electric hookup, 140 level pitches, 345 static caravans, 32 🚿, 16 WCs, 2 CWPs
🛒
➡ At ¼ mile S of Belford on A1 turn E on B1342. Site in 2½ miles.

BANBURY Oxfordshire   4B1

Barnstones Caravan & Camping Site
Great Bourton, Banbury OX7 2BB.
☎ 01295-750289
Open all year ▲ 🚐 🚛

Beautiful award winning park situated on the edge of a pretty village close to the Cotswolds. Delightfully landscaped with trees and flower beds. Immaculate toilet block, free showers, laundry room and children's play area.

Size 2½ acres, 49 touring pitches, 49 with electric hookup, 49 level pitches, 3 🚿, 5 WCs, 1 CWP
£ car/tent £5, car/caravan £5, motorhome £5, motorbike/tent £5, children £0.50
🛒¼ ✕¼ 🍽¼ 🔌 🗄 🏧   Calor Gaz ♿ 🐕
➡ From junction 11 of M40 (Chipping Norton) continue to third roundabout and take A423 to Southam. After 3 miles turn right to Great Bourton. Site is 100 yards on right.

Bo Peep Caravan Park

Aynho Road, Adderbury, Banbury OX17 3NP
☎ 01295-810605 Fax 01295-810605
Open April-October A 🚐 🚏

Beautiful six acre site with 56 all-electric pitches, surrounded by farmland. Excellent campsite facilities. Central for Oxford, Blenheim, Stratford-on-Avon and Warwick Castle. Access M40 junctions 10 and 11.

Size 6 acres, 76 touring pitches, 76 with electric hookup, 40 level pitches, 12 🚿, 13 WCs, 4 CWPs
£ car/tent £6.50-£7.50, car/caravan £7.50-£10.50, motorhome £7.50-£10.50, motorbike/tent £6.50-£7.50, children £1.10
🛒 📷 🔌 🔥 🖂 Calor Gaz ♿ 🐕 WS
Last arrival time: 8:00
➡ From Banbury(M40 jn 11) follow signs for Adderbury A4260. From S (jn10) or Oxford follow signs to Adderbury. At Adderbury traffic lights take B4100, look for caravan sign, approx half mile.

Mollington Touring Caravan Park

The Yews, Mollington, Banbury OX17 1AZ
☎ 01295-750731
Open March-November A 🚐 🚏

Located on the edge of a lovely village within easy reach of many National Trust properties, the Cotswolds, Stratford-upon-Avon, Warwick, Oxford and more.

Size 2 acres, 24 touring pitches, 24 with electric hookup, 20 level pitches, 4 🚿, 4 WCs, 1 CWP
£ car/tent £4-£5, car/caravan £5-£6, motorhome £5-£6, motorbike/tent £4
🛒¼ ✕¼ 🔌 🖂 ♿ 🐕
Last arrival time: 11:00
➡ Site is directly off A423 Banbury to Southam road, 200 yards past Mollington, turn left from Banbury direction. Signposted close to site.

BANHAM Norfolk   9E3

Farm Meadow Caravan & Camping Park

The Grove, Banham Zoo, Banham NR16 2HB
☎ 01953-888370 Fax 01953-887445
Open all year A 🚐 🚏
Size 13 acres, 123 touring pitches, 123 with electric hookup, 123 level pitches, 6 🚿, 12 WCs, 1 CWP
£ car/tent £5-£7, car/caravan £6.50-£9, motorhome £6.50-£9, motorbike/tent £7
CC MasterCard Visa
🛒 ✕ 🍴 🔌 🔥 🖂 🏧 🎯 🔌 Calor ♿ 🐕 WS
➡ Banham is situated on B1113 Norwich to Bury St Edmunds road, halfway between Attleborough and Diss.

BARNARD CASTLE Co. Durham   10C2

Camping & Caravanning Club Site

Dockenflatts Lane, Lartington, Barnard Castle DL12 9DG
☎ 01833-630228
Open March-November A 🚐 🚏
Size 90 touring pitches, 39 with electric hookup, 90 level pitches, 8 🚿, 10 WCs, 1 CWP

£ car/tent £5.20-£7.80, car/caravan £5.20-£7.80, motorhome £5.20-£7.80, motorbike/tent £5.20-£7.80, children £1.50
CC MasterCard Visa
⊟ C Ⅲ & ✚
Last arrival time: 11:00
➡ Take A66 from Scotch Corner, then B6277 for Barnard Castle, cross A67 and head for Lartington, turn left at site sign before reaching Lartington.

BARNSTAPLE Devon — 2C2

Midland Caravan Park
Braunton Road, Barnstaple EX31 4AU
📞 01271-43691 Fax 01271-43691
Open April-30 September ▲ ⊕ ⊞

Level, well protected grass park overlooking the River Taw Estuary. Ideally situated to enjoy all of North Devon's beaches and attractions, and Exmoor.

Size 8½ acres, 35 touring pitches, 35 with electric hookup, 35 level pitches, 62 static caravans, 8 ⚿, 24 WCs, 1 CWP
£ car/tent £5-£7, car/caravan £7-£9, motorhome £7-£9, motorbike/tent £7, children £1.50
Rental ⊕ £90-£349
✕ ⊟ C ⊟ ⊺⊽ Ⅲ   ⊕ Calor Gaz ✚
Last arrival time: 9:00
➡ Take A361 through Barnstaple and follow Braunton and Ilfracombe signs. Park is 2 miles W of Barnstaple on right of dual carriageway.

BARTON-ON-HUMBER Lincolnshire — 11E4

Silver Birches Tourist Park
Waterside Road, Barton-on-Humber DN18 5BA
📞 01652-632509
Open 1 April-October ▲ ⊕ ⊞
Size 1½ acres, 24 touring pitches, 24 with electric hookup, 24 level pitches, 4 ⚿, 6 WCs, 1 CWP
£ car/tent £5.50, car/caravan £5.50, motorhome £5.50, motorbike/tent £5.50, children £0.50
⚡¼ ✕¼ ⦿¼ C ⊟ Ⅲ   Calor Gaz & ✚
Last arrival time: 11:00
➡ From A15 or A107, follow signs for Humber Bridge viewing area, just past The Sloop public house.

BATH Somerset — 3F1

Bath Marina & Caravan Park
Brassmill Lane, Bath BA1 3JT
📞 01225-428778 Fax 01225-428778
Open all year ⊕ ⊞
Size 4 acres, 88 touring pitches, 88 with electric hookup, 88 level pitches, 9 ⚿, 23 WCs, 2 CWPs
£ car/caravan £12, motorhome £12, children £0.75
CC MasterCard Visa
⚡ ✕¼ ⊟ C Ⅲ   Calor Gaz & ✚
Last arrival time: 12:00
➡ Two miles W of Bath on A4 at Newbridge.

Newton Mill Touring Centre
Newton St Loe, Bath BA2 9JF
📞 01225-333909
Open all year
Size 43 acres, 195 touring pitches, 90 with electric hookup, 195 level pitches, 18 ⚿, 32 WCs, 1 CWP
CC Visa
⚡ ⦿ C &
➡ SE from junction of A4 and A39 on B3110 to site on left.

Hints & Tips
In winter take your seat cushions home. Not only will they keep dry but thieves won't be able use or sell a caravan without upholstery

BEACONSFIELD Buckinghamshire   4C2

Highclere Farm Country Touring Park

Newbarn Lane, Seer Green, Beaconsfield HP9 2QZ

☎ 01494-874505 Fax 01494-875238

Open 1 March-31 January ▲ ⚏

A quiet meadowland site, one mile from the railway station. Cheap travel cards for London. Legoland 11 miles. Pub food ¼ mile, swimming 1½ miles.

Size 2 acres, 45 touring pitches, 45 with electric hookup, 45 level pitches, 6 ♺, 8 WCs, 2 CWPs
£ car/tent £8.50-£9.50, car/caravan £8.50-£9.50, motorhome £8.50-£9.50, motorbike/tent £8.50-£9.50
Rental Chalet. B & B - £35 single, £48 double.
℃ MasterCard Visa
⚐ ✕¼ ☂¼ ▣ ▯ ⚏   Calor Gaz ♿ ♯
Last arrival time: 10:00
➡ Leave M40 at jn 2 onto A40 to Gerrards Cross. Turn left after ¼ mile to Seer Green and follow tourist signs.

BEADNELL Northumberland   13F3

Camping & Caravanning Club Site

Anstead, Beadnell NE67 5BX

☎ 01665-720586

Open end March-end September ▲ ⚏ ⛺
Size 12 acres, 150 touring pitches, 150 level pitches, 6 ♺, 17 WCs, 1 CWP
£ car/tent £5.20-£7.80, car/caravan £5.20-£7.80, motorhome £5.20-£7.80, motorbike/tent £5.20-£7.80
℃ MasterCard Visa
▣ ⚐ ♯
Last arrival time: 11:00
➡ From A1 to Alnwick take a right fork (B1340). This takes you to Beadnell itself, the site is on coastal front on left, after a left hand bend.

BEAMISH Co. Durham   11D1

Bobby Shafto Caravan Park

Cranberry Plantation, Beamish

☎ 01370-1776

Open March-October
Size 8 acres, 55 touring pitches, 24 with electric hookup, 40 static caravans, 6 ♺, 6 WCs, 1 CWP
⚐ ☂ Gaz
➡ From NW: A68 to Castleside, near Consett, then left onto A692, follow Beamish Museum signs onto A693.

BELLINGHAM Northumberland   13E3

Brown Rigg Caravan & Camping Park

Bellingham NE48 2JY

☎ 01434-220175

Open Easter-31 October ▲ ⚏ ⛺

A family run site within Northumberland National Park. ½ mile south of Bellingham. Walking, golf, fishing nearby. Hadrian's Wall and Kielder 9 miles.

Size 6 acres, 60 touring pitches, 26 with electric hookup, 60 level pitches, 6 ♺, 10 WCs, 1 CWP
£ car/tent £5-£6.50, car/caravan £6.50, motorhome £6.50, motorbike/tent £2-£5, children £0.75
⚐ ⚐¼ ✕¼ ☂¼ ▣ ▯ ⚏ GR ◪ TV ⚠   Calor Gaz ♿ ♯
Last arrival time: 8:30
➡ From A69 ½ mile W of Hexham to Chollerford. At Chollerford take B6318, left over N Tyne River to roundabout signposted B6329 Bellingham.

BERE REGIS Dorset   4A4

Rowlands Wait Touring Park

Rye Hill, Bere Regis BH20 7LP

☎ 01929-471958

Open 16 March-31 October ▲ ⚏ ⛺

Family-run site in area of outstanding natural beauty with direct access to heathlands, woods, numerous walks, cycle ways and nature trails.

Size 8½ acres, 71 touring pitches, 40 with electric hookup, 40 level pitches, 10 ♺, 10 WCs, 1 CWP
£ car/tent £5.80-£8.80, car/caravan £5.80-£8.80, motorhome £5.80-£8.80, motorbike/tent £5.80-£8.80
⚐ ✕¼ ☂¼ ▣ ▯ GR ◪ ⚠   Calor Gaz ♯
Last arrival time: 9:30
➡ At Bere Regis turn S off A35 onto Wool/Bovington Tank Museum road. At top of Rye Hill turn right. Park is 200 yards ahead.

BERKELEY Gloucestershire 7E4

Hogsdown Farm
Lower Wick, Dursley GL11 6DS
☎ 01453-810224
Open all year A ⌂ ⇌

Ideal base for exploring the beauty of Cotswold Edge country, visiting historic market towns, picturesque villages, riverside meadows of Berkeley Vale and Severn Estuary.

Size 4 acres, 40 touring pitches, 25 with electric hookup, 40 level pitches, 2 ⓕ, 7 WCs, 2 CWPs
£ car/tent £5.50, car/caravan £7, motorhome £7, children £0.50
Rental ⌂
⧉ ⧉¼ ⊡ ⓚ ⧄ ⑤ ⚎   Calor ⅂ WS
Last arrival time: 10:30
➔ Between junctions 13 and 14 on A38. One mile off A38 opposite Berkeley turning.

BERWICK-UPON-TWEED Northumberland 13F2

Berwick Holiday Centre
Magdalene Fields, Berwick-upon-Tweed TD15 1NE
☎ 01289-307113 fax 01289-306276
Open March-October ⌂ ⇌

A family holiday park close to excellent beaches and with indoor and outdoor heated pools, leisure facilities, kids clubs, live entertainment, bars and food. A 'British Holidays Park'.

Size 58 acres, 35 touring pitches, 35 with electric hookup, 35 level pitches, 819 static caravans, 1 CWP
£ car/caravan £8-£14, motorhome £8-£14
Rental ⌂
⟪ Visa
⧉ ✕ ⧉ ⊡ ⓚ ⑤ ⑤ ⧈ ⚎   ⧇ Calor ⅁ ⅂
➔ Signposted on A1 from both N and S, signs directing you to Berwick Holiday Centre in town.

Haggerston Castle Caravan Park
Boal, Berwick-upon-Tweed TD15 2RA
☎ 01289-381333
Open 9 March-9 January ⌂ ⇌

'Toweringly' different family holiday park set around lakes and trees with heated indoor and outdoor pools, kids clubs, tennis and bowling included in the wide range of leisure facilities, restaurants and bars, cabaret entertainment. A 'British Holidays Park'.

Size 220 acres, 159 touring pitches, 159 with electric hookup, 800 static caravans, 16 ⓕ, 16 WCs, 2 CWPs
£ car/caravan £6.50-£17.50, motorhome £6.50-£17.50
Rental ⌂
⟪ MasterCard Visa
⧉ ✕ ⧉ ⊡ ⓚ ⧄ ⑤ ⑤ ⧈ ⧉ ⌁ ⅂ ⧑ ⧈ ⧉ GR ⧇ TV ⚎   ⧇
Calor ⅁ ⅂ WS
➔ 7½ miles S of Berwick on A1.

Ord House Caravan Park

East Ord, Berwick-upon-Tweed TD15 2NS
☎ 01289-305288 Fax 01289-330832
Open 1 March-9 January Å ⊕ ⇴

40 acre tree-lined estate dominated by an 18th century mansion containing a licensed club. Luxury toilet and shower facilities. Recreation and play area. Practice golf.

Size 41 acres, 70 touring pitches, 60 with electric hookup, 34 level pitches, 220 static caravans, 8 ℞, 16 WCs, 1 CWP
£ car/tent £5.20-£11.90, car/caravan £7.25-£11.90, motorhome £7.25-£11.90
Rental ⊕ £130-£385 p.w.
ℂℂ MasterCard Visa
🜨 🜨¼ ✕ ⊕ ⊚ 🜨 🜨 ⚠   ⊞ Calor Gaz & ⭢
Last arrival time: 11:00
➡ On A1 Berwick bypass. Turn off at second roundabout at East Ord and follow caravan symbol.
See advert on previous page

BEXHILL-ON-SEA East Sussex   5E4

Kloofs Caravan Park

Sandhurst Lane, Whydown, Bexhill-on-Sea TN39 4RG
☎ 01424-842839
Open March-January Å ⊕ ⇴

Family run camp site set in tranquil and secluded surroundings with sheltered, level open grass or shaded pitches. Within easy reach of Bexhill, Hastings and Eastbourne.

Size 22 acres, 50 touring pitches, 16 with electric hookup, 40 level pitches, 75 static caravans, 6 ℞, 9 WCs, 1 CWP
£ car/tent £6, car/caravan £6, motorhome £6, motorbike/tent £6, children £0.80
Rental ⊕
🜨 🜨 Calor Gaz ⭢ WS
➡ On A259 from Hastings

BICESTER Oxfordshire   4B1

Heyford Leys Farm

Camp Road, Upper Heyford, Bicester OX6 3LU
☎ 01869-232048 Fax 01869-232048
Open 1 April-31 October Å ⊕ ⇴

Quiet family run park in rural area. Ideal base for Oxfordshire, Cherwell Valley, central Midlands, Bicester Retail Village. Great for weekend breaks and journey stop-overs.

Size 10 acres, 22 touring pitches, 10 with electric hookup, 22 level pitches, 47 static caravans, 2 ℞, 4 WCs, 1 CWP
£ car/tent £5-£9, car/caravan £6.50-£8.50, motorhome £6.50-£8.50, motorbike/tent £5
ℂℂ MasterCard Visa
🜨 ⊚ 🜨 ⊕ ▢ ⚠   Calor Gaz & ⭢
➡ From junction 10 M40 follow B430 for 1½ miles.

BIDEFORD Devon   2C2

Steart Farm Touring Park

Bideford EX39 5DW
☎ 01237-431836
Open Easter-30 October Å ⊕ ⇴
Size 10 acres, 60 touring pitches, 29 with electric hookup, 25 level pitches, 4 ℞, 6 WCs, 1 CWP
£ car/tent £7, car/caravan £7, motorhome £7, motorbike/tent £5
ℂℂ MasterCard Visa
🜨¼ ⊕¼ ⊚ 🜨 ⚠   Calor Gaz ⭢ WS
Last arrival time: 11:00
➡ Follow A39 from Bideford through Fairy Cross and Horns Cross. Site is 2 miles past Horns Cross. From Bude, take A39 past Clovelly Cross and Bucks Cross. Site is ½ mile past Bucks Cross on left.

BILLINGSHURST West Sussex   4C3

Limeburner Arms Site
Newbridge, Billingshurst RH14 9JA
📞 01403-782311
Open 1 April-end October
Size 2¾ acres, 42 touring pitches, 21 with electric hookup, 42 level pitches, 6 ⛉, 6 WCs, 1 CWP
£ car/tent £7, car/caravan £7, motorhome £7, motorbike/tent £7,
🛒 ✕ 🍺 📞 🗑 ⛑ Calor Gaz. ⌀ ⛉ WS
Last arrival time: 10.00
➜ 1½ miles W of Billinghurst on A272, turn left on B2133, site 400 yards on left.

BIRCHINGTON Kent   5F2

Two Chimneys Caravan Park
Five Acres, Shottendane Road, Birchington CT7 0HD
📞 01843-841068 **fax** 01843-848099
Open Easter-end October ⛺ 🚐 🚙

A lovely country site near sandy beaches and close to the city of Canterbury.

Size 10 acres, 90 touring pitches, 60 with electric hookup, 140 level pitches, 50 static caravans, 13 ⛉, 22 WCs, 1 CWP
£ car/tent £6.50-£14, car/caravan £6.50-£14, motorhome £6.50-£14, motorbike/tent £6.50-£14
Rental ⛺ Chalet. £140-£390
《 MasterCard Visa
🛒 ✕¼ 🍺 🗑 📞 🗑 ⛑ 🔲 🔲 🔲 GR 🔲 ⛏ ⛑ Calor Gaz
⛉ ⌀ WS
Last arrival time: 10:00
➜ From the A299 follow A28 to Birchington Square, turn right at church into Park Lane (B2048). Left at Manston Road (B2050), first left into Shottendane Road. Site is 300 yards on right.

BIRMINGHAM West Midlands   7F3

BISHOP'S CASTLE Shropshire   7D3

Daisy Bank Caravan Park
Snead, Bishop's Castle SY15 6EB
📞 01588-620471
Open February-November ⛺ 🚐

Situated in the heart of the beautiful Camlad Valley. Absolutely fabulous views. Numerous water points and individual waste points. An ideal base for touring.

Size 6 acres, 40 touring pitches, 40 with electric hookup, 21 level pitches, 4 ⛉, 4 WCs, 1 CWP
£ car/caravan £5.50-£7, motorhome £5.50-£7, children £1
⛑ Calor ⛉ ⌀ WS
Last arrival time: 9:00
➜ 2 miles E of Churchstoke on A489.

BLACKPOOL Lancashire   10B3

Kneps Farm Holiday Park

River Road, Thornton Cleveleys, Blackpool FY5 5LR
☎ 01253-823632 Fax 01253-863967
Open 1 March-15 November ▲ 🚐 ��

Situated in the Wyre Estuary Country Park with easy access to the premier resorts of Blackpool, Wyre and Fylde, the Trough of Bowland, the Yorkshire Dales, the English Lake District and many more places of interest.

Size 10 acres, 70 touring pitches, 60 with electric hookup, 70 level pitches, 90 static caravans, 11 🚿, 17 WCs, 1 CWP
£ car/tent £8-£10.50, car/caravan £8-£10.50, motorhome £8-£10.50, motorbike/tent £8-£10.50, children £1-£1.50
Rental 🚐 £150-£300 per week
CC MasterCard Visa
🛒 🖶 🚻 🍴 ♨   Calor Gaz ♿ 🐕
Last arrival time: 8:00
➡ Leave M55 at junction 3 and follow A585 for Fleetwood. At the first roundabout turn right onto B5412. After 1 mile, turn right after the school into Stanah Road, which leads to River Road.

Maaruig Caravan Park

71 Pilling Lane, Preesall, Blackpool FY6 0HB
☎ 01253-810404
Open 1 March-4 January ▲ 🚐 🚚

We can offer the enjoyment of a peaceful holiday on a quiet, friendly, small site. Pleasant local walks along the sea wall with views around Morecambe Bay.

Size 1 acre, 28 touring pitches, 28 with electric hookup, 28 level pitches, 4 🚿, 6 WCs, 1 CWP

£ car/tent £7.50, car/caravan £7.50, motorhome £7.50, children £0.50
🛒¼ 🖶 🐕
Last arrival time: 9:30
➡ M6 (jn 32) join M55 (jn 3) exit onto A585 for Fleetwood. At third set of traffic lights turn right onto A588 for Lancaster. 5 miles to Ford garage on left. Follow signs for Knott-End onto B5377 up to T-junction. Turn left then first right onto Pilling Lane. Round the corner, second caravan park on left.

Marton Mere Holiday Park

Mythope Road, Blackpool FY4 4XN
☎ 01253-767544 Fax 01253-791544
Open March-end of illuminations ▲ 🚐 🚚

A family holiday park set in 93 acres just three miles from Blackpool. Heated indoor pool, kids clubs, tennis and bowling included in the wide range of leisure facilities, restaurants and bars, excellent cabaret entertainment. A 'British Holidays Park'.

Size 93 acres, 420 touring pitches, 420 with electric hookup, 420 level pitches, 900 static caravans, 36 🚿, 40 WCs, 20 CWPs
£ car/tent £9-£12, car/caravan £14-£16, motorhome £14-£16, motorbike/tent £12
Rental 🚐 £90-£454
CC MasterCard Visa
🛒 🍴 🚗 🖶 🚻 🍴 🔲 🔳 🔲 🔳 🔲 GR 🔲 📺 ♨   🍴 Calor Gaz ♿ 🐕 WS
Last arrival time: 10:00
➡ Take junction 4 off M55 (A583) towards Blackpool. At second set of traffic lights turn right into Mythop Road. Site is 100 yards on left.

Stanah House Caravan Park

River Road, Thornton, Blackpool FY5 5LW
☎ 01253-824000 Fax 01253-863060
Open March-October ▲ 🚐 🚚
Size 6 acres, 55 touring pitches, 50 with electric hookup, 55 level pitches, 4 🚿, 6 WCs, 1 CWP
£ car/tent £8.50, car/caravan £8.50, motorhome £8.50, motorbike/tent £8.50
CC MasterCard Visa
🛒 🛒¼ 🍴¼ 🚗¼ 🖶 🚻 🍴 ♨   Calor Gaz ♿ 🐕 WS
➡ Leave M55 junction 3 onto A585. After 6 miles at roundabout by River Wyre Hotel, turn right onto B5415 signposted Little Thornton and Stanah picnic area. Follow picnic area signs and continue to very end of River Road, turn right into caravan site nearest river.

Stanah House
CARAVAN PARK

A small select touring site, overlooking the River Wyre with good views of the Fells and Lake District mountains. Close access to a slipway for sailing and water-skiing.

Open March – October

River Road, Thornton, Blackpool FY5 5LR
Tel: 01253-824000
Fax: 01253-863060

THE INSIDE PARK
Touring Caravan & Camping Park

One of Dorset's Premier Touring Parks

Surrounded by farm and woodland rich in wildlife, this peaceful and beautiful setting is an ideal central location from which to explore Dorset's varied and fascinating countryside. Comfortable and fully equipped modern facilities are housed in 18th Century coach and stable building.

Brochure & Information
BLANDFORD FORUM, DORSET
Tel: 01258 453719 Fax: 01258 454026

Willowgrove Caravan Park
Sandy Lane, Preesall, Blackpool FY6 0EJ
☎ 01253-811306
Open March-November ⚏ ⚏

Enjoy the tranquillity of pitches alongside the lake with its island bird sanctuary, fishing and bird watching. Level site for bikes and wheelchairs, with childrens play area.

Size 25 acres, 80 touring pitches, 80 with electric hookup, 80 level pitches, 100 static caravans, 8 🚿, 10 WCs, 2 CWPs
£ car/caravan £8, motorhome £8, children £1
⚏¼ ✕¼ ⚏¼ 🗇 ⚏ 🗇 /Ⅱ   Calor 👤 🐕 WS
Last arrival time: 9:00
➔ From M55 junction 3, take A585 Fleetwood, right at A588 Knott End over Shard Bridge, near Preesall continue on B5377, right at T junction onto B5270, site on left.

BLANDFORD FORUM Dorset   3F2

Inside Park Caravan & Camping
Blandford Forum DT11 9AP
☎ 01258-453719 **Fax** 01258-459921
Open Easter-31 October ▲ ⚏ ⚏
Size 13 acres, 120 touring pitches, 90 with electric hookup, 12 🚿, 14 WCs, 1 CWP
£ car/tent £7-£12, car/caravan £7-£12, motorhome £7-£12, motorbike/tent £7-£12, children £1.25
CC MasterCard Visa
⚏ 🗇 ⚏ 🗇 GR 🗇 /Ⅱ   Calor Gaz 👤 🐕 WS
Last arrival time: 8:30
➔ From junction of A354 and A350, take Blandford St Mary exit and follow signs to park.

BODIAM East Sussex   5E3

Bodiam Caravan and Camping Park
Park Farm, Bodiam TN32 5XA
☎ 01580-830514 **Fax** 01580-830514
Open April-October ▲ ⚏ ⚏
Size 7 acres, 50 touring pitches, 50 level pitches, 5 🚿, 7 WCs, 1 CWP
£ car/tent £5-£6, car/caravan £6, motorhome £6, motorbike/tent £6, children £0.50
⚏ 🗇 🗇 /Ⅱ   🐕 WS
Last arrival time: 10:00
➔ 3 miles S of Hawkhurst on B2244 and 3 miles N of Sedlescombe.

BODMIN Cornwall   2B3

Camping & Caravanning Club Site
Old Callywith Road, Bodmin PL31 2DZ
☎ 01208-73834
Open March-November 🛆 ⛺ 🚐
Size 10½ acres, 175 touring pitches, 53 with electric hookup, 8 ☂, 18 WCs, 1 CWP
£ car/tent £4.60-£6.80, car/caravan £4.60-£6.80, motorhome £4.60-£6.80, motorbike/tent £4.60-£6.80, children £1.40
ℂℂ MasterCard Visa
⊡ 🗋 Gaz 🐕
Last arrival time: 11:00
➔ From A389 follow signs for site.

Glenmorris Park
Longstone Road, St Mabyn, Bodmin PL30 3BY
☎ 01208-841677 Fax 01208-841677
Open April-October 🛆 ⛺ 🚐
Size 11 acres, 100 touring pitches, 50 with electric hookup, 100 level pitches, 6 static caravans, 8 ☂, 11 WCs, 1 CWP
£ car/tent £5-£7, car/caravan £5-£7, motorhome £5-£7, motorbike/tent £5-£7
Rental 🚐 Chalet. £75-£260.
ℂℂ MasterCard Visa
🛒 🛒¼ ⊡ 🗋 ⊡ 🗐 GR 🔲 ⚠   Calor Gaz 🐕 WS
Last arrival time: 10:30
➔ ½ mile SW of Camelford on A39 fork left on B3266 for 6½ miles. Turn right (signposted St Mabyn), ¼ mile to site, 5½ miles from Bodmin on B3266.

BOROUGHBRIDGE North Yorkshire   11D3

Camping & Caravanning Club Site
Bar Lane, Roecliffe, Boroughbridge YO5 9LS
☎ 01423-322683
🛆 ⛺ 🚐
Size 6 acres, 80 touring pitches, 52 with electric hookup, 6 ☂, 14 WCs, 1 CWP
£ car/tent £5.20-£7.80, car/caravan £5.20-£7.80, motorhome £5.20-£7.80, motorbike/tent £5.20-£7.80, children £1.50
ℂℂ MasterCard Visa
🛒 ⊡ 🗐 GR 🔲 ⚠   🐕
Last arrival time: 11:00
➔ Leave A1 signposted Boroughbridge, turn W off main street signposted Roecliffe. Site is on right.

Old Hall Caravan Park
Skelton Road, Langthorpe, Boroughbridge YO5 9BZ
☎ 01423-322130
Open April-October 🛆 ⛺ 🚐
Size 10 acres, 12 touring pitches, 8 with electric hookup, 12 level pitches, 99 static caravans, 4 ☂, 5 WCs, 1 CWP
➔ From junction of A1 and B6265, take B6265 for 1½ miles, then right for 400 yards to site on left

BOSTON Lincolnshire   9D2

White Cat Park
Shaw Lane, Old Leake PE22 9LQ
☎ 01205-870121
Open March-November 🛆 ⛺ 🚐
Size 2½ acres, 40 touring pitches, 36 with electric hookup, 40 level pitches, 5 static caravans, 2 ☂, 6 WCs, 1 CWP
£ car/caravan £5-£6, motorhome £5-£6, motorbike/tent £5-£6
Rental 🚐 £115-£130
🛒 🛒¼ ✗¼ 🍴¼ 🗋 ⊡ ⚠   Calor Gaz 🐕 WS
Last arrival time: 10:00
➔ Take A52 Skegness Road as far as the Old Leake cross roads, turn right opposite B1184 Sibsey Road. Park is 300 yards on left.

BOURNEMOUTH & BOSCOMBE Dorset   3F3

Cara Touring Park
Old Bridge Road, Iford, Bournemouth BH6 5RQ
☎ 01202-482121 Fax 0118-945 2063
Open all year ⛺ 🚐
Size 3 acres, 36 touring pitches, 36 with electric hookup, 36 level pitches, 6 ☂, 6 WCs,
£ car/caravan £7.50-£11, motorhome £7-£11
Rental 🚐 £90-£270
ℂℂ MasterCard Visa
🛒 ✗¼ 🍴¼ 🗋 ⊡ Calor
➔ A35 between Christchurch and Boscombe. One mile from Christchurch and 1½ miles from Boscombe.

St Leonards Farm Camping & Caravan Park

West Moors, Bournemouth BH22 OAQ
☎ 01202-872637
Open Easter-30 September ▲ ⛺ 🚐

Quiet, level site near Bournemouth, Poole, cross channel ferries and the New Forest. Easy access off A31. Electric hook-ups, modern facilities including those for disabled, launderette.

Size 8 acres, 110 touring pitches, 40 with electric hookup, 110 level pitches, 12 ⁿ, 2 CWPs
£ car/tent £8-£12, car/caravan £8-£12, motorhome £8-£12, motorbike/tent £8-£12, children £1
🛁¼ ✗¼ 🚻¼ 🔲 🔌 🎣 ⚠   Calor Gaz 🔥 WS
➡ On A31 4 miles W of Ringwood, opposite West Moors garage.

BRANDS HATCH Kent   5D3

Thriftwood Camping & Caravanning Park

Plaxdale Green Road, Stansted, Brands Hatch TN15 7PB
☎ 01732-822261 **Fax** 01732-822261
▲ ⛺ 🚐
Size 22 acres, 160 touring pitches, 102 with electric hookup, 160 level pitches, 10 static caravans, 9 ⁿ, 18 WCs, 1 CWP
£ car/tent £8-£10.75, car/caravan £8-£10.75, motorhome £8-£10.75, motorbike/tent £6-£8, children £1.50
Rental ⛺ £125-£320
℃ MasterCard Visa
🛁 ✗¼ 🚻¼ 🔲 🔌 🔌 🎣 ⚠   ⚡ Calor Gaz 🔥 WS
Last arrival time: 10:00
➡ M26 junction 2A and M20 junction 2. Follow caravan & camping signs N on A20.

BRANSGORE Hampshire   4A4

Harrow Wood Farm Caravan Park

Poplar Lane, Bransgore
☎ 01425-672487 **Fax** 01425-672487
Open 1 March-6 January ⛺ 🚐

Situated in a pleasant village right on the edge of the New Forest, this six acre site offers the perfect centre from which to explore the surrounding area. Christchurch, Highcliffe and the market town of Ringwood are but a short drive away.

Size 6 acres, 60 touring pitches, 60 with electric hookup, 60 level pitches, 6 ⁿ, 12 WCs, 3 CWPs
£ car/caravan £9-£12.75, motorhome £9-£12.75
🛁¼ ✗¼ 🚻¼ 🔲 🔌 🔌 🎣 Calor Gaz WS
➡ Take Ringwood Road into Bransgore. Follow signs to site, between Three Tuns Pub and the Crown Inn.

BRAUNTON Devon   2C2

Chivenor Caravan Park

Chivenor, Barnstaple
☎ 01271-812217
Open March-October ▲ ⛺ 🚐
Size 1½ acres, 30 touring pitches, 4 ⁿ, 6 WCs
➡ 3½ miles from Barnstaple on A361 to Ilfracombe. Entrance off the only roundabout.

Lobb Fields Caravan & Camping Park

Saunton Road, Braunton EX33 1EB
☎ 01271-812090 Fax 01271-812090
Open Easter-October Å 🚐 🚐

A large, level, grassy park facing south with panoramic views across to the Taw/Torridge Estuary. One mile from Saunton Golf Club and 1½ miles from a large beach. Dishwashing facilities are available, as are hairdryer and razor points.

Size 14 acres, 100 touring pitches, 33 with electric hookup, 180 level pitches, 18 🚿, 50 WCs, 2 CWPs
£ car/tent £4-£6.50, car/caravan £5.50-£8, motorhome £4-£6.50, motorbike/tent £4-£6.50, children £0.50
🛒 ⓘ 📞 🔲 ⚠   Calor Gaz 🐕
➜ In Braunton at traffic lights, turn W off A361 to B3231, towards Saunton and Croyde. The site is one mile on the right.

BRENTWOOD Essex   5D2

Camping & Caravanning Club Site

Warren Lane, Frog Street, Kelvedon Hatch, Brentwood CM15 0JD
☎ 01277-372773
Open March-September Å 🚐 🚐
Size 12 acres, 150 touring pitches, 60 with electric hookup, 6 🚿, 13 WCs, 1 CWP
£ car/tent £5.20-£7.80, car/caravan £5.20-£7.80, motorhome £5.20-£7.80, motorbike/tent £5.20-£7.80, children £1.50
℃ MasterCard Visa
ⓘ 📞 ♿ 🐕 WS
Last arrival time: 11:00
➜ A12 N at junction 28 of M25, join A1023 then turn right onto A128 and site is on right.

BRIDGNORTH Shropshire   7E3

Stanmore Hall Touring Park

Stourbridge Road, Bridgnorth WV15 6DT
☎ 01746-761 761
Open all year Å 🚐 🚐

A 12½ acre touring park, with 131 electrically supplied pitches, surrounding a two acre lake and located near to Bridgnorth in Shropshire.

Size 12½ acres, 131 touring pitches, 131 with electric hookup, 131 level pitches, 13 🚿, 14 WCs, 4 CWPs
£ car/tent £9.80-£11.40, car/caravan £10.20-£11.80, motorhome £10.20-£11.80, motorbike/tent £8.60-£10.20, children £1.35-£1.45
🛒 ⓘ 📞 🔲   Calor Gaz ♿ 🐕
Last arrival time: 9:00
➜ From Bridgnorth take A458 to Stourbridge. Within two miles turn right into Stanmore Hall.

BRIDGWATER Somerset   3E2

Mill Farm Caravan & Camping Park

Fiddington, Bridgwater TA5 1JQ
☎ 01278-732286
Open all year Å 🚐 🚐

Inland family holiday park situated in a picturesque valley between the beautiful Quantock Hills and the sea. Children's paradise, swimming pool with slides, boating, riding, large sandpit, games and TV rooms, trampolines, holiday cottage.

Size 10 acres, 125 touring pitches, 125 with electric hookup, 125 level pitches, 18 🚿, 56 WCs, 3 CWPs
£ car/tent £6-£8, car/caravan £6-£8, motorhome £6-£8, motorbike/tent £6-£8, children £0.50
🛒 🏊 ⓘ 📞 🔲 🎣 📞 📺 ⚠   Calor Gaz 🐕 WS
➜ Leave M5 at Bridgwater, junction 23 or 24, take A39 W for 6 miles. Turn right to Fiddington, then follow camping signs. Camp is 1 mile from main road.

BRIDLINGTON East Yorkshire — 11F3

Thorpe Hall Caravan Site
Rudston, Driffield YO25 0JE
📞 01262-420393 **Fax** 01262-420588
Open March-October ▲ 🚐 🚏

Quiet and sheltered within Thorpe Hall's kitchen garden's brick walls, in the beautiful East Riding countryside of the great Wold valley of the Gypsy race.

Size 4½ acres, 90 touring pitches, 53 with electric hookup, 6 🚿, 19 WCs, 1 CWP
£ car/tent £4.50-£8.70, car/caravan £4.70-£9.10, motorhome £4.70-£9.10
🔌 🖸 📞 🖩 📂 GR 🔍 TV ⚠ Calor Gaz ⚅ 🐾
Last arrival time: 10:00
➤ 4½ miles W of Bridlington on B1253

BRIDPORT Dorset — 3E3

Binghams Farm Touring Caravan Park
Melplash, Bridport DT6 3TT
📞 01308-488234
Open all year ▲ 🚐 🚏
Size 5 acres, 60 touring pitches, 40 with electric hookup, 60 level pitches, 5 🚿, 7 WCs, 1 CWP
£ car/tent £8-£10.50, car/caravan £8-£10.50, motorhome £8-£10.50, motorbike/tent £8-£10.50, children £0.50-£1
🖸 📞 🖩 🖽 GR 🔍 ⚠ Calor Gaz ⚅ 🐾
Last arrival time: 9:00
➤ From A35 at Bridport take A3066 to Beaminster. After 2 miles, turn left into Binghams Farm.

Eype House Caravan & Camping Park
Eype, Bridport DT6 6AL
📞 01308-424903
Open Easter-October ▲ 🚏

A small, quiet, family run park in an area of outstanding natural beauty, on the coastal path, with the beach only 300 yards away. Dogs welcome.

Size 4 acres, 20 touring pitches, 20 level pitches, 35 static caravans, 4 🚿, 10 WCs, 1 CWP
£ car/tent £6-£10, motorhome £6-£10
Rental 🚐 £90-£299
🔌 ✕¼ 🍴 🖸 📞 🖩 Calor Gaz 🐾
Last arrival time: 9:00
➤ A35 (1¼ miles from Bridport) signposted to Eypes Mouth.

Freshwater Beach Holiday Park
Burton Bradstock, Bridport DT6 4PT
📞 01308-897317 **Fax** 01308-897336
Open 21 March-9 November ▲ 🚐 🚏

➤

← Freshwater Beach Holiday Park

*Situated at the mouth of the River Bride with its own
private beach, and nightly entertainment in the high
season. A golf course adjoins the site.*

Size 40 acres, 425 touring pitches, 171 with electric
hookup, 425 level pitches, 250 static caravans, 34 ⋒,
171 WCs, 4 CWPs
£ car/tent £6.50-£16, car/caravan £6.50-£16,
motorhome £6.50-£16, motorbike/tent £6.50-£16
Rental ⚐
CC MasterCard Visa
⚑ ✕ ⬤ ⬛ ⬛ ⬛ ⬛ ⬛ TV ⚲ ⬤ Calor Gaz ⟊ ✚
Last arrival time: 11:30
➜ At Bridport take B3157 Weymouth road. Site
entrance 1½ miles on right from Crown roundabout.

Highlands End Farm Holiday Park
Eype, Bridport DT6 6AR
☎ 01308-422139 **Fax** 01308-425672
Open March-October ▲ ⚐ 🚐
Size 28 acres, 120 touring pitches, 120 with electric
hookup, 120 level pitches, 160 static caravans, 15 ⋒,
24 WCs, 2 CWPs
£ car/tent £7.50-£11.75, car/caravan £7.50-£11.75,
motorhome £7.50-£11.75, motorbike/tent £7.50-
£11.75, children £1.25-£1.40
Rental ⚐ Chalet.
CC MasterCard Visa
⚑ ✕ ✕¼ ⬤ ⬤¼ ⬤ ⬛ ⬛ ⬛ ⬛ ⬛ ⬛ GR ⚲ ⬛ ⬤ Calor
Gaz ⟊ ✚
Last arrival time: 11:00
➜ One mile W of Bridport on A35. Turn S for village
of Eype at picnic area.

BRISTOL   3E1

Brook Lodge Camping & Caravan Park
Cowslip Green, Redhill, Bristol BS18 7RD
☎ 01934-862311
Open 1 March-31 October ▲ ⚐ 🚐
Size 3.2 acres, 29 touring pitches, 25 with electric
hookup, 29 level pitches, 4 ⋒, 8 WCs, 1 CWP
£ car/tent £8.50-£10.50, car/caravan £8.50-£10.50,
motorhome £8.50-£9.50, motorbike/tent £7.50
Rental ⚐ Chalet.
⚑ ⬤ ⬛ ⬤ ⬛ ⚲ Calor WS
Last arrival time: 11:00
➜ From Bristol take A38 SW for 7 miles, park
signposted on left. From Bath take A4 to Bristol and
turn left at Southern Ring Road onto A38. From M5 S
junction 19 take A369/B3129/B3130 to A38, 3 miles S.

Oak Farm Touring Park
Weston Road, Congresbury, Weston-super-Mare BS19
5EB
☎ 01934-833246
Open April-October ▲ ⚐ 🚐
Size 2 acres, 27 touring pitches, 20 with electric
hookup, 4 ⋒, 6 WCs, 1 CWP
£ car/tent £7.50-£8.50, car/caravan £7.50-£10.50,

motorhome £7.50-£8.50, motorbike/tent £7.50
⚑¼ ✕¼ ⬤¼ ⬤ ⬛ ✚ WS
Last arrival time: 11:00
➜ On A370, midway between Weston-super-Mare and
Bristol, 4 miles from M5 junction 21.

Salthouse Farm Caravan Site
Severn Beach, Bristol
☎ 01454-632274
Open 1 April-end October ▲ ⚐ 🚐

*Set in a farm courtyard with level, grassy pitches.
Located 200 yards off the main road, beside the
estuary and close to the new Severn Bridge.*

Size 8 acres, 60 touring pitches, 20 with electric
hookup, 60 level pitches, 30 static caravans, 6 ⋒, 9
WCs, 1 CWP
£ car/tent £7-£7.50, car/caravan £7-£7.50, motorhome
£7-£7.50, motorbike/tent £6.50-£7, children £0.90
⚑¼ ✕¼ ⬤¼ ⬤ ⬤ ⬤ ⬤ ⚲ Calor Gaz ⟊ ✚ WS
Last arrival time: 10:00
➜ From M5 jn 17 take B4055 for 3 miles to Pilning,
straight across lights to B4064. Entrance 1 mile on right.

BRIXHAM Devon   3D4

Hillhead Camp
Brixham TQ5 0HH
☎ 01803-853204
Open Easter-October ▲ ⚐ 🚐

*Centrally situated family site with live nightly
entertainment plus separate childrens entertainment.
Individual pitches and terraced areas, many with sea
views. Colour brochure available.*

Size 20 acres, 300 touring pitches, 200 with electric
hookup, 260 level pitches, 37 ⋒, 49 WCs, 2 CWPs
£ car/tent £6-£10, car/caravan £6-£11.50, motorhome
£6-£10, motorbike/tent £6-£10, children £1.30
⚑ ✕ ⬤ ⬤ ⬤ ⬛ ⬛ GR TV ⚲ ⬤ Calor Gaz ✚

Last arrival time: 9:00

➡ From A380 towards Brixham, turn onto A379 (Dartmouth) at Prouts Garage, avoiding Brixham town centre. After the BP garage, take the left fork (Kingswear) and the camp is 200 yards ahead.

Upton Manor Farm Camping Site

St Mary's Road, Brixham TQ5 9QH

☎ **01803-882384 Fax 01803-882384**

Open end May-start September **⚠ ⛺ 🚐**

Size 10 acres, 250 touring pitches, 8 with electric hookup, 250 level pitches, 20 🚿, 20 WCs, 1 CWP

£ car/tent £6.20-£8.50, car/caravan £6.20-£8.50, motorhome £6.20-£8.50, motorbike/tent £6.20-£8.50, children £1-£1.25

🛒 ✕ 🅿 🗑 🔌 🚽 Calor Gaz 🐕

Last arrival time: 9:00

➡ From Brixham town centre, turn right into Bolton Street and continue until next traffic lights (½ mile). Take second turning on left into Castor Road leading to St Mary's Road or follow signs on outskirts of Brixham.

BROADWAY Worcestershire　　7F4

Leedons Park

Childswickham Road, Broadway WR12 7HB

☎ **01905-795999 Fax 01905-794012**

Open all year

Size 40 acres, 400 touring pitches, 200 with electric hookup, 400 level pitches, 13 static caravans, 22 🚿, 22 WCs, 1 CWP

🛒 ✕ 🅿 🗑 🔌 🚽 Calor Gaz ♿

➡ Signposted off A44 Broadway to Evesham road. 1 mile from Broadway village

BROMYARD Worcestershire　　7E3

Boyce Caravan Park

Stanford Bishop, Bringsty, Nr Worcester WR6 5UB

☎ **01885-483439**

Open March-December **⚠ ⛺ 🚐**

A peaceful, family run, top grade farm park ideal for exploring the Heart of England and the Welsh Border Country. Coarse fishing available.

Size 10 acres, 24 touring pitches, 10 with electric hookup, 24 level pitches, 70 static caravans, 6 🚿, 12 WCs, 1 CWP

£ car/tent £7.50, car/caravan £7.50, motorhome £7.50, motorbike/tent £7.50

✕¼ 🗑 🔌 🚽 🛁 ⚠　Calor Gaz ♿ 🐕

Last arrival time: 6:00

➡ Take B4220 (Bromyard to Malvern). After 1¾ miles turn sharp left at Linley Green signpost, then turn right and follow the signs.

BRUTON Somerset   3E2

Batcombe Vale Caravan Park
Batcombe, Shepton Mallet BA4 6BW
☎ 01749-030246
Open 1 May-30 September ⚊ 🚐 🚚

Small, peaceful site in a secluded valley of lakes and wild gardens. Close to Longleat, Stourhead, Wells and Glastonbury.

Size 5 acres, 32 touring pitches, 16 with electric hookup, 32 level pitches, 2 🚿, 4 WCs, 1 CWP
£ car/tent £7-£8, car/caravan £7-£8, motorhome £7-£8, motorbike/tent £7, children £1
🔋 🗑 ☑ Calor Gas 🐕 WS
➡ Off B3081 between Bruton and Evercreech, from where it is well signed.

BUCKFAST Cornwall   2C3

Churchill Farm
Buckfastleigh, Buckfast TQ11 0EZ
☎ 01364 642884
Open Easter-November ⚊ 🚐 🚚
Size 2 acres, 25 touring pitches, 8 with electric hookup, 20 level pitches, 2 🚿, 4 WCs, 1 CWP
£ car/tent £5.50-£9, car/caravan £5.50-£9, motorhome £5.50-£9, motorbike/tent £5.50-£9, children £0.50-£2
🍴¼ ✗¼ 🛒¼ 🔋 🗑 🐕
Last arrival time: 10:00
➡ From A38 exit at Dart Bridge, junction for Buckfastleigh/Totnes, head towards Buckfast Abbey. At mini-roundabout, drive up hill towards Holne. Turn left at junction (into no-through road) towards Holy Trinity Church. Entrance is opposite the church.

BUDE Cornwall   2B3

Budemeadows Touring Holiday Park
Poundstock, Bude EX23 0NA
☎ 01288-361646 Fax 01288-361646
Open all year ⚊ 🚐 🚚
Size 10 acres, 139 touring pitches, 80 with electric hookup, 70 level pitches, 13 🚿, 22 WCs, 1 CWP
£ car/tent £4-£11, car/caravan £4-£11, motorhome £4-£11, motorbike/tent £4-£11, children £2-£2.75
Rental Chalet. £200-£350
Ⓒ MasterCard Visa
🍴 🛒 🔋 🗑 🔳 GR 🔲 TV 🎮   Calor Gaz ♿ 🐕 WS
Last arrival time: 9:00
➡ 3 miles S of Bude on A39.

Camping & Caravanning Club Site

Gillards Moor, St Gennys, Bude EX23 0BG

☎ 01840-230650

Open end March-end September ▲ ⛺ 🚐

Size 100 touring pitches, 33 with electric hookup, 8 🚿, 11 WCs, 1 CWP

£ car/tent £5.20-£7.80, car/caravan £5.20-£7.80, motorhome £5.20-£7.80, motorbike/tent £5.20-£7.80, children £1.50

CC MasterCard Visa

🖪 📻 📺 ⚠ 🐕 🐾

Last arrival time: 11:00

➡ From Wadebridge heading N on A39 towards Bude. Site is on left, signposted.

Cornish Coasts Caravan Park

Middle Penlean, Poundstock, Widemouth Bay, Bude EX23 0EE

☎ 01288-361380

Open Easter-31 October ▲ ⛺ 🚐

Size 4 acres, 78 touring pitches, 25 with electric hookup, 50 level pitches, 3 static caravans, 4 🚿, 5 WCs, 1 CWP

£ car/tent £5.50-£7, car/caravan £5.50-£7, motorhome £5.50-£7, motorbike/tent £5.50-£7, children £0.80-£1

Rental 🚐 £50-£225

🛒 🛍 📻 📺 🖪 ⚠ ☒ Calor Gaz 🐾

Last arrival time: 9:00

➡ On the coastal side of the A39, 5½ miles S of Bude. ½ mile S of Treskinnick Cross. Good access from layby.

Hedley Wood Caravan & Camping Park

Bridgerule, Holsworthy EX22 7ED

☎ 01288-381404 Fax 01288-381404

▲ ⛺ 🚐

Size 16½ acres, 120 touring pitches, 110 with electric hookup, 60 level pitches, 12 static caravans, 12 🚿, 14 WCs, 2 CWPs

£ car/tent £5.50-£8.50, car/caravan £5.50-£8.50, motorhome £5.50-£8.50, motorbike/tent £8.50, children £0.75-£1

Rental 🚐 from £85-£285

🛒 ✗ 🛍 📻 🖪 🆖 📺 ⚠ 🚿 Calor Gaz 🐾 WS

➡ From A3072 (midway between Holsworthy and Bude), at red post and roads, turn S on B3254 for 2½ miles, turn right, the site is in 500 yards.

Red Post Inn & Holiday Park

Launcells, Bude EX23 9NW

☎ 01288-381305

Open Easter-end October ▲ ⛺ 🚐

Size 4 acres, 50 touring pitches, 11 with electric hookup, 50 level pitches, 4 🚿, 5 WCs, 1 CWP

£ car/tent £3-£6, car/caravan £4-£7.50, motorhome £4-£7.50, motorbike/tent £6, children £0.75

🛒 🛒¼ ✗ 🛍 📻 🖪 📺 ⚠ 🚿 🐾 WS

Last arrival time: 11:00

➡ From junction of A39 and A3072 at Stratton, travel E on A3072 to Red Post (three miles) to site on right.

Sandymouth Bay Holiday Park
Bude EX23 9HW
📞 01288-352563 Fax 01288-352563
Open April-October 🛆 🚐 🚍

Family park set in 14 acres overlooking beautiful heritage coastline and award winning sandy beaches. 3 miles from Bude. 6-8 berth caravans, lodges and bungalows.

Size 14 acres, 55 touring pitches, 120 static caravans, 14 ⌂, 15 WCs, 1 CWP
Rental 🚐 Chalet.
℅ MasterCard Visa
🧍✕🐾🖲🔌🗄🔲🔳🔲 GR ⚠   🔌 Calor Gaz ♿ 🐕 WS
Last arrival time: 10:00
➡ A39 from Kilkampton to Bude. Turn right immediately after Penstone turning through Stibb. 3 miles from Bude.

Widemouth Bay Caravan Park
Widemouth Bay, Bude
📞 01288-361208 Fax 01271-866791

idemouth Bay
Near Bude, Cornwall

BARGAIN PRICES

Graded Very Good

Caravan Parc

Overlooking beautiful Widemouth Bay

50 acre parc a few minutes from safe sandy beach
NEW Indoor Tropical Heated Pool & Childrens club & Licensed club with FREE entertainment

Electric hook-up's Playground, Laundrette, shop, bistro & take-away

FREE awning space
FREE hot showers/toilet blocks

ESTABLISHED 1953

JOHN FOWLER HOLIDAYS
40 YEARS OF HAPPY FAMILY HOLIDAYS

Tel: 01271866766 Dept RAC

Open March-October 🛆 🚐 🚍
Size 56 acres, 80 with electric hookup, 140 static caravans
£ car/tent £4-£8, car/caravan £5-£10.50, motorhome £5-£10.50, motorbike/tent £8
Rental 🚐
℅ MasterCard Visa
🧍✕🐾🖲🔌🗄 GR TV ⚠ 🔳 🔌 Calor 🐕 WS
Last arrival time: 10:00
➡ Take A39 past Bude and turn right to Widemouth Bay. Turning to Millook in Widemouth Bay.

Wooda Farm Caravan & Camping Park
Wooda Farm, Poughill, Bude EX23 9HJ
📞 01288-352069 Fax 01288-355258
Open April-October 🛆 🚐 🚍

A quiet, family run farm park, overlooking Bude Bay and the countryside. Excellent for touring and camping. Luxury holiday homes for hire. Sandy beaches 1½ miles. 'Splash' indoor pool nearby.

Size 15 acres, 200 touring pitches, 122 with electric hookup, 100 level pitches, 54 static caravans, 22 ⌂, 36 WCs, 2 CWPs
£ car/tent £6.50-£10, car/caravan £6.50-£10, motorhome £6.50-£10, motorbike/tent £6.50-£10, children £0.50-£1
Rental 🚐 £99-£395
℅ MasterCard Visa
🧍✕🐾🖲🔌🗄🔲🔳🔲🔲 GR 🔳 TV ⚠ 🔌 Calor Gaz 🐕 WS
Last arrival time: 9:00
➡ From A39 at Stratton take road to Poughill/Coombe Valley. Drive 1 mile through crossroads. Wooda is 200 yards on right.

BUDLEIGH SALTERTON Devon   **3D3**

Ladram Bay Holiday Centre
Budleigh Salterton, Budleigh Salterton EX9 7BX
📞 01395-568398 Fax 01395-568338
Open 1 April-30 September 🛆 🚐 🚍
Size 52 acres, 304 touring pitches, 42 with electric hookup, 474 static caravans, 12 ⌂, 52 WCs, 1 CWP
£ car/tent £7-£14, car/caravan £8-£12, motorhome £7-£10, motorbike/tent £14
Rental 🚐
℅ MasterCard Visa
🧍✕🐾🖲🔌🗄🔲 GR ⚠ 🔳 🔌 Calor Gaz 🐕
Last arrival time: 8:00
➡ Two miles N of Budleigh Salterton on B3178, turn E into Otterton. Ladram Bay is signposted.

BUNGAY Suffolk   9F3

Outney Meadow Caravan Park
Bungay NR35 1HG
☎ 01986-892338
Open March-October Å 🚐 🚏
Size 8 acres, 45 touring pitches, 45 with electric
hookup, 45 level pitches, 30 static caravans, 4 🚾, 10
WCs, 1 CWP
£ car/tent £6.50-£10.50, car/caravan £6.50-£10.50,
motorhome £6.50-£10.50, motorbike/tent £6.50-
£10.50, children £1
🛒¼ ✕¼ 🛒¼ 🖥 🔌 🖵 ▯ Calor Gaz 🦴 WS
Last arrival time: 10:00
➡ Park is signposted from roundabout of junction
A144/A143.

BURNHAM-ON-SEA Somerset   3E2

Burnham on Sea Holiday Village
Marine Drive, Burnham-on-Sea TA8 1LA
☎ 01278-783391
Open mid March-mid November Å 🚐 🚏

*Burnham Holiday Village is situated near the town
centre with access onto the esplanade and beach and
offers superb facilities for the perfect family holiday. A
'British Holidays Park'.*

Size 95 acres, 52 touring pitches, 29 with electric
hookup, 52 level pitches, 500 static caravans
£ car/tent £7-£16, car/caravan £7-£16, motorhome £7-
£16, motorbike/tent £7-£16, children £1.50
Rental 🚐 Chalet.
⊂⊂ MasterCard Visa
🛒✕ 🖥 🔌 🖥 🖵 📺 🖵 🔌 🖵 🔌 🛢 ⚮ 🎛 🔌 ⚡ ♿
Last arrival time: 10:00
➡ Off M5 jn 22, A38 to Highbridge, B3139 to
Burnham. Signposted from there.

Diamond Farm Caravan & Touring Park
Weston Road, Brean, Burnham on Sea
☎ 01278-751041
Open March-October Å 🚐 🚏
Size 5 acres, 100 touring pitches, 100 with electric
hookup, 120 level pitches, 12 🚾, 28 WCs, 1 CWP
£ car/tent £4-£8, car/caravan £4-£8, motorhome £4-
£8, motorbike/tent £4-£8
🛒 🛒¼ ✕ ✕¼ 🖥 🔌 🖵 🔌 🔌 🖵 ⚮ Calor Gaz ♿ 🦴 WS
Last arrival time: 11:00

➡ From M5 junction 22 take B3139 to Brean. Through
village and site is 2 miles down coast road.

BURTON UPON TRENT Staffordshire   7F2

THE
BASS
MUSEUM
Horninglow St.,
Burton upon Trent,
Staffs DE14
Tel: 01283 511000

Museum of the history of Bass, Brewing and Beer. Features
include a working 'N' Gauge model of Burton upon Trent
dated 1921. An Edwardian Bar, "The Story of Brewing",
historical fleet of horse drawn and motorised vehicles. Also
the home of the famous "Bass Shire Horses". Fully licensed
bars, restaurant and souvenir shop.
Open everyday except Christmas, Boxing and New Years
day from 4pm-5pm (last admission 4pm).

BUXTON Derbyshire   8A1

Cottage Farm Caravan Park
Blackwell In The Peak, Taddington, Buxton SK17
9TQ
☎ 01298-85330
Open 1 March-31 October Å 🚐 🚏

*Extra space for tents and motor caravans. 24 level
hardstandings. Winter opening with tap and hookup.*

Size 3 acres, 29 touring pitches, 30 with electric
hookup, 24 level pitches, 5 🚾, 5 WCs, 1 CWP
£ car/tent £6, car/caravan £6, motorhome £5.50,
children £0.50
🛒 🖥 Calor Gaz 🦴
➡ Six miles from Buxton on A6 to Bakewell. Turn left
on unclassified road. Signposted.

Pomeroy Caravan & Camping Park
Street House Farm, Pomeroy, Flagg, Buxton SK17
9QG
☎ 01298-83259
Open Easter/April-October Å 🚐 🚏

A well maintained level park adjoining the High Peak Trail with a large rally field available. Good access from the A515.

Size 2 acres, 30 touring pitches, 24 with electric hookup, 30 level pitches, 1 static caravans, 4 🚿, 6 WCs, 1 CWP
£ car/tent £4.50-£6.50, car/caravan £6-£6.50, motorhome £5.50-£6, motorbike/tent £4.50-£5, children £0.50
Rental 🚐
✗¼ 🚐¼ 🔲 🔲 Calor Gaz 🐕
Last arrival time: 10:00
➡ On A515 Buxton/Ashbourne road 5 miles from Buxton, 16 miles from Ashbourne. Entrance over cattle grid with 100 yards of tarmac drive to site.

CAISTER-ON-SEA Norfolk 9F3

Old Hall Caravan Park
High Street, Caister-on-Sea NR30 5JL
📞 01493-720400
Open Easter-October 🚐 🚏

A small family park with outstanding facilities including free swimming pool. Close to beach, Great Yarmouth and Norfolk Broads - ideal base for touring.

Size 4 acres, 30 touring pitches, 30 with electric hookup, 30 level pitches, 33 static caravans, 6 🚿, 9 WCs, 1 CWP
£ car/caravan £6-£10, motorhome £6-£10, children £0.50
Rental 🚐 Chalet.
CC MasterCard Visa
🚿¼ ✗ 🚐 🔲 🔲 🔲 🔲 🔲 🔲 /🔺 🚐 Calor
Last arrival time: 11:00
➡ Take A149 from Great Yarmouth, follow tourist signs from Yarmouth Stadium. Park is opposite Caister church.

Scratby Hall Caravan Park
Scratby, Caister-on-Sea NR29 3PH
📞 01493-730283
Open Easter-mid October 🛆 🚐 🚏

Quiet, well-kept, level, grassy site near the sea with children's playground, shop, payphone and disabled facilities.

Size 4½ acres, 108 touring pitches, 64 with electric hookup, 108 level pitches, 10 🚿, 18 WCs, 1 CWP
£ car/tent £4.50-£9.90, car/caravan £4.50-£9.90, motorhome £4.50-£9.90, motorbike/tent £4.50-£9.90
🚿 ✗¼ 🚐¼ 🔲 🔲 🔲 🔲 /🔺 Calor Gaz 🚹 🐕
Last arrival time: 10:00
➡ At roundabout, junction of A149 and B1159, 1½ miles N of Caister, turn N along B1159 for 1 mile to site on the left.

CALNE Wiltshire 4A2

Blackland Lakes Holiday & Leisure Centre
Stockley Lane, Calne SN11 0NQ
📞 01249-813672 **Fax** 01249-813672
Open all year 🛆 🚐 🚏

An interesting family run site in a scenic location, ideal for children. Bikes, kitchen with Turkish oven and licensed bar for groups all available. New 20 x 10m covered swimming pool, and 15 'Superpitches'. Colour brochure. Bookings advised.

Size 17 acres, 180 touring pitches, 120 with electric hookup, 100 level pitches, 13 🚿, 23 WCs, 2 CWPs
🚿 🚐 🔲 🔲 🔲 🔲 🔲 🔲 🔲 🔲 /🔺 Calor Gaz 🚹 🐕 WS
Last arrival time: 11:00
➡ Signposted from A4 E of Calne.

CAMBORNE Cornwall 2A4

Magor Farm Caravan Site
Tehidy, Camborne TR14 0JF
☎ 01209-713367
Open April-Easter ▲ 🚐 🚛
Size 7½ acres, 160 touring pitches, 160 level pitches, 12 🚿, 18 WCs, 1 CWP
£ car/tent £6-£6.50, car/caravan £6, motorhome £6, motorbike/tent £6, children £0.50
© Visa
✗¼ 🅿¼ 🔲 🔲 🔲 🔲
➔ At junction of A30 and A3047, W of Camborne, travel N on unclassified road for 1½ miles.

CAMBRIDGE Cambridgeshire 9D4

Apple Acre Park
London Road, Fowlmere, Royston SG8 7RU
☎ 01763-208354
Open all year ▲ 🚐 🚛
Size 3½ acres, 20 touring pitches, 20 with electric hookup, 20 level pitches, 12 static caravans, 2 🚿, 4 WCs, 1 CWP
£ car/tent £4-£5.50, car/caravan £6.50-£7, motorhome £5-£6.50, motorbike/tent £5
🔲¼ ✗¼ 🅿¼ 🔲 🔲 🔲 🔲 🔲
Last arrival time: 10:00
➔ From Cambridge, A10 to Harston, turn left onto B1368 to site through village of Fowlmere on left. From Royston, A505 to Flint Cross Road, turn left onto B1358, site is on right after Fowlmere village sign.

Stanford Park
CAMBRIDGE
Telephone: 01638 741547 or 0802 439997

Quiet, family-run park, offering excellent facilities including a children's playground, in an attractive country setting.
Situated on the edge of the Fens, ideal for picturesque walks and cycling. Within close proximity of local rivers offering the opportunity for boating and fishing.
Superb modern toilet block and launderette, including facilities for the disabled.
Close to the university city of Cambridge and also Newmarket racing.
OPEN 52 WEEKS OF THE YEAR

Camping & Caravanning Club Site
Behind 19 Cabbage Moor, Great Shelford, Cambridge CB2 5NB
☎ 01223-841185
Open end March-start November ▲ 🚐 🚛
Size 12 acres, 120 touring pitches, 68 with electric hookup, 8 🚿, 11 WCs, 1 CWP
£ car/tent £5.60-£8.60, car/caravan £5.60-£8.60, motorhome £5.60-£8.60, motorbike/tent £5.60-£8.60, children £1.50
© MasterCard Visa
🔲¼ 🔲 🔲 🔲 🔲 🔲 WS
Last arrival time: 11:00
➔ From M11 junction 11 turn N onto A10. At traffic lights turn right onto A1301 for ¼ mile to site on left.

Highfield Farm Camping Park
Long Road, Comberton, Cambridge CB3 7DG
☎ 01223-262308 **Fax** 01223-262308
Open 1 April-31 October ▲ 🚐 🚛

A popular award winning park with an exellent grading, close to the historic university city of Cambridge. Other nearby attractions include the Imperial War Museum at Duxford and Wimpole Hall.

Size 8 acres, 120 touring pitches, 100 with electric hookup, 80 level pitches, 16 🚿, 23 WCs, 3 CWPs
£ car/tent £7-£8.25, car/caravan £7-£8.50, motorhome £7-£8.25, motorbike/tent £5.75-£6.75, children £1-£1.50
🔲 🔲 🔲 🔲 🔲 Calor Gaz 🔲
Last arrival time: 10:00
➔ From M11 jn 12 take A603 to Sandy for ½ mile, then turn right on B1046 to Comberton. From A428 leave at Hardwick roundabout and follow signs to Comberton.

Stanford Park Camping and Caravanning
Weirs Road, Burwell, Cambridge CB5 0BP
☎ 01638-741547 **Fax** 01638-743508
Open all year ▲ 🚐 🚛
Size 20 acres, 120 touring pitches, 40 with electric hookup, 120 level pitches, 3 static caravans, 5 🚿, 13 WCs, 1 CWP
£ car/tent £7.50-£9, car/caravan £7.50-£9, motorhome £7.50-£9, motorbike/tent £7.50
Rental 🚐 £100-£120
🔲¼ ✗¼ 🅿¼ 🔲 🔲 🔲 🔲 Calor Gaz 🔲 🔲 WS
Last arrival time: 8:00
➔ From Cambridge at Stow Cum Quy roundabout take B1102 to Burwell. From Newmarket turn off A14 onto A142 following signs to Burwell via Exning.

CANTERBURY Kent 5E3

Ashfield Farm Camping & Caravanning Site
Waddenhall, Petham, Nr. Canterbury CT4 5PX
☎ 01227-700624
Open 1 April - 31 October ▲ ⟐ ⟐

Quiet family touring park situated in an area of outstanding natural beauty with views over open countryside. Easy reach of Canterbury and Kent coastline.

Size 4 acres, 20 touring pitches, 16 with electric hookup, 3 ⋒, 5WCs
£ car/tent £6-£7.50, car/caravan £6-£7.50, motorhome £6-£7.50

Camping & Caravanning Club Site
Bekesbourne Lane, Canterbury CT3 4AB
☎ 01227-463216
Open all year ▲ ⟐ ⟐
Size 20 acres, 210 touring pitches, 85 with electric hookup, 19 ⋒, 22 WCs, 1 CWP
£ car/tent £5.60-£8.60, car/caravan £5.60-£8.60, motorhome £5.60-£8.60, motorbike/tent £5.60-£8.60, children £1.50
℀ MasterCard Visa
▢ ▣ ⚠ ⊁ WS
Last arrival time: 11:00
➡ At 1½ miles E of Canterbury centre on A257 to Sandwich. Turn opposite Canterbury Golf Club.

Red Lion Caravan Park
Old London Road, Dunkirk, Canterbury ME13 9LL
☎ 01227-750661
⟐ ⟐
Size 1 acre, 15 touring pitches, 12 with electric hookup, 11 level pitches, 2 ⋒, 5 WCs, 1 CWP
£ car/caravan £7, motorhome £7, children £1
▲¼ ✕¼ ⟐¼ ▣ ⊁ WS
➡ From A2 London bound follow signs. Turn off ½ mile at Dunkirk. From A2 Dover bound take Dunkirk turning immediately after joining from M2 junction 7. Follow signs. Car park 3 miles.

South View Caravan Park
Maypole Lane, Hoath, Canterbury CT3 4LL
☎ 01227-860280
Open all year ▲ ⟐ ⟐

A small, family run country park ideal for visiting Canterbury, East Kent seaside towns and Channel Ports.

Size 3 acres, 45 touring pitches, 28 with electric hookup, 45 level pitches, 4 ⋒, 8 WCs, 1 CWP
£ car/tent £8.50, car/caravan £8.50, motorhome £8.50, motorbike/tent £8.50, children £1
▲¼ ✕¼ ⟐¼ ▢ ▣ ▢ Calor Gaz ♿ WS
➡ Well signed off A28 and A299.

CARLISLE Cumbria 10B1

Dalston Hall Caravan Park
Dalston Road, Carlisle CA5 7J
☎ 01228-710165
Open 1 March-31 October ▲ ⟐ ⟐
Size 4½ acres, 40 touring pitches, 40 with electric hookup, 40 level pitches, 17 static caravans, 4 ⋒, 15 WCs, 1 CWP
£ car/tent £6-£6.50, car/caravan £7-£7.50, motorhome £7-£7.50, motorbike/tent £6-£6.50, children £0.75
▲ ✕ ⟐ ▣ ▢ ▢ ▣ ⚠ ⊟ Calor Gaz ⊁ WS
Last arrival time: 9:00
➡ Leave M6 at junction 42 and follow sign for Dalston. Turn right for Carlisle and site is on right after 1½ miles.

Dandy Dinmont Caravan & Camping Park
Blackford, Carlisle CA6 4EA
☎ 01228-574611
Open 1 March-31 October ▲ ⟐ ⟐

A quiet rural park yet only 1½ miles north of the M6 (44). A good overnight halt or a base for a longer stay to visit the Lake District, historic Carlisle, Roman Wall or romantic Scottish Border.

➡

← Dandy Dinmont Caravan & Camping Park

Size 4½ acres, 27 touring pitches, 20 with electric hookup, 27 level pitches, 4 ⚟, 14 WCs, 1 CWP
£ car/tent £5.75-£6.25, car/caravan £7-£7.25, motorhome £7-£7.25, motorbike/tent £5.75-£6
🗑 🔌 🍳 Calor ⚡
Last arrival time: 12:00
➡ Just N of Carlisle leave M6 junction 44 and take A7 Galashiels road. From here the park is approximately 1½ miles on the right. After Blackford village sign, follow the road directional signs to the park.

Orton Grange Caravan Park
Wigton Road, Carlisle CA5 6LA
📞 01228-710252 **Fax** 01228-710252
Open all year ▲ 🚐 🚕
Size 7 acres, 50 touring pitches, 30 with electric hookup, 50 level pitches, 22 static caravans, 6 ⚟, 11 WCs, 1 CWP
£ car/tent £6.90-£8.60, car/caravan £6.90-£8.60, motorhome £6.90-£8.60, motorbike/tent £4.40-£5, children £0.60-£0.80
Rental 🚐 £99-£185
((MasterCard Visa
🛒 ✕¼ 🍺 🗑 🔌 🍳 🔲 GR TV ⚠ Calor Gaz ⚙ ⚡ WS
Last arrival time: 10:00
➡ 4 miles W of Carlisle on A595.

CARNFORTH Lancashire   10B3

Detron Gate Caravan Site
Bolton-le-Sands, Carnforth LA5 9TN
📞 01524-732842
Open 1 March-30 September ▲ 🚐 🚕
Size 10 acres, 150 touring pitches, 98 with electric hookup, 50 level pitches, 42 static caravans, 12 ⚟, 18 WCs, 2 CWPs
£ car/tent £4, car/caravan £6, motorhome £6, children £0.75
🛒 ✕¼ 🍺¼ 🗑 🔌 🍳 GR 🔲 ⚠ Calor Gaz ⚡
Last arrival time: 10:00
➡ 1½ miles S of Carnforth on A6. Once you pass a large lay by on left, site is next turning on right off A6.

Sandside Caravan & Camping Site
The Shore, Bolton-le-Sands, Carnforth LA5 8JS
📞 01524-822311 **Fax** 01524-822311
Open 1 March-31 October ▲ 🚐 🚕
Size 6 acres, 130 touring pitches, 100 with electric hookup, 55 level pitches, 35 static caravans, 10 ⚟, 18 WCs, 2 CWPs
£ car/tent £8-£12, car/caravan £8-£12, motorhome £8-£12, motorbike/tent £8-£10
((MasterCard Visa
🛒 ✕¼ 🍺¼ 🗑 🔌 🍳 Calor ⚡
Last arrival time: 10:00
➡ From junction 35 follow signs for Morecambe, after 3 miles turn right at Little Chef for a further ½ mile. Entrance on right hand side.

CASTLE DONINGTON Leicestershire   7F2

Donington Park Farmhouse
Melbourne Road, Isley Walton, Castle Donington DE74 2RN
📞 01332-862409 **Fax** 01332-862364
▲ 🚐 🚕

Well screened grassland site adjacent mature woods in farmhouse hotel grounds. Perfect base for touring southern Derbyshire.

Size 8 acres, 60 touring pitches, 40 with electric hookup, 45 level pitches, 3 ⚟, 10 WCs, 2 CWPs
£ car/tent £8-£12, car/caravan £8-£12, motorhome £8-£12, motorbike/tent £7, children £1
((MasterCard Visa
✕ 🍺 🔌 ⚙ ⚡ WS
Last arrival time: 9:00
➡ Take the Melbourne turn at Isley Walton on the A453 and the site is ½ mile on the right.

CHARD Somerset   3E2

Alpine Grove Touring Park
Forton, Chard TA20 4HD
📞 01460-63479
Open Easter-30 September ▲ 🚐 🚕
Size 7½ acres, 40 touring pitches, 20 with electric hookup, 40 level pitches, 12 ⚟, 5 WCs, 1 CWP
£ car/tent £5.50-£7, car/caravan £5-£7, motorhome £6-£8, motorbike/tent £5.50-£7, children £1
Rental 🚐
🛒 🗑 🔌 🍳 🔲 ⚠ Calor Gaz ⚙ ⚡
Last arrival time: 10:00
➡ Leave M5 at junction 25 and follow signs for Crinkley Bottom at Crickley St Thomas. Turn right immediately before Crinkley Bottom entrance onto B3167. Turn right at second signpost for Forton. Site on right.

CHARMOUTH Dorset   3E3

Manor Farm Holiday Centre
Charmouth DT6 6QL
📞 01297-560226 **Fax** 01297-560429
Open all year ▲ 🚐 🚕

A large, open site in an area of outstanding natural beauty at Charmouth. A 10 minute level walk to a beach famous for its fossils and safe for bathing.

Size 32 acres, 302 touring pitches, 30 with electric hookup, 100 level pitches, 15 static caravans, 30 ℞, 42 WCs, 2 CWPs

£ car/tent £6.50-£9, car/caravan £6.50-£9, motorhome £6.50-£9, motorbike/tent £6.50-£9, children £1-£1.50

Rental ⬛ Chalet. caravans - £100-£350, houses - £145-£450

℃ MasterCard Visa

🐾 🐾¼ ✗ ✗¼ ➡ ➡¼ 🔲 🔳 🔲 🔲 🔲 GR ⚠ ⬛ Calor Gaz ♿ 🐕 WS

Last arrival time: 11:00

➡ On main A35 from Bridport travelling west, Charmouth is 6 miles. Enter Charmouth from A35, Manor Farm Holiday Centre is ¾ mile on the right in Charmouth.

CHEADLE Staffordshire 7E1

Hales Hall Caravan & Camping Park
Oakamoor Road, Cheadle ST10 1BU

☎ **01538-753305 Fax 01782-202316**

Open 1 March-30 October ▲ ⬛ 🚐

Size 8 acres, 48 touring pitches, 30 with electric hookup, 10 level pitches, 4 ℞, 8 WCs, 3 CWPs

£ car/tent £7-£8, car/caravan £7-£8, motorhome £7-£8, motorbike/tent £7-£8, children £1

🐾 ✗ ➡ 🔲 🔲 🔲 🔲 🔲 ⚠ ⬛ Calor Gaz 🐕 WS

➡ From Cheadle take the B5417 signposted Oakamoor. The site is ½ mile on the left.

CHEDDAR Somerset 3E1

Broadway House Caravan & Camping Park
Axbridge Road, Cheddar BS27 3DB

☎ **01934-742610 Fax 01934-744950**

Open March-November ▲ ⬛ 🚐

Size 30 acres, 200 touring pitches, 190 with electric hookup, 200 level pitches, 35 static caravans, 29 ℞, 64 WCs, 2 CWPs

£ car/tent £5-£12, car/caravan £5-£12, motorhome £4-£10, motorbike/tent £4-£12, children £1-£2

Rental ⬛ £110-£485

℃ MasterCard Visa

🐾 ➡ 🔲 🔲 🔲 🔲 🔲 GR ⚠ TV ⚠ ⬛ Calor Gaz ♿ 🐕

Last arrival time: 12:00

➡ Leave M5 at junction 22, and continue for 8 miles to park, following brown tourist signs to Cheddar Gorge and Caves. Midway between Cheddar and Axbridge on A371

Bucklegrove Caravan Park

Rodney Stoke, Cheddar BS27 3UZ
☎ 01749-870261 Fax 01749-870865
Open 1 March-31 October ▲ ⊕ ⊠

Family run park near Cheddar. First class facilities with free indoor pool. Nestling on the south side of Mendip with picturesque views of Somerset.

Size 7½ acres, 125 touring pitches, 69 with electric hookup, 95 level pitches, 35 static caravans, 16 ⋔, 21 WCs, 3 CWPs
£ car/tent £5-£10, car/caravan £5-£10, motorhome £5-£10, children £1.25
Rental ⊕ £110-£350
CC MasterCard Visa
⊠ ⬤ ⊡ ⬤ ⬦ GR TV ⚠ ⊟ Calor Gaz WS
Last arrival time: 10:00
➜ Leave M5 at junction 22. Proceed N on A38. Join A371 at Axbridge, proceed through Cheddar to Rodney Stoke, Bucklesgrove is on left.

Froglands Farm

Cheddar BS27 3RH
☎ 01934-742058
Open Easter-October ▲ ⊕ ⊠

A small, family site situated in an area of outstanding natural beauty, within walking distance of village shops, pubs, restaurants, swimming pool, leisure centre, gorge and caves.

Size 3 acres, 60 touring pitches, 30 with electric hookup, 50 level pitches, 6 ⋔, 12 WCs, 1 CWP
£ car/tent £5.50-£7.50, car/caravan £6.50-£8.50, motorhome £5.50-£7.50
⊠ ⊠¼ ✕¼ ⬤¼ ⊡ ⬤ ⊟ Calor Gaz �?? ⋔
Last arrival time: 10:30
➜ On the main A371 Wells/Cheddar road, 100 yards past Cheddar Church.

Longwillows C&C Park

Station Road, Woodmancote, Cheltenham GL52 4HN
☎ 01242-674113 Fax 01242-678731
Open 14 March-30 September ▲ ⊕ ⊠
Size 4 acres, 80 touring pitches, 56 with electric hookup, 80 level pitches, 7 ⋔, 14 WCs, 2 CWPs
£ car/tent £5.50-£6, car/caravan £5.50-£6, motorhome £5.50-£6, motorbike/tent £5.50-£6
⊠¼ ✕ ⬤ ⊡ ⬤ ⬦ ⚠ ⊟ Calor Gaz ⅗ ⋔
Last arrival time: 11:00
➜ Turn off A435 at Bishop's Cleeve or B4632 at Southam, park is next to Staddlestones Restaurant.

Camping & Caravanning Club Site

Bridge Road, Chertsey KT16 8JX
☎ 01932-562405
Open end March-start November ▲ ⊕ ⊠
Size 12 acres, 200 touring pitches, 96 with electric hookup, 12 ⋔, 21 WCs, 1 CWP
£ car/tent £5.60-£8.60, car/caravan £5.60-£8.60, motorhome £5.60-£8.60, motorbike/tent £5.60-£8.60, children £1.50
CC MasterCard Visa
⊠ ✕¼ ⬤¼ ⬤ ⬦ ⬤ TV ⅗ ⋔ WS
Last arrival time: 11:00
➜ Leave M25 (jn 11) and follow signs to Chertsey. Site is 200 yards from Chertsey Bridge on B375.

Chester Southerly Caravan Park

Balderton Lane, Marlston-cum-Lache, Chester CH4 9LF
☎ 01829-270697
Open 1 March-30 November ▲ ⊕ ⊠
Size 8 acres, 90 touring pitches, 65 with electric hookup, 90 level pitches, 8 ⋔, 12 WCs, 1 CWP
£ car/tent £6.20-£8.80, car/caravan £6.20-£8.80, motorhome £6.20-£8.80, motorbike/tent £6.20-£8.80, children £1.10-£1.20
⊠ ⊠¼ ✕¼ ⬤¼ ⊡ ⬤ ⊟ ⚠ Calor Gaz ⅗ ⋔
Last arrival time: 9:00
➜ Leave A55 at A483 junction towards Wrexham. After 300 yards at roundabout double back to Balderton Lane.

Camping & Caravanning Club Site

343 Main Road, Southbourne PO10 8JH
☎ 01243-373202
Open end March-start November ▲ ⊕ ⊠
Size 3 acres, 60 touring pitches, 10 ⋔, 8 WCs, 1 CWP
£ car/tent £5.20-£7.80, car/caravan £5.20-£7.80, motorhome £5.20-£7.80, motorbike/tent £5.20-£7.80,

children £1.50
CC MasterCard Visa
▣ ⴟ 🛈
Last arrival time: 11:00
➡ From Chichester, heading W on A259, site is on right immediately before Travellers Joy pub.

Red House Farm
Earnley, Chichester PO20 7JG
📞 01243-514216 Fax 01243-514216
Open April-October ▲ ⛺ 🚐
Size 4 acres, 100 touring pitches, 100 level pitches, 4 ⏏, 12 WCs, 1 CWP
£ car/tent £6-£7.50, car/caravan £6-£7.50, motorhome £6-£7.50, motorbike/tent £6-£7.50
⛽¼ ✕¼ 📞 ▣ ⚠ Gaz ⴟ 🛈 WS
Last arrival time: 10:00
➡ Take A286 from Chichester to Witterings. Turn left at Birdham garage onto B2198 to Bracklesham Bay. After ½ mile turn left again to Earnley on sharp right hand bend. Site is 500 yards on left.

Southern Leisure Centre
Vinnetrow Road, Chichester PO20 6LB
📞 01243-787715 Fax 01243-533643
Open March-October ▲ ⛺ 🚐

A family holiday park set in 220 acres and amongst 12 lakes, excellent for watersports, heated outdoor pool, kids clubs, tennis and bowling included in the wide range of leisure facilities, restaurants and bars, entertainment. A 'British Holidays Park.'

Size 220 acres, 1,500 touring pitches, 420 with electric hookup, 1500 level pitches, 32 ⏏, 66 WCs, 5 CWPs
£ car/tent £5, car/caravan £6.50-£12.50, motorhome £6.50-£12.50, motorbike/tent £5, children £1.50
CC MasterCard Visa
⛽ ⛴ ▣ 📞 ⏩ ▣ ⚠ ⛽ Calor Gaz ⴟ 🛈 WS
➡ At roundabout junction of A27 (Chichester by-pass) and A259, 1 mile SE of Chichester, turn into Vinnetrow Lane and it's ¼ mile to the park.

Hints & Tips
Make sure your mirrors are adjusted correctly before moving off.

CHIPPING NORTON Oxfordshire   **4B1**

Camping & Caravanning Club Site
Chipping Norton Road, Chadlington, Chipping Norton OX7 3PE
📞 01608-641993
Open end March-start November ▲ ⛺ 🚐
Size 75 touring pitches, 50 with electric hookup, 4 ⏏, 5 WCs, 1 CWP
£ car/tent £5.60-£8.60, car/caravan £5.60-£8.60, motorhome £5.60-£8.60, motorbike/tent £5.60-£8.60, children £1.50
CC MasterCard Visa
▣ 📞 ⚠ ⴟ 🛈
Last arrival time: 11:00

CHRISTCHURCH Dorset   **3F3**

Hoburne Park
Christchurch BH23 4HU
📞 01425-273379 Fax 01425-270705
Open March-October ⛺ 🚐

A family holiday park with an extensive range of quality family and sporting entertainment facilities. Close to the beach, New Forest and Bournemouth.

Size 40 acres, 285 touring pitches, 285 with electric hookup, 285 level pitches, 287 static caravans, 23 ⏏, 38 WCs, 4 CWPs
£ car/caravan £9.50-£23.50, motorhome £9.50-£23.50
CC MasterCard Visa
⛽ ✕ ⛴ ▣ 📞 ⏩ ⏩ ▣ ⏩ ⏩ GR TV ⚠ ⛽ Calor ⴟ
Last arrival time: 9:00
➡ From Lyndhurst, take A35 signed Bournemouth for 13 miles to roundabout. Take first exit left onto A337, then take first left at roundabout. The site is 100 yards on left.

CHUDLEIGH Devon   **3D3**

Finlake Leisure Park
Chudleigh TQ13 0EJ
📞 01626-853833 Fax 01626-854031
Open all year ▲ ⛺ 🚐

➡

← **Finlake Leisure Park**

Situated in a 130 acre park, encompassing hills, valleys, woodland and lakes. Facilities include indoor and outdoor pools with waterslide, tennis, bar, restaurant and entertainment.

Size 130 acres, 450 touring pitches, 377 with electric hookup, 450 level pitches, 19 static caravans, 50 ⓡ, 93 WCs, 7 CWPs
£ car/tent £4.50-£11.25, car/caravan £6.25-£14.50, motorhome £6.25-£14.50, motorbike/tent £4.50-£11.25, children £1.25-£2
Rental 🚐 Chalet. caravans £150-£550, lodge £180-£630
ℂ MasterCard Visa
🜂 ✕ ☏ 🜄 🄫 🔃 🔢 🔥 ▣ 🔲 ▨ ▨ GR ⏃ ▣   🔥 Calor Gaz 🏕 WS
Last arrival time: 10:00
➡ From A38 take Chudleigh/Knighton exit (B3344). Site is ½ mile on right.

Holmans Wood Tourist Park
Chudleigh TQ13 0DZ
☎ 01626-853785
Open March-end November Ⓐ 🚐 🏕

Set amongst beautiful Devon countryside with breathtaking views on all sides, Holmans Wood is an immaculately well kept site. Peaceful and relaxing for all the family. Graded excellent. Winner of 1996 Calor award.

Size 20 acres, 125 touring pitches, 125 with electric hookup, 125 level pitches, 10 ⓡ, 15 WCs, 3 CWPs

£ car/tent £5.70-£7.95, car/caravan £5.70-£8.95, motorhome £5.70-£8.95, motorbike/tent £5.70-£7.95, children £1.50
ℂ MasterCard Visa
🜂 ✕¼ ☏¼ 🜄 🔃 🔲 ▣ ⏃   Calor Gaz 🜂 🏕 WS
Last arrival time: 11:00
➡ Follow M5 to Exeter and take A38 towards Plymouth. After the racecourse (about ½ mile on the left) is an exit signposted to Chudleigh. Site entrance is at end of this short slip road.

CHURCH STRETTON Shropshire   7D3

Small Batch Site
Ashes Valley, Little Stretton, Church Stretton SY6 6PW
☎ 01694-723358
Open 17 April-30 September Ⓐ 🚐 🏕
Size 32 touring pitches, 1 ⓡ, 5 WCs, 1 CWP
£ car/tent £7, car/caravan £7, motorhome £7
🜂¼ 🏕
➡ Off A49 into Little Stretton, onto B4370. Left at Ragleth Inn and site is ¼ mile on right.

CIRENCESTER Gloucestershire   7F4

Cotswold Hoburne
Broadway Lane, South Cerney, Cirencester GL7 5UQ
☎ 01285-860216 **Fax** 01285-862106
Open Easter-31 October Ⓐ 🚐 🏕

Set in the Cotswold Water Park, this quality site has fish-stocked lakes, a magnificent indoor pool and a licensed lakeside lounge with seasonal entertainment.
Size 70 acres, 302 touring pitches, 302 with electric hookup, 302 level pitches, 158 static caravans, 18 ⓡ, 54 WCs, 6 CWPs
£ car/tent £8.50-£21, car/caravan £8.50-£21, motorhome £8.50-£21
Rental 🚐 Chalet.
ℂ MasterCard Visa
🜂 ✕ ☏ 🜄 🄫 🔃 🔢 🔥 🔲 ▣ GR ▣ 📺 ⏃   🔥 Calor Gaz 🜂
Last arrival time: 9:00
➡ The park is signposted from A419, 4 miles S of Cirencester.

Mayfield Touring Park

Cheltenham Rd, Perrotts Brook, Cirencester GL7 7BH

☎ 01285-831301 Fax 01285-831301

Open March-October **A** 🚐 🚑

Size 12 acres, 72 touring pitches, 42 with electric hookup, 20 level pitches, 2 static caravans, 4 🚿, 5 WCs, 1 CWP

£ car/tent £5.30-£9.30, car/caravan £6.80-£9.30, motorhome £5.80-£9.30, children £2

Rental 🚐 £80-£210

🧍 ✗¼ 🔲 🔋 🔲 Calor Gaz WS

Last arrival time: 10:30

➡ Immediately off main A435 Cirencester to Cheltenham road, 2 miles N of Cirencester.

CLACTON-ON-SEA Essex   5E1

Orchards Holiday Park

Point Clear, St. Osyth, Clacton-on-Sea CO16 8LJ

☎ 01255-820651

Open March-October **A** 🚐 🚑

A family holiday park surrounded on three sides by water, ideal for watersports and the active family. New indoor heated pool, outdoor pool, kids club, tennis and bowling included in the wide range of leisure facilities, restaurants and bars, excellent cabaret entertainment. A 'British Holidays Park'.

Size 160 acres, 85 touring pitches, 85 with electric hookup, 85 level pitches, 1,400 static caravans, 14 🚿, 10 WCs, 1 CWP

🧍 ✗ 🔲 🔲 🔲 🔲 🔲 Calor Gaz 🐕

➡ From Clacton take B1027 (signposted Colchester). Turn left after Pump Hill petrol station, then over crossroads in St Osyth to park entrance.

Weeley Bridge Holiday Park

Weeley, Clacton-on-Sea CO16 9DH

☎ 01255-830403 Fax 01255-831544

Open March-October 🚐 🚑

Size 16 acres, 25 touring pitches, 25 with electric hookup, 25 level pitches, 200 static caravans, 4 🚿, 4 WCs, 2 CWPs

£ car/caravan £8.50-£11.50, motorhome £8.50-£11.50

Rental 🚐

₡ MasterCard Visa

🧍 ✗ 🔲 🔲 🔲 🔲 📺 🔲 🔲 Calor 🐕 WS

Last arrival time: 10:00

➡ Take A12 from London onto A133. Follow signs for Clacton/Weeley.

CLEETHORPES Lincolnshire   11F4

Thorpe Park Holiday Centre

Humberton, Cleethorpes DN36 4HG

☎ 01472-813395

Open March-October **A** 🚐 🚑

A family holiday park close to excellent beaches with a new indoor heated pool, kids clubs, coarse fishing lake, kids pets corner - a wide range of leisure facilities, hot food, bars and cabarets. A 'British Holidays Park'.

Size 279 acres, 115 touring pitches, 115 with electric hookup, 80 static caravans, 78 🚿, 22 WCs, 19 CWPs

₡ MasterCard Visa

🧍 🔲 🔲 🔲 🔲 🔲 🔲 🔲 🔲 Calor 🐕

➡ Follow A180 from M180, following signs for Grimsby and Cleethorpes. In Cleethorpes town centre, with seafront on left, follow signs for 'Fitties'. At the mini roundabout you will see Thorpe Park's entrance straight ahead.

CLIPPESBY Norfolk   9F3

Clippesby Holidays

Clippesby, Great Yarmouth NR29 3BJ

☎ 01493-369367 Fax 01493-368181

Open May-September & Easter week ▲ ⬤ ⬤

Size 34 acres, 100 touring pitches, 70 with electric hookup, 70 level pitches, 10 ⬤, 20 WCs, 3 CWPs

£ car/tent £8.50-£15, car/caravan £8.50-£15, motorhome £8.50-£15, motorbike/tent £8.50-£13, children £0.50-£0.75

Rental Chalet. £130-£495

℃ MasterCard Visa

⬤ ✕ ⬤ ⬤ ⬤ ⬤ ⬤ ⬤ ⬤ ⬤ ⬤ ⬤ Calor Gaz ⬤ ⬤

➡ Take A47 to Acle, then A1064 for 3 miles and turn left at Clippesby. After ½ mile, turn left again and then first right after 200 yards.

CLITHEROE Lancashire   10C3

Camping & Caravanning Club Site

Edisford Bridge, Edisford Road, Clitheroe BB7 3LA

☎ 01200-425294

Open end March-start November ▲ ⬤ ⬤

Size 6 acres, 80 touring pitches, 32 with electric hookup, 6 ⬤, 14 WCs, 1 CWP

£ car/tent £4.60-£6.80, car/caravan £4.60-£6.80, motorhome £4.60-£6.80, children £1.40

℃ MasterCard Visa

✕¼ ⬤ ⬤ ⬤   Gaz ⬤

Last arrival time: 11:00

➡ From A59, take A671 to Clitheroe. In Clitheroe take B6243, Edisford Road, 1 mile to site.

CLOVELLY Devon   2C2

Dyke Green Farm Camping Site

Higher Clovelly, Clovelly

☎ 01237-431279

Open Easter-October

Size 40 touring pitches, 2 ⬤, 3 WCs, 1 CWP

⬤ ⬤¼ ⬤ ⬤ Calor

➡ On roundabout A39 turn onto Clovelly road and immediately right to site.

COCKERMOUTH Cumbria   10A1

Wyndham Hall Caravan Park

Old Keswick Road, Cockermouth CA13 9SF

☎ 01900-822571

Open 1 March-15 November ▲ ⬤ ⬤

Size 12½ acres, 32 touring pitches, 24 with electric hookup, 32 level pitches, 105 static caravans, 9 ⬤, 21 WCs, 2 CWPs

£ car/tent £7, car/caravan £7, motorhome £7, motorbike/tent £7, children £0.50

Rental ⬤ Chalet.

⬤ ✕ ⬤ ⬤ ⬤ ⬤ ⬤ ⬤ ⬤ Calor Gaz ⬤ WS

➡ Off A66 on Old Keswick Road.

CLIPPESBY HOLIDAYS

Family-run Touring Park Camping and Holiday Cottages in the beautiful wooded grounds of Clippesby Hall, with lots of family things to do.

"DAVID BELLAMY CONSERVATION AWARD"

"BEST PARK IN ENGLAND"
1996 CALOR AWARD

"BEST FAMILY PARK"
2 years running, Practical Caravan

Clippesby, Nr Gt. Yarmouth NR29 3BJ
Tel: 01493 369367 Fax: 01493 368181

COMBE MARTIN Devon   2C2

Stowford Farm Meadows

Combe Martin, Ilfracombe EX34 0PW

☎ 01271-882476 Fax 01271-883053

Open Easter-31 October ▲ ⬤ ⬤

Set in 500 acres of glorious Devon countryside, and on the fringe of Exmoor National Park, this family orientated touring park has a superb range of facilities and amenities. Renowned as a high quality park offering outstanding value for money.

Size 500 acres, 570 touring pitches, 550 with electric hookup, 250 level pitches, 60 ⬤, 110 WCs, 10 CWPs

£ car/tent £4.25-£9, car/caravan £4.25-£9, motorhome £4.25-£9, motorbike/tent £4.25-£9, children £2

℃ MasterCard Visa

⬤ ✕ ⬤ ⬤ ⬤ ⬤ ⬤ ⬤ ⬤ ⬤ ⬤ ⬤ ⬤ ⬤ Calor Gaz ⬤ ⬤ WS

Last arrival time: 8:00

➡ M5 jn 27, follow North Devon Link to Barnstaple, then A39 (for Lynton) through Barnstaple centre. 1 mile from Barnstaple turn left onto B3230. Turn right at garage onto A3123. Site 1½ miles on right.

CORFE CASTLE Dorset 3F3

Woodland Camping Park

Glebe Farm, Corfe Castle, Wareham BH20 5NS
01929-480280
Open Easter-October

A quiet family site with all essential facilities, direct access to the Purbeck Hills and lovely safe walk to Corfe Castle by public footpath.

Size 7 acres, 65 touring pitches, 65 level pitches, 5 , 1 CWP
£ car/tent £8, car/caravan £8, motorhome £8, motorbike/tent £6, children £1.25
Calor Gaz
Last arrival time: 9:00
➜ Take Church Knowle road at Castle ruins off A351. The site is ¾ mile on right hand side.

COVENTRY West Midlands 8B3

Somers Wood Caravan & Camping Park

Somers Road, Meriden, Coventry CV7 7PL
01676-522978
Open all year

Located near Meriden in the centre of England, this family run park is set amongst mature woodland. Adjacent to 18 hole golf course/driving range and Somers Coarse Fishery and Packington Trout Fishery.

Size 6 acres, 48 touring pitches, 42 with electric hookup, 4 , 7 WCs
£ car/tent £8-£10, car/caravan £8-£10, motorhome £8-£10
See advert under Birmingham

CRANTOCK Cornwall   2A4

Quarryfield
Crantock
☎ 01637-872792
Open March-October 🏕 🚐 🚚

An ideal touring site, 15 minutes walk from the beach and close to the village. A level site with all modern amenities.

Size 20 acres, 20 touring pitches, 20 with electric hookup, 125 level pitches, 40 static caravans, 18 🚿, 20 WCs, 2 CWPs
£ car/caravan £4.30-£5.50, motorhome £4.30-£5.50, children £0.50-£1.25
Rental 🚐 Chalet. apply for free brochure
🔌 🛒 🗑 🔧 🍴 GR 🅰 🕹 Calor 🐕
Last arrival time: 9:30
➡ Off A3075 Redruth road to Crantock to bottom of village. There is a red telephone kiosk, a road up on right of kiosk. The site is at top.

CREDITON Devon   3D3

Yeatheridge Farm Caravan Park
East Worlington, Crediton EX17 4TN
☎ 01884-860330 **Fax** 01884-860330
Open Easter-30 September 🏕 🚐 🚚

A genuine working family farm, plenty of animals and panoramic views from a spacious park. Coarse fishing, lakes and horse riding. Two indoor heated swimming pools and 20 acres of woodland.

Size 9 acres, 85 touring pitches, 75 with electric hookup, 2 static caravans, 12 🚿, 17 WCs, 1 CWP
£ car/tent £6.50-£8, car/caravan £6.50-£8, motorhome £6.50-£8, motorbike/tent £6.50-£8, children £1.50
CC MasterCard Visa
🔌 📺 🗑 🔧 🍴 GR 🅰 🕹 Calor Gaz 🐕 WS
➡ Leave M5 at junction 27 onto B3137 out of Finerton. Take B3042 before Witheridge. The site is 3½ miles on the left.

CROMER Norfolk   9F2

Camping & Caravanning Club Site
Holgate Lane, West Runton, Cromer NR27 9NW
☎ 01263-837544
Open late March-early November 🏕 🚐 🚚
Size 11½ acres, 224 touring pitches, 101 with electric hookup, 20 🚿, 30 WCs, 1 CWP
£ car/tent £5.60-£8.60, car/caravan £5.60-£8.60, motorhome £5.60-£8.60, motorbike/tent £5.60-£8.60, children £1.50
CC MasterCard Visa
🔌 🗑 🛒 🅰 ♿ 🐕
Last arrival time: 11:00
➡ On A148 from N past 'Aylemerton' sign in ¾ mile turn left at Roman Camp Inn, site at crest of hill opposite National Trust sign.

Manor Farm Caravan & Camp Site
East Runton, Cromer NR27 9PR
☎ 01263-512858 **Fax** 01263-512858

Peaceful family run site with glorious sea and woodland views. Well equiped toilet facilites. Separate field for dog owners. Ideal for families. Tents welcome. Beach one mile.

Size 20 acres, 200 touring pitches, 128 with electric hookup, 200 level pitches, 20 🚿, 55 WCs, 5 CWPs
£ car/tent £6.60-£8.20, children £0.75
🔌¼ ✖¼ 📺¼ 🗑 🛒 🍴 🅰 Calor Gaz 🐕
Last arrival time: 10:00
➡ 1½ miles west of Cromer turn off A148 at signpost "East Runton"

Seacroft Camping & Caravan Park
Runton Road, Cromer NR27 9JN
☎ 01263-511722 **Fax** 01263-511512
Open 20 March-30 October 🏕 🚐 🚚

The pitches are individually marked with shrubs forming boundaries. Within easy walking distance from Cromer.

Size 7 acres, 120 touring pitches, 110 with electric hookup, 120 level pitches, 15 ⏢, 30 WCs, 1 CWP
£ car/tent £7-£11.50, car/caravan £7-£11.50, motorhome £7-£11.50, motorbike/tent £7-£11.50, children £0.50-£1.50
℃ MasterCard Visa
⚥ ✕ 🛒 🖥 🔧 🚾 📺 ⚠ 🔌 Calor Gaz ♿ ♞
Last arrival time: 11:00
➡ 1 mile W of Cromer on A149 coast road.

CROSTHWAITE Cumbria   10B2

Lambhowe Caravan Park
Crosthwaite LA8 8JE
📞 015395-68483 **Fax** 01539-723339
Open 1 March-15 November 🔌 🚐

Ideal for touring the many attractions of the Lake District National Park. A secluded wooded site located between Lancaster and Windermere.

Size 14 touring pitches, 14 with electric hookup, 14 level pitches, 111 static caravans, 4 ⏢, 14 WCs, 1 CWP
£ car/caravan £10, motorhome £10
⚥¼ 🖥 📞 🔧 🔌 Calor ♞
Last arrival time: 7:30
➡ Leave M6 N at junction 36 onto A590, then A5074 to Bowness, just opposite Damson Dene hotel.

CROWBOROUGH East Sussex   5D3

Camping & Caravanning Club Site
Goldsmith Recreation Ground, Crowborough TN6 2TN

📞 **01892-664827**
Open end February-start November 🅰 🔌 🚐
Size 60 touring pitches, 24 with electric hookup, 4 ⏢, 7 WCs, 2 CWPs
£ car/tent £5.20-£7.80, car/caravan £5.20-£7.80, motorhome £5.20-£7.80, motorbike/tent £5.20-£7.80, children £1.50
℃ MasterCard Visa
🖥 📞 ⚠ ♿ ♞
Last arrival time: 11:00
➡ From Tunbridge Wells on A26 S. Before reaching Crowborough town centre, site is adjacent to major sports and leisure centre.

CROYDE BAY Devon   2C2

Bay View Farm
Braunton, Croyde Bay EX33 1PN
📞 **01271-890501**
Open March-October 🅰 🔌 🚐
Size 10 acres, 70 touring pitches, 24 with electric hookup, 70 level pitches, 3 static caravans, 16 ⏢, 18 WCs
⚥ 🖥 ⚠ Calor Gaz ♿ ♞
Last arrival time: 9:30
➡ From Braunton take B3231. Site on right.

DARLINGTON Co. Durham   11D2

Winston Caravan Park
Winston, Darlington DL2 3RH
📞 **01325-730228** **Fax** 01325-730228
Open 1 March-31 October 🅰 🔌 🚐

A pleasant family site ideally situated for exploring the surrounding countryside. Grassy, level and sheltered with tourers and tents welcome. Holiday caravans for hire, one with wheelchair access. ETB grading 4 ticks.

Size 2½ acres, 20 touring pitches, 16 with electric hookup, 20 level pitches, 11 static caravans, 5 ⏢, 5 WCs, 1 CWP
£ car/tent £7-£9, car/caravan £7-£9, motorhome £7-£9, motorbike/tent £7
Rental 🔌 £25-£30 nightly, £165-£195 weekly.
⚥¼ ✕¼ 🛒¼ 📞 🖥 Calor Gaz ♞
Last arrival time: 11:00
➡ Ten miles W of Darlington on A67, turn left into Winston Village and the site is 400 yards on right.

DARTMOUTH Devon   3D4

Deer Park Holiday Estate
Stoke Fleming, Dartmouth TQ6 0RF
☎ 01803-770253 Fax 01803-770320
Open March-November ▲ ⊕ ⇄
Size 12 acres, 160 touring pitches, 100 with electric
hookup, 160 level pitches, 12 ℞, 18 WCs, 1 CWP
℅ Visa
⚡ ✕ ☛ ⊡ ⬗ ➔ GR ⚠ Calor Gaz ⚒ ✕
Last arrival time: 10:00
➡ Situated 2 miles S of Dartmouth on A379. Observe
bus stop at site entrance.

Newlands Farm Camp Site
Newlands Farm, Slapton, Dartmouth TQ7 2RB
☎ 01548-580366
Open Whitsun-mid September ▲ ⊕ ⇄
Size 10 acres, 30 touring pitches, 8 with electric
hookup, 30 level pitches, 3 ℞, 7 WCs, 1 CWP
£ car/tent £6, car/caravan £6, motorhome £6,
motorbike/tent £6, children £0.50
Rental ▲ caravans £110-£200, tents £110-£160
⊡ ✕ WS
Last arrival time: 10:00
➡ From Totnes take A381 towards Kingsbridge
through Harbertonford and Halwell villages, past Esso
garage, take the 4th left turning, signposted Slapton,
go 4 miles, campsite on left. (Caravans must come
this way!)

DAWLISH Devon   3D3

Cofton Country Holiday Park

Starcross, Dawlish EX6 8RP

☎ **01626-890111** Fax **01626-891572**

Open Easter-31 October Å 🚐 🚐

Landscaped park with green meadows, bright flower beds, mature trees, woodlands and extensive countryside views. Only a short drive to Dawlish Warren beach.

Size 16 acres, 450 touring pitches, 300 with electric hookup, 62 static caravans, 46 🚿, 97 WCs, 2 CWPs
£ car/tent £5.50-£10, car/caravan £5.50-£10, motorhome £5.50-£10, motorbike/tent £5.50-£10, children £1-£1.75
Rental 🚐 £85-£410, cottages £170-£499.
℃ MasterCard Visa
🛒 ✗ 🍴 🗑 🔌 🚻 🎣 🎡 🅿 🔥 GR 🅼 🍴 Calor Gaz ♿ 🐕 WS
Last arrival time: 8:00
➡ From M5 junction 30 take A379 to Dawlish. Park is on left, ½ mile after small harbour at Cockwood Village.
See advert on previous page

Lady's Mile Touring & Camping Park

Exeter Road, Dawlish EX7 0LX

☎ **01626-863411** Fax **01626-888689**

Open mid March-end October Å 🚐 🚐
Size 20 acres, 300 touring pitches, 300 with electric hookup, 300 level pitches, 40 🚿, 80 WCs, 3 CWPs
£ car/tent £8-£11.50, car/caravan £8-£11.50, motorhome £8-£11.50, motorbike/tent £11.50, children £1.50-£2.30
Rental Chalet.
℃ MasterCard Visa
🛒 ✗ 🍴 🗑 🔌 🚻 🎣 🎡 🅿 🔥 GR TV 🅼 🍴 Calor Gaz ♿ 🐕 WS
Last arrival time: 8:00
➡ 1 mile N of Dawlish on A379.
See advert on previous page

Leadstone Camping

Warren Road, Dawlish EX7 0NG

☎ **01626-872239** Fax **01626-873833**

Open 19 June-4 September Å 🚐 🚐

Seven acres of rolling grassland in a natural secluded bowl within ½ mile of Dawlish Warren Beach and nature reserve. Ideally situated for exploring Devon.

Size 8 acres, 15 touring pitches, 32 with electric hookup, 100 level pitches, 12 🚿, 12 WCs, 1 CWP
£ car/tent £6.80-£8, car/caravan £8.80-£10.50, motorhome £6.80-£8, motorbike/tent £6.80, children £1.10-£1.30
🛒 ✗¼ 🗑 🔌 🅼 Calor Gaz 🐕
➡ From M5 junction 30 take A379 to Dawlish. As you approach Dawlish, turn left on the brow of hill signposted Dawlish Warren. Site is ½ mile on right.

Peppermint Park

Warren Road, Dawlish Warren EX7 0PQ

☎ **01626-863436**

Open Easter-October Å 🚐 🚐

Grassland park with some level terraces, all sheltered by mature trees. Nearest touring park to Dawlish Warren beach (600 yards). Free family entertainment nightly in licensed club.

Size 26 acres, 300 touring pitches, 190 with electric hookup, 250 level pitches, 35 static caravans, 39 🚿, 37 WCs, 2 CWPs
£ car/tent £5-£10.50, car/caravan £5-£10.50, motorhome £5-£10.50, motorbike/tent £5-£9.50, children £0.50-£1.75
Rental 🚐 holiday homes £55-£410
℃ MasterCard Visa
🛒 ✗ 🍴 🗑 🔌 🚻 🎣 🎡 🅿 🔥 GR 🅼 🍴 Calor Gaz ♿ 🐕
➡ From M5 (jn 30) take A379 to Dawlish. Turn left to Dawlish Warren, 7 miles on, just before entering Dawlish. Park is on left at bottom of hill.

DEAL Kent 5F3

Sutton Vale Caravan Club
Sutton-by-Dover, Deal, Kent CT15 5DH
☎ 01304-374155 Fax 01304-381132
Open March-January ▲ ⚏ ⌂

A beautiful rural park set in a conservation area shrouded by trees section off in 3 fields.

Size 6 acres, 14 touring pitches, 14 with electric hookup, 100 level pitches, 100 static caravans, 8 ⍾, 8 WCs, 1 CWP
£ car/caravan £9.50-£13.50, motorhome £9.50-£13.50
Rental ⚏ Chalet. £105-£335
⚑ ✕ ⚑ ⍾ ⚑ ⌂ ⍾ ⌂ ⚑ Calor & ⚑ WS
Last arrival time: 11:00
➜ From A2. 5 miles from Dover, exit Whitfield roundabout A256, then after 20 yards turn right opposite McDonalds. Site is 4 miles on left.

DEVIZES Wiltshire 4A3

Lakeside
Rowde, Devizes SN10 2LX
☎ 01380-722767

A beautiful, landscaped, rural setting with excellent facilities surrounding a large well stocked spring fed lake.

Size 6½ acres, 55 touring pitches, 50 with electric hookup, 55 level pitches, 4 ⍾, 6 WCs, 1 CWP
£ car/tent £6.50-£7, car/caravan £7-£9.45, motorhome £6.50-£9.45, motorbike/tent £6.50, children £1
⚑ ⚑¼ ✕¼ ⚑¼ ⚑ ⌂ ⚑ Calor Gaz & ⚑
Last arrival time: 10:00
➜ 1 mile N of Devizes on A342.

Lower Foxhangers Farm
Rowde, Devizes
☎ 01380-828254 Fax 01380-828254
Open Easter-October ▲ ⚏ ⌂

Quietly located working farm alonside canal flight of 29 locks. Fishing, boating, walking and cycling. Self catering in 4 holiday homes of farmhouse bed and breakfast

Size 2 acres, 10 touring pitches, 4 with electric hookup, 10 level pitches, 4 static caravans, 1 ⍾, 2 WCs, 1 CWP
£ car/tent £6, car/caravan £6, motorhome £6, motorbike/tent £6-£7
Rental Chalet.
⚑ ⌂ Calor Gaz ⚑
➜ 2 miles W of Devizes on A361. ½ mile E of junction of A361/A365.

DISS Norfolk 9E3

Willows Camping & Caravan Park
Diss Road, Scole IP21 4DH
☎ 01379-740271
Open May-September ▲ ⚏ ⌂
Size 4 acres, 32 touring pitches, 18 with electric hookup, 32 level pitches, 2 ⍾, 7 WCs, 2 CWPs
£ car/tent £7, car/caravan £7, motorhome £7, motorbike/tent £7, children £0.25
⚑¼ ✕¼ ⚑¼ ⌂ ⚑ ⚑ Calor Gaz ⚑
Last arrival time: 11:00
➜ 200 yards off the A140 roundabout at Scole, in the direction of Diss on A1066.

DORCHESTER Dorset 3E3

Giant's Head Caravan & Camping Park
Old Sherborne Road, Dorchester DT2 7TR
☎ 01300-341242
Open 17 April-31 October ▲ ⚏ ⌂
Size 3½ acres, 60 touring pitches, 20 with electric hookup, 60 level pitches, 2 ⍾, 8 WCs, 1 CWP
£ car/tent £5-£6.50, car/caravan £5-£6.50, motorhome £5-£6.50, motorbike/tent £5-£6.50, children £1
Rental Chalet.
⌂ ⚑ ⌂ Calor Gaz ⚑ WS
➜ Into Dorchester, avoiding bypass, at Top o' Town roundabout take Sherborne road. After 500 yards take right fork at Loders (BP) Garage and follow signs.

Home Farm Camping & Caravan Site
Puncknowle, Dorchester DT2 9BW
☎ 01308-897258
Open April-October **A ⚑ ☂**

Small secluded site in beautiful area. Good food at village inn. Sea fishing nearby.

Size 5 acres, 5 touring pitches, 22 level pitches, 14 static caravans, 4 ⛌, 8 WCs, 1 CWP
£ car/tent £4-£5, car/caravan £5-£6, motorhome £5, motorbike/tent £4-£5
Rental ⚑
☎¼ ⛁ ☎ ⛁ ⚠ Calor Gaz ⛏
Last arrival time: 9:00
➜ From Dorchester take A35 towards Bridport. Drive through Winterbourne Abbas and turn left just before the dual carriageway to Lilton Cheney. Follow signs to Puncknowle.

DOVER Kent   5F3

Hawthorn Farm
Martin Mill, Dover CT15 5LA
☎ 01304-852658 Fax 01304-853417
Open 1 March-31 October

Award winning park set in 28 acres. A quiet, peaceful base from which to discover the delights of Kent and only one hour from France.

Size 250 touring pitches, 100 with electric hookup, 24 ⛌, 21 WCs, 2 CWPs
CC Visa
☎ Calor Gaz WS
➜ Well signposted on A258 from Dover to Deal.

DUNWICH Suffolk   9F4

Cliff House
Minsmere Road, Dunwich IP17 3DQ

☎ 01728-648282 Fax 01728-648282
Open Easter-October **A ⚑ ☂**
Size 30 acres, 121 touring pitches, 75 with electric hookup, 7 level pitches, 78 static caravans, 8 ⛌, 12 WCs, 3 CWPs
£ car/tent £8-£12, car/caravan £8-£12, motorhome £8-£12, motorbike/tent £0-£12
Rental ⚑ Chalet. £120-£260
CC MasterCard Visa
☎ ✕ ⛻ ⛁ ☎ ⛁ ⛏ GR ⛉ ⚠ ⛁ Calor Gaz ⛏ WS
Last arrival time: 9:00
➜ From A12, 5 miles N of Saxmundham, follow signs to Dunwich Heath. Site is on left.

EAST HORSLEY Surrey   4C3

Camping & Caravanning Club Site
Ockham Road North, East Horsley KT24 6PE
☎ 01483-283273
Open end March-start November **A ⚑ ☂**
Size 12 acres, 135 touring pitches, 60 with electric hookup, 10 ⛌, 16 WCs, 1 CWP
£ car/tent £5.60-£8.60, car/caravan £5.60-£8.60, motorhome £5.60-£8.60, motorbike/tent £5.60-£8.60, children £1.50
CC MasterCard Visa
⛁ ⛏ GR ⚠ ♿ ⛏ WS
Last arrival time: 11:00
➜ Leave M25 (jn 10) and head S on A3, then take B2039 towards East Horsley, site is signposted.

ESKDALE GREEN Cumbria   10A2

Fisherground Farm
Eskdale Green CA19 1TF
☎ 01946-723319
Open mid March-mid November **A ☂**

Peaceful family site in a beautiful location. Adventure playground, children's raft pool, 7 mile miniature railway, (station on site). Brand new toilet block. Camp fires allowed. Brochure on request.

Size 3 acres, 30 touring pitches, 4 with electric hookup, 30 level pitches, 8 ⛌, 10 WCs, 1 CWP
£ car/tent £7-£8, motorhome £7-£8, motorbike/tent £7-£8, children £2
Rental Chalet.
✕¼ ⛁ ⛏ ⛁ ⚠ ♿ ⛏
➜ At King George IV inn, turn up valley towards Hard Knott pass. Fisherground is 400 yards on left.

EXETER Devon 3D3

Haldon Lodge Farm Caravan & Camping Park

Kennford, Near Exeter EX6 7YG
☎ 01392-832312
Open all year **⚊ ⊞ ⇶**

Peaceful family site with beautiful forest scenery, nature walks, fishing lakes, riding holidays, barbecues plus friendly country inns. Excellent facilities with hook-ups. Sea and Exeter 15 minutes.

Size 7½ acres, 40 touring pitches, 80 with electric hookup, 60 level pitches, 4 static caravans, 8 ☂, 14 WCs, 2 CWPs
£ car/tent £5-£7.50, car/caravan £5-£7.50, motorhome £5-£8, motorbike/tent £5-£7.50
Rental ⊞ Chalet. £70-£195
⚊ ✗ ⛝ ▣ ⚊ ⛁ ⛝ ▣ ▦ ⑰ ⚠ Calor Gaz ⚑ WS
Last arrival time: 10:00
➡ Off A38 at Kennford services, follow signs to Haldon Lodge turning left into village. Proceed passing post office and over motor bridge turning left. 1¼ miles to site.

Springfield Holiday Park

Tedburn Road, Tedburn St Mary, Exeter EX6 6EW
☎ 01647-24242 Fax 01647-24131
Open 15 March-15 November **⚊ ⊞ ⇶**

A quiet family owned park set in nine acres of beautiful countryside on the fringe of Dartmoor National Park. Eight miles west of Exeter and approximately 30 minutes drive to the beaches.

Size 9 acres, 88 touring pitches, 50 with electric hookup, 88 level pitches, 13 static caravans, 8 ☂, 16 WCs, 2 CWPs

£ car/tent £6-£7.50, car/caravan £5.50-£8.50, motorhome £5.50-£9.50, motorbike/tent £6-£7
Rental ⊞ £100-£260
⚊ ⚊¼ ✗ ⛝ ▣ ⚊ ⛁ ▣ ⑃ ▦ ▣ ⚠ Calor Gaz ⚑ WS
Last arrival time: 9:30
➡ From M5 (jn 31) take A30 to Okehampton. Leave A30 at second exit, signposted Tedburn St Mary. Turn left at roundabout and drive through village to site on right, 1¾ miles from village.

EXFORD Somerset 3D2

Westermill Farm

Exford, Minehead TA24 7NJ
☎ 01643-831238 Fax 01643-831660
Open April-October **⚊ ⇶**

Beautiful secluded site for tents by shallow river. Heart of Exmoor National Park. Four waymarked walks over 500 acre working farm. Natural and uncommercialised. Quality Scandinavian log cottages for hire. Silver David Bellamy award for conservation

Size 6 acres, 60 touring pitches, 60 level pitches, 6 ☂, 14 WCs, 1 CWP
£ car/tent £7, motorhome £7, motorbike/tent £7, children £1
Rental Chalet. Cottages £140-£399
⚊ ▣ ⚊ ⛁ ⚊ Calor Gaz ⚑
➡ Leave Exford on Porlock road, after ¼ mile fork left. Continue 2 miles past another campsite until 'Westermill' seen on tree, then fork left.

EXMOUTH Devon 3D3

Webbers Farm Caravan Park

Castle Lane, Woodbury, Exeter EX5 1EA
☎ 01395-232276 Fax 01395-233389
Open Easter-end September **⚊ ⊞ ⇶**
Size 7½ acres, 100 touring pitches, 100 with electric hookup, 20 level pitches, 14 ☂, 17 WCs, 6 CWPs
£ car/tent £6.95-£9.50, car/caravan £6.95-£9.50, motorhome £6.95-£9.50, children £1.50
CC MasterCard Visa
⚊ ⚊¼ ✗¼ ⛝¼ ▣ ⚊ ⛁ ⚊ ⚠ Calor Gaz ♿ ⚑ WS
Last arrival time: 10:00
➡ From M5 junction 30 take A376 to Exmouth. At second roundabout take B3179 to Woodbury and follow signs from village centre.

EYE Suffolk   9E3

Honeypot Camp & Caravan Park
Wortham, Eye IP22 1PW
☎ 01379-783312 Fax 01379-783293
Open April-September ▲ ⛺ 🚐

A quiet, well organised landscaped country site, part of which surrounds two lakes, on well grassed, level, free draining land, facing due south. Under the personal supervision of the owners for over 20 years.

Size 6½ acres, 35 touring pitches, 22 with electric hookup, 35 level pitches, 2 🚿, 4 WCs, 1 CWP
£ car/tent £6.50-£7.50, car/caravan £7.50, motorhome £7.50, motorbike/tent £6.50, children £1
✕¼ 🌢¼ 🗑 🛒 🔥 ▨ ⚠ Calor Gaz 🐕 WS
Last arrival time: 11:00
➡ South side of A143, 4 miles W of Diss, 17 miles E of Bury St Edmunds. Main 'A' road entrance opposite the tea pot sign.

FAIRFORD Gloucestershire   4A2

Second Chance Touring Park
Castle Eaton SN6 6SZ
☎ 01285-810675
Open 1 March-30 November ▲ ⛺ 🚐
Size 2 acres, 26 touring pitches, 26 with electric hookup, 26 level pitches, 4 🚿, 5 WCs, 1 CWP
£ car/tent £6, car/caravan £6, motorhome £6, motorbike/tent £6, children £1
✕¼ 🌢¼ 🗑 🔥 ▨ Calor 🐕
Last arrival time: 9:00
➡ Follow A419 from Cirencester or Swindon, turn off at Fairford signpost and proceed 3 miles. Turn left at first Castle Eaton signpost. Site is 200 yards on left.

FAKENHAM Norfolk   9E2

Crossways Caravan Site
Holt Road, Little Snoring, Fakenham NR21 0AX
☎ 01328-878335 Fax 01328-878335
Open March-October ▲ ⛺ 🚐

A quiet caravan site with provision for some tents. Handy for touring the north Norfolk coast.

Size 2 acres, 26 touring pitches, 13 with electric hookup, 2 🚿, 7 WCs, 1 CWP
£ car/tent £6-£9.50, car/caravan £6-£9.50, motorhome £6-£9.50, motorbike/tent £6-£9.50
🛒 🔥 Calor Gaz 🐕
➡ On A148, 3 miles N of Fakenham.

FALMOUTH Cornwall   2A4

Calamankey Farm
Longdowns, Penryn TR10 9DL
☎ 01209-860314
Open April-end October ▲ 🚐
Size 4 static caravans, 3 🚿, 14 WCs, 1 CWP
£ car/tent £5, motorhome £5, motorbike/tent £5, children £1.25
Rental 🚐 £80-£150
🌢¼ ✕¼ 🌢¼ 🔥 🗑 🐕
Last arrival time: 10:00
➡ From Truro, take A39 to Treluswell roundabout and go straight across onto A394 towards Helston. Calamankey Farm is in Longdowns village, opposite Murco filling station.

Menallack Farm Caravan & Camping Site
Treverva, Penryn, Falmouth TR10 9BP
☎ 01326-340333 Fax 01326-340333
Open April-October ▲ ⛺ 🚐
Size 1½ acres, 30 touring pitches, 4 with electric hookup, 30 level pitches, 2 🚿, 6 WCs, 1 CWP
£ car/tent £5-£5.50, car/caravan £5-£5.50, motorhome £5-£5.50, motorbike/tent £5-£5.50, children £0.70-£0.80
🌢 🌢 🗑 Calor Gaz 🐕
Last arrival time: 9:00
➡ From Truro go towards Falmouth for 10 miles. Follow A39 over double mini roundabouts. At next roundabouts go straight across first roundabout and take second exit from second roundabout. Do not take the Helston road. In Mabe Burnthouse go straight over crossroads. 2 miles further on at next crossroads turn right towards Gweek. Go through Lamanva and Treverva. Farm is ¾ mile beyond Trevera on left going towards Gweek.

FAREHAM Hampshire 4B4

Ellerslie Camping & Caravan Park
Down End Road, Fareham PO16 8TS
☎ 01329-822248 Fax 01329-822248
Open March-October ▲ ⊞ ⊞

A small, attractive wooded site on the southern slopes of Portsdown Hill with space for approxiately 40 caravans and cars. Positioned close to the M27.

Size 4 acres, 40 touring pitches, 30 with electric hookup, 4 level pitches, 8 ☂, 2 WCs, 1 CWP
£ car/tent £6, car/caravan £6.50, motorhome £6.50, motorbike/tent £5.50, children £0.50
CC MasterCard Visa
⚡¼ ⊞¼ ⊡ ⊠ ⊡ ⅙ ☂ WS
Last arrival time: 10:00
➜ From M27 junction 11 take A27 to Portsmouth. After ½ mile turn left at traffic lights into Down End Road. Site ½ mile on right.

FARNHAM Surrey 4C3

Tilford Touring
Tilford, Farnham GU10 2DF
☎ 01252-792199 Fax 01252-781027
Open all year
Size 4 acres, 75 touring pitches, 50 with electric hookup, 75 level pitches, 3 ☂, 4 WCs, 1 CWP
£ car/tent £6-£7.50, car/caravan £8
Rental ⊞
⚡¼ ☎
➜ From Farnham railway station, head S over level crossing and immediately turn right. Then 3 miles to Tilford village, site beside The Hankley Pub.

FENSTANTON Cambridgeshire 9D4

Crystal Lakes Caravan Park
Low Road, Fenstanton PE18 9W
☎ 01480-497728 Fax 01480-497728
Open 1 March-31 October
Size 40 acres, 50 touring pitches, 45 with electric hookup, 72 level pitches, 16 ☂, 16 WCs, 1 CWP
⚡ ✗ ⚑ ⊡ ⊠ GR ⊡ TV ⊿ Calor Gaz ⅙ WS
Last arrival time: 24 hrs
➜ Halfway between Cambridge and Huntingdon, off A14. Signposted in village.

FOLKESTONE Kent 5F3

Little Satmar Holiday Park
Winehouse Lane, Capel-le-Ferne, Folkestone CT18 7JF
☎ 01303-251188 Fax 01303-251188
Open April-October ▲ ⊞ ⊞

Situated inland of the B2011. Quiet country setting. Holiday homes for hire, excellent facilities for touring caravans and camping. Rose award winning park. Satisfaction guaranteed.

Size 8 acres, 60 touring pitches, 60 with electric hookup, 60 level pitches, 70 static caravans, 6 ☂, 15 WCs, 2 CWPs
£ car/tent £6.25-£8.25, car/caravan £6.25-£8.25, motorhome £6.25-£8.25, motorbike/tent £4.50, children £0.75
Rental Chalet. £130-£235
⚡ ✗¼ ⊞¼ ⊡ ⊠ ⊡ GR ⊿ Calor Gaz ⅙ ☂ WS
Last arrival time: 11:00
➜ Leave A20 at junction of B2011, signposted Capel-le-Ferne. In Capel-le-Ferne, turn right into Winehouse Lane and site is immediately ahead.

Camping & Caravanning Club Site

The Warren, Folkestone CT19 6PT
☎ **01303-255093**
Open end March-end September **A** 🚐 🚍
Size 4 acres, 82 touring pitches, 6 🍴, 17 WCs, 1 CWP
£ car/tent £4.60-£6.80, car/caravan £4.60-£6.80,
motorhome £4.60-£6.80, motorbike/tent £4.60-£6.80,
children £1.40
ℂℂ MasterCard Visa
🔌 ⊀
Last arrival time: 11:00
➡ From M20 and A20 turn S to Folkestone and
follow signs to site.

Little Switzerland Caravan Site

Wear Bay Road, Folkestone CT19 6PS
☎ **01303-252168**
Open 1 March-31 October **A** 🚐 🚍

*Quiet site in cliffs east of town with magnificent views
of Dover Straits.*

Size 2 acres, 18 touring pitches, 12 with electric
hookup, 13 static caravans, 4 🍴, 12 WCs, 1 CWP
£ car/tent £8.85, car/caravan £9.50, motorhome £9.50,
motorbike/tent £8.50
🔌¼ ✕ 💧 🔲 🔋 🛢 🄶🄡 🔌 Calor Gaz ⊀
➡ On A20 over first two roundabouts. At third
roundabout at foot of Folkestone Hill turn right along
A2033 (Hill Road), then ½ mile further continue
ahead into Wear Bay Road for ¼ mile, site on left.

FOLKINGHAM Lincolnshire   8C2

Low Farm Touring Park

Spring Lane, Folkingham, Sleaford NG34 0SJ
☎ **01529-497322**
Open Easter-end October **A** 🚐 🚍
Size 2½ acres, 36 touring pitches, 25 with electric
hookup, 36 level pitches, 4 🍴, 6 WCs, 1 CWP
£ car/tent £6.50-£7.50, car/caravan £6.50-£7.50,
motorhome £6.50-£7.50, motorbike/tent £6.50-£7.50,
children £1
🔌¼ ✕¼ ⬤¼ 🛢 🔌 & ⊀ WS
➡ Signposted from A15. Folkingham is midway
between towns of Bourne and Sleaford. Turn
opposite petrol station.

FORDINGBRIDGE Hampshire   4A4

Sandy Balls Holiday Centre

Godshill, Fordingbridge SP6 2JY
☎ **01425 653042** **Fax** **01425-653067**
Open all year **A** 🚐 🚍
Size 120 acres, 350 touring pitches, 340 with electric
hookup, 350 level pitches, 250 static caravans, 40 🍴,
50 WCs, 9 CWPs
£ car/tent £10.50-£18.50, car/caravan £12-£20.50,
motorhome £12-£20, motorbike/tent £10.50-£18.50,
children £1
Rental Lodge £157-619, caravan £117-£544 per week
ℂℂ MasterCard Visa
🔌 ✕ 🍴 🔌 🔲 🔲 🔳 🔳 🔳 🔳 🔌 🄶🄡 🔋 TV 🄼 🔳 🔌
Calor Gaz & ⊀
Last arrival time: 8:00
➡ From A338 take B3078 to Cadnam. 1½ miles from
M27 take B3078 to Fordingbridge 9 miles.

GARSTANG Lancashire   10B3

Bridge House Marina & Caravan Park

Nateby Crossing Lane, Nateby, Garstang PR3 0JJ
☎ **01995-603207** **Fax** **01995-601612**
Open March-January **A** 🚐 🚍

*Family owned, sheltered level grassy site, with
centrally heated toilet block. Close to Blackpool, the
Lake District and Bowland Fells. An 18 hole golf
course is just one mile away.*

Size 6 acres, 50 touring pitches, 50 with electric
hookup, 50 level pitches, 20 static caravans, 8 🍴, 12
WCs, 2 CWPs
£ car/caravan £7.70, motorhome £7.70
ℂℂ MasterCard Visa
🔌 ✕¼ 🛢 🔌 🄼 Calor Gaz ⊀ WS
Last arrival time: 10:30
➡ From M6 junction 32 take A6 to N. After 9 miles
turn left at Chequered Flag. After 100 yards turn left
to site 400 yards on left.

Six Arches Holiday Caravan Park

Scorton, Garstang PR3 1AC

☎ 01524-791683

Open 1 March-31 October

Family run riverside park within easy reach of Blackpool, Morecambe, Lake District and Bowland. Family entertainment in club house. Colour brochure available on request.

Size 16 acres, 16 touring pitches, 16 with electric hookup, 16 level pitches, 275 static caravans, 4 ☗, 8 WCs, 1 CWP
£ car/caravan £9-£10, motorhome £9-£10
Rental 6 berth caravans/flats £125-£250
Calor
Last arrival time: 10:00
➡ Turn E off A6 by Little Chef, ¼ mile N of junction with B6430. After 200 yards turn left under railway bridge to site.

GATESHEAD Tyne & Wear 13F4

Derwent Park Caravan and Camping Site

Gateshead

☎ 01207-543383

Open 1 April-30 September

This beautiful riverside park offers tennis, crazy golf, bowling green and adventure playground. Ideally placed for touring Northumbria and near to the Gateshead Metro Centre and Beamish museum.

Size 9 acres, 47 touring pitches, 35 with electric hookup, 25 static caravans, 12 ☗, 13 WCs, 1 CWP
£ car/tent £5.50-£9.50, car/caravan £8-£9, motorhome £8.50-£9.50, motorbike/tent £6, children £1
℀ MasterCard Visa
Calor Gaz
Last arrival time: 11:30
➡ Situated seven miles south west of Newcastle at the junction of the A694 and B6314, 3 miles from A1.

GISBURN Lancashire 10C3

Rimington Caravan Park

Hardacre Lane, Gisburn BB7 4EE

☎ 01200 445355

Open March-October

Peaceful, family-run site in the beautiful Ribble Valley. A high standard of facilities and amenities ensure a pleasant stay.

Size 12 acres, 25 touring pitches, 16 with electric hookup, 20 level pitches, 130 static caravans, 6 ⚲, 16 WCs, 2 CWPs

⚲ ▣ ▣ ▣ ▣ ▣ Calor Gaz WS

Last arrival time: 9:00

➜ From Gisburn, travel S on A682 for 1½ miles, turn right at sign. Site on right in 400 yards.

GLASTONBURY Somerset 3E2

Old Oaks Touring Park

Wick Farm, Wick, Glastonbury BA6 0JS

☎ 01458-831437

Open 1 March-31 October ▲ ⛺ ⛺

A family run park, set in delightfully tranquil and unspoilt countryside with lovely views and walks, offering excellent amenities in an outstanding environment.

Size 4 acres, 40 touring pitches, 40 with electric hookup, 40 level pitches, 6 ⚲, 9 WCs, 2 CWPs

£ car/tent £7-£8.50, car/caravan £7-£8.50, motorhome £7-£8.50, motorbike/tent £7-£8.50, children £1.50-£1.75

CC MasterCard Visa

⚲ ▣ ▣ ▣ ▣ ▣ ▣ ▣ Calor Gaz ⚲ ⚲

Last arrival time: 9:00

➜ 1½ miles from Glastonbury on A361 Shepton Mallet road, turn left at sign for Wick. Park on left in 1 mile; or from A39 Wells Road, left off roundabout approaching Glastonbury, at sign for Wick park is 1½ miles on right.

GLOSSOP Derbyshire 10C4

Camping & Caravanning Club Site

Crowden, Hadfield, Hyde

☎ 01457-866057

Open end February-start November ▲ ⛺ ⛺

Size 2½ acres, 46 touring pitches, 2 ⚲, 6 WCs, 1 CWP

£ car/tent £4.60-£6.80, car/caravan £4.60-£6.80, motorhome £4.60-£6.80, motorbike/tent £4.60-£6.80, children £1.30

CC MasterCard Visa

⚲ ▣ ⚲

Last arrival time: 1:00

➜ From M67 (Hyde) take A628. Site is on left.

GOATHLAND North Yorkshire 11E2

Brow House Farm

Goathland YO22 5NP

☎ 01947-896274

Open March-November ▲ ⛺ ⛺

Excellent location for exploring the National Park and the Moors.

Size 3 acres, 50 touring pitches, 50 level pitches, 2 ⚲, 2 WCs, 1 CWP

£ car/tent £4-£5, car/caravan £4-£5, motorhome £4-£5, motorbike/tent £4-£5

⚲¼ ✗¼ ▣¼ ▣ ▣ ⚲

Last arrival time: 11:00

➜ Turn W off A169 at ¼ mile N of Eller Beck Bridge. Site 1 mile S of Goathland.

GOONHAVERN Cornwall 2B4

Rose Hill Farm Tourist Park
Goonhavern TR4 9LA
☎ 01872-572448
Open Easter-September ▲ ⚐ ⏚
Size 7 acres, 65 touring pitches, 40 with electric hookup, 65 level pitches, 7 ♺, 9 WCs, 1 CWP
£ car/tent £5-£8.50, car/caravan £5-£8.50, motorhome £5-£8.50, motorbike/tent £5-£8.50, children £0.75
🛉 ✕¼ ☛¼ ▣ ☒ ▣ GR ◉ TV ⚠ Calor Gaz ♜
Last arrival time: dusk
➜ From A30 take B3285 signposted Perranporth to village of Goonhavern. Turn right at New Inn. Site is on right.

Silverbow Park
Goonhavern TR4 9NX
☎ 01872-572347 **Fax** 01872-572347
Size 24 acres, 90 touring pitches, 54 with electric hookup, 80 level pitches, 12 ♺, 15 WCs, 1 CWP
£ car/tent £5.50-£13.50, car/caravan £5.50-£13.50, motorhome £5.50-£13.50, motorbike/tent £5.50-£13.50, children £1.50-£2.60
🛉 ▣ ☒ ▣ ☒ ▣ GR ◉ ⚠ Calor Gaz ♿
Last arrival time: 10:30
➜ From A30 take B3285 Perranporth road. At T junction in Goonhavern village, turn left onto A3075 for ½ mile. Silverbow entrance is on the left.

GORRAN Cornwall 2B4

Trelispen Camping & Caravaning Park
Gorran, St Austell PL26 6NS
☎ 01726-843501 **Fax** 01726-843501

Open 1 April-31 October ▲ ⚐ ⏚
Size 2 acres, 40 touring pitches, 8 with electric hookup, 40 level pitches, 2 ♺, 7 WCs, 1 CWP
£ car/tent £7-£10, car/caravan £8-£10, motorhome £8-£10, motorbike/tent £7-£9, children £1-£3
🛉¼ ✕¼ ☛¼ ▣ ☒ ▣ ♜
➜ From St Austell take B3273 for Mevagissey. Follow signs for park.

GOSFORTH Cumbria 10A2

Church Stile Camp Site
Wasdale, Seascale, Gosforth CA20 1ET
☎ 01946-726388
Open March-October ▲ ⏚

Set on a working family farm within easy reach of Scafell and many other mountains. An ideal walking and climbing area.

Size 4 acres, 50 touring pitches, 50 level pitches, 30 static caravans, 4 ♺, 9 WCs, 1 CWP
£ car/tent £5-£6, motorhome £5-£6, motorbike/tent £5-£6, children £1
✕¼ ☛¼ ▣ ☒ ▣ ⚠ ☒ ♜ WS
Last arrival time: 10:00
➜ Off A595, 4½ miles E of Gosforth to Nether Wasdale village.

GOSPORT Hampshire 4B4

Kingfisher Caravan Park

Browndown Road, Stokes Bay, Gosport PO13 9BE
☎ 01705-502611 Fax 01705-583583
Open February-November Å ⊄ ⊅

A family run site situated on the South Coast within easy reach of Portsmouth with ferries to the continent and Isle of Wight.

Size 14 acres, 120 touring pitches, 100 with electric hookup, 120 level pitches, 100 static caravans, 12 ⚑, 17 WCs, 2 CWPs
£ car/tent £13-£16.50, car/caravan £13-£16.50, motorhome £13-£16.50, motorbike/tent £9-£16.50
Rental ⊄ £45 per night.
ℂ MasterCard Visa
⚡ ✗ 🚻 🗑 🔌 GR ⚠ 🗙   ⚑ Calor & ⚞ WS
Last arrival time: 11:00
➡ From M27 junction 11 take A32 to Gosport. Seafront road into Browndown Road.

GRANGE-OVER-SANDS Cumbria   10B3

Lakeland Leisure Park

Moor Lane, Flookburgh LA11 7LT
☎ 015395-58556 Fax 015395-58559
Open March-October Å ⊄ ⊅

A family holiday park, just a few minutes drive from picturesque Grange Over Sands and within easy driving distance of the Lakes. Indoor/outdoor pools, kids clubs, tennis and bowling. Live family entertainment, bars, great food. A 'British Holidays Park'.

Size 105 acres, 100 touring pitches, 90 with electric hookup, 100 level pitches, 750 static caravans, 7 ⚑, 1 CWP
£ car/tent £8-£14, car/caravan £8-£14, motorhome £8-£14, motorbike/tent £8-£14, children £2

Rental ⊄
ℂ MasterCard Visa
⚡ 🚐 🚻 🔌 🗑 🗙 🗙 🗙 GR 🔍 ⚠ ⚑ Calor Gaz ⚞
Last arrival time: 9:00
➡ From M6 junction 36 take A590 to Barrow-in-Furness. Then take B5277 through Grange over Sands and into Flookburgh. Turn left at the village square and travel 2 miles down this road to park.

Old Park Wood Caravan Park

Holker, Cark-in-Cartmel LA11 7PP
☎ 015395-58266 Fax 015395-58101
Open March-October ⊄ ⊅

Overlooking the estuary of the River Leven with exceptional view of the hills. Facilities are provided for both touring and motor caravans. No tents allowed.

Size 36 acres, 42 touring pitches, 42 with electric hookup, 32 level pitches, 325 static caravans, 8 ⚑, 12 WCs, 2 CWPs
£ car/caravan £12.75, motorhome £12.75
⚡ 🚻 🔌 🗑 🗙 ⚠ Calor ⚞
➡ At 4¾ miles W of Grange, or 1 mile N of Cark on B5277, turn W.

GRASSINGTON North Yorkshire   10B3

Hawkswick Cote Caravan Park

Arncliffe, Skipton BD23 5PX
☎ 01756-770226 Fax 01756-770327
Open March-October Å ⊄ ⊅
Size 50 touring pitches, 50 with electric hookup, 50 level pitches, 90 static caravans, 5 ⚑, 6 WCs, 1 CWP
£ car/tent £8, car/caravan £8-£12, motorhome £8-£12, motorbike/tent £8, children £1.50
⚡ 🚻 🔌 🗑 ⚠ Calor Gaz & ⚞
➡ B6160 Threshfield to Grassington Road. Half a mile N of Kilnsey take road to Arncliffe. Park is on left, 1½ miles.

HAILSHAM East Sussex   5D4

Old Mill Caravan Park

Chalvington Road, Golden Cross, Hailsham BN27 3SS
☎ 01825-872532
Open 1 April-31 October ⊄ ⊅
Size 2 acres, 25 touring pitches, 17 with electric hookup, 25 level pitches, 2 ⚑, 5 WCs, 1 CWP

£ car/caravan £5.50-£6

🔄¼ ✕¼ 🚐¼ ★

➡ Turn off A22 4 miles NW of Hailsham at Golden Cross by Golden Cross inn into Chalvington road. Park in 150 yards.

HALESOWEN West Midlands   8A3

Camping & Caravanning Club Site
Clent Hills, Fieldhouse Lane, Romsey, Halesowen B62 0NH

📞 **01562-710015**

Open end March-start November **A 🚐 🚍**

Size 6½ acres, 130 touring pitches, 48 with electric hookup, 8 🚿, 13 WCs, 1 CWP

£ car/tent £5.20-£7.80, car/caravan £5.20-£7.80, motorhome £5.20-£7.80, motorbike/tent £5.20-£7.80, children £1.50

CC MasterCard Visa

🔲 🔳 GR 🔺 ♿ ★ WS

Last arrival time: 11:00

➡ Take B4551, then road by Sun Hotel, turn left at Bell End Broughten junction. Left turn after ¼ mile. Site on left.

HALTWHISTLE Northumberland   10B1

Camping & Caravanning Club Site
Burnfoot Park Village, Haltwhistle NE49 0JP

📞 **01434-320106**

Open end September-start November **A 🚐 🚍**

Size 3 acres, 60 touring pitches, 34 with electric hookup, 4 🚿, 9 WCs, 1 CWP

£ car/tent £4.60-£6.80, car/caravan £4.60-£6.80, motorhome £4.60-£6.80, motorbike/tent £4.60-£6.80, children £1.40

CC MasterCard Visa

🔲 🔳 🔳 ★

Last arrival time: 11:00

➡ Turn S of A69 immediately W of Haltwhistle, site is on right.

HARROGATE North Yorkshire   11D3

High Moor Farm Park
Skipton Road, Harrogate HG3 2LZ

📞 **01423-563637 Fax 01423-529449**

Open 1 April-31 October **A 🚐 🚍**

Size 22 acres, 250 touring pitches, 200 with electric hookup, 250 level pitches, 151 static caravans, 10 🚿, 25 WCs, 2 CWPs

£ car/tent £8.75-£9, car/caravan £8.75-£9, motorhome £8.75-£9, motorbike/tent £8.75-£9

Rental 🚐

CC MasterCard Visa

🔳 ✕ 🚐 🔲 🔳 🔳 🔳 P 🔳 🔳 GR 🔺 🍴 Calor Gaz ♿ ★ WS

Last arrival time: 11:00

➡ On A59, 4 miles W of Harrogate.

Ripley Caravan Park
Ripley, Harrogate HG3 3AU
Tel: 01423-770050

Luxury touring park in the countryside. First class facilities: Indoor heated swimming pool, sauna, sunbed, games room, nursery playroom, playground, tennis net, football pitch, shop, laundry and disabled unit. At a crossroads for the Yorkshire Dales, only three miles to Harrogate and the Yorkshire Dales. At junction of A61/B6165. Park 300 yards towards Knaresborough.

Maustin Caravan Park
The Riddings, Spring Lane, Kearby-with-Netherby, Wetherby LS22 4DP

📞 **0113-288 6234 Fax 0113-288 6234**

Open March-October **A 🚐 🚍**

Award winners for their peaceful environment. Catering for adults only. Situated close to Harrogate and Harewood House. Spacious tourer pitches, hire luxury holiday homes. Excellent facilities.

Size 6 acres, 16 touring pitches, 16 with electric hookup, 16 level pitches, 70 static caravans, 2 🚿, 6 WCs, 1 CWP

£ car/tent £8-£8.50, car/caravan £8.50-£9, motorhome £8.50

Rental 🚐 from £195 per week

CC Visa

🔳 ✕ 🚐 🔲 🍴 Calor Gaz ★

➡ From A61, after crossing River Wharfe, bottom of Harewood Bank, take first right signposted Kirkby Overblow. Then right again to Kearby, then right to caravan park.

Ripley Caravan Park

Ripley, Harrogate HG3 3AU
☎ 01423-770050 Fax 01423-770050
Open Easter-31 October ▲ 🚐 🚏
Size 18 acres, 100 touring pitches, 75 with electric hookup, 100 level pitches, 15 ☔, 18 WCs, 1 CWP
£ car/tent £6.25-£7.25, car/caravan £6.25-£7.25, motorhome £6.25-£7.25, motorbike/tent £7.25, children £1
⚌ ✕¼ 🛒¼ 🔌 🔋 🔲 🔺 🖳 GR 🔳 🗘 Calor Gaz ⅃ ⚐ WS
Last arrival time: 9:00
➡ About 3 miles N of Harrogate, access is 300 yards down B6165 Knaresborough Road from roundabout junction with A61.
See advert on previous page

Rudding Holiday Park

Follifoot, Harrogate HG3 1JH
☎ 01423-870439 Fax 01423-870859
Open March-November ▲ 🚐 🚏
Size 50 acres, 141 touring pitches, 141 with electric hookup, 76 level pitches, 16 ☔, 24 WCs, 2 CWPs
£ car/tent £7-£10, car/caravan £9-£20, motorhome £9-£20, motorbike/tent £7-£10
Rental Cottages & lodges available from £150 p.w.
СС MasterCard Visa
⚌ ✕ 🛒 🔌 🔋 🔲 🔺 GR 🗘 🗘 Calor Gaz ⅃ ⚐ WS
Last arrival time: 10:00
➡ Between A61 and A661 on A658, 1½ miles SE of Harrogate, turn NW ½ mile on right.

Shaws Trailer Park

Knaresborough Road, Harrogate HG2 7NE
☎ 01423-884432
Open all year ▲ 🚐 🚏
Very slightly sloping on the A59 opposite hospital. Car park and caravan parking. Daily and up to 8 months holiday site. Baths, showers and laundry.
Size 11 acres, 30 with electric hookup, 65 level pitches, 120 static caravans, 4 ☔
£ car/tent £7.50, car/caravan £7.50, motorhome £6.50
🔌 Calor Gaz ⚐ WS
➡ On the A59 off Grand Hospital. 1 mile from centre of Harrogate. 3 miles from centre of Knaresborough.

Village Farm

Old Bilton, Harrogate HG1 4DH
☎ 01423-863121
Open April-October ▲ 🚐 🚏
Size 10 acres, 25 touring pitches, 25 with electric hookup, 25 level pitches, 4 ☔, 17 WCs, 1 CWP
Rental 🚐
⚌ 🔋 🔲 🗒 Calor Gaz ⚐ WS
➡ A59 in Harrogate between A661 and A61. Turn at Dragon Inn. Park 1 mile.

HAWES North Yorkshire   10C2

Bainbridge Ings Farm

Hawes DL8 3NU
☎ 01969-667354
Open 1 April-31 October ▲ 🚐 🚏
Size 5 acres, 80 touring pitches, 25 with electric hookup, 15 static caravans, 6 ☔, 15 WCs, 1 CWP
£ car/tent £6, car/caravan £6.50, motorhome £6, motorbike/tent £6, children £0.30
Rental 🚐 £95-£15/
🗒 Calor Gaz ⚐
Last arrival time: 9:30
➡ Approaching Hawes from Bainbridge on A684, turn left at sign post marked Gayle 300 yards on left.

HAYFIELD Cheshire   7F1

Camping & Caravanning Club Site

Kinder Road, Hayfield SK12 5LE
☎ 01663-745394
Open end March-start November ▲ 🚏
Size 7 acres, 90 touring pitches, 6 ☔, 12 WCs, 1 CWP
£ car/tent £5.20-£7.80, car/caravan £5.20-£7.80, motorhome £5.20-£7.80, motorbike/tent £5.20-£7.80, children £1.50
СС MasterCard Visa   ⅃
Last arrival time: 11:00
➡ From A624 follow signs for Hayfield and then international camping signs.

HAYLE Cornwall   2A4

Callouse Caravan & Camping Park

Leedstown, Paythorne, Hayle TR27 5ET
☎ 01736-850431 Fax 01736-850431
Open 15 April-30 October ▲ 🚐 🚏

Award winning secluded family park in suntrap valley offering, superb facilities for tourers.

Size 12½ acres, 120 touring pitches, 99 with electric hookup, 120 level pitches, 17 static caravans, 15 ☔, 21 WCs, 2 CWPs
£ car/tent £6.50-£11, car/caravan £6.50-£11, motorhome £6.50-£11, motorbike/tent £6.50-£11, children £0.75-£1.75
Rental 🚐 £100-£450
СС MasterCard Visa
⚌ ✕ 🛒 🔋 🔌 🔲 🗒 🔲 GR 🔳 TV 🔺 🗘 Calor Gaz ⅃ ⚐
Last arrival time: 10:00
➡ Take B3302 towards Helston. Turn left at approach to Leedstown opposite village hall.

Parbola Holiday Park

Wall, Gwinear, Nr Hayle TR27 5LE
☎ 01209-831503 Fax 01209-831503
Open Easter-October ▲ 🚐 �"

Secluded family woodland park. Rose Award caravans/pre-erected tents for hire. Large, spacious pitches for campers. Close to glorious beaches.

Size 17½ acres, 115 touring pitches, 70 with electric hookup, 115 level pitches, 19 static caravans, 12 🚿, 16 WCs, 2 CWPs
£ car/tent £7.25-£11.50, car/caravan £7.25-£11.50, motorhome £7.25-£11.50, motorbike/tent £7.25-£11.50
Rental ▲ 🚐 Chalet. £99-£439
℃ MasterCard Visa
🍴 🛒 🖻 🍲 🔧 🅿 GR TV ⚠ Calor Gaz ♿ WS
Last arrival time: 10:00
➜ Take A30 to Hayle. At roundabout leave first exit to Connor Downs. At end of village turn right to Carnhell Green and turn right at T junction. Parbola is 1 mile on left.

St Ives Bay Holiday Park

73 Loggans Road, Upton Towans, Hayle TR27 5BH
☎ 01736-752274 Fax 01736-754523
Open 1 May-1 October ▲ 🚐 �"

Set in sand dunes with private access to a fabulous sandy beach. Two bars and a large indoor pool. Family and children oriented.

Size 75 acres, 250 touring pitches, 130 with electric hookup, 200 level pitches, 250 static caravans, 26 🚿, 38 WCs, 5 CWPs
£ car/tent £5-£18, car/caravan £5-£18, motorhome £5-£18, motorbike/tent £5-£18
Rental 🚐 Chalet. £99-£450
℃ MasterCard Visa
🍴 🛒 🖻 🍲 🔧 🔧 GR 🍲 TV ⚠ 🍴 Calor Gaz ♦
➜ Exit A30 at Hayle and take B3301 coast road. Park entrance is 600 yards on left.

HAYLING ISLAND Hampshire 4B4

Lower Tye Farm Camp Site

Copse Lane, Hayling Island PO11 0RQ
☎ 01705-462479 Fax 01705-462479
Open 1 March-1 November ▲ 🚐 �"

Quiet family site near family pub. An excellent touring base for Portsmouth, Isle of Wight and the New Forest. Long term parking is available on site.

Size 5 acres, 150 touring pitches, 150 with electric hookup, 150 level pitches, 13 🚿, 18 WCs, 1 CWP
£ car/tent £7, car/caravan £7, motorhome £7, motorbike/tent £7, children £1
Rental 🚐
🍴 🍴¼ ✗ 🛒 🖻 🔧 🍲 🔧 GR ⚠ Calor Gaz ♦ WS
Last arrival time: 12:00
➜ Exit M27 or A3M motorways at Havant and follow A3023. Lower Tye site is indicated, turn left into Copse Lane 1½ miles after crossing bridge onto Hayling Island. Site is on right ½ mile from main road.

HELMSLEY North Yorkshire 11D2

Foxholme Touring Caravan Park

Harome, Helmsley YO6 5JG
☎ 01439-770416 Fax 01439-771744
Open 1 March-31 October ▲ 🚐 �"

Quiet, sheltered and level wooded site. All pitches attractively situated among evergreen trees and well spaced to ensure peace, quiet and privacy. Hard roads throughout the site give good all-weather access.

Size 6 acres, 60 touring pitches, 60 with electric hookup, 60 level pitches, 8 🚿, 16 WCs, 2 CWPs
£ car/tent £6.50-£7, car/caravan £6.50-£7, motorhome £6.50-£7, motorbike/tent £6.50-£7
🍴 🖻 🔧 🍲 Calor Gaz ♿ ♦ WS
➜ On A170 for ½ mile, turn right on road to Harome, 2 miles turn left at church, ½ mile further keep left, then take first turn on left to site in 350 yards.

Golden Square Caravan Park

Oswaldkirk, Helmsley YO6 5YQ
01439-788269
Open 1 March-31 October

A quiet secluded site with excellent facilities, hidden from the outside world. Storage and seasonal pitches available.

Size 12 acres, 129 touring pitches, 100 with electric hookup, 129 level pitches, 14, 18 WCs, 2 CWPs
£ car/tent £6-£7.70, car/caravan £6-£7.70, motorhome £6-£7.70, motorbike/tent £6-£7.70
Rental Chalet. £90-£300
¼ GR Calor Gaz WS
Last arrival time: 10:00
2 miles S of Helmsley off B1257 road to Ampleforth.

Wrens Of Ryedale Caravan Site

Gale Lane, Nawton, Helmsley YO6 5SD
01439-771260
Open Easter-31 October

Very attractive, well-sheltered, level site. Ideal for North York National Park, Dales, York and the coast. 5% discount with this advert.

Size 2½ acres, 45 touring pitches, 21 with electric hookup, 45 level pitches, 4, 10 WCs, 1 CWP
£ car/tent £5-£6.50, car/caravan £5-£6.50, motorhome £5-£6.50, motorbike/tent £5-£6.50, children £0.50
Rental £120-£180 weekly
Calor Gaz WS
Last arrival time: 10:00
Take A170 from Helmsley to Pickering. 3 miles E of Helmsley in Beadlam turn right into Gale Lane. Site is 600 yards on right.

HELSTON Cornwall 2A4

Boscrege Caravan Park

Ashton, Helston TR13 9TG
01736-762231 Fax 01736-762231
Open Easter-end October
Size 7½ acres, 50 touring pitches, 25 with electric hookup, 50 level pitches, 26 static caravans, 8, 8 WCs, 1 CWP
£ car/tent £5-£10, car/caravan £5-£10, motorhome £5-£10, motorbike/tent £5-£10
Rental from £70-£350
CC MasterCard Visa
GR TV Calor Gaz WS
Last arrival time: 10:00
Leave A30 at Hayle roundabout. Take the Hayle Town turn-off (B3301). After ½ mile drive under viaduct, turn left onto B3302, signposted Helston. After 2 miles, turn right just past Smugglers Inn, signposted Townshend and Breage. Straight over crossroads at Townshend, follow signs to Godolphin, turn right at pub. Boscrege is straight across junction at top of hill.

Franchis Holiday Park

Cury Cross Lanes, Nr Mullion, Helston TR12 7AZ
01326-240301
Open 1 March-31 October

Rose award park in an area of outstanding natural beauty. Close mown grass and woodland. Excellent facilities.

Size 17 acres, 70 touring pitches, 37 with electric hookup, 65 level pitches, 7 static caravans, 11, 11 WCs, 1 CWP
£ car/tent £6-£7, car/caravan £6-£7, motorhome £6-£7, motorbike/tent £6-£7, children £0.50
Rental Bungalows £115-315, caravans £135-400
Calor Gaz
Last arrival time: 10:00
6 miles from Helston on A3083 Helston to Lizard road

Mullion Holiday Park
Penhale Cross, Ruan Minor, Helston TR12 7LJ
☎ 01326-240000 Fax 01326-241141
Open Easter-September Å ⚏ ⇄
Size 49 acres, 159 touring pitches, 87 with electric
hookup, 295 static caravans, 15 ☂, 15 WCs, 1 CWP
£ car/tent £7.50-£14.50, car/caravan £7.50-£14.50,
motorhome £7.50-£14.50, motorbike/tent £7.50-£14.50
Rental ⚏ Chalet. £105-£599
℃ MasterCard Visa
⚑ ✕ ☛ ⊡ ☎ ⅃ ⅃ 🅰 GR ▣ TV 🅰 ⊟ Calor Gaz ⤚
Last arrival time: 9:00
➡ From A30, take A39 from Fraddon to Truro and
continue on Falmouth road. Take A394 to Helston,
then A3083 for Lizard. After 7 miles site is on left
opposite Mullion turning.

Swiss Farm Camping International
Marlow Road, Henley-on-Thames RG9 2HY
☎ 01491-573419
Å ⚏ ⇄
Size 7 acres, 200 touring pitches, 10 ☂, 21 WCs
⚑ ✕ ☛
➡ Site ½ mile N of Henley, W side of A4155.

Bowdens Crest Caravan Park
Bowden, Henstridge TA12 6AE
☎ 01458-250553
Open 16 March-30 November

Tranquil site in the heart of South Somerset. Excellent
location for touring many local attractions. 10½ acres
of vineyard and woodland. Walking & fishing nearby.

Size 16 acres, 12 with electric hookup, 30 level
pitches, 4 ☂, 6 WCs
⚑ ✕¼ ☎ ⊡ 🅰 ⊟ Calor Gaz ♿
➡ A303 from Langport. A372 from Bridgewater.

Poston Mill Park
Golden Valley, Peterchurch HR2 0SF
☎ 01981-550225 Fax 01981-550885
Open all year Å ⚏ ⇄
Size 25 acres, 60 touring pitches, 60 with electric
hookup, 60 level pitches, 40 static caravans, 8 ☂, 12
WCs, 2 CWPs
£ car/tent £6-£8.50, car/caravan £6.50-£7.50,
motorhome £6.50-£7.50, motorbike/tent £6, children
£0.50
Rental ⚏ holiday home £130-£240
⚑¼ ✕ ✕¼ ☛ ☛¼ ⊡ ☎ ⅃ 🅰 ⅃ GR ▣ 🅰 ⊟ Calor Gaz
♿ ⤚ WS
Last arrival time: 10:00
➡ Site on B4348 Hereford to Hay-on-Wye road.

Camping & Caravanning Club Site
Mangrove Road, Hertford SG13 8QF
☎ 1992-586696
Open end March-start November Å ⚏ ⇄
Size 32 acres, 150 touring pitches, 100 with electric
hookup, 2 ☂, 10 WCs, 1 CWP
£ car/tent £5.20-£7.80, car/caravan £5.20-£7.80,
motorhome £5.20-£7.80, motorbike/tent £5.20-£7.80,
children £1.50
℃ MasterCard Visa
☎ 🅰 ⤚ WS
Last arrival time: 11:00
➡ Take A414 from A1 jn 4. In Hertford take Mangrove
Road on left by fire station. Site is ¾ mile.

HEXHAM Northumberland   13F4

Causey Hill Caravan Park
Bensonsfell Farm, Hexham NE46 2JN
☎ 01434-604647 Fax 01434 604647
Open 1 April-31 October Å ⚎ ⇄
Size 7½ acres, 35 touring pitches, 22 with electric
hookup, 22 level pitches, 68 static caravans, 12 ☌, 32
WCs, 2 CWPs
£ car/tent £7.50-£8.50, car/caravan £9, motorhome
£9, motorbike/tent £7.50, children £1
⚑ 🖭 📞 Calor ⚲
Last arrival time: 9:00

HIGH BENTHAM Lancashire   10B3

Riverside Caravan Park
Wenning Avenue, High Bentham LA2 7HS
☎ 01524-261272
Open March-October Å ⚎ ⇄

*Peaceful riverbank site with free fishing, dingby
sailing and swimming in River Wenning. Excellent
children's play area. Easy walk to shops in High
Bentham. Table tennis and pool, golf 2 miles. Booking
always advisable.*

Size 12 acres, 30 touring pitches, 30 with electric
hookup, 30 level pitches, 170 static caravans, 8 ☌, 7
WCs, 1 CWP
£ car/tent £6.50, car/caravan £7.80, motorhome £7.80
⚑¼ ✕¼ 🍴¼ 🖭 📞 📂 GR 🔲 ⚞
Last arrival time: 9:00
➔ Turn S on B4680 at Black Bull Hotel in High Bentham.

HINKLEY Leicestershire   8B3

Wolvey Villa Farm Caravan & Camp Site
Wolvey, Hinkley LE10 3HF
☎ 01455-220493
Open all year Å ⚎ ⇄
Size 7 acres, 55 with electric hookup, 110 level
pitches, 8 ☌, 11 WCs, 1 CWP
£ car/tent £5.40-£5.60, car/caravan £5.50-£5.70,
motorhome £5.50-£5.70, motorbike/tent £5.40,
children £1
⚑ 📂 📺 Calor Gaz ⚲ WS
Last arrival time: 11:00
➔ M6 junction 2 to B4065 and follow Wolvey signs.
M69 junction 1, then follow Wolvey signs.

HODDESDON Hertfordshire   5D2

Lee Valley Caravan Park
Charlton Meadows, Essex Road, Dobbs Weir,
Hoddesdon EN11 0AS
☎ 01992-462090
Open March (Easter)-October Å ⚎ ⇄
Size 23 acres, 100 touring pitches, 36 with electric
hookup, 100 level pitches, 100 static caravans, 20 ☌,
16 WCs, 2 CWPs
£ car/tent £13.90, car/caravan £13.90, motorhome
£13.90, motorbike/tent £13.90, children £2
℃ MasterCard Visa
⚑¼ 🍴¼ 🖭 📞 📂 ⚞ Calor ♿ ⚲ WS
➔ Take Hoddesdon turn off A10. At second
roundabout turn left and site is 1½ miles on right.

HOLBEACH Lincolnshire   9D2

Matopos Touring Park
Main Street, Fleet Hargate, Holbeach, Spalding PE12
8LL
☎ 01406-22910
Open 16 March-16 October Å ⚎ ⇄
Size 3 acres, 45 touring pitches, 22 with electric
hookup, 45 level pitches, 4 ☌, 5 WCs, 1 CWP
£ car/tent £6, car/caravan £6, motorhome £6,
children £0.80
⚑¼ ✕¼ 🍴¼ 🖭 📞 🖩 🔳 Calor Gaz ⚲ WS
Last arrival time: 10:30
➔ From Spalding take A151 to Holbeach. Continue
further 3 miles to Fleet Hargate. Turn right into
village just before A151 joins A17.

HOLMFIRTH West Yorkshire   10C4

Holme Valley Camping & Caravan Park
Thongsbridge, Holmfirth HO7 2TD
☎ 01484-665819 Fax 01484-663870
Å ⚎ ⇄

*In the heart of beautiful 'Summerwine' country. The
park is regularly chosen by the BBC for water and
woodland shots. See display advert for description.*

Size 8½ acres, 62 touring pitches, 62 with electric
hookup, 56 level pitches, 4 static caravans, 4 ☌, 8

WCs, 1 CWP
£ car/tent £5.50-£6.50, car/caravan £6.50-£7.50,
motorhome £5.50-£6.50, motorbike/tent £5.50
Rental 🚐 £75-£180
🛒 🗑 💺 🔳 ⚠ Calor Gaz ♿ 🐕
Last arrival time: 10:00
➡ Entrance to private lane is off A6024, one mile N
of Holmfirth.

Camping & Caravanning Club Site
Otter Valley Park, Northcote, Honiton EX14 8ST
📞 01404-44546
Open end March-start November 🏕 🚐 🚏
Size 6 acres, 90 touring pitches, 35 with electric
hookup, 10 🚿, 15 WCs, 2 CWPs
£ car/tent £5.20-£7.80, car/caravan £5.20-£7.80,
motorhome £5.20-£7.80, motorbike/tent £5.20-£7.80,
children £1.50
CC MasterCard Visa
🗑 💺 🐕 WS
Last arrival time: 11:00
➡ From A30 follow Honiton signposts, then follow
caravan and tent signs. Drive through public site to
reach Club site.

Don't forget to mention the guide
When booking, please remember to tell
the site that you chose it from
RAC Camping & Caravanning 1998

HOLME VALLEY
Camping & Caravan Park

On the fringe of the Peak District National Park.
*Open all year, the park enjoys a picturesque setting in a
peaceful valley bottom, surrounded by woodland and
meadows.. The 62 level pitches all have optional 16-amp
hookups. Fishing is available in the former mill dam and
the River Holme. The excellent, clean on-site amenities
include extra roomy showers. The well-stocked food shop
is licensed for off-sales and a hot meal takeaway service
operates at peak periods. Rally fields adjacent to the park
are available year-round to clubs.*

Free brochure from:

**THONGSBRIDGE, HOLMFIRTH,
WEST YORKSHIRE HD7 2TD
Tel: 01484-665819**

Hopton Holiday Village
Hopton on Sea
📞 0345-508508 **Fax** 01442-254956
Open March-mid October

*Hopton is a garden village alongside the sea, an ideal
family park offering facilities and activities to suit all
age groups. A 'British Holidays Park'.*

Size 80 acres, 350 static caravans for hire
Rental 🚐 £78-£594
CC MasterCard Visa
🛒 ✕ 💺 🗑 💺 GR 💺 💺 🔳 🔳 🔳 🔳 ⚠ Calor ♿ 🐕
➡ Situated just off A12 between Great Yarmouth and
Lowestoft. Turn off A12 at sign for Hopton.

Horam Manor Touring Park
Horam, Near Heathfield TN21 0YD
📞 01435-813662
Open March-mid October 🏕 🚐 🚏

*A tranquil rural site in an area of outstanding
natural beauty. Plenty of space. Special mother and
toddler room. Free hot water and showers.*

Size 7 acres, 90 touring pitches, 52 with electric
hookup, 75 level pitches, 7 🚿, 10 WCs, 1 CWP
£ car/tent £9-£11, car/caravan £9-£11, motorhome £9-
£11, motorbike/tent £9-£11, children £0.85
🛒¼ ✕¼ 💺¼ 🗑 💺 🗑 🔳 🔳 Calor Gaz ♿ 🐕
➡ Site is on A267, S of Horam village. 3 miles S of
Heathfield, 13 miles N of Eastbourne.

HORSHAM West Sussex   4C3

Honeybridge Park
Dial Post, Horsham RH13 8NX
☎ 01403 710923 Fax 01403 710923
Å ⊕ ⇄

Size 15 acres, 100 touring pitches, 62 with electric hookup, 100 level pitches, 6 ⚲, 20 WCs, 1 CWP
£ car/tent £7.50-£9.50, car/caravan £9.50-£11.50, motorhome £9.50-£11.50, motorbike/tent £5.50-£7.50, children £1
⚲ ✕¼ ⬛ 🔌 ⬛ 📶 ⚲ Calor Gaz ♿ ♥ WS
Last arrival time: 9:30
➡ 300 yards off A24. Follow international camping signs to Ashurst ¼ mile S of Dial Post village.

Raylands Caravan Park
Jackrells Lane, Southwater, Horsham RH13 7HA
☎ 01403-730218 Fax 01403-732828
Open 1 March-31 October
Size 11 acres, 80 touring pitches, 60 with electric hookup, 40 level pitches, 65 static caravans, 6 ⚲, 14 WCs, 1 CWP
⚲ 🔌 ⬛ GR ⬛ ⚲ Calor Gaz ♿
Last arrival time: 10:00
➡ Leave the A24 Worthing-London road for Southwater and follow signs to park. OS TQ 170265

HUNSTANTON Norfolk   9D2

Searles Holiday Centre
3 South Beach Road, Hunstanton PE36 5BB
☎ 01485-534211 Fax 01485-533815
Open March-October Å ⊕ ⇄
Size 60 acres, 350 touring pitches, 202 with electric hookup, 350 level pitches, 200 static caravans
£ car/tent £7-£16, car/caravan £7-£20, motorhome £7-£20, motorbike/tent £16
Rental ⊕ Chalet.
ℂℂ MasterCard Visa
⚲ ✕ ⬛ 🔌 ⬛ ⬛ ⬛ ⬛ ⬛ ⬛ ⬛ GR ⬛ 📶 ⚲ Calor ♿ ♥
Last arrival time: 9:00
➡ From King's Lynn take A149 to Hunstanton. Turn left at roundabout signposted South Beach.

HUNTINGDON Cambridgeshire 8C4

Houghton Mill Caravan & Camping Park
Mill Street, Houghton., Huntingdon
☎ 01480-462413
Open April-September ▲ ⚏ ⛺
Size 10 acres, 65 touring pitches, 30 with electric hookup, 65 level pitches, 6 ⏄, 8 WCs, 1 CWP
£ car/tent £9-£9.50, car/caravan £9-£9.50, motorhome £9-£9.50, motorbike/tent £8-£8.50, children £1-£1.25
⚑¼ ✕¼ ⚏¼ ☎ ⍟ Calor Gaz ♿ ⌁
Last arrival time: 8:00
➨ Site on A1123.

Old Manor Caravan Park
Church Lane, Grafham, Huntingdon PE18 0BB
☎ 01480-810264
Open February-November ▲ ⚏ ⛺
Size 6½ acres, 80 touring pitches, 60 with electric hookup, 80 level pitches, 20 static caravans, 6 ⏄, 10 WCs, 1 CWP
£ car/tent £9-£11, car/caravan £9-£11, motorhome £9-£11, motorbike/tent £6, children £1-£1.50
⚑ ✕¼ ⌑ ☎ ⍟ ⍓ ⚠ Calor Gaz ♿ ⌁
Last arrival time: 10:00
➨ Leave A1 at Buckden for B661. Take A14 to Ellington.

Park Lane Touring Park
Park Lane, Godmanchester, Huntingdon PE18 8AF
☎ 01480-453740 Fax 01480-453740
Open March-October ▲ ⚏ ⛺
Size 2½ acres, 50 touring pitches, 50 with electric hookup, 50 level pitches, 4 ⏄, 8 WCs, 1 CWP
£ car/tent £8, car/caravan £8, motorhome £8, motorbike/tent £8, children £1
⚑¼ ✕¼ ⚏¼ ⌑ ☎ ⍟ Calor Gaz ♿ ⌁ WS
Last arrival time: 10:30
➨ From A14 turn off to Godmanchester and pick up camp signs on lamp post. Turn right at Black Bull pub. Entrance on left.

Quiet Waters Caravan Park
Hemingford Abbots, Huntingdon PE18 9AJ
☎ 01480-463405
Open April-October ▲ ⚏ ⛺
Size 5 acres, 20 touring pitches, 20 with electric hookup, 20 level pitches, 9 static caravans, 6 ⏄, 6 WCs, 1 CWP
£ car/tent £8-£9, car/caravan £8-£9, motorhome £8-£9, motorbike/tent £8-£9
Rental ⚏
⊂⊃ Visa
⚑ ✕¼ ☎ ⍟ Calor Gaz ⌁
Last arrival time: 8:00
➨ From A14 turn off at Hemingford Abbotts. 1 mile into village follow signs.

HUNTLEY Gloucestershire 7E4

Forest Gate Campsite
Huntley GL19 3EU
☎ 01452-831192 Fax 01452-831192
Open 1 March-31 October ▲ ⚏ ⛺
Size 2½ acres, 30 touring pitches, 24 with electric hookup, 30 level pitches, 2 ⏄, 6 WCs, 1 CWP
£ car/tent £8.40, car/caravan £8.40, motorhome £8.40, motorbike/tent £8.40, children £2.10
⊂⊃ MasterCard Visa
⚑ ⚑¼ ✕¼ ⚏¼ ☎ Calor Gaz ♿ ⌁
Last arrival time: 10:30
➨ On A40 at junction with A4136 (Monmouth Road), 7 miles from Gloucester, 9 miles from Ross-on-Wye.

ILFRACOMBE Devon 2C2

Hele Valley Holiday Park
Hele Bay, Ilfracombe EX34 9RD
☎ 01271-862460 Fax 01271-862460
Open Easter-end October ▲ ⚏ ⛺
Size 17 acres, 12 touring pitches, 12 with electric hookup, 12 level pitches, 77 static caravans, 8 ⏄, 16 WCs, 1 CWP
£ car/tent £5-£8, car/caravan £5.50-£10, motorhome £5-£8, motorbike/tent £5-£8, children £1
Rental ⚏ £70-£375, cottages £140-£460
⊂⊃ MasterCard Visa
⚑ ⚑¼ ✕¼ ⚏¼ ⌑ ☎ ⍟ ⚠ Calor Gaz ♿ ⌁
Last arrival time: 10:00
➨ At 1½ miles E of Ilfracombe on A399. Turn S as signposted to Hele Village.

Mullacott Cross Caravan Park

Ilfracombe EX34 8NB
☎ 01271-862212 Fax 01271-862979
Open Easter-end October

Our site is situated between Ilfracombe and Woolacombe with views to the coast. A quieter park with bar and restaurant and all main facilities.

Size 20 acres, 65 touring pitches, 34 with electric hookup, 150 static caravans, 16 🚿, 42 WCs, 1 CWP
£ car/tent £5-£8, car/caravan £6-£9, motorhome £5-£8
《 Visa
🛒 ✕ 🍽 🔋 🔌 🛢 ⚠ 🗑 Calor Gaz ♿
Last arrival time: 9:00
➡ On A361, 2 miles S of Ilfracombe.

Napps Camp Site

Old Coast Road, Berrynarbor, Ilfracombe EX34 9SW
☎ 01271-882557 Fax 01271-882557
Open 1 April-31 October 🏕 🚐 🚛

A well kept site in a peaceful setting right on the beautiful North Devon coast, with woodland and coastal footpaths to the beach. Breathtaking coastal views and excellent facilities.

Size 15 acres, 200 touring pitches, 90 with electric hookup, 200 level pitches, 10 🚿, 20 WCs, 1 CWP
£ car/tent £5-£9, car/caravan £5-£9, motorhome £5-£9, motorbike/tent £5-£9
Rental 🚐
《 MasterCard Visa
🛒 ✕ 🔋 🛢 🔌 🗑 📮 GR 🔍 TV ⚠ 🗑 Calor Gaz ♿ 🐕 WS
➡ Take A399 1½ miles W of Combe Martin. Site is signposted on right, 300 yards along old coast road.
See advert on previous page

IPSWICH Suffolk   **5E1**

Low House Touring Caravan Centre

Bucklesham Road, Foxhall, Ipswich IP10 0AU
☎ 01473-659437 Fax 01473-659880
Open all year 🏕 🚐 🚛
Size 3 acres, 30 touring pitches, 30 with electric hookup, 3 level pitches, 4 🚿, 5 WCs, 1 CWP
£ car/tent £4.25-£6.50
✕¼ 🛢 🔋 🗑 📮 🔍 ⚠ 🗑 Calor Gaz ♿ 🐕 WS
➡ Turn off A14 Ipswich ring road onto A1156 (signposted Ipswich East). Follow road over bridge which crosses A14 and almost immediately turn right

(no sign). After ½ mile turn right again (signposted Bucklesham) and site is on left after ¼ mile.

Priory Park

Off Nacton Road, Ipswich IP10 0JT
☎ 01473-727393 Fax 01473-278372
Open all year 🏕 🚐 🚛

Set in 85 acres on the banks of the River Orwell, with woodland, a golf course, swimming pool, tennis and foreshore access for small boats. Bar with food. Open all year.

Size 85 acres, 75 touring pitches, 75 with electric hookup, 75 level pitches, 75 static caravans, 16 🚿, 15 WCs, 2 CWPs
£ car/tent £13, car/caravan £13, motorhome £13, motorbike/tent £1313
Rental Chalet. From £200 per week.
🛒¼ ✕ 🛢 🔋 🗑 📮 🔍 GR 🔍 ⚠ 🗑 Calor Gaz 🐕
Last arrival time: 9:00
➡ Leave A14 Ipswich southern bypass at Nacton interchange (east of Orwell Bridge). Turn towards Ipswich, after 300 yards turn left, following signs to Priory Park.

ISLE OF WIGHT   **4B4**

Adgestone Camping Park

Lower Road, Adgestone, Sandown PO36 0HL
☎ 01983-403432 Fax 01983-404955
Open Easter-September 🏕 🚐 🚛

Superb award winning park in glorious countryside, 1½ miles from beach. Facilities include swimming pool, takeaway, adventure playground, river and pond fishing. Special ferry inclusive package holidays, plus park fee concessions for over 50's.

Size 15½ acres, 200 touring pitches, 200 with electric hookup, 200 level pitches, 15 ⚲, 30 WCs, 2 CWPs
£ car/tent £7-£10, car/caravan £7-£10, motorhome £7-£10, motorbike/tent £7-£10, children £1.75-£2.95
℃ MasterCard Visa
⚲ ⚑ ⊡ ⚲ ⊡ ⚲ ⚲ ⚲ ⚲ Calor Gaz ⚲ ⚲
Last arrival time: dusk
➥ Turn off A3055 at Manor House pub in Lake. Go past golf club to T-junction and turn right. Site is 200 yards on right.

Beaper Farm
Ryde PO33 1QJ
☎ 01983-615210
Open April-October ⚲ ⚑ ⚲

Beautiful, quiet uncrowded site of 13 acres for tents, caravans and motor homes. Good clean facilities, shop, off licence, near out of town Tesco. Electric hook-ups.

Size 13 acres, 250 touring pitches, 16 with electric hookup, 8 static caravans, 12 ⚲, 22 WCs, 2 CWPs
Rental ⚑ from £140
⚲ ⊡ ⚲ ⊡ ⚲ Calor Gaz ⚲ ⚲ WS
Last arrival time: 9:00
➥ Situated 3 miles from Ryde on left of A3055.

Comforts Farm
Pallance Road, Northwood, Cowes
☎ 01983-293888
Open May-October ⚲ ⚑ ⚲

Set on a 60 acre working farm near the sea at Cowes, with excellent views and good amenities. No charge for children or dogs.

Size 9 acres, 50 touring pitches, 25 with electric hookup, 25 level pitches, 6 ⚲, 11 WCs, 1 CWP
£ car/tent £4.50, car/caravan £5.80-£6.80, motorhome £5.80-£6.80, motorbike/tent £2-£2.50, children £2.75
⚲ ⊡ ⚲ ⊡ ⚲ GR ⚲ Calor Gaz ⚲ ⚲

➥ From Cowes take A3020, turn right into Three Gates Road at Plessy Road and after ¼ mile, right into Pallance Road.

Heathfield Farm Camping Site
Heathfield Road, Freshwater PO40 9SH
☎ 01983-752480 **Fax** 01983-752480
Open May-end September ⚲ ⚑ ⚲

Peaceful family site with sea and downland views. High standard of cleanliness maintained in modern toilet block. Close to the beach, shops and buses. Ferry inclusive holidays.

Size 5 acres, 60 touring pitches, 16 with electric hookup, 60 level pitches, 4 ⚲, 7 WCs, 1 CWP
£ car/tent £5.50-£6.50, car/caravan £5.50-£6.50, motorhome £5.50-£6.50, motorbike/tent £5.50-£6.50
⚲¼ ✕ ⚑ ⊡ Gaz ⚲
Last arrival time: 10:00
➥ 2 miles W from Yarmouth ferry port on A3054 turn left into Heathfield Road. Site is 200 yards on right.

Landguard Camping Park

Landguard Manor Road, Shanklin PO37 7PH

📞 01983-867028

Open May-September ⚏ 🚐 🚍

Countryside setting only ½ mile from town centre. Heated swimming pool. Licensed club with evening entertainment. Cafe. Horse riding. Marked pitches, all with electric hook-up.

Size 6 acres, 150 touring pitches, 150 with electric hookup, 140 level pitches, 10 🚿, 16 WCs, 1 CWP

£ car/tent £6.50-£11, car/caravan £6.50-£11, motorhome £6.50-£11, motorbike/tent £6.50-£11, children £1.90-£2.80

℃ MasterCard Visa

🛒 ✕ 🍺 🖥 📭 🛒 📅 🖾 🛠 GR ⚙ 🔌 Calor Gaz ♿

Last arrival time: 9:00

➡ From Newport take A3056 to Sandown. Do not turn off at A3020 to Shanklin. Continue on the Sandown road past Safeway and take next turning right into Whitecross Lane. Follow signs.

Ninham Country Holidays

Shanklin PO37 7PL

📞 01983-864243 **Fax** 01983-868881

Open Easter-September ⚏ 🚐 🚍

Country park setting overlooking a wooded valley and small lakes. Adjacent to the island's main resort of Shanklin.

Size 5 acres, 98 touring pitches, 40 with electric hookup, 90 level pitches, 4 static caravans, 8 🚿, 12 WCs, 1 CWP

£ car/tent £7.20-£9.50, car/caravan £7.20-£9.50, motorhome £7.20-£9.50, motorbike/tent £9.50, children £1.80-£2.50

Rental 🚐 £185-£345

℃ MasterCard Visa

🛒¼ ✕¼ 🍺¼ 🖥 📭 🛒 🖾 🛠 📅 GR 🔍 ⚙ Calor Gaz WS

Last arrival time: 10:00

➡ Main site entrance is 1½ miles W of Lake on Newport-Sandown road (A3056). Private drive on left past mini-roundabout outside 'Safeway' superstore.

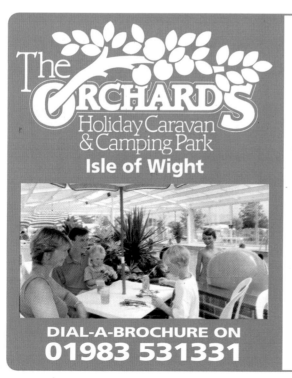

Orchards Holiday Caravan & Camping Park

Newbridge, Yarmouth PO41 0TS

☎ 01983-531331 Fax 01983-531666

Å ⇶ ⇌

Size 15 acres, 175 touring pitches, 175 with electric hookup, 40 level pitches, 61 static caravans, 14 🖧, 25 WCs, 3 CWPs

£ car/tent £6.85-£9.95, car/caravan £6.85-£9.95, motorhome £6.85-£9.95, motorbike/tent £6.85-£9.95, children £1.30-£2.70

CC MasterCard Visa

🕮 💌 🗄 📞 🔄 🔄 ⬜ 🔍 ⚠ Calor Gaz 🐕

Last arrival time: 11:00

➡ 4 miles E of Yarmouth and 6 miles W of Newport on B3401. Entrance is opposite Newbridge village post office.

Pondwell Caravan & Camping Park

Pondwell Hill., Ryde

☎ 01983-612330 Fax 01983-613511

Open May-September Å ⇶ ⇌

Size 8 acres, 150 touring pitches, 20 with electric hookup, 45 level pitches, 20 🖧, 30 WCs, 2 CWPs

£ car/tent £4-£7, car/caravan £4-£7, motorhome £4-£7, children £1-£1.75

Rental Chalet. £73-£381

CC MasterCard Visa

🕮 ✗¼ 💌¼ 🗄 📞 🔲 🔳 📺 ⚠ Calor Gaz

Last arrival time: 11:30

➡ Take A3054 to Ryde, then A3055 turning left along B3330 to Seaview. Park is next to Well pub.

Southland Camping Park

Newchurch, Sandown PO36 0LZ

☎ 01983-865385 Fax 01983-867663

Open Easter-end September Å ⇶ ⇌

Size 6 acres, 100 touring pitches, 100 with electric hookup, 100 level pitches, 7 🖧, 14 WCs, 1 CWP

£ car/tent £6.60-£8.80, car/caravan £6.60-£8.80, motorhome £6.60-£8.80, motorbike/tent £6.60-£8.80, children £1.20-£1.70

CC MasterCard Visa

🕮 ✗¼ 🗄 📞 ⚠ Calor Gaz ♿ 🐕

Last arrival time: 10:30

➡ Park is signposted from A3055/6 Newport to Sandown road, SE of Arreton.

Waverley Park Holiday Centre

Old Road, East Cowes

☎ 01983-293452 Fax 01983-200494

Open Easter-October Å ⇶ ⇌

Size 12 acres, 45 touring pitches, 28 with electric hookup, 42 static caravans, 12 🖧, 15 WCs, 1 CWP

£ car/tent £6.80-£10, car/caravan £6.80-£10, motorhome £6.80-£10, motorbike/tent £10, children £1.70-£2.20

Rental ⇶ £100-£380

CC MasterCard Visa

🕮 ✗ 💌 🗄 📞 🔲 🔳 ⬜ 🔍 ⚠ 🔌 Calor 🐕 WS

Last arrival time: 10:30

➡ Signposted from the Red Funnel terminal, East Cowes and also from York Avenue, coming from Newport or Ryde.

See advert on previous page

Whitecliff Bay Holiday Park

Hillway, Bembridge PO35 5PL

☎ 01983-872671 Fax 01983-872941

Open March-31 October Å ⇶ ⇌

➡

← **Whitecliff Bay Holiday Park**

Set in an area of outstanding natural beauty, and an ideal base for the family to explore the Isle of Wight. Facilities available close by include outdoor pools, shops, entertainment and snack bars.

Size 40 acres, 400 touring pitches, 130 with electric hookup, 200 level pitches, 14 static caravans, 38 ♟, 68 WCs, 15 CWPs
£ car/tent £6.20-£9.40, car/caravan £6.20-£9.40, motorhome £6.20-£9.40, motorbike/tent £6.20-£9.40, children £1.80-£2.50
Rental ⚠ ⛺ Chalet.
⟨⟨ MasterCard Visa
⚡ ✗ ⛟ ⛁ ⟨ ⛅ ⛶ ⛯ ⛱ ⟨ GR ⛲ ⟨ ⚠ ⛓ Calor Gaz WS
Last arrival time: 10:00
➜ Take A3055, turn onto B3395 at Brading and follow signs to Whitecliff Bay
See advert on previous page

See advert on previous page

KENDAL Cumbria   10B2

Camping & Caravanning Club Site
Millcrest, Shap Road, Kendal
☎ 01539-741363
Open end March-start November ⚠ ⛺ ⛴
Size 3 acres, 55 touring pitches, 30 with electric hookup, 4 ♟, 6 WCs, 1 CWP
£ car/tent £5.20-£7.80, car/caravan £5.20-£7.80, motorhome £5.20-£7.80, motorbike/tent £5.20-£7.80, children £1.50
⟨⟨ MasterCard Visa
⛁ ⟨ ⚠ ⛓
Last arrival time: 11:00
➜ Situated on A6, 1½ miles N of Kendal.

Millness Hill Park
Omit, Crooklands, Milnthorpe LA7 7NU
☎ 01539-567306 **Fax** 01539-567306
Open 1 March-mid November ⚠ ⛺ ⛴
Size 5 acres, 15 touring pitches, 15 with electric hookup, 15 level pitches, 6 static caravans, 2 ♟, 5 WCs, 1 CWP
£ car/tent £6-£7.50, car/caravan £6-£7.50, motorhome £6-£7.50, motorbike/tent £6-£7.50
Rental ⛺ Chalet. caravans £135-£340, chalets £200-£540
✗¼ ⛟¼ ⛁ ⟨ ⛶ ⚠ Calor ⛓
Last arrival time: 9:00
➜ Exit M6 junction 36 onto A65 to Kirkby Lonsdale. Turn left at next roundabout signposted Endmoor and Crooklands. Site is 100 yards on left.

Waters Edge Caravan Park
Crooklands, Kendal LA7 7NN
☎ 015395-67708 **Fax** 015395-67610
Open 1 March-14 November ⚠ ⛺ ⛴
Size 3 acres, 30 touring pitches, 30 with electric hookup, 30 level pitches, 5 ♟, 8 WCs, 1 CWP
£ car/tent £6.50, car/caravan £7.95-£13.50, motorhome £7.95-£13.50, motorbike/tent £6.50

Rental ⛺ £150-£230
⟨⟨ MasterCard Visa
⚡ ✗¼ ⛁ ⟨ ⛅ GR ⛶ ⛓ Calor Gaz ⚠ ⛓ WS
Last arrival time: 11:00
➜ Located at Crooklands ¾ miles along A65, M6 junction 36

KENNACK SANDS Cornwall   2A4

Silver Sands Holiday Park
Gwendreath, Kennack Sands, Helston TR12 7LZ
☎ 01326-290631
Open May-September ⚠ ⛺ ⛴
Size 6 acres, 34 touring pitches, 18 with electric hookup, 34 level pitches, 16 static caravans, 4 ♟, 8 WCs, 1 CWP
£ car/tent £5.50-£7, car/caravan £5.50-£7, motorhome £5.50-£7, motorbike/tent £5.50-£7, children £1.10-£1.50
Rental ⛺ £90-£315
⚡¼ ✗¼ ⛟¼ ⛁ ⟨ ⛅ ⚠ Calor Gaz ⛓
Last arrival time: 10:00
➜ Take A3083 "The Lizard" out of Helston. Past Naval Air Station Culdrose, turn left onto B3293 (St Keverne) past Goonhilly Satellite Station. Turn right at crossroads, after 1½ miles sign on left indicating "Gwendreath." Site is 1 mile down lane on right.

KESSINGLAND Suffolk   9F3

Heathland Beach Caravan Park
London Road, Kessingland NR33 7PJ
☎ 01502-740337 **Fax** 01502-742355
Open Easter-October ⚠ ⛺ ⛴

Flat, grassy park surrounded by farmland, with private beach access.

Size 30 acres, 106 touring pitches, 65 with electric hookup, 106 level pitches, 168 static caravans, 25 ♟, 44 WCs, 2 CWPs
£ car/tent £9.50-£11.50, car/caravan £9.50-£11.50, motorhome £9.50-£11.50, motorbike/tent £9.50-£11.50, children £0.50
Rental ⛺ £185-£335
⟨⟨ Visa
⚡ ✗ ⛟ ⛁ ⟨ ⛅ ⛶ ⛯ ⟨ ⚠ ⛓ Calor Gaz ⚠ WS
Last arrival time: 10:00
➜ 1 mile N of Kessingland on B1437. 3 miles S of Lowestoft off A12.

KESWICK Cumbria 10B2

Camping & Caravanning Club Site

Derwentwater, Keswick CA12 5EP

☎ 01768-772392

Open start February-start December Ⓐ 🚐 🚑

Size 14 acres, 250 touring pitches, 130 with electric hookup, 17 🚿, 35 WCs, 2 CWPs

£ car/tent £5.60-£8.60, car/caravan £5.60-£8.60, motorhome £5.60-£8.60, motorbike/tent £5.60-£8.60, children £1.50

CC MasterCard Visa

🏊 ✗¼ 🍴¼ 🗑 🔌 💾 🅿 🔥 👤 🐕

Last arrival time: 11:00

➡ From Penrith take A66, ignore Keswick signs and follow road to roundabout, turn right onto A5271, take first right at bottom of road, site is adjacent to Rugby Club.

Castlerigg Hall

Keswick

☎ 017687-72437 **Fax** 017687-72437

Open Easter-mid November Ⓐ 🚐 🚑

Castlerigg Hall Caravan & Camping Park overlooks Derwentwater with panoramic views of the surrounding fells. Fully serviced touring pitches available. Luxury holiday caravan for hire.

Size 53 touring pitches, 53 with electric hookup, 53 level pitches, 30 static caravans, 12 🚿, 26 WCs, 1 CWP

£ car/tent £6.50-£7.50, car/caravan £8.50-£10, motorhome £7.50, motorbike/tent £5.70-£6.30, children £1.80-£2

🏊 ✗¼ 🗑 🔌 🗑 Calor Gaz 🐕

Last arrival time: 9:00

➡ 1½ miles SE of Keswick. Turn right off A591, 50 yards past Heights Hotel on the right.

Derwentwater Caravan Park

Crowe Park Road, Keswick CA12 5EN

☎ 017687-72579

Open 1 March-14 November 🚐 🚑

Situated on the shores of Derwentwater, with its own lake frontage and excellent views of the surrounding fells, yet convenient for the town.

Size 17½ acres, 50 touring pitches, 50 with electric hookup, 50 level pitches, 160 static caravans, 10 🚿, 12 WCs, 2 CWPs

£ car/caravan £9.20-£9.60, motorhome £9.20-£9.60, children £2.30-£2.40

🏊¼ ✗¼ 🍴¼ 🗑 🔌 💾 🅿 Calor Gaz 👤 🐕

Last arrival time: 10:00

➡ From M6 (jn 40) take A66 signposted Keswick for 13 miles and at roundabout signed Keswick turn left. At the T-junction turn left to Keswick town centre. At the mini roundabout turn right. In 200 yards bear right, and in 400 yards turn right. Park is right after the bend in the road.

Gill Head Farm
Troutbeck, Keswick CA11 0ST
☎ 01768-779652
Open 1 April-10 November A 🚐 🚎

Pleasant, very well kept rural site containing a small stream with ducks. Bed & breakfast available at farm. Dog walk alongside adjacent river.

Size 1½ acres, 17 touring pitches, 17 with electric hookup, 17 level pitches, 17 static caravans, 4 🚿, 8 WCs, 1 CWP
£ car/tent £7-£10, car/caravan £7-£10, motorhome £7, motorbike/tent £7, children £3.50
🎱 ✕¼ 🍴¼ 🔲 🔋 🔲 Calor Gaz 🚭 🐕
Last arrival time: 10:00
➡ From A66 take A5091 for Ullswater. 100 yards through Troutbeck take right turn, then first right again.

Scotgate Holiday Park
Braithwaite, Keswick
☎ 017687-78343 Fax 017687-78099
Open March-November A 🚐 🚎
Size 9 acres, 15 touring pitches, 15 with electric hookup, 15 level pitches, 27 static caravans, 8 🚿, 32 WCs, 1 CWP
£ car/tent £6.70-£7, car/caravan £10-£13, motorhome £5.25-£5.50, motorbike/tent £7, children £1.50-£1.60
Rental 🚐 Chalet.
🎱 ✕ 🍴 🔲 🔋 🔲 GR Calor Gaz 🐕
Last arrival time: 11:00
➡ 2 miles W of Keswick, just off A66 (Keswick-Cockermouth road) on B5292.
See advert on previous page

KIDDERMINSTER Worcestershire   7E3

Camp Easy
The Old Vicarage Activity Centre, Stottesdon, Kidderminster DY14 8UH
☎ 01746-718436 Fax 01746-718420

Camp Easy is based in Ginny Hole Nature Reserve, situated on the outskirts of the village of Stottesdon. When you arrive a tent can be pitched and ready for you.

Size 27 acres

Camping & Caravanning Club Site
Brown Westhead Park, Wolverley, Kidderminster
☎ 01562-850909
Open late March-early November A 🚐 🚎
Size 8.2 acres, 124 touring pitches, 60 with electric hookup, 6 🚿, 12 WCs,
£ car/tent £5.20-£7.80, car/caravan £5.20-£7.80, motorhome £5.20-£7.80, motorbike/tent £5.20-£7.80, children £1.50
CC MasterCard Visa
🎱 🔲 🔋 🔲 GR 🏛 🐕
Last arrival time: 11:00
➡ From Kidderminster A449 to Wolverhampton turn left at traffic lights, B4189 SP Wolverley look for brown camping sign, turn left, entrance on right.

Shorthill Caravan & Camping Centre

Worcester Road, Crossway Green, Stourport, Kidderminster DY13 9SH

☎ 01299-250571

Å ⚌ ⛺

Size 7 acres, 30 touring pitches, 20 with electric hookup, 30 level pitches, 3 🚿, 5 WCs, 1 CWP
£ car/tent £6.50-£8.50, car/caravan £6.50-£10, motorhome £6.50-£10, motorbike/tent £6.50-£8.50
🚻¼ ✗ 🍴 ⚌¼ 🔌 🖬 ⚠ 🐕 WS
Last arrival time: 10:00
➡ On A1449 Kidderminster to Worcester road, 200 yards after Hartlebury service station island is Little Chef restaurant. Turn into restaurant entrance and site is located at rear.

KING'S LYNN Norfolk   9D3

Pentney Park Caravan Site

Gayton Road, Narborough, King's Lynn PE32 1HU

☎ 01760-337479 Fax 01760-338118

Å ⚌ ⛺

Size 16 acres, 200 touring pitches, 156 with electric hookup, 190 level pitches, 16 🚿, 44 WCs, 3 CWPs
£ car/tent £8-£10, car/caravan £8-£10, motorhome £8-£10, motorbike/tent £1010, children £1.10-£1.40
Rental ⚌ from £100
CC MasterCard Visa
🚻 ✗ 🍴 🖬 🔌 🖬 🔌 🖬 GR 🖬 ⚠ 🍴 Calor Gaz ⚕ 🐕 WS
Last arrival time: 10:00
➡ On A47, midway between King's Lynn and Swaffham. Entrance on B1153, 150 yards from junction.

Rickels Caravan Site

Bircham Road, Stanhoe, King's Lynn PE31 8PU

☎ 01485-518671 Fax 01485-518671

Open March-October Å ⚌ ⛺
Size 2 acres, 30 touring pitches, 26 with electric hookup, 20 level pitches, 4 🚿, 7 WCs, 1 CWP
£ car/tent £7.50-£8.50, car/caravan £7.50-£8.50, motorhome £7.50-£8.50, motorbike/tent £8.50, children £0.50
Rental ⚌
🔌 🖬 ⚠ Calor Gaz 🐕 WS
Last arrival time: 10:00
➡ Take A148 (Cromer road) for 4 miles to Hillington. Continue through village and turn left onto B1153 to Great Bircham. Proceed through Bircham and on a left hand bend fork right onto B1155, follow to main crossroads (Fakenham right, Docking left). Continue straight over and site is situated 200 yards on left.

KINGSBRIDGE Devon   2C4

Camping & Caravanning Club Site

Middle Grounds, Slapton, Kingsbridge

☎ 01548-580538

Open late March-early November Å ⚌ ⛺
Size 5½ acres, 115 touring pitches, 24 with electric hookup, 6 🚿, 9 WCs, 1 CWP
£ car/tent £5.60-£8.60, car/caravan £5.60-£8.60, motorhome £5.60-£8.60, motorbike/tent £5.60-£8.60, children £1.50
CC MasterCard Visa
🚻¼ 🍴 🔌 🖬 ⚕ 🐕
Last arrival time: 11:00
➡ A381 to Totnes, left onto B3207 to Dartmouth, right onto A379 to Street, right to Slapton.

Karrageen Camping & Caravan Park

Bolberry, Malborough, Kingsbridge TQ7 3EN

☎ 01548-561230 Fax 01548-560192

Open 15 March-15 November Å ⚌ ⛺

A small family park offering panoramic rural and sea views - the closest park to the beaches at Hope Cove and only ¾ mile from the National Trust Coastal Path. Level pitches with a view, disabled/family shower room.

Size 7½ acres, 75 touring pitches, 54 with electric hookup, 75 level pitches, 20 static caravans, 9 🚿, 10 WCs, 1 CWP
£ car/tent £6-£8.50, car/caravan £7-£10, motorhome £6-£8.50, motorbike/tent £6-£7.50, children £0.50
🚻 🍴 🖬 🔌 🖬 Calor Gaz ⚕ 🐕
➡ Take A381 from Kingsbridge to Salcombe. Turn sharp right through Malborough, after 0.6 mile turn right (S.P. Bolberry). After 0.9 mile site is on right. Reception on left at Karrageen House.

KNARESBOROUGH North Yorkshire   11D3

Scotton Holiday Park

New Road, Scotton, Knaresborough HG5 9HH

☎ 01423-864413 Fax 01423-864413

Open 1 March-7 January Å ⚌ ⛺
Size 8½ acres, 100 touring pitches, 85 with electric hookup, 60 level pitches, 29 static caravans, 10 🚿, 16 WCs, 2 CWPs
£ car/tent £6-£7.50, car/caravan £7.50-£8.50, motorhome £7.25-£8.50, motorbike/tent £6-£7.50, children £1
Rental ⚌ Chalet. caravans - £98-£180, chalets - £150-£320
CC MasterCard Visa
🚻 ✗ 🍴 🔌 ⚠ 🖬 Calor Gaz ⚕ 🐕
Last arrival time: 9:00
➡ 1½ miles NW of Knaresborough on B6165.

LACOCK Wiltshire   4A3

Piccadilly Caravan Site
Folly Lane West, Lacock SN15 2LP
☎ 01249 730260
Open 1 April-31 October Å 🚐 🚍

Located in countryside half a mile from the historic National Trust village of Lacock, the site is an ideal touring centre for Bath and the Cotswolds.

Size 2½ acres, 40 touring pitches, 34 with electric hookup, 40 level pitches, 4 🚿, 6 WCs, 1 CWP
£ car/tent £7-£8.50, car/caravan £7-£8.50, motorhome £7-£8.50, motorbike/tent £7-£8.50
🛒¼ ✗¼ 🖪 🔌 🖥 Calor Gaz 🐕
Last arrival time: 10:00
➜ Turn right off A350 Chippenham to Melksham road signposted Gastard (with caravan symbol) into Folly Lane West. Site on left in 300 yards.

LAMPLUGH Cumbria   10A2

Inglenook Caravan Park
Lamplugh CA14 4SH
☎ 01946-861240
Open all year Å 🚐 🚍
Size 3½ acres, 36 touring pitches, 20 with electric hookup, 36 level pitches, 22 static caravans, 4 🚿, 8 WCs, 1 CWP
£ car/tent £6.50-£8.50, car/caravan £7.50-£8.50, motorhome £7.50-£8.50, motorbike/tent £6.25-£7.25, children £1.25
Rental 🚐 £140-£250
🛒 📞 🔌 🖥 ⚠ Calor Gaz 🐕 WS
Last arrival time: 8:00
➜ Leave A5086 at sign for Lampugh Green. Site ½ mile on right-hand corner.

LANCASTER Lancashire   10B3

Cockerham Sands Caravan Park
Cockerham, Lancaster LA2 0BB
☎ 01524-751387 Fax 01524-752275
Open March-October 🚐 🚍

A country club and caravan park with a cabaret suite, lounge bar, snooker TV room, play area and pool.

Size 5 acres, 9 touring pitches, 9 with electric hookup, 9 level pitches, 220 static caravans, 2 🚿, 3 WCs, 1 CWP
£ car/caravan £10.50-£11.50, motorhome £10.50-£11.50
Rental 🚐 £145-£230
🛒 📞 🖪 🔌 🌀 🔣 GR ⚠ 🔌 Calor ♿ 🐕
Last arrival time: 11:00
➜ From M6 junction 33 take A6 to Glasson Dock for 1¼ miles. Turn right onto Cockerham Road and right again for Thurnham Hall. Turn left opposite hall at signpost.

LAND'S END Cornwall   2A4

Cardinney Caravan & Camping Park
Land's End TR19 6HJ
☎ 01736-810880
Open February-November Å 🚐 🚍
Size 4½ acres, 105 touring pitches, 50 with electric hookup, 40 level pitches, 2 static caravans, 6 🚿, 11 WCs, 1 CWP
£ car/tent £4-£7, car/caravan £4-£7, motorhome £4-£7, motorbike/tent £4-£7, children £0.50-£0.75
Rental 🚐 from £75-£195
ℂℂ MasterCard Visa
🛒 ✗ 📞 🖪 🔌 🖥 GR 📺 ⚠ 🔌 Calor Gaz 🐕
Last arrival time: 12:00
➜ 5 miles W of Penzance on A30. Towards Land's End, park on right before village of Crows-an-Wra.

LANGPORT Somerset   3E2

Thorney Lakes Caravan Park
Muchelney., Langport TA10 0DW
☎ 01458-250811
Open March-November Å 🚐 🚍
Size 7 acres, 16 touring pitches, 16 with electric hookup, 16 level pitches, 4 🚿, 5 WCs, 1 CWP
£ car/tent £6, car/caravan £6, motorhome £6
🔋 ♿ 🐕
➜ 2 miles S of Langport on Crewekerne road follow sign to Muchelney Pottery. Pass Mulchelney Pottery around a sharp corner, a big lay-by, Thorney Lakes and caravan site on left.

LECHDALE Gloucestershire 4A2

St John's Priory Parks
Faringdon Road, Lechlade GL7 3EZ
☎ 01367-252360
Open 1 March-31 October ▲ ⊕ ⊐

100 yards to the River Thames. Next to the famous Trout Inn. Ideal base to explore Cotswolds, Stratford, Stowe, Burford etc. Fishing, boating, river walks.

Size 3 acres, 25 touring pitches, 15 with electric hookup, 25 level pitches, 6 ℟, 12 WCs, 1 CWP
£ car/tent £5-£10, car/caravan £5-£10, motorhome £5-£10, motorbike/tent £5-£10
♨¼ ✕¼ ♥¼ ⚡ ⚠ Calor Gaz ✿ WS
➡ ½ mile on left-hand side of Lechlade to Faringdon road (A417).

LEEDS West Yorkshire 11D3

Moor Lodge Caravan Park
Blackmoor Lane, Bardsey, Leeds LS17 9DZ
☎ 01937-572424
Open all year ▲ ⊕ ⊐

Peaceful, immaculate, countryside park.

Size 7½ acres, 12 touring pitches, 12 with electric hookup, 12 level pitches, 60 static caravans, 4 ℟, 4 WCs, 1 CWP
£ car/tent £6.50, car/caravan £6.50, motorhome £6.50, motorbike/tent £6.50
♨¼ ✕¼ ♥¼ ⚡ ⊟ Calor Gaz ♿ ✿ WS
➡ Take A58 from Leeds towards Wetherby. Cross over roundabout on outskirts of Leeds. After one third of a mile when street lights finish, turn left at next crossroad and follow caravan signs.

LEEK Staffordshire 7E1

Camping & Caravanning Club Site
Blackshaw Grange, Blackshaw Moor, Leek
☎ 01538-300285
Open end March-start November ▲ ⊕ ⊐
Size 6 acres, 60 touring pitches, 30 with electric hookup, 6 WCs
£ car/tent £5.20-£7.80, car/caravan £5.20-£7.80, motorhome £5.20-£7.80, motorbike/tent £5.20-£7.80, children £1.50
℀ MasterCard Visa
♨¼ ⊟ GR ⚠ ♿ ✿
Last arrival time: 11:00
➡ M6 junction 15, join A500 then turn left onto A53, go past Leek and turn left.

Glencote Caravan Park
Churnet Valley, Station Road, Cheddleton, Leek ST13 7EE
☎ 01538-360745 Fax 01538-361788
Open April-October ▲ ⊕ ⊐

A pleasant, well sheltered, level park to the south of Leek to the Churnet Valley. Railway museum and canal-side pub close by. Central for the Potteries, Alton Towers, Staffordshire moorlands and Peak District.

Size 6 acres, 48 touring pitches, 60 with electric hookup, 60 level pitches, 6 static caravans, 7 ℟, 8 WCs, 3 CWPs
£ car/tent £8, car/caravan £8, motorhome £8, motorbike/tent £8, children £1.50
Rental ⊕
℀ Visa
✕¼ ⊟ ⚡ ▣ ⚠ Calor Gaz ✿ WS
Last arrival time: 9:30
➡ Turn left off A520 (Leek-Stone) at foot of hill in Cheddleton into Station Road (sign- N. Staffs Rly Museum). Park is on right in ¾ mile.

Hints & Tips
Caravans are stolen from laybys and motorway service stations. Even if you are just stopping for a cup of tea or to stretch your legs make sure you secure your caravan.

LEISTON Suffolk   9F4

Cakes & Ale Park

Abbey Lane, Theberton, Leiston IP16 4TE

☎ **01728 831655** Fax **01473-736270**

Open 1 April-31 October ▲ 🚐 🚏

A fully serviced site in tranquil parkland with a golf driving range and practice nets, and a large mown recreation area. Nearby is an indoor pool and the area offers superb walking and cycling. Minsmere, Dunwich, Southwold, Aldeburgh and Snape are within easy distance.

Size 45 acres, 50 touring pitches, 50 with electric hookup, 50 level pitches, 150 static caravans, 20 🚿, 20 WCs, 2 CWPs

£ car/tent £8-£10, car/caravan £8-£10, motorhome £8-£10, motorbike/tent £8-£10

Rental 🚐 from £180 weekly.

CC MasterCard Visa

🛒 🗑 🔌 🔲 🔳 🔲 🔲 ⚠ ⊞ Calor Gaz 🐾 WS

Last arrival time: 9:00

➡ From A12 take B1121 to Saxmundham. At the crossroads in Saxmundham, take B1119 to Leiston. Turn onto minor road 3 miles from Saxmundham and follow signs.

LEOMINSTER Herefordshire   7D3

Shobdon Airfield Touring Site

Leominster HR6 9NR

☎ **01568-708369** Fax **01568-708935**

Open February-6 January ▲ 🚐 🚏

Size 5 acres, 35 touring pitches, 4 with electric hookup, 35 level pitches, 12 static caravans, 8 🚿, 8 WCs, 1 CWP

£ car/tent £2-£6, car/caravan £3.50-£5, motorhome £3.50-£5, motorbike/tent £2-£6, children £2-£6

CC MasterCard Visa

🛒¼ ✗ 🔲 🗑 ⅋ 🐾 WS

Last arrival time: 9:00

LEWES East Sussex   5D4

Bluebell Holiday Park

The Broyle, Shortgate, Ringmer, Lewes BN8 6PJ

☎ **01825-840407**

Open 1 April-31 October ▲ 🚐 🚏

Quiet rural park sheltered by trees. No club, swimming pool or playground, just peace and quiet, and an abundance of wild life. Luxury caravans for hire.

Size 2½ acres, 10 touring pitches, 10 with electric hookup, 20 level pitches, 4 static caravans, 4 🚿, 7 WCs, 1 CWP

£ car/tent £7.50, car/caravan £7.50, motorhome £7.50, motorbike/tent £7.50

Rental 🚐 £90-£250

✗¼ 🛒¼ 🔌 ⊞ Calor 🐾

Last arrival time: 9:00

➡ From A22 Halland roundabout take B2192 to Ringmer. Site is 1½ miles on left behind Bluebell Inn.

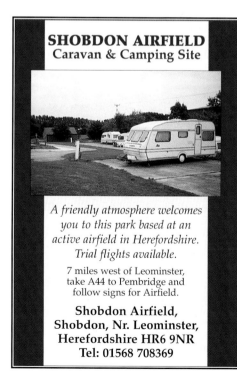

LEYBURN North Yorkshire   10C2

Constable Burton Hall Caravan Park
Leyburn DL8 5LJ
☎ 01677-450428 Fax 01677-450622
Open April-October ▲ ⊞ ⊞
Size 10 acres, 120 touring pitches, 120 with electric hookup, 120 level pitches, 9 ⋒, 13 WCs, 3 CWPs
£ car/tent £7.50-£8.50, car/caravan £7.50-£8.50, motorhome £7.50-£8.50, children £0.75
✗¼ ⚑¼ ▐ ⊟ Calor Gaz ⋔
Last arrival time: 10:00
➤ 8 miles W of A1 on A684 between Bedale and Leyburn.

LINCOLN Lincolnshire   8C1

Hartsholme Country Park
Skellingthorpe Road, Lincoln LN6 OEY
☎ 01522-686264
Open 1 March-31 October ▲ ⊞ ⊞
Size 3 acres, 50 touring pitches, 20 with electric hookup, 50 level pitches, 4 ⋒, 5 WCs, 1 CWP
£ car/tent £6.50, car/caravan £6.50, motorhome £6.50
⚑¼ ✗¼ ⚑ ⅋ ⋔
Last arrival time: 9:00
➤ 3 miles SW of city centre, signposted from A46 bypass.

LINGFIELD Surrey   5D3

Long Acres Caravan & Camping Park
Newchapel Road., Lingfield RH7 6LE
☎ 01342-833205
Open all year ▲ ⊞ ⊞
Size 40 acres, 60 touring pitches, 60 with electric hookup, 50 level pitches, 6 ⋒, 10 WCs, 2 CWPs
£ car/tent £8, car/caravan £8, motorhome £8, motorbike/tent £8, children £1.50
⚑ ⚑¼ ✗¼ ⚑¼ ▐ ⊟ ▨ ⟁ Calor Gaz ⋔ WS
➤ From M25 junction 6 take A22 to East Grinstead. At Newchapel roundabout turn left onto B2028 to Lingfield. Site is on right (700 yards).

Hints & Tips

If you have any information concerning caravan theft contact the confidential freephone Crimestoppers Line on 0800 555111.
You may be entiled to a reward and there is no need to give your name if you don't want to.

LISKEARD Cornwall   2B3

Pine Green Caravan Park
Doublebois, Liskeard PL14 6LE
☎ 01271-328981
Open Easter-31 October ▲ ⊞ ⊞

Off the A38, near Dobwalls, an elevated site tastefully landscaped with rural views, and within easy reach of Plymouth, the sea and the moors. Warden on site.

Size 2 acres, 50 touring pitches, 25 with electric hookup, 16 level pitches, 4 ⋒, 6 WCs, 1 CWP
£ car/tent £4-£7, car/caravan £5-£9, motorhome £5-£9, motorbike/tent £4-£7
Rental ⊞ £80-£210
⊟ ▐ Calor Gaz ⋔ WS
Last arrival time: 10:00
➤ From Liskeard W on A38 to Dobwalls. Keep right and ¾ mile further turn left onto B3360, site ¼ mile on right.

LONDON, NORTH   5D2

Lee Valley Campsite
Sewardstone Road, Chingford, London E4 7RA
☎ 0181-529 5689 Fax 0181-559 4070
Open Easter-October ▲ ⊞ ⊞
Size 13 acres, 200 touring pitches, 100 with electric hookup, 100 level pitches, 28 ⋒, 30 WCs, 3 CWPs
£ car/tent £14.40, car/caravan £14.40, motorhome £14.40, motorbike/tent £14.40, children £2.20
℅ MasterCard Visa
⚑ ⚑ ⊟ ▐ ⟁ Calor ⅋ ⋔ WS
➤ Leave M25 junction 26, follow signs to Waltham Abbey, turn left at traffic lights. Site 2 miles on right.

Lee Valley Cycle Circuit Campsite
Lee Valley Sports Centre, Temple Mills Lane, Leyton, London E15 2EN
☎ 0181-534 6085 Fax 0181-536 0959
Open March (Easter)-October ▲ ⊞ ⊞
Size 2 acres, 80 touring pitches, 80 level pitches, 20 ⋒, 10 WCs, 1 CWP
£ car/tent £14.80, car/caravan £14.80, motorhome £14.80, motorbike/tent £14.80, children £2.20
℅ MasterCard Visa
⚑¼ ✗¼ ⚑¼ ⊟ ▐ ⊞ ▨ ⊞ ⅋ ⅋ ⋔

Lee Valley Leisure Centre Campsite

Picketts Lock Lane, Edmonton, London N9 0AS
☎ 0181-345 6666 fax 0181-884 4975
Open all year ▲ ⛺ 🚐
Size 6 acres, 200 touring pitches, 60 with electric
hookup, 200 level pitches, 6 ♠, 17 WCs, 2 CWPs
£ car/tent £14.80, car/caravan £14.80, motorhome
£14.80, motorbike/tent £14.80, children £2.20
CC MasterCard Visa
⚡ ✗ ⛽ ⊡ 🔌 🔲 🔲 🔲 🔲 🔲 🔲 🔲 🔲 🔲 ⚲ 🔲 ⚠ 🔲 Calor
Gaz & 🔥 WS
➡ From M25 junction 25 follow signs for City. At first
set of traffic lights take slip road signposted
'Feezywater', continue along this road (A1055) for 6
miles, site is at rear of Leisure Centre complex.

Tent City Camping

Millfields Road, Hackney, London E5
☎ 0181-985 7656 fax 0181-749 9074
Open 1 June-30 August ▲ ⛺ 🚐
Size 3 acres, 60 touring pitches, 200 level pitches, 20
♠, 12 WCs
£ car/tent £10, car/caravan £10, motorhome £10,
motorbike/tent £10, children £5
Rental ▲
⚡ ✗¼ ⛽ ⊡ 🔌 🔲 🔲 GR TV ⚠ Calor 🔥
➡ A102 or A104 to Lower Clapton Road. Down
Millfields Road, over hump bridge to Hackney
Camping.

Camelot Caravan Park

Sandysike, Longtown CA6 5SZ
☎ 01228-/91248
Open March-October ▲ ⛺ 🚐
Size 5 acres, 20 touring pitches, 6 with electric
hookup, 20 level pitches, 1 static caravans, 2 ♠, 4
WCs, 1 CWP
£ car/tent £5.70, car/caravan £6.70, motorhome £6.70,
motorbike/tent £5.70, children £0.50
⚡ 🔌 ⊡ Calor Gaz 🔥 WS
Last arrival time: flexible
➡ Leave M6 at junction 44. Site on right off A7 in 4
miles, 1 mile S of Longtown.

Camping Caradon

Trelawne Gardens, Looe PL13 2NA
☎ 01503-272388
Open Easter-end October ▲ ⛺ 🚐
Size 3½ acres, 85 touring pitches, 37 with electric
hookup, 85 level pitches, 4 ♠, 12 WCs, 1 CWP
£ car/tent £5-£8, car/caravan £5-£8, motorhome £5-
£8, children £0.30-£1
⚡ 🔌 ⛽ 🔲 ⚲ ⚠ 🔲 Calor Gaz 🔥
Last arrival time: 10:00
➡ 2¼ miles W of Looe on A387, turn N on B3359
and take first on right. Site ¼ mile on left.

Polborder House Caravan & Camping Park

Bucklawren Road, St Martins, Looe PL13 1QR

☎ 01503-240265

Open April-October △ ⊕ ⊞

Size 3 acres, 31 touring pitches, 28 with electric hookup, 36 level pitches, 5 static caravans, 9 ⋒, 16 WCs, 1 CWP

£ car/tent £6-£8, car/caravan £6-£8, motorhome £6-£8, motorbike/tent £4-£5, children £0.75-£1

Rental ⊕ £120-£280

⊒ ⊡ ⊠ ⊟ Calor Gaz ⅙ ⋔

Last arrival time: 10:00

➡ 2½ miles E of Looe, turn off B3253 signposted Polborder & Monkey Sanctuary. Site ½ mile on right.

Tencreek Caravan Park

Looe PL13 2JR

☎ 01503-262447 **Fax** 01503-262447

Open all year △ ⊕ ⊞

Size 16 acres, 250 touring pitches, 200 with electric hookup, 250 level pitches, 62 static caravans, 24 ⋒, 40 WCs, 2 CWPs

£ car/tent £7-£11.50, car/caravan £7-£11.50, motorhome £7-£11.50, motorbike/tent £7-£11.50, children £1.20-£1.75

Rental ⊕ £95-£340 weekly

⊄ MasterCard Visa

⊒ ⊌ ⊡ ⊠ ⊟ ⊠ ⊞ ⊿ ⊟ Calor Gaz ⅙ ⋔ WS

Last arrival time: 11:00

➡ From A38 turn right onto A387 for Looe. Travel through Looe town, over bridge and up hill. Approximately 1½ miles from bridge.

Tencreek
Caravan & CampingPark

Perfectly situated for Looe & Polperro. The nearest park to Looe. Families and couples only.
FREE Family facilities include:
Heated swimming pool • Modern toilets & showers • Adventure park • Shop • Launderette • Licensed club with nightly entertainment • Two bars • Cafe/takeaway • Dog exercise area • Apartments available in Looe • Golf • Sea, Coarse & shark fishing • Boating • Horse riding etc. - all nearby.
— OPEN ALL YEAR —
Free Brochure:

LOOE, CORNWALL PL13 2JR
Tel: (01503) 262447/262757

Treble B Holiday Centre

Polperro Road, Looe PL12 2JS

☎ 01503-262425 **Fax** 01503-262425

Open May-end September △ ⊕ ⊞

Size 22 acres, 557 touring pitches, 265 with electric hookup, 450 level pitches, 30 static caravans, 44 ⋒, 100 WCs, 4 CWPs

£ car/tent £6.80-£10, car/caravan £6.80-£10, motorhome £6.80-£10, motorbike/tent £6.80-£10, children £0.75-£1.50

Rental ⊕ Chalet. £63-£350

⊄ MasterCard Visa

⊒ ✕ ⊌ ⊡ ⊠ ⊟ ⊠ ⊞ ⊠ ⊡ ⊿ ⊟ Calor Gaz ⅙ WS

Last arrival time: 11:00

➡ 2 miles W of Looe on A387. Observe sign.

Trelay Farmpark

Pelynt, Looe PL13 2JX

☎ 01503-220 900

Open Easter-end October △ ⊕ ⊞

Size 5 acres, 55 touring pitches, 23 with electric hookup, 27 level pitches, 20 static caravans, 5 ⋒, 11 WCs, 1 CWP

£ car/tent £7-£8.50, car/caravan £7-£8.50, motorhome £7-£8.50, motorbike/tent £7-£8.50, children £1-£1.50

Rental ⊕ £140-£250

⊡ ⊠ ⊟ ⅙ ⋔

Last arrival time: 11:00

➡ From A38 2 miles W of Liskeard at Dobwalls turn onto A390 for Lostwithiel. Shortly after East Taphouse turn left onto B3359 to Pelynt. Trelay is ½ mile past Pelynt on left. Or from A387 Polperro/Looe road, take A3359 ½ mile before Pelynt on right.

LOSTWITHIEL Cornwall 2B4

Powderham Castle Touring Park

Lanlivery, Lostwithiel PL30 5BU

☎ 01208-872277

Open 1 April-31 October △ ⊕ ⊞

A quiet, select uncommercialised park appealing to the more discerning camper. Spacious pitches in enclosed paddocks. Approved and recommended by all relevant touring authorities.

Size 10 acres, 75 touring pitches, 75 with electric hookup, 75 level pitches, 38 static caravans, 8 ⋒, 20

➡

← Powderham Castle Touring Park

WCs, 1 CWP
£ car/tent £6.50-£8.50, car/caravan £6.50-£8.50, motorhome £6.50-£8.50, motorbike/tent £4-£5.50, children £0.50-£1
✕¼ ➡¼ ▣ 🄲 🄳 🄸 🄰 GR 🄰 TV 🄸 Calor Gaz & ➤ WS
Last arrival time: 10:00
➡ 1½ miles SW of Lostwithiel on A390 turn right at signpost to Lanlivery. Go up road for 400 yards.

LOTHERSDALE North Yorkshire	10C3

Springs Farm Caravan Park
Lothersdale, Nr Skipton BD20 8HH
☎ **01535-632533**
Open 1 April-15 October ▲ ⛺ 🚐
Size 4 acres, 17 touring pitches, 17 with electric hookup, 10 level pitches, 2 ⛒, 5 WCs, 1 CWP
£ car/tent £5-£6, car/caravan £7-£9, motorhome £7-£9, motorbike/tent £5-£6, children £1-£1.20
Calor Gaz WS
Last arrival time: 7
➡ From A629 Keighley-Skipton road, take A6068 at Crosshills. Turn right onto Lothersdale road. After 2 miles, turn left at crossroads, go through village, past church, shop and school. Then take next left, then first left and continue past lakes up hill to Springs.

LOUGHTON Essex	5D2

Debden House Campsite
Debden Green, Loughton IG10 2PA
☎ **0181-508 3008** Fax **0181-508 0284**

Set within the beautiful countryside of Epping Forest, but within easy reach of London by road or Underground. Newly refurbished toilet blocks on site.

Size 48½ acres, 150 touring pitches, 60 with electric hookup, 150 level pitches, 10 ⛒, 18 WCs, 2 CWPs 🛁
🛁¼ ➡ 🄲 🄳 🄰 🄰 Calor Gaz &
Last arrival time: 11:30
➡ From M25 junction 26 take A121 to Loughton. At double mini roundabout, turn left onto A1168 Rectory Lane, then take second left into Pyrles Lane.

LOWESTOFT Suffolk	9F3

Camping & Caravanning Club Site

Suffolk Wildlife Park, Whites Lane, Kessingland, Lowestoft

☎ **01502-742040**

Open end March-start November **A ⊡ ⊞**

Size 6½ acres, 90 touring pitches, 53 with electric hookup, 10 ♠, 12 WCs, 1 CWP

£ car/tent £5.60-£8.60, car/caravan £5.60-£8.60, motorhome £5.60-£8.60, motorbike/tent £5.60-£8.60, children £1.50

℃ MasterCard Visa

▣ ☎ ⚠ ⛟ ⚓

Last arrival time: 11:00

➡ From Lowestoft towards London on A12 follow signs to Wildlife Park.

Carlton Manor Caravan Site

Chapel Road, Carlton Colville, Lowestoft NR33 8BL

☎ **01502-566511** Fax **01502-573949**

Open 1 April-October **A ⊡ ⊞**

Size 9½ acres, 90 touring pitches, 60 with electric hookup, 6 ♠, 10 WCs, 2 CWPs

£ car/tent £5.50-£8.25, car/caravan £7-£9.75, motorhome £7.50, motorbike/tent £5.50-£8.25

℃ MasterCard Visa

✕ ⛟ ⚓ ▣ ⚠ Calor ⚓ WS

➡ From A12 or A146 follow signs to Transport Museum. Site next door on B1384.

Kessingland Beach Holiday Village

Kessingland, Lowestoft NR33 7RN

☎ **01502-740636** Fax **01502-740907**

Open 17 April-31 October **A ⊡ ⊞**

Full sports and entertainment programme with nightly cabarets, live bands, a disco and three clubrooms. 108 caravans and 97 chalets for hire (own WCs). Calor gas only. No single-sex parties U25.

Size 66 acres, 90 touring pitches, 40 with electric hookup, 90 level pitches, 222 static caravans, 6 ♠, 16 WCs, 1 CWP

£ car/tent £7-£15, car/caravan £7-£15, motorhome £7-£15, motorbike/tent £7-£15

Rental ⊡ Chalet.

℃ MasterCard Visa

⚓ ✕ ⛟ ▣ ☎ ▣ ⛊ ⛊ ⛊ ⛊ ⛊ GR ⛊ ⚠ ⛊ Calor ⚓ ⚓ WS

➡ Follow Kessingland Beach signs from roundabout on A12 at southern end of the village.

Whitehouse Farm

Gisleham, Kessingland NR33 8DX

☎ **01502-740248**

Open Easter-October **A ⊡ ⊞**

Size 4.5 acres, 40 touring pitches, 34 with electric hookup, 40 level pitches, 4 ♠, 5 WCs, 1 CWP

£ car/tent £6-£7, car/caravan £6-£7, motorhome £6-£7, motorbike/tent £6-£7

⚓¼ ✕¼ ⛟¼ ⛊ ⚠ Gaz ⚓ ⚓ WS

Last arrival time: 11:00

➡ In Kessingland (A12), turn W opposite Wildlife Park. Right at second junction. Site 250 yards.

LYME REGIS Dorset   **3E3**

Hook Farm Camping & Caravan Park

Gole Lane, Uplyme, Lyme Regis DT7 3UU

☎ **01297-442801** Fax **01297-442801**

Open all year **A ⊡ ⊞**

Size 10 acres, 100 touring pitches, 24 with electric hookup, 50 level pitches, 17 static caravans, 8 ♠, 24 WCs, 1 CWP

£ car/tent £6-£8, car/caravan £6-£9, motorhome £6-£8, motorbike/tent £5.50-£6.50, children £1

Rental A ⊡ tents £15 night, caravans £110-£175 week

⚓ ▣ ☎ ▣ ⚠ Calor Gaz ⚓ ⚓

Last arrival time: flexible

➡ From A3052 turn right 2 miles W of Lyme Regis.

Shrubbery Caravan Park

Rousdon, Lyme Regis DT7 3XW

☎ **01297-442227**

Open March-November **A ⊡ ⊞**

Size 10½ acres, 120 touring pitches, 90 with electric hookup, 120 level pitches, 14 ♠, 21 WCs, 1 CWP

£ car/tent £5.75-£7.25, car/caravan £5.75-£7.25, motorhome £5.75-£7.25, motorbike/tent £5-£6.50, children £4.50-£6.50

⚓ ▣ ☎ ▣ ⚠ ⛊ Calor Gaz ⚓ ⚓ WS

Last arrival time: 9:00

➡ 3 miles W of Lyme Regis on A3052 at village of Rousdon.

LYMINGTON Hampshire   **4B4**

Lytton Lawn Camping & Caravan Park

Lymore, Milford-on-Sea, Lymington

☎ **01590-642513**

Open Easter-October **A ⊡ ⊞**

Size 5 acres, 126 touring pitches, 92 with electric hookup, 30 level pitches, 24 ♠, 24 WCs, 2 CWPs

£ car/tent £9.50-£22, car/caravan £9.50-£22, motorhome £9.50-£22, motorbike/tent £9.50-£22

℃ MasterCard Visa

⚓ ✕ ⛟ ▣ ☎ ▣ ⛊ ⛊ ⛊ ⛊ ⛊ GR ⛊ ⚠ ⛊ Calor Gaz ⚓ ⚓

Last arrival time: 10:00

➡ From Lymington take A337 to Everton, then left onto B3058 towards Milford-on-Sea. Lytton Lawn is ¼ mile on left.

See advert inside front cover

LYNTON Devon   2C2

Camping & Caravanning Club Site
Caffyns Cross, Lynton EX35 6JS
☎ 01598-752379
Open end March-start November ▲ ⊕ ⊒
Size 5½ acres, 105 touring pitches, 50 with electric hookup, 10 ⓕ, 14 WCs, 1 CWP
£ car/tent £5.20-£7.80, car/caravan £5.20-£7.80, motorhome £5.20-£7.80, motorbike/tent £5.20-£7.80, children £1.50
CC MasterCard Visa
◌ ⚡ ⚠ ⴕ
Last arrival time: 11:00
➔ Turn N off A39, signposted Caffyns, then turn right.

Channel View Caravan Park
Manor Farm, Barbrook, Lynton EX35 6LD
☎ 01598-753349
Open March-October ▲ ⊕ ⊒

A warm welcome awaits you from Robin & Pat Wren at this quiet family run site. Situated on the edge of Exmoor National Park with spectacular views.

Size 9 acres, 70 touring pitches, 40 with electric hookup, 40 level pitches, 29 static caravans, 11 ⓕ, 20 WCs, 1 CWP
£ car/tent £7-£7.50, car/caravan £7.50-£8, motorhome £7-£7.50, motorbike/tent £7-£7.50, children £0.50
Rental ⊕ £30 per night
CC MasterCard Visa
⚡ ✕¼ ⬤¼ ◌ ⚡ ⚠ Calor Gaz ⴕ ⴕ
Last arrival time: 10:00
➔ On main A39, ½ mile from Barbrook village.

LYTHAM ST ANNES Lancashire   10B4

Bank Lane Caravan Park
Warton, Preston
☎ 01772-633513
Open March-October ▲ ⊕ ⊒

Bank Lane Caravan Park has been architecturally designed, popular and highly praised by visitors. With modern facilities all holiday homes are situated in spacious cul-de-sacs. Tourers very welcome.

Size 15 acres, 50 touring pitches, 50 with electric hookup, 40 level pitches, 160 static caravans, 5 ⓕ, 8 WCs, 2 CWPs
£ car/tent £7-£8, car/caravan £7, motorhome £7, motorbike/tent £7, children £7
⚡ ✕¼ ⬤¼ ◌ ⚡ ⚠ Calor ⴕ ⴕ WS
Last arrival time: 8:00
➔ M6 (jn 31) to Blackpool. Join A584 Freckleton/Lytham, past BAE. Turn left at art gallery/ladies hairdressers. Follow the lane to site.

Eastham Hall Caravan Park
Saltcotes Road, Lytham St Annes FY8 4LS
☎ 01253-737907
Open 1 March-31 October ⊕ ⊒
Size 25 acres, 140 touring pitches, 72 with electric hookup, 140 level pitches, 250 static caravans, 10 ⓕ, 52 WCs, 10 CWPs
£ car/caravan £9-£10.50, motorhome £9-£10.50, children £0.75-£1
⚡ ⚡¼ ◌ ⚡ ⚠ Calor Gaz ⴕ ⴕ WS
Last arrival time: 8:00
➔ Take A584 from Preston, turn right onto B5259 and site is ¾ mile on the right.

MABLETHORPE Lincolnshire   11F4

Camping & Caravanning Club Site
Highfield, Church Lane, Mablethorpe LN12 2NU
☎ 01507-472374
Open end March-end September ▲ ⊕ ⊒
Size 6 acres, 105 touring pitches, 60 with electric hookup, 4 ⓕ, 11 WCs, 1 CWP
£ car/tent £4.60-£6.80, car/caravan £4.60-£6.80, motorhome £4.60-£6.80, motorbike/tent £4.60-£6.80, children £1.40
CC MasterCard Visa
◌ ⚡ ⚠ ⴕ WS
Last arrival time: 11:00
➔ From A1104 turn into Church Lane. Site is ¼ mile on right.

Kirkstead Holiday Park

North Road, Trusthorpe, Mablethorpe LN12 2QD

📞 01507-441483

Open March-December ▲ 🚐 🚏

Size 6 acres, 60 touring pitches, 40 with electric hookup, 60 level pitches, 45 static caravans, 6 🚿, 10 WCs, 1 CWP

£ car/tent £5, car/caravan £6.50-£9, motorhome £6.50-£9, motorbike/tent £5

Rental 🚐 £80-£200

🦮 🦮¼ ✕ ✕¼ 🍽 🍽¼ 🔲 📞 🗄 🖼 GR TV 🍴 Calor ♿ 🐾 WS

➔ On A52 coast road between Mablethorpe and Sutton-on-Sea. Turn off Trusthorpe Island for signs to Kirkstead Holiday Park.

Trusthorpe Springs Leisure Park

Trusthorpe Hall, Mile Lane, Trusthorpe, Mablethorpe LN12 2QQ

📞 01507-441333 **Fax** 01507-441333

Open 1 March-30 November 🚐 🚏

Size 4 acres, 22 touring pitches, 22 with electric hookup, 22 level pitches, 109 static caravans, 8 🚿, 30 WCs, 5 CWPs

£ car/caravan £6-£7.50

Rental ▲ 🚐 £25 daily, £185 weekly.

ℂℂ MasterCard Visa

🦮 ✕ 🍽 🔲 📞 🗄 ⚠ 🍴 Calor ♿ 🐾

Last arrival time: 5:00

➔ Enter Mablethorpe on A1104, right at Cross Inn public house into Mile Lane. Site on corner, 1 mile from Cross Inn.

TRUSTHORPE
Springs

Being less than a mile from the coast, the Park offers seaside location but in a woodland setting in the grounds of Trusthorpe Hall, a fine Georgian House built in 1830.

The park has it's own licensed club – The Cartwheel – which throughout the season has much live entertainment for all ages. Children too, are important and facilities are provided for their needs.

The heated swimming pool located in the centre of the park, always catches the sun and provides an ideal focal point during the day for those who just want to relax.

Trusthorpe Hall, Mile Lane, Trusthorpe, Mablethorpe, Lincolnshire LN12 2QQ Tel: (01507) 441384

Pine Lodge Touring Park

Ashford Road, Hollingbourne, Maidstone ME17 1XH

📞 01622-730018 **Fax** 01622-734498

Open all year ▲ 🚐 🚏

Ideally placed for touring Kent (Leeds Castle is only a mile away) and within easy reach of the Channel ports and the Channel Tunnel. New facilities block. Open all year. Sorry no dogs.

Size 7 acres, 100 touring pitches, 95 with electric hookup, 100 level pitches, 8 🚿, 11 WCs, 1 CWP

£ car/tent £8.50-£9.50, car/caravan £8.50-£9.50, motorhome £8.50-£9.50, motorbike/tent £7, children £0.50

ℂℂ MasterCard Visa

🦮 ✕¼ 🔲 📞 🗄 ⚠ Calor Gaz ♿ WS

Last arrival time: 10:00

➔ From junction 8 on A20 roundabout turn off towards Bearsted and Maidstone. Pine Lodge is on left after 1 mile.

Burton Hill Caravan & Camping Park

Burton Hill, Malmesbury SN16 0EH

📞 01666-822585 **Fax** 01666-822585

Open 1 April-30 November ▲ 🚐 🚏

Size 2 acres, 30 touring pitches, 18 with electric hookup, 30 level pitches, 2 🚿, 4 WCs, 1 CWP

£ car/tent £7, car/caravan £7, motorhome £7, motorbike/tent £7, children £0.50

🔲 📞 🗄 📶 Calor Gaz 🐾 WS

Last arrival time: 12:00

➔ 200 yards S of roundabout at junction of A429, B4014 and B4042, turn W off A429 opposite Malmesbury Hospital (Arches Lane) and follow signs.

Hints & Tips

When braking it will take you an average of 20% more distance to stop. Always avoid violent braking

MALVERN Worcestershire   7E4

Camping & Caravanning Club Site

Blackmore Camp Site No. 2, Hanley, Swan WR8 OEE

☎ 01684 310280

Open end March-end November ▲ ⊕ ⇱

Size 12 acres, 200 touring pitches, 102 with electric hookup, 12 ⌂, 14 WCs, 2 CWPs

£ car/tent £5.60-£8.60, car/caravan £5.60-£8.60, motorhome £5.60-£8.60, motorbike/tent £5.60-£8.60, children £1.50

℄ MasterCard Visa

⊟ ▮ GR ⚠ & ↰ WS

Last arrival time: 11:00

➡ Watch for Blackmore camp sign at junction of B4211. All approaches to site are well signposted.

MANSFIELD Nottinghamshire   8B2

Sherwood Forest Caravan Park

Cavendish Lodge, Old Clipstone, Mansfield NG21 9HW

☎ 0800-146505 **Fax** 01623-823132

Open March-October ▲ ⊕ ⇱

Quiet country park in the heart of Robin Hood country. Some pitches overlook lake and river. Rural atmosphere with wildlife around. Excellent area for walking and cycling.

Size 22 acres, 180 touring pitches, 137 with electric hookup, 21 ⌂, 25 WCs, 5 CWPs

£ car/tent £9.35-£10.20, car/caravan £9.35-£10.20, motorhome £9.35-£10.20, motorbike/tent £9.35-£10.20, children £1.20

℄ MasterCard Visa

⚍¼ ✗¼ ⬤¼ ⊟ ▮ GR ▣ TV ⚠   Calor Gaz & ↰

➡ Best approach is via Ollerton-Mansfield road A6075; turn S towards Old Clipstone opposite turning to Warsop and ½ mile to park. From M1 take exit 27 from S and 30 from N.

MANSTON Kent   5F2

Pine Meadow Caravan Park

Spratling Court Farm, Manston CT12 5AN

☎ 01843-587770 **Fax** 01843-851177

Open April-end September ▲ ⊕ ⇱

Size 3 acres, 40 touring pitches, 40 with electric

hookup, 40 level pitches, 4 ⌂, 4 WCs, 1 CWP

£ car/tent £8-£11.20, car/caravan £8-£11.20, motorhome £8-£11.20

⚍¼ ✗¼ ⬤¼ ▮ ▣ ⚠   Calor

Last arrival time: 10:00

➡ From A256 junction take B2050 W towards Manston village, in 300 yards turn right, signposted Greensole Lane/Pine Meadow.

MARDEN Kent   5E3

Tanner Farm Caravan & Camping Park

Goudhurst Road, Marden TN12 9ND

☎ 01622-832399 **Fax** 01622-832472

Open all year ▲ ⊕ ⇱

Secluded park in centre of 150 acre farm. Ideal touring centre. Shire horses in use.

Size 15 acres, 100 touring pitches, 100 with electric hookup, 95 level pitches, 13 ⌂, 21 WCs, 3 CWPs

£ car/tent £7.50-£11, car/caravan £6-£11, motorhome £6-£11, motorbike/tent £7.50-£11, children £1.10-£1.20

CC MasterCard Visa

🔋 🗄 🔌 🚻 ⬛ /M̄\　Calor Gaz ♿ ⚓ WS

Last arrival time: 8:00

➡ From A229 or A262 onto B2079 midway between villages of Marden and Goudhurst.

MARGATE Kent　　　5F2

Frost Farm Caravan Site

St Nicholas-at-Wade, Birchington, Margate

☎ **01843-847219**

Open March-October 🚐 🚍

Size 3 acres, 12 touring pitches, 8 with electric hookup, 6 level pitches, 48 static caravans, 2 🚿, 8 WCs, 1 CWP

£ car/caravan £6-£8, motorhome £6-£8

🔋¼ ✕¼ 🍴¼ 🔌 /M̄\　Calor ⚓ WS

Last arrival time: 10:00

➡ Site on A299, to St Nicholas roundabout, return on London side ¼ mile.

St Nicholas Camping Site

Court Road, St Nicholas-at-Wade, Birchington, Margate

☎ **01843-847245**

Open 1 March-31 October ⚑ 🚐 🚍

Size 3 acres, 75 touring pitches, 16 with electric hookup, 75 level pitches, 4 🚿, 8 WCs, 1 CWP

£ car/tent £7-£7.50, car/caravan £6.50-£8.50, motorhome £6.50-£7.50, motorbike/tent £7-£7.50

🔋 🔋¼ ✕¼ 🍴¼ 🗄 /M̄\ ⬛　Calor Gaz ♿ ⚓

➡ Signposted off A299 and off A28 near Birchington.

MARKET RASEN Lincolnshire　　　8C1

Market Rasen Racecourse

Legsby Road, Market Rasen LN8 3EA

☎ **01673-842307 Fax 01673-844532**

Open 9 April-5 October ⚑ 🚐 🚍

Rural site, with phone, TV room, playground, games area, reduced admission to racing, 9 hole pay and play golf course. Shop and restaurant one mile. Swimming pool 15 miles.

Size 2 acres, 55 touring pitches, 35 with electric hookup, 55 level pitches, 6 🚿, 6 WCs, 1 CWP

£ car/tent £5.50-£6.70, car/caravan £5-£6.20, motorhome £5-£6.20, motorbike/tent £5.50-£6.70, children £1-£1.10

CC MasterCard Visa

🔋 🗄 🔌 🅿 🇬🇧 /M̄\　Calor Gaz ⚓

Last arrival time: 8:00

➡ S off A631 on E outskirts of Market Rasen. Site is on left after ¾ mile.

MARTOCK Somerset　　　3E2

Southfork Caravan Park

Parrett Works, Martock TA12 6AE

☎ **01935-825661 Fax 01935-825122**

Open all year ⚑ 🚐 🚍

A small family-run park in open countryside near the River Parrett, clean and well-maintained with a modern heated toilet block and free hot showers. Numerous places of interest are nearby for all ages.

Size 2 acres, 30 touring pitches, 20 with electric hookup, 30 level pitches, 3 static caravans, 4 🚿, 5 WCs, 1 CWP

£ car/tent £7, car/caravan £7, motorhome £7, motorbike/tent £7, children £1

Rental 🚐 £90-£220

CC MasterCard Visa

🔋 🗄 🔌 🗄 /M̄\　Calor Gaz ♿ ⚓

Last arrival time: 10:00

➡ From A303 E of Ilminster at South Petherton roundabout, take first exit towards South Petherton and follow camping signs.

Hints & Tips

Tyres are your only contact with the road. Look after them and you will improve the safety and behaviour of your unit. Never mix cross ply and radials on the same axis.

MATLOCK Derbyshire   8A2

Darwin Forest Country Park
Two Dales, Matlock DE4 5LN
☎ 01629-732428 Fax 01629-735015
Open March-December 🚐 🚅

A luxurious family park set in 44 acres of magnificent woodland, featuring every comfort in a spacious and peaceful environment. Pine lodges for hire.

Size 44 acres, 48 touring pitches, 48 with electric hookup, 48 level pitches, 16 🚿, 21 WCs, 1 CWP
£ car/caravan £10-£12, motorhome £10-£12
Rental Chalet. £190
€ MasterCard Visa
🧍✗ 🗣 🔲 🔳 🔲 GR TV ⚠   🔌 Calor 🚹 🐕
Last arrival time: 9:00
➜ M1, junction 29 to Chesterfield - A632 towards Matlock, turn right on to B5057 towards Two Dales. Park is on right, 2 miles before village.

Packhorse Farm
Tansley, Matlock DE4 5LF
☎ 01629-580950 Fax 01629-580950
🏕 🚐 🚅
Size 2 acres, 30 touring pitches, 17 with electric hookup, 30 level pitches, 2 🚿, 4 WCs, 1 CWP
£ car/tent £6-£8, car/caravan £6-£8, motorhome £6-£8, motorbike/tent £6-£8
🧍 🧍¼ 🗣 🗣¼ 🔲 🔳 🚹 🐕
➜ On A615 Alfreton to Matlock road. Turn right in Tansley village.

Wayside Farm Caravan Site
Matlock Moor, Matlock DE4 5LF
☎ 01629-582967
Open all year 🏕 🚐 🚅

A working farm, with a hard road around a well-kept site and trees and hedges beginning to establish. B&B and holiday cottages also available.

Size 1½ acres, 30 touring pitches, 19 with electric hookup, 12 level pitches, 6 🚿, 10 WCs, 1 CWP
£ car/tent £7, car/caravan £7, motorhome £7, motorbike/tent £7, children £1
🧍✗ 🗣 🔲 🔳 🔲 ⚠ 🔳   Calor Gaz 🚹 🐕
Last arrival time: 10:00
➜ Wayside is two miles from Matlock on the A632 Matlock to Chesterfield road. Wayside is well signed off A632

MERSEA ISLAND Essex   5E1

Waldegraves Farm Holiday Park
West Mersea, Mersea Island CO5 8SE
☎ 01206-382898 Fax 01206-385359
Open March-November 🏕 🚐 🚅
Size 25 acres, 120 touring pitches, 120 with electric hookup, 120 level pitches, 205 static caravans, 20 🚿, 20 WCs, 4 CWPs
£ car/tent £8-£12, car/caravan £8-£12, motorhome £8-£12, motorbike/tent £8-£12
Rental 🚐 £150-290
€ MasterCard Visa
🧍✗ 🗣 🔲 🗣 🔲 🔳 🔳 🔲 GR 🔲 TV ⚠   🔌 Calor Gaz 🚹 🐕 WS
Last arrival time: 10:00
➜ B1025 from Colchester to Mersea. Follow brown tourist signs to East Mersea and on to Waldegraves.

TREGARTON PARK

A warm friendly welcome awaits you on our exclusive sheltered touring park, situated in pleasant countryside, just a short drive from the sea.

For colour brochure and full park details please telephone or fax

Tel: 01726-843666
Fax: 01726-844481

Proprietors: Mr. & Mrs. B.A. Hicks & Mr. R.A. Hicks

A peaceful, landscaped, level park close to beautiful beaches. Acres of recreational space with badminton, tennis court, volleyball and putting green.

Size 16 acres, 165 touring pitches, 150 with electric hookup, 165 level pitches, 38 static caravans, 15 ⚐; 30 WCs
£ car/tent £7.50-£16.50, car/caravan £7.50-£16.50, motorhome £7.50-£16.50, children £2-£2.50
Rental Å ⚐ Chalet. £100-£495
℃ MasterCard Visa
⚐ ⚐ ⚐ ⚐ ⚐ ⚐ GR ⚐ ⚐   Calor Gaz ⚐ ⚐
Last arrival time: 10:00
➡ From St Austell take B3273 signed Mevagissey. Prior to village follow brown tourism signs and turn right signed Gorran. After 6 miles follow directional signs on right.

Tregarton Park

Gorran, St Austell PL26 6NF
📞 01726-843666 Fax 01726-844481ep
Open 1 April-30 September Å ⚐ ⚐

Possibly the least commercialised park in Cornwall, with free hot water, swimming and paddling pools.

Size 12 acres, 150 touring pitches, 100 with electric hookup, 80 level pitches, 10 ⚐, 15 WCs, 1 CWP
£ car/tent £6-£12, car/caravan £6-£12, motorhome £6-£12, motorbike/tent £6-£12, children £1.20-£1.50
℃ MasterCard Visa
⚐ ⚐ ⚐ ⚐ ⚐ ⚐ ⚐   Calor Gaz ⚐
Last arrival time: 9:00
➡ From St Austell take B3273 to Mevagissey. After Pentewan turn right to Gorran.

MEVAGISSEY Cornwall   2B4

Penhaven Touring Park

Pentewan PL26 6DL
📞 01726-843687 Fax 01726-843
Open Easter-31 October Å ⚐ ⚐
Size 13 acres, 105 touring pitches, 78 with electric hookup, 105 level pitches, 10 ⚐, 17 WCs, 2 CWPs
£ car/tent £7.50-£12.50, car/caravan £7.50-£16, motorhome £7.50-£16, motorbike/tent £7.50-£12.50, children £1.40
℃ MasterCard Visa
⚐ ✕ ⚐ ⚐ ⚐ ⚐ ⚐ ⚐ ⚐   Calor Gaz ⚐ ⚐ WS
Last arrival time: 9:00
➡ S of St Austell, on B3273 turning on left.

Sea View International

Boswinger, Gorran, St Austell PL26 6LL
📞 01726-843425 Fax 01726-843358
Open April-October Å ⚐ ⚐

MILNTHORPE Cumbria   10B2

Fell End Caravan Park

Slackhead Road, Near Hale, Milnthorpe LA7 7BS
☎ 015395-62122 Fax 015395-63810
Open all year ▲ ⬛ 🚐

A warm welcome awaits you at this family owned award winning park. Peace and tranquillity in a beautiful garden setting with all luxury facilities. Winner 'Calor Best Park in England 1994'. 1995 Best Kept Parks Award. Located in an area of oustanding natural beauty.

Size 28 acres, 68 touring pitches, 68 with electric hookup, 60 level pitches, 215 static caravans, 13 ⛊, 44 WCs, 3 CWPs
£ car/tent £9.50-£10.50, car/caravan £11.50-£12.50, motorhome £11.50-£12.50, children £1.50
⚡ ✕ 🚾 🛢 🔌 ⚠   ♨ Calor Gaz ♿
Last arrival time: 9:00
➔ Leave M6 at junction 35 and head N up A6 for 3¼ miles. Turn left onto unclassified road at brown sites sign and follow road ¾ mile, pick up Fell End Caravan Park signs.

MINEHEAD Somerset   3D2

Blue Anchor Bay Caravan Park

Minehead TA24 6JT
☎ 01643-821360 Fax 01643-821572
Open March-October ▲ ⬛ 🚐

Peaceful beach side location bordered by the West Somerset Railway. Ideal for exploring Exmoor and the beautiful Somerset coast.

Size 29 acres, 103 touring pitches, 103 with electric hookup, 103 level pitches, 300 static caravans, 8 ⛊, 15 WCs, 1 CWP
£ car/caravan £6-£14.50, motorhome £6-£14.50
Rental ⬛
Ⅱ MasterCard Visa
⚡ ⚡¼ ✕¼ 🚾 🛢 🔌 🔲 ⚠   Calor Gaz ♿
Last arrival time: 11:00
➔ From junction 25 on M5, take A358 signed Minehead. After about 12 miles, turn left onto A39 at Williton. After about four miles, turn right onto B3191 at Carhampton. Park is 1½ miles on right.

Camping & Caravanning Club Site

Hill Road, North Hill, Minehead TA24 5SF
☎ 01643-704138
Open end March-end September ▲ ⬛ 🚐
Size 3¾ acres, 60 touring pitches, 12 with electric hookup, 3 ⛊, 8 WCs, 1 CWP
£ car/tent £4.60-£6.80, car/caravan £4.60-£6.80, motorhome £4.60-£6.80, motorbike/tent £4.60-£6.80, children £1.40
Ⅱ MasterCard Visa
🔌 ✝
Last arrival time: 11:00
➔ From A39 turn into The Parade, then left into Blenheim Road and left again into Martlett Road. Follow road past church into Moor Road and then Hill Road. Site is ¼ mile on right.

MINSTERLEY Shropshire   7D2

Old School Caravan Park

Shelve, Minsterley SY5 0JQ
☎ 01588-650410
Open March-October ▲ ⬛ 🚐

A small, quiet, family-run park, situated in the Shropshire Hills and offering first class facilities. Close to the legendary Stiperstones and Long Mynd.

Size 1.25 acres, 12 touring pitches, 10 with electric hookup, 6 level pitches, 1 ⛊, 2 WCs, 1 CWP
£ car/tent £5.50, car/caravan £5.50, motorhome £5.50, motorbike/tent £5.50, children £1.25
✕¼ 🚾¼ 🔌 🛢 ✝
Last arrival time: 10:30
➔ From A488 16 miles S of Shrewsbury through village of Hope. Park is on the left, past the More Arms public house.

MODBURY Devon 2C4

Camping & Caravanning Club Site
California Cross, Ivybridge, Modbury PL21 0SG
☎ 01548-821297
Open end March-start November Å ⊕ ⊞
Size 3.66 acres, 80 touring pitches, 40 with electric
hookup, 6 ☊, 9 WCs, 1 CWP
£ car/tent £5.20-£7.80, car/caravan £5.20-£7.80,
motorhome £5.20-£7.80, motorbike/tent £5.20-£7.80,
children £1.50
℅ MasterCard Visa
🚿¼ 🗑 ⚠ ⚿ ⌕
Last arrival time: 11:00
➜ On B3196 towards Kingsbridge. Site is behind Gulf
service station.

*Immaculate, peaceful site with panoramic views.
Close to many beaches, towns and numerous
attractions. Childrens equipped play area. Shop.
electric hook-up. Superb toilet/showers block. Luxury
caravans for hire.*

Size 12 acres, 154 touring pitches, 50 with electric
hookup, 120 level pitches, 70 static caravans, 15 ☊,
28 WCs, 2 CWPs
£ car/tent £5.50-£9, car/caravan £5.50-£9, motorhome
£4.50-£8, motorbike/tent £5
Rental ⊕ from £80-£310
🚿 🗑 ⚿ 🗑 ⚠ Calor Gaz ⚿
Last arrival time: 10:00
➜ From Exeter, leave A38 at Wrangaton Cross, left
then straight ahead at next crossroads. Continue for 4
miles. Pass garage on left, then 2nd left, site is 1 mile.

Moor View Touring Park
California Cross, Nr Modbury PL21 0SG
☎ 01548-821485 **fax** 01548-821485
Open 1 May-end September Å ⊕ ⊞

*Quiet country park, superb moorland views, sheltered
spacious level pitches, modern and scrupulously
clean toilets and showers with free hot water. Shop
and take-away. Dogs welcome.*

Size 5½ acres, 68 touring pitches, 68 with electric
hookup, 68 level pitches, 6 ☊, 9 WCs, 1 CWP
£ car/tent £6.50-£9.50, car/caravan £6.50-£9.50,
motorhome £6.50-£9.50, motorbike/tent £6.50-£9.50,
children £1.50
℅ MasterCard Visa
🚿 ✕¼ ⚿ 🗑 ⚿ ⚿ ⚿ ⚿ 📺 ⚠ Gaz ⌕
Last arrival time: 10:00
➜ From A38, 25 miles W of Exeter, leave at
Wrangaton Cross (A3121). After 3 miles after
Loddiswell Road leave BP garage on left and follow
Modbury (B3207) road. Park is ½ mile on left.

Pennymoor Camping & Caravan Park
Modbury PL21 0SB
☎ 01548-830269
Open 15 March-15 November Å ⊕ ⊞

MORECAMBE Lancashire 10B3

Melbreak Caravan Park
Carr Lane, Middleton, Morecambe LA3 3LH
☎ 01524-852430
Open 1 March-30 October Å ⊕ ⊞

*Small family site with modern fully-tiled toilet blocks
situated four miles from Morecambe and six miles
from Lancaster, within reach of the Lake District and
Yorkshire Dales.*

Size 2 acres, 30 touring pitches, 40 with electric
hookup, 40 level pitches, 10 static caravans, 4 ☊, 7
WCs, 1 CWP
£ car/tent £6-£6.50, car/caravan £6.50-£7, motorhome
£6.75-£7, motorbike/tent £5.75-£6
🚿 ⚿ 🗑 Calor Gaz ⌕
Last arrival time: 9:00
➜ Take A589 S from Lancaster. At second large
roundabout turn left to Middleton. Follow signs for site.

Ocean Edge Family Park

Moneyclose Lane, Heysham, Morecambe LA3 2AX

☎ 01524-855657

Open March-October

Size 20 acres, 86 touring pitches

🛒)(🛥 🔌 ⛽ OR ♿

➜ From M6 jn 34 take A683 to Heysham for 5 miles. Site signposted

Riverside Caravan Park

Oxcliffe Hill Farm, Heaton-with-Oxcliffe, Morecambe LA3 3ER

☎ 01524-844193

Open March-October 🛖 🚐 🚍

Size 2½ acres, 50 touring pitches, 50 with electric hookup, 50 level pitches, 4 🚿, 8 WCs, 1 CWP

£ car/tent £6-£8, car/caravan £6-£8, motorhome £6-£8, motorbike/tent £6-£8

🛒¼ ✕¼ 🔘 🔌 ⚠   🍴 Calor ♿ 🐕 WS

Last arrival time: 10:00

➜ Leave M6 junction 34, follow signs for Morecambe. Cross river and follow signs for Overton and Middleton. Site gate next to Golden Ball Inn, where river and road run next to each other.

Venture Caravan Park

Langridge Way, Westgate, Morecambe LA4 4TQ

☎ 01524-412986 **Fax** 01524-855884

Open all year 🛖 🚐 🚍

18 acre site with level grass pitches. Quiet, but only three quarters of a mile to all town amenities.

Size 18 acres, 100 touring pitches, 70 with electric hookup, 100 level pitches, 200 static caravans, 20 🚿, 20 WCs, 2 CWPs

£ car/tent £8-£13, car/caravan £8-£13, motorhome £8-£13, motorbike/tent £8-£13

Rental 🚐

🛒 🛥 🔘 🔌 ⛽ 🔲 📺 ⚠   🍴 Calor Gaz ♿ 🐕 WS

➜ M6 junction 34 to Lancaster, then A589 to Morecambe. At third roundabout by Shrimp Public House, take left along Westgate, ½ mile right at school into Langridge Way. Straight on ahead for site.

Percy Wood Caravan Park

Swanland, Morpeth NE65 9JW

☎ 01670-787649 **Fax** 01670-787034

Open 1 March-31 January 🛖 🚐 🚍

Secluded woodland site with plenty of wildlife, adjacent to forest walks

Size 67 acres, 60 touring pitches, 60 with electric hookup, 60 level pitches, 60 static caravans, 6 🚿, 10 WCs, 1 CWP

£ car/tent £8, car/caravan £9.50, motorhome £9.50, motorbike/tent £8, children £1

Rental 🚐 £85-£290

ℂℂ MasterCard Visa

🛒 🛒¼ ✕¼ 🛥¼ 🔘 🔌 ⛽ GR 🔲 ⚠   Calor Gaz 🐕

Last arrival time: 10:00

➜ 2 miles off A1 to Swarland, 6 miles S of Alnwick.

Mill Farm Holiday Park

Hughley SY5 6NT
☎ 01746-785208 Fax 01746-785208
Open 1 March-31 October ▲ ⊞ ⊞

*Family run site in an area of outstanding natural
beauty. Mill Farm offers peace, tranquillity, an
abundance of bird and wildlife, excellent walking,
riding and fishing.*

Size 10 acres, 40 touring pitches, 35 with electric
hookup, 30 level pitches, 85 static caravans, 6 ⋒, 12
WCs, 2 CWPs
£ car/tent £7, car/caravan £7, motorhome £7,
children £1
Rental ⊞
⊡ ⋐ ⊟ ⊠ ⊡ Calor Gaz ⧫ ✝ WS
Last arrival time: 8:00
➡ A4169 from Telford to Much Wenlock. From Much
Wenlock take A468 to Shrewsbury. Turn left at
Harley, left again and follow signs for Hughley.

Sandy Gulls Clifftop Touring Park

Cromer Road, Mundesley-on-Sea NR11 8DF
☎ 01263-720513
Open March-November ▲ ⊞ ⊞

*Set on a clifftop with panoramic sea views, half a
mile from the village. Only a ten minute drive to the
Broads National Park and centrally situated for all
attractions.*

Size 20 acres, 40 touring pitches, 40 with electric
hookup, 20 level pitches, 100 static caravans, 10 ⋒,
20 WCs, 2 CWPs
£ car/tent £5-£10, car/caravan £5-£10, motorhome £5-
£10
Rental ⊞ Chalet. £140-£200
⊒¼ ✗¼ ⊡¼ ⊡ ⋐ ⊟ ⚠   Calor ⧫ ✝ WS
Last arrival time: 10:00
➡ 5 miles S of Cromer on the coast road.

Woodland Caravan Park

Trimingham, Mundesley NR11 8AL
☎ 01263-579208 Fax 01263-833071
Open March-October ⊞ ⊞
Size 43 acres, 150 touring pitches, 80 with electric
hookup, 100 level pitches, 150 static caravans, 14 ⋒,
30 WCs, 2 CWPs
£ car/caravan £6.50-£10.50, motorhome £5.50-£7
CC MasterCard Visa
⊒ ✗ ⊡ ⊡ ⋐ ⊟ GR ⊡ ⚠   ⊟ Calor ⧫ ✝ WS
➡ On coast road between Cromer and Mundesley.

Brookfield Caravan Park

Shrewbridge Road, Nantwich
☎ 01270-69176 Fax 01270-650756
Open Easter-end September ▲ ⊞ ⊞

*Touring caravans and tents are welcome at this site,
which is situated only five minutes walk away from
the historical town of Nantwich and the shops.*

Size 12 touring pitches, 12 with electric hookup, 24
level pitches, 2 ⋒, 4 WCs,
£ car/caravan £6.20, motorhome £3.60
⊒¼ ✗¼ ⊡¼ ⋐ ⊡ ⊡ ⊡ ⚠   ⧫ ✝
➡ From M6 junction 16 take A500 into Nantwich.

Bashley Park

Sway Road, New Milton BH25 5QR
☎ 01425-612340 Fax 01425-612602
Open 1 March-31 October ⊞ ⊞

➡

← Bashley Park

Set in a wooded country estate close to Bournemouth, the New Forest and Solent Beaches, this family park has a vast range of sporting and entertainment facilities

Size 100 acres, 420 touring pitches, 420 with electric hookup, 350 level pitches, 380 static caravans, 37 ⚑, 72 WCs, 4 CWPs
£ car/caravan £9.50-£26, motorhome £9.50-£26
Rental ⚐
ℂ MasterCard Visa
⚑ ✕ ☝ ▤ ⬛ ⬛ ⬛ ⬛ ⬛ ⬛ GR ⬛ TV ⚠ ⬛ Calor ⚓
Last arrival time: 9:00
➜ Take A35 Lyndhurst to Bournemouth for 10 miles. Take B3055 signed Swayford for 2½ miles, then straight over at crossroads. Park is ¼ mile on left.

Delightful site in the heart of the Peak District with excellent facilities and free hot water. Alton Towers, Chatsworth House, Haddon Hall, Harwick Hall, all within easy reach.

Size 30 acres, 125 touring pitches, 73 with electric hookup, 80 level pitches, 70 static caravans, 8 ⚑, 18 WCs, 1 CWP
£ car/tent £6.75-£8, car/caravan £6.75-£8, motorhome £6.75-£8, motorbike/tent £6.75-£8
⚑ ✕¼ ▤ ⬛ ⬛ GR ⚠ Calor Gaz ⚓ WS
➜ Halfway between Ashbourne and Buxton on A515 at junction with A5012.

NEWBY BRIDGE Cumbria   10B2

Newby Bridge Caravan Park
Canny Hill, Newby Bridge LA12 8NF
📞 **015395-31030 Fax 015395-30105**
Open March-October ⚐ 🚐
Size 25 acres, 20 touring pitches, 20 with electric hookup, 20 level pitches, 69 static caravans, 4 ⚑, 8 WCs, 1 CWP
£ car/caravan £8.50-£12, motorhome £8.50-£12
Rental ⚐ Chalet. £75-£385
⚑¼ ✕¼ ☝¼ ▤ ⬛ Calor ♿ ⚓ WS
Last arrival time: 8:00
➜ Just before entering Newby Bridge from motorway turn left at Canny Hill signpost. Park entrance is 200 yards on right.

Oak Head Caravan Park
Ayside, Newby Bridge LA11 6JA
📞 **01539-531475**
Open March-October ⚑ ⚐ 🚐
Size 3½ acres, 60 touring pitches, 30 with electric hookup, 50 level pitches, 71 static caravans, 8 ⚑, 33 WCs, 1 CWP
£ car/tent £5-£7, car/caravan £7-£8, motorhome £5-£7, motorbike/tent £5
Rental ⚐
▤ ⬛ ⬛ Calor Gaz ♿ ⚓ WS
Last arrival time: flexible
➜ M6 junction 36 onto A590. Follow signs for Newby Bridge for 14 miles. Caravan sign is on left of A590. Site is 1½ miles S of Newby Bridge.

NEWHAVEN Derbyshire   8A2

Newhaven Caravan & Camping Park
Newhaven SK17 0DT
📞 **01298-84300**
Open 1 March-31 October ⚑ ⚐ 🚐

NEWMARKET Suffolk   9D4

Camping & Caravanning Club Site
Rowley Mile Racecourse, Newmarket CB8 8JL
📞 **01638-663235**
Open end March-end September ⚑ ⚐ 🚐
Size 90 touring pitches, 36 with electric hookup, 6 ⚑, 14 WCs, 1 CWP
£ car/tent £5.20-£7.80, car/caravan £5.20-£7.80, motorhome £5.20-£7.80, motorbike/tent £5.20-£7.80, children £1.50
ℂ MasterCard Visa
▤ GR ⚠ ⚓
Last arrival time: 11:00
➜ On A1304 in Newmarket, follow signs for Hospital Racecourse.

NEWQUAY Cornwall   2A3

Camping & Caravanning Club Site
Tregurrian, Watergate Bay, Newquay TR8 4AE
📞 **01637-860448**
Open late March-late September ⚑ ⚐ 🚐
Size 4½ acres, 106 touring pitches, 31 with electric hookup, 6 ⚑, 16 WCs, 2 CWPs
£ car/tent £4.60-£6.80, car/caravan £4.60-£6.80, motorhome £4.60-£6.80, motorbike/tent £4.60-£6.80, children £1.40
ℂ MasterCard Visa
⬛ ⚓
Last arrival time: 11:00
➜ From B3056 take road signed Airport, left at B3276 then follow signs.

Gwills Holiday Park

Newquay TR8 4PE

📞 01637-873617 **Fax** 01637-873617

Open Easter-December ▲ ⊕ ⊞

Riverside family park only 2 miles from Newquay. Luxury lodges and caravans for hire. Tourers/tents are welcome. Electrical hook-ups available. Domed heated pool, lounge bar and river fishing. Families and couples only.

Size 14 acres, 150 touring pitches, 45 with electric hookup, 150 level pitches, 32 static caravans, 13 ⁛, 10 WCs, 1 CWP

£ car/tent £5.20-£9, car/caravan £5.20-£9, motorhome £4.60-£8, motorbike/tent £4.90-£8.50, children £1.20-£2.10

Rental ⊕ Chalet. £90-£500

₵ MasterCard Visa

🛒 ✕ 🖤 🗑 📞 🔄 🔲 🔳 GR TV 🛆 🍴 Calor ⅋ ⚓ WS

➔ Take M5 to Exeter, then A30, then A392 to Newquay. At Quintrell Downs go straight across at roundabout, then take second turning on left signposted 'Gwills'. Go past Lane Theatre, turn right at crossroads and site is 400 yards on right.

Hendra Holiday Park

Newquay TR8 4NY

📞 01637-875778 **Fax** 01637-879017

Open April-October ▲ ⊕ ⊞

Size 49 acres, 600 touring pitches, 250 with electric hookup, 600 level pitches, 187 static caravans, 3 CWPs

£ car/tent £7.25-£11.15, car/caravan £7.25-£11.15, motorhome £7.25-£11.15, motorbike/tent £7.25-£11.15, children £3.25

Rental ⊕ from £110-£595

₵ MasterCard Visa

🛒 ✕ 🖤 🗑 📞 🔄 🔲 🔳 🔲 GR 🔲 TV 🛆 🍴 Calor Gaz ⅋ ⚓ WS

➔ A30 to Indian Queens, A392 to Newquay. Hendra is 1½ miles before Newquay town centre.

Newquay Holiday Park

Newquay TR8 4HS

📞 01637-871111 **Fax** 01637-850818

Open 17 May-19 September ▲ ⊕ ⊞

Size 23 acres, 357 touring pitches, 156 with electric hookup, 10 level pitches, 140 static caravans, 24 ⁛, 30 WCs, 4 CWPs

£ car/tent £7-£11.80, car/caravan £7-£11.80, motorhome £7-£11.80, motorbike/tent £7-£11.80, children £3.60

Rental ⊕ £95-£495

₵ MasterCard Visa

🛒 🖤 🗑 📞 🔳 🔲 GR 🔲 TV 🛆 🍴 Calor Gaz

Last arrival time: 10:00

➔ 2 miles from Newquay on A3059 toward St Columb, signposted.

See advert on next page

Trekenning Tourist Park
Newquay TR8 4JF
☎ 01637-880462 Fax 01637-880462
Open March-October Å 🚐 🚎
Size 6½ acres, 75 touring pitches, 68 with electric hookup, 9 ⛺, 11 WCs, 1 CWP
£ car/tent £6.80-£9.40, car/caravan £6.80-£9.40, motorhome £6.80-£9.40, motorbike/tent £6.80-£9.40, children £2.30-£3.40
Rental Å 🚐
℃ MasterCard Visa
🔋 ✗ 📞 🅰 🔌 🔲 🔲 GR TV ⚠ 🔲 Calor Gaz WS
➡ Adjacent to A39 by St Columb Major roundabout.
See advert on previous page

Treloy Farm Tourist Park
Newquay TR8 4JN
☎ 01637-872063
Open April-end September Å 🚐 🚎
Size 11½ acres, 141 touring pitches, 98 with electric hookup, 100 level pitches, 14 ⛺, 24 WCs, 1 CWP
£ car/tent £5-£9, car/caravan £5-£9, children £1.50-£2.50
℃ MasterCard Visa
🔋 ✗ 📞 🅰 🔌 🔲 🔲 GR 🔲 TV ⚠ 🔲 Calor Gaz 🐕
Last arrival time: 11:00
➡ Just off A3059 (main St Columb Major to Newquay road). 5 minutes to Newquay.

Trenance Caravan Park
Edgcumbe Avenue, Newquay TR7 2JY
☎ 01637-873447 Fax 01637-873447
Open 1 April-31 October Å 🚐 🚎

Situated on partly sloping ground and only one mile from Newquay's centre with all amenities.

Size 12 acres, 50 touring pitches, 36 with electric hookup, 16 level pitches, 134 static caravans, 22 ⛺, 3 CWPs
£ car/tent £6-£10, car/caravan £6-£10, motorhome £6-£10, motorbike/tent £6-£10, children £1.50-£2.50
Rental 🚐 Chalet. £80-£340
℃ MasterCard Visa
🔋 ✗ 📞 🅰 🔌 🔲 GR Calor Gaz
Last arrival time: 9:00
➡ On the main A3075 Newquay/Truro road. 1 mile from Newquay town centre.

Trethiggey Touring Park
Quintrell Downs, Newquay TR8 4LG
☎ 01637-877672
Open 1 March-1 January Å 🚐 🚎
Size 15 acres, 145 touring pitches, 100 with electric hookup, 145 level pitches, 12 static caravans, 8 ⛺, 21 WCs, 1 CWP
£ car/tent £5.15-£7.75, car/caravan £5.15-£7.75, motorhome £4.40-£7, motorbike/tent £4.40-£7, children £1-£1.75
Rental 🚐 £80-£300
℃ MasterCard Visa
🔋 🔋¼ ✗¼ 📞 📞¼ 🅰 🔌 🔲 🔲 🔲 🔲 GR TV ⚠ Calor Gaz ♿ 🐕 WS
Last arrival time: 10:30
➡ From A30 at Indian Queens take A392 Newquay road. Follow this road for 5 miles to Quintrell Downs roundabout. The site is signposted left on A3058 ½ mile.

Trevornick Holiday Park
Holywell Bay, Newquay TR8 5PW
☎ 01637-830531 Fax 01637-831000
Open 1 May-14 September **Å ♙ ⌥**

*Just ½ mile from beach, stunning sea views from
immaculately maintained 5 tick park.
Daytime/evening entertainment programme. Fully
equipped tents to sleep 6, to rent.*

Size 30 acres, 450 touring pitches, 250 with electric
hookup, 200 level pitches, 40 ⌂, 70 WCs, 8 CWPs
£ car/tent £6-£10.40, car/caravan £6-£10.40,
motorhome £6-£10.40, motorbike/tent £6-£10.40,
children £2.90
Rental Å Eurotents, fully equipped £80-£250 weekly.
CC MasterCard Visa
🛒 ✕ ☕ ▣ 🔌 ⌗ 🖼 🔯 🅿 🔳 🔲 📷 GR TV ⚠ 🔳   🔥
Calor ♿ 🐾
➡ Take A3075 Newquay to Perranporth road. Turn left
for Cubert/Holywell. Go through Cubert and site is ½
mile on right.

Watergate Bay Holiday Park
Tregurrian, Watergate Bay, Newquay TR8 4AD
☎ 01637-860387 Fax 01637-860387
Open 1 March-30 November **Å ♙ ⌥**

*For a relaxing holiday in beautiful countryside by the
sea. Heated pool, licensed club, cafeteria, electronics,
laundrette, adventure playground and evening
entertainment.*

Size 30 acres, 171 touring pitches, 100 with electric
hookup, 171 level pitches, 32 ⌂, 43 WCs, 7 CWPs
£ car/tent £6.50-£10.50, car/caravan £6.50-£10.50,
motorhome £6.50-£10.50, motorbike/tent £6.50-£10.50
CC MasterCard Visa
🛒 ✕ ☕ ▣ 🔌 ⌗ 🔳 GR TV ⚠   🔥 Calor Gaz ♿ 🐾 WS
➡ 4 miles N of Newquay on B3276 coast road to
Newquay.

Dornafield Caravan Park
Two Mile Oak, Newton Abbot TQ12 6DD
☎ 01803-812732 Fax 01803-812032
Open 20 March-31 October **Å ♙ ⌥**

*Beautiful 14th century farmhouse located in peaceful
Devon countryside. Superb facilities for the
discerning caravanner with 135 pitches (including
64 full service). Tennis, games room, children's
adventure areas and shop. Our brochure is only a
phone call away*

Size 30 acres, 135 touring pitches, 135 with electric
hookup, 135 level pitches, 19 ⌂, 28 WCs, 32 CWPs

£ car/tent £8-£12.50, car/caravan £8-£12.50,
motorhome £8-£12.50, motorbike/tent £8-£12.50,
children £1.10-£1.25
🛒 ✕¼ ☕¼ ▣ 🔌 ⌗ 🔳 GR 🔍 ⚠   Calor Gaz ♿ 🐾
WS
Last arrival time: 10:00
➡ Take A381, Newton Abbot to Totnes road. From
Newton Abbot after 2½ miles turn right at 'Two Mile
Oak Inn'. After 5 miles take first turning on left and
site is 200 yards on right.

Lemonford Caravan Park
Bickington, Newton Abbot TQ12 6JR
☎ 01626-821242
Open March-October **Å ♙ ⌥**

*One of the prettiest parks in South Devon, landscaped
with hedges and trees, with easy access to Torbay,
Dartmoor and many major attractions.*

Size 7½ acres, 90 touring pitches, 62 with electric
hookup, 90 level pitches, 18 static caravans, 6 ⌂, 12
WCs, 3 CWPs

£ car/tent £5-£8, car/caravan £5-£8, motorhome £5-£8, motorbike/tent £8, children £1.10

⚡ ✗¼ 🔲 🔳 🔲 /⚡   Calor Gaz 🔥 WS

Last arrival time: 10:00

➡ From Exeter take A38 towards Plymouth to B382. At roundabout, take third exit to Bickington. From Plymouth take A383 turn off to Bickington.

Ross Park

Park Hill Farm, Ipplepen, Newton Abbot TQ12 5TT

📞 01803-812983 Fax 01803-812983

Open all year Å 🚐 🚏

Welcoming, tranquil, rural site with private pitches and splendid views of Dartmoor. Easy access from all major routes. Magnificent floral displays. Heated tropical conservatory. Restaurant.

Size 26 acres, 110 touring pitches, 110 with electric hookup, 110 level pitches, 11 🏠, 19 WCs, 1 CWP
£ car/tent £6.80-£10.20, car/caravan £6.80-£10.20, motorhome £6.80-£10.20, children £1.75

⚡ ✗ 🔲 🔳 🔲 🔳 🔲 📺 /⚡   Calor Gaz ⚡ 🔥 WS

Last arrival time: 9:00

➡ 3 miles from Newton Abbot, 6 miles from Totnes on A381. At Park Hill crossroads and Jet filling station, take road sign to Woodlands and brown tourist road sign Ross Park.

Stover International Caravan Park

Lower Staple Hill, Newton Abbot TQ12 6JD

📞 01626-821446 Fax 01626-821606

Open Easter-31 October Å 🚐 🚏

Quiet secluded touring park on the edge of Dartmoor. Excellent facilities including free indoor heated swimming pool. Also holiday homes for sale or rent.

Size 15 acres, 220 touring pitches, 200 with electric hookup, 200 level pitches, 4 static caravans, 26 🏠, 60 WCs, 3 CWPs
£ car/tent £4.25-£8.75, car/caravan £4.25-£8.75, motorhome £4.25-£8.75, children £1.30
Rental 🚐 Chalet. caravans £115-£320, chalets £100-£280
ℂℂ MasterCard Visa

⚡ 🔳 🔲 🔳 🔲 🔳 🔲 /⚡   🔲 Calor Gaz ⚡ 🔥 WS

Last arrival time: dusk

➡ From A38 take A382 signed Newton Abbot. 800 yards follow signs to Stover International and Trago Mills.

NORTHALLERTON North Yorkshire	11D2

Cote Ghyll Caravan Park

Osmotherley, Northallerton OL6 3AH

📞 01609-883425

Open April-October Å 🚐 🚏

Size 7 acres, 57 touring pitches, 57 with electric hookup, 27 level pitches, 17 static caravans, 10 🏠, 17 WCs, 2 CWPs
£ car/tent £5.25-£6, car/caravan £6, motorhome £5.50, motorbike/tent £5, children £0.50

⚡¼ ✗¼ 🔲 🔲 Calor Gaz 🔥

Last arrival time: 10:00

➡ Take A19 to A684. Follow signpost for Osmotherley to village centre. Turn left up hill. Site is ½ mile on right.

NORTHAMPTON Northamptonshire   8B4

Billing Aquadrome
Little Billing, Northampton NN3 4DA
☎ 01604 408181 Fax 01604 784412
Open 23 March-1 November ▲ ⌁ ⇋
Size 237 acres, 999 touring pitches, 450 with electric hookup, 999 level pitches, 1,000 static caravans, 66 ☔, 217 WCs, 14 CWPs
£ car/tent £10-£12, car/caravan £10-£12, motorhome £10-£12, motorbike/tent £10-£12
Rental ⌁ from £140 weekly.
✕ MasterCard Visa
⚡ ✕ ➤ ⛽ ⬚ ⟐ ⟐ ⟐ ⬚ ⟐ ⬚ ⟐ ⬚ ⟐ Calor Gaz ♿ ☂ WS
➜ Junction 15 M1, 10 miles away, follow signpost.

NORWICH Norfolk   9F3

Camping & Caravanning Club Site
Martineau Lane, Lakenham, Norwich NR1 2HX
☎ 01603-620060
Open end March-start September ▲ ⌁ ⇋
Size 2½ acres, 50 touring pitches, 16 with electric hookup, 4 ☔, 6 WCs, 1 CWP
£ car/tent £5.20-£7.80, car/caravan £5.20-£7.80, motorhome £5.20-£7.80, motorbike/tent £5.20-£7.80, children £1.50
✕ MasterCard Visa
⚡¼ ⬚ ☂
Last arrival time: 11:00
➜ From A47 turn into Long John Hill (under low bridge 10' 6"), left into Martineau Lane and site is on right.

Dower House Touring Park
East Harling, Norwich NR16 2SE
☎ 01953-717314 Fax 01953-717843
Open 15 March-31 October ▲ ⌁ ⇋

This family run touring park deep in the heart of the Thetford Forest provides the ideal break. Set in rural tranquillity with excellent facilities, including a pub and outdoor pool.

Size 20 acres, 80 with electric hookup, 160 level pitches, 11 ☔, 20 WCs, 3 CWPs
£ car/tent £6.95-£9, car/caravan £6.95-£9, motorhome £6.95-£9, motorbike/tent £6.95-£9
✕ MasterCard Visa
⚡ ✕ ➤ ⬚ ⬚ ⬚ ⬚ ⬚ ⟐ Calor Gaz ♿ ☂ WS

Last arrival time: 9:00
➜ From Thetford, take A1066 E for 5 miles, fork left at camping sign onto East Harling road. Site is on left after 2 miles.

Haveringland Hall Caravan Park
Cawston, Norwich NR10 4PN
☎ 01603-871302
Open March-October ▲ ⌁ ⇋
Size 35 acres, 40 touring pitches, 20 with electric hookup, 20 level pitches, 55 static caravans, 10 ☔, 18 WCs, 1 CWP
£ car/tent £6-£8.50, car/caravan £7-£8.50, motorhome £7-£8.50, motorbike/tent £6-£8.50, children £1
Rental ⌁
⚡¼ ✕¼ ⬚ ⬚ ⬚ ⬚ ⬚   Calor Gaz ♿ ☂ WS
Last arrival time: 8:00
➜ From Norwich N on A140 for 3¾ miles, fork left on B1149 for 2¾ miles. 3 miles past turn left into unclassified road, after 1¼ miles turn right and continue to site on right in ½ mile.

Swans Harbour Caravan Park
Barford Road, Marlingford, Norwich NR9 4BE
☎ 01603-759658
Open all year ▲ ⌁ ⇋

Situated just outside the historic city of Norwich, this site is perfectly placed for touring Norfolk and the Broads.

Size 4 acres, 25 touring pitches, 25 with electric hookup, 25 level pitches, 2 ☔, 6 WCs, 1 CWP
£ car/tent £5, car/caravan £5, motorhome £5, motorbike/tent £5, children £0.50
⚡¼ ✕¼ ➤¼ ⬚ ⬚ ☂
➜ Take B1108 Norwich-Watton. 2½ miles past Norwich southern bypass, turn right at crossroads to Marlingford. Follow tourist signs to site.

NOTTINGHAM Nottinghamshire   8B2

Thornton's Holt Camping Park
Stragglethorpe, Radcliffe-on-Trent, Nottingham NG12 2JZ
☎ 0115-933 2125 Fax 0115-933 3318
Open all year ▲ ⌁ ⇋
Size 14 acres, 90 touring pitches, 64 with electric

hookup, 90 level pitches, 9 ⬧, 12 WCs, 1 CWP
£ car/tent £7-£8, car/caravan £7-£8, motorhome £7-£8, motorbike/tent £7-£8, children £0.50-£0.75
⬧ ⬧¼ ✗¼ ⬧ ⬧ ⬧ ⬧ GR ⬧ �ᐃ ⬧ Calor Gaz ⬧ ⬧ WS
Last arrival time: 9:00
➡ From A52, 3 miles E of Nottingham, turn S at traffic lights towards Cropwell Bishop. Park is ½ mile on left. From A46, 5 miles SE of Nottingham turn N signposted Stragglethorpe. Park is 2½ miles on right.

THORNTON'S HOLT
CAMPING PARK

'The Indoor Swimming Pool and Patio'

Situated where the peace of the countryside meets the culture and life of the City of Nottingham, this sheltered Park offers the following attractions:

☆ 90 pitches, most with electric H.U.
☆ Good central amenities
☆ Outdoor play area & games barn
☆ Indoor heated swimming pool
☆ Shop & information centre
☆ Pub & restaurant within 150 metres
☆ Regular & frequent bus service to Nottingham.

STRAGGLETHORPE, RADCLIFFE-ON-TRENT, NOTTINGHAM NG12 2JZ
Tel: 0115 9332125 Fax: 0115 9333318

OAKHAM Rutland   8C3

Ranksborough Hall Camping & Caravan Park

Langham, Oakham
☎ 01572-722984
Open all year ⬧ ⬧ ⬧
Size 34 acres, 140 touring pitches, 100 with electric hookup, 260 level pitches, 65 static caravans, 12 ⬧, 16 WCs, 2 CWPs
£ car/tent £7.50-£10.50, car/caravan £7.50-£10.50, motorhome £6.50, motorbike/tent £7.50
Rental Chalet. £30-£55 per day
⬧ ✗ ⬧ ⬧ ⬧ ⬧ ⬧ ⬧ GR �ᐃ ⬧ Calor Gaz ⬧ WS
Last arrival time: 11:00
➡ Main A606 from Oakham towards Melton Mowbray. 1½ miles from Oakham.

OKEHAMPTON Devon   2C3

Bridestow Caravan Park

Bridestowe, Okehampton EX20 4ER
☎ 01837-86261
Open March-end December ⬧ ⬧ ⬧
Size 5½ acres, 13 touring pitches, 13 with electric hookup, 13 level pitches, 36 static caravans, 4 ⬧, 9 WCs, 1 CWP
£ car/tent £6.50, car/caravan £6.50, motorhome £6.50, motorbike/tent £4.50, children £0.50
Rental ⬧ from £85
⬧ ⬧¼ ✗¼ ⬧¼ ⬧ ⬧ ⬧ GR ⬧ �ᐃ Calor Gaz ⬧ WS
Last arrival time: 10:30
➡ Turn off A30 at Sourton Cross junction, follow signs to Bridestowe Village. In the village follow signs to the park.

Camping & Caravanning Club Site

Lydford, Nr Okehampton EX20 4BE
☎ 01822-820275
Open end March-end September ⬧ ⬧ ⬧
Size 4 acres, 70 touring pitches, 30 with electric hookup, 8 ⬧, 18 WCs, 1 CWP
£ car/tent £5.20-£7.80, car/caravan £5.20-£7.80, motorhome £5.20-£7.80, motorbike/tent £5.20-£7.80, children £1.50
((MasterCard Visa
⬧ ⬧ �ᐃ ⬧
Last arrival time: 11:00
➡ From Okehampton on A386 turn right at Lydford, follow road past school and turn right past war memorial. Site is on left.

Dartmoor View Caravan & Camping Park

Whiddon Down, Okehampton EX20 2QL
☎ 01647-231545 Fax 01647-231654
Open March-November ⬧ ⬧ ⬧

A quiet, friendly and superbly maintained family holiday park within easy reach of the A30 and the perfect base for touring glorious Devon and Cornwall. Letterboxing centre with licensed bar, heated outdoor pool and take-away.

Size 5½ acres, 75 touring pitches, 40 with electric hookup, 31 static caravans, 4 ⬧, 8 WCs, 1 CWP
£ car/tent £6.50-£8.80, car/caravan £6.50-£8.80, motorhome £6.50-£8.80, motorbike/tent £6.50-£8.80, children £1.50
Rental ⬧ Chalet. £110-£295
((MasterCard Visa
⬧ ✗¼ ⬧ ⬧ ⬧ ⬧ GR TV �ᐃ ⬧ Calor Gaz ⬧
Last arrival time: 10:00
➡ A30 from Exeter to Merry Meet roundabout (17 miles) turn left. Park ½ mile from roundabout on right

Olditch Farm Caravan & Camping Park
Sticklepath, Okehampton EX20 2NT
☎ 01837-840734 Fax 01837-840877
Open 14 March-14 November ▲ ⊕ ⇝

A small family run site, within the Dartmoor National Park - direct walking access to the moor, small play area for children, dogs welcome approximately one hour from the coast.

Size 5 acres, 35 touring pitches, 15 with electric hookup, 12 level pitches, 20 static caravans, 4 ⏃, 12 WCs, 1 CWP
£ car/tent £5.50-£6.50, car/caravan £5.50-£6.50, motorhome £5.50-£6.50, motorbike/tent £6.50
Rental ⊕ £75-£195
🛒¼ ✗ ✗¼ ▣ 🔋 ⊟ ⏰ ▣ ▣ Calor Gaz ⊺ WS
Last arrival time: 10:00
➡ 3 miles E of Okehampton turn off A30 at Merry Meet roundabout. Site is 3 miles down Old Road.

Yertiz Caravan and Camping Park
Exeter Road, Okehampton EX20 1QF
☎ 01837-52281
Open all year ▲ ⊕ ⇝
Size 3½ acres, 30 touring pitches, 22 with electric hookup, 8 level pitches, 4 static caravans, 3 ⏃, 5 WCs, 1 CWP
£ car/tent £4-£6.50, car/caravan £4.50-£6.50, motorhome £4.50-£6.50, motorbike/tent £4.50-£5.50, children £0.50
Rental ⊕ £80-£200
🛒¼ ✗¼ ▣ 🔋 ⊟ Calor Gaz ♿ ⊺
Last arrival time: 11:30

Emberton Country Park
Olney MK46 5DB
☎ 01234-711575 Fax 01234-711575
Open 1 April-31 October ▲ ⊕ ⇝

A quiet grassy site within a country park. Containing five lakes and the River Ouse. The market town of Olney is within easy walking distance.

Size 175 acres, 200 touring pitches, 10 with electric hookup, 200 level pitches, 115 static caravans, 10 ⏃, 15 WCs, 4 CWPs
£ car/tent £6.50-£8.50, car/caravan £8-£11, motorhome £8-£11, motorbike/tent £6.50-£8.50
🛒 ▣ 🔋 ▣ ▣ ⏏ Calor Gaz ♿ ⊺
Last arrival time: 24 hrs
➡ From M1 junction 14 follow A504 towards Newport Pagnell. Follow A509/422 towards Olney. Site is ½ mile S of Olney.

Royal Hill Inn
Edgerley, Kinnerley, Oswestry SY10 8ES
☎ 01743-741242
Open April-October ▲ ⊕ ⇝
Size 2.5 acres, 25 touring pitches, 6 static caravans, 2 ⏃, 2 WCs, 1 CWP
£ car/tent £4, car/caravan £4, motorhome £4, motorbike/tent £4
Rental ⊕ £80-£100
🔋 ⊟ ▣ ▣ ⏏ Calor ⊺
Last arrival time: 10:00
➡ From A5 (Shrewsbury), left at Melverley sign, left out of Pentre at post office. Site 1 mile from Pentre next to Severn River.

Green Pastures Farm
Ower, Romsey SO51 6AJ
☎ 01703-814444
Open 15 March-31 October ▲ ⊕ ⇝
Size 4 acres, 45 touring pitches, 45 with electric hookup, 45 level pitches, 4 ⏃, 7 WCs, 1 CWP
£ car/tent £7.50, car/caravan £7.50, motorhome £7.50, motorbike/tent £7.50, children £0.75

🛒 🗗 Calor Gaz ⚊ ⚓ WS

➡ Site signposted from A36 and A3090 at Ower. From M27 exit 2 follow signs for Paultons Park, then our own signs.

OWERMOIGNE Dorset   3F3

Sandyholme Holiday Park

Moreton Road, Owermoigne DT2 8HZ
📞 01305-852677 **Fax** 01305-854677
Open Easter-31 October 🛆 ⚐ ⛟
Size 6 acres, 65 touring pitches, 58 with electric hookup, 65 level pitches, 35 static caravans, 8 🚿, 20 WCs, 1 CWP
£ car/tent £5.50-£10.50, car/caravan £5.50-£10.50, motorhome £5.50-£10.50, motorbike/tent £5-£10
Rental ⚐ £115-£310
CC MasterCard Visa
🛒 ✕ 🍳 🗗 📵 🗓 🔧 🗺 GR 🔍 🅰 🍴 Calor Gaz ⚓ WS
Last arrival time: 10:00
➡ Turn off A352 Dorchester/Wareham road through village of Owermoigne for 1 mile.

OXFORD Oxfordshire   4B2

Cassington Mill Caravan Park

Eynsham Road, Cassington, Oxford OX8 1DB
📞 01865-881081 **Fax** 01865-880577
Open 1 April-31 October 🛆 ⚐ ⛟

A quiet, grassy site, with the River Evenlode running through the park. Restaurant one mile. Swimming pool seven miles.

Size 4 acres, 83 touring pitches, 70 with electric hookup, 83 level pitches, 35 static caravans, 4 🚿, 30 WCs, 2 CWPs
£ car/tent £7.50-£9, car/caravan £7.50-£9, motorhome £7.50-£9, motorbike/tent £5.50-£6.50, children £2
CC MasterCard Visa
🛒 🗓 🎵 🅰   Calor Gaz ⚊ ⚓ WS
Last arrival time: 9:00
➡ A40 W of Oxford, second left, signposted.

Diamond Farm Caravan & Camping Park

Bletchingdon, Oxford OX5 3DR
📞 01869-350909 **Fax** 01869-350918
Open all year 🛆 ⚐ ⛟

A small family run site set in the heart of the countryside. Offering first class facilities. Only 3 miles from junction 9 of the M40.

Size 3 acres, 37 touring pitches, 26 with electric hookup, 37 level pitches, 4 🚿, 8 WCs, 1 CWP
£ car/tent £8-£10, car/caravan £8-£10, motorhome £8-£10, motorbike/tent £8-£10, children £1-£1.50
🛒 ✕ 🍳 🗗 🗓 🔧 🗺 GR 🅰 🍴 Calor Gaz ⚓ WS
Last arrival time: 10:00
➡ From M40 junction 9 follow A34 for about 2 miles towards Oxford. Take second exit off A34 and follow signs for Bletchingdon.

Oxford Camping International

426 Abingdon Road, Oxford OX1 4XN
📞 01865-246551 **Fax** 01865-240145
Open all year 🛆 ⚐ ⛟

Situated on the edge of Oxford, just over one mile from the historic centre and ½ mile from the River Thames, with good access to the M4/M40.

Size 5 acres, 129 touring pitches, 90 with electric hookup, 129 level pitches, 10 🚿, 21 WCs, 1 CWP
£ car/tent £8, car/caravan £8, motorhome £8, motorbike/tent £7.10
CC MasterCard Visa
🛒 🛒¼ ✕¼ 🍳¼ 🗗 🗓 Calor Gaz ⚊ ⚓
Last arrival time: 10:00
➡ On S side of Oxford, take A4144 to city centre from ring road, ¼ mile on left. Rear of Touchwoods Outdoor Life Centre.

PADSTOW Cornwall   2B3

Carnevas Holiday Park
St. Merryn, Padstow PL28 8PN
☎ 01841-520230 Fax 01041-520230
Open April-October A 🚐 🚚
Size 12 acres, 195 touring pitches, 40 with electric hookup, 75 level pitches, 9 static caravans, 10 🚿, 21 WCs, 1 CWP
£ car/tent £5-£8.50, car/caravan £5-£8.50, motorhome £4.50-£8.50, motorbike/tent £5-£8.50, children £0.80
Rental 🚐 Chalet. £100-£395
🛒 🖲 📞 🖨 GR ⚠ 🔦 Calor Gaz 🔦
➡ From village of St Merryn take B3276 towards Porthcothan Bay, turn right off Tredrea Inn and park is ¼ mile on right.

Maribou Holidays
St Merryn, Padstow PL28 8QA
☎ 01841-520520 Fax 01841-521154
Open Easter-October A 🚐 🚚
Size 22 acres, 100 touring pitches, 20 with electric hookup, 80 level pitches, 100 static caravans, 6 🚿, 20 WCs, 1 CWP
£ car/tent £6-£8, car/caravan £6-£8, motorhome £6-£8, motorbike/tent £8
Rental 🚐 Chalet. £95-£295
🛒 💬 🖲 📞 ▨ ▦ GR ⚠ 🔌 🔦
Last arrival time: 9:00
➡ From Wadebridge SW on A39 to first roundabout. Right onto B3274. Second left to St Merryn, over crossroads to site in 1 mile.

Music Water Touring Site
Rumford, Padstow PL27 7SJ
☎ 01841-540257
Open April-October A 🚐 🚚
Size 8 acres, 140 touring pitches, 40 with electric hookup, 130 level pitches, 7 static caravans, 8 🚿, 18 WCs, 2 CWPs
£ car/tent £4-£6.95, car/caravan £4-£6.95
Rental 🚐
🛒 ✗ 💬 🖲 📞 🖨 GR 🔲 ⚠ Calor Gaz 🔦 WS
➡ From junction of A39 and B3274 (N of St Columb Major), N on B3274 signed Padstow for 2 miles, turn left to site on right in just over ¼ mile.

Trevean Farm Caravan & Camping Site
St Merryn, Padstow PL28 8PR
☎ 01841-520772
Open 1 April-31 October A 🚐 🚚
Size 2 acres, 36 touring pitches, 12 with electric hookup, 36 level pitches, 3 static caravans, 4 🚿, 7 WCs, 1 CWP
£ car/tent £5.50, car/caravan £5.50, motorhome £5.50, motorbike/tent £4, children £0.50
Rental 🚐 £100-£260
🛒 🖲 📞 🖨 ⚠ Calor Gaz 🔦 WS
Last arrival time: 10:00
➡ From St Merryn village take B3276 Newquay road for 1 mile. Turn left for Rumford. Site is ¼ mile right.

PAIGNTON Devon   3D3

Beverley Park Holiday Centre
Goodrington Road, Paignton TQ4 7JE
☎ 01803-843887 Fax 01803-84542/
Open Easter-November A 🚐 🚚

Superb holiday park overlooking Torbay, offering the very best in touring park facilities. The perfect centre for exploring Devon.

Size 21 acres, 194 touring pitches, 190 with electric hookup, 40 level pitches, 198 static caravans, 24 🚿, 48 WCs, 3 CWPs
£ car/tent £7-£12, car/caravan £8.50-£13.50, motorhome £8.50-£13.50, motorbike/tent £7, children £1.60
Rental 🚐 £88-£497
((C MasterCard Visa
🛒 ✗ 💬 🖲 📞 🖨 🖳 ▧ ▨ ▦ GR 🔲 ⚠ ▦ 🔌 Calor Gaz ♿
Last arrival time: 10:00
➡ 2 miles S of Paignton on A380, then take A3022 and turn left into Goodrington Road.

Byslades Camping & Caravan Park

Totnes Road, Paignton TQ4 7PY

☎ 01803-555072 Fax 01803-555072

Open April-October ▲ ⚑ ⛺

Friendly, well-run, family park, set in 23 acres of beautiful rolling Devon countryside with 7 acres of level, terraced pitches. Excellent amenities are offered by this award-winning site.

Size 23½ acres, 170 touring pitches, 100 with electric hookup, 170 level pitches, 17 🚿, 17 WCs, 2 CWPs

£ car/tent £5.50-£10, car/caravan £6-£11, motorhome £5.50-£10, motorbike/tent £5.50-£10, children £0.80-£1.50

🛒 ✕ 🛒 🗑 🔌 🗒 🖃 🔲 GR 🔲 ⚠ ⛽ Calor Gaz 🔑 🐾 WS

Last arrival time: 10:00

➡ On the main Paignton-Totnes road (A385). 2 miles from Paignton, 4 miles from Totnes.

Grange Court Holiday Centre

Grange Road, Goodrington, Paignton TQ4 7JP

☎ 01803-558010 Fax 01803-663336

Open 15 February-15 January ▲ ⚑ ⛺

Superb family park with extensive entertainment and leisure facilities including a new indoor pool complex and licensed club. Panoramic view across Torbay.

Size 65 acres, 157 touring pitches, 157 with electric hookup, 90 level pitches, 530 static caravans, 33 🚿, 35 WCs, 3 CWPs

£ car/tent £8.50-£21, car/caravan £8.50-£21, motorhome £8.50-£21

Rental ⚑

₡ MasterCard Visa

🛒 ✕ 🛒 🔌 🗒 🖃 🔲 GR 🔲 ⚠ ⛽ Calor Gaz

Last arrival time: 10:00

➡ From junction of A380 (Paignton ring road) and A385, travel S on A380 for 1 mile. Turn left into Goodrington Road. After ¾ mile turn left into Grange Road. The park is signposted.

r Well Farm Holiday Park

Stoke Gabriel, Paignton TQ9 6RN

☎ 01803-782289

Open Easter-October **Å ⊕ ⊞**

Size 12 acres, 30 touring pitches, 30 with electric hookup, 28 level pitches, 18 static caravans, 12 ℞, 18 WCs, 1 CWP

£ car/tent £6, car/caravan £6, motorhome £6, children £1

Rental ⊕ £120-£290 weekly. £17 nightly.

⚑ ▣ ▣ ▣ Calor Gaz **⚲**

➡ Take A385 from Paignton to Totnes and turn left at Parker Arms pub. Head straight on for 1½ miles and turn left.

Holly Gruit Camp

Brixham Road, Paignton TQ4 7BA

☎ 01803-550763

Open end May-end September **Å**

Size 3 acres, 70 touring pitches, 70 level pitches, 4 ℞, 11 WCs

£ car/tent £8-£9, motorbike/tent £8-£9

⚑ ▣ ▣ ▣ ▣ GR ▣ TV ⚠ ▣ Calor Gaz **⚲**

Last arrival time: 11:00

➡ From junction of A3022 and A385 (1 mile W of Paignton), travel S on A3022 for ¾ mile. Site signposted.

Lower Yalberton Holiday Park

Long Road, Lower Yalberton, Paignton TQ4 7PQ

☎ 01803-558127 Fax 01803-558127

Open May-September **Å ⊕ ⊞**

Size 25 acres, 550 touring pitches, 90 with electric hookup, 8 static caravans, 22 ℞, 3 CWPs

£ car/tent £7-£8.50, car/caravan £8-£10.50, motorhome £7.25-£8.75, motorbike/tent £8, children £1-£1.60

Rental ⊕ £130-£330 weekly.

℀ MasterCard Visa

⚑ ▣ ▣ ▣ ▣ ▣ TV ⚠ ▣ Calor Gaz **⚲**

Last arrival time: 8:30

➡ 2½ miles from Paignton. 5 miles from Torquay. 3 miles from Brixham. 1 mile S of intersection of A385 and A3022 Paignton ring road. Turn W off the A3022 into Long Road for ¾ mile

See advert on previous page

Ramslade Touring Park

Stoke Road, Stoke Gabriel TQ9 6QB

☎ 01803-782575 Fax 01803-782828

Open mid March-31 October **Å ⊕ ⊞**

Size 8½ acres, 135 touring pitches, 135 with electric hookup, 135 level pitches, 12 ℞, 20 WCs, 4 CWPs

£ car/tent £8-£11.50, car/caravan £8-£11.50, motorhome £8-£11.50, motorbike/tent £8-£11.50, children £1.10-£1.20

℀ MasterCard Visa

⚑ ⚑¼ ▣¼ ▣ ▣ ▣ GR ▣ TV ⚠ Calor Gaz **⚲ ⚲ WS**

Last arrival time: 9:00

➡ Turn off A385 Paignton to Totnes road at Parkers Arms, Ramslade is 1½ miles on right, near Stoke Gabriel.

Whitehill Farm Holiday Park

Stoke Road, Paignton TQ4 7PF

☎ 01803-782338 Fax 01803-782722

Open May-September **Å ⊕ ⊞**

Whitehill is beautifully situated in rolling Devon countryside, and only 2½ miles from the sea. No dogs allowed. Mixed couples and families only.

Size 30 acres, 400 touring pitches, 225 with electric hookup, 200 level pitches, 60 static caravans, 52 ℞, 81 WCs, 3 CWPs

£ car/tent £6.50-£9, car/caravan £6.50-£9, motorhome £6.50-£9, motorbike/tent £6.50-£9

Rental ⊕ from £70-£395

℀ MasterCard Visa

⚑ ✕ ▣ ▣ ▣ ▣ GR ▣ ⚠ ▣ Calor Gaz

Last arrival time: 10:00

➡ Turn off A385 at Parkers Arms pub and site is ½ mile from Paignton Zoo.

See advert on previous page

Widend Touring Park

Berry Pomeroy Road, Marldon, Paignton TQ3 1RT

☎ 01830-550116

Open Easter-October **Å ⊕ ⊞**

Size 22 acres, 184 touring pitches, 119 with electric hookup, 174 level pitches, 17 ℞, 28 WCs, 3 CWPs

£ car/tent £5.50-£9.50, car/caravan £5.50-£10, motorhome £5.50-£10, children £1-£1.50

℀ MasterCard Visa

⚑ ▣ ▣ ▣ ▣ ▣ ▣ GR ▣ ⚠ ▣ Calor Gaz **⚲**

Last arrival time: 9:00

➡ Follow A380 Torbay ring road. At second roundabout turn towards Marldon. At next roundabout turn second left into Five Lanes - Singmore Hotel on corner. Head towards Berry Pomeroy and Totnes following camping signs. Widend is 1 mile from ring road.

Hints & Tips

Hill starts need more throttle than normal to get going and you will need delicate clutch control to avoid stalling

PAR Cornwall   2B4

Par Sands Holiday Park
Par Beach, Par PL24 2AS
☎ 01726-812868 Fax 01726-817899
Open 1 April-31 October Å ⚟ ⛺

A flat, grassy site alongside a large, safe, sandy beach. Ideal position for touring Cornwall. Modern toilet and shower facilities, electric hook-ups, super pitches and baby's bathroom.

Size 23 acres, 199 touring pitches, 114 with electric hookup, 199 level pitches, 210 static caravans, 20 ⓡ, 26 WCs, 2 CWPs
£ car/tent £5-£11, car/caravan £5-£11, motorhome £5-£11, motorbike/tent £5-£11, children £1
Rental ⚟ Holiday homes - £110-£420
ℂℂ MasterCard Visa
⚡ ✕ 🛒 🗑 🔌 🗑 🔲 🔲 GR 🛗   Calor Gaz ⅋ 🐾
➥ Signposted ½ mile E of Par on A3082, heading towards Fowey.

PATELEY BRIDGE North Yorkshire   10C3

Studfold Farm
Lofthouse, Harrogate HG3 5SG
☎ 01423-755210
Open April-October Å ⚟ ⛺
Size 3 acres, 20 touring pitches, 6 with electric hookup, 20 level pitches, 60 static caravans, 8 ⓡ, 15 WCs, 1 CWP
£ car/tent £5, car/caravan £6
Rental ⚟ £100
⚡ ✕¼ ⚡¼ 🔌 🗑 Calor Gaz ⅋ 🐾 WS
➥ 7 miles from Pateley Bridge.

PENRITH Cumbria   10B1

Lowther Caravan Park
Eamont Bridge, Penrith CA10 2JB
☎ 01768-63631 Fax 01768-868126
Open March-November Å ⚟ ⛺
Size 50 acres, 221 touring pitches, 175 with electric hookup, 200 level pitches, 403 static caravans, 25 ⓡ, 30 WCs, 2 CWPs
£ car/tent £10-£12, car/caravan £10-£12, motorhome £10-£12, motorbike/tent £10-£12
Rental ⚟ from £150-£325

ℂℂ MasterCard Visa
⚡ ✕ ⚡ 🗑 🔌 🗑 🔲 GR 🛗   ⛽ Calor Gaz ⅋ 🐾 WS
Last arrival time: 11:00
➥ From roundabout (junction of A6, A66 and A686) S of Penrith, travel on A6 for ½ mile, then right along W bank of River Lowther to site.

Thacka Lea Caravan Site
Penrith CA11 9HX
☎ 01768-863319
Open March-October ⚟ ⛺
Size 25 touring pitches, 24 with electric hookup, 25 level pitches, 2 ⓡ, 7 WCs, 1 CWP
£ car/caravan £6, motorhome £6
⚡¼ Calor Gaz 🐾
➥ Off A6 N of Penrith.

PENZANCE Cornwall   2A4

Bone Valley Caravan Park
Heamoor, Penzance TR20 8UJ
☎ 01736-360313
Open March-December Å ⚟ ⛺
Size 1 acre, 17 touring pitches, 17 with electric hookup, 17 level pitches, 2 ⓡ, 3 WCs, 1 CWP
£ car/tent £7-£8, car/caravan £7-£8, motorhome £6-£7, motorbike/tent £7-£8, children £1
⚡ ✕¼ ⚡¼ 🗑 🗑 Calor Gaz
Last arrival time: 10:00
➥ From A30 Penzance by-pass turn off to Heamoor. Drive through village to caravan/camp sign on right. To next caravan/camp sign on left. Site is 200 yds on left.

Camping & Caravanning Club Site

Higher Tregiffian Farm, St Buryan, Penzance
☎ 01736-871588
Open end March-end September ▲ ⛟ ⛺
Size 4 acres, 75 touring pitches, 24 with electric hookup, 6 ⌂, 9 WCs, 1 CWP
£ car/tent £4.60-£6.80, car/caravan £4.60-£6.80, motorhome £4.60-£6.80, motorbike/tent £4.60-£6.80, children £1.40
℃ MasterCard Visa
▣ 🔌 ♿ ⛽
Last arrival time: 11:00
➡ Follow A30 from Penzance to Land's End, site is signed off B3306 (St Just Airport road).

Kenneggy Cove Holiday Park

Higher Kenneggy, Rosudgeon, Penzance TR20 9AU
☎ 01736-763453 Fax 01736-763453
Open 31 March-31 October ▲ ⛟ ⛺

In a superb location overlooking Mount's Bay and Lizard Penninsula this is a quiet family site ideally situated for walking and exploring West Cornwall.

Size 4 acres, 60 touring pitches, 21 with electric hookup, 50 level pitches, 9 static caravans, 6 ⌂, 12 WCs, 1 CWP
£ car/tent £4.30-£7.50, car/caravan £4.30-£7.50, motorhome £4.30-£7.50, motorbike/tent £4.30-£7.50, children £0.75
Rental ⛟ £110-£285
🔌 ▣ 🔌 ⛺ ⚷ Calor Gaz ⚓ WS
Last arrival time: 11:00
➡ 3 miles E of Marazion on A394 just E of Rosudgeon. Turn S for ½ mile to park.

River Valley Caravan Park

Relubbus, Penzance TR20 9ER.
☎ 01736-763398 Fax 01736-763398
Open 1 March-6 January ▲ ⛟ ⛺

Set in a sheltered valley with a small trout stream half mile from any main road. All roads on site are tarmac and all the pitches are level. Separate dog area near to the footpath.

Size 18 acres, 90 touring pitches, 60 with electric hookup, 90 level pitches, 12 static caravans, 12 ⌂, 30 WCs, 1 CWP
£ car/tent £6.50-£10, car/caravan £6.50-£10, motorhome £6.50-£10, motorbike/tent £6.50
Rental ⛟ £150-£460
℃ MasterCard Visa
🔌 ▣ 🔌 ⚷ Calor Gaz ⚓ WS
Last arrival time: 8:00
➡ From A30 at St Michael's Mount roundabout, take A394 to Helston. At next roundabout turn left to Relubbus, travel three miles, over a small bridge, park on left.

Tower Park Camping and Caravanning

St Buryan, Penzance TR19 6BZ

☎ **01736-810286**

Open April-October 人 ⇩ ⇱

*Quiet, rural park between Penzance and Land's End.
Nr. Minack Theatre, Sennen Blue Flag Beach,
unspoilt coves and coastal walks. Cleanliness ensured
by resident owners.*

Size 12 acres, 102 touring pitches, 30 with electric
hookup, 102 level pitches, 5 static caravans, 10 🚿, 12
WCs, 2 CWPs
£ car/tent £5-£8, car/caravan £5-£8, motorhome £5-
£8, motorbike/tent £5-£7.50, children £1
🛒 🛒¼ ✕¼ ☎ ⊡ 🔋 🗇 GR 🔋 TV ⚠ Calor Gaz ⅋ 🐕
Last arrival time: 10:00
➡ 3 miles from Penzance on A30 fork self on B3283
to St Buryan. In village take first right and right
again. Park is 300 yards on the right on St Just Road.

PERRANPORTH Cornwall   **2A4**

Blue Seas Holidays

Newquay Road, Goonhavern TR4 9QD

☎ **01872-572176**

Open Easter-October

*Eight static luxury caravans with sea and beach
views on a quiet family park, overlooking
Perranporth. Only ten minutes walk to golden sands,
lake and shops.*

Size 8 static caravans
Rental ⇩ £85-£330 weekly
🛒 ✕¼ ✎¼ ☎ 🔋 Calor
➡ In Perranporth on B3285, 800 yards on right from
town centre.

Penrose Farm Touring Park

Goonhavern TR4 9QF

☎ **01872-573 185**

Open April-October 人 ⇩ ⇱

*Quiet family park on 9 acres. No club/no bar.
Families and couples only. Very clean facilities.
Adventure play area. Just 2½ miles from Perranporth
Beach. All hot water free. Dogs are welcome.*

Size 9 acres, 100 touring pitches, 50 with electric
hookup, 97 level pitches, 11 🚿, 16 WCs, 1 CWP
£ car/tent £5-£9, car/caravan £5-£9, motorhome £5-
£9, children £1-£2
《 MasterCard Visa
🛒 🛒¼ ✕¼ ✎¼ ☎ 🔋 🗇 ⚠ Calor Gaz ⅋ 🐕 WS
Last arrival time: 11:00
➡ From A30, take B3285 to Perranporth. Park is
about 1½ miles on left.

Perranporth Camping & Touring Park

Budnick Road, Perranporth TR6 0AQ

☎ **01872-572174**

Open Easter-end September 人 ⇩ ⇱
Size 7 acres, 160 touring pitches, 24 with electric
hookup, 9 static caravans, 10 🚿, 19 WCs, 1 CWP
£ car/tent £8-£11, car/caravan £8-£11, motorhome £8-
£11, motorbike/tent £8-£11, children £1-£1.50
Rental ⇩ Chalet.
《 MasterCard Visa
🛒 ✕ ✎ ☎ 🔋 🗇 🔄 GR TV ⚠ ⅋ Calor Gaz ⅋ 🐕
Last arrival time: 11:00
➡ ½ mile NE of Perranporth centre.

PETWORTH West Sussex   **4C3**

Camping & Caravanning Club Site

Great Bury, Graffham, Petworth GU28 0QJ

☎ **01798-867476**

Open end March-start November 人 ⇩ ⇱
Size 20 acres, 90 touring pitches, 18 with electric
hookup, 6 🚿, 11 WCs, 2 CWPs
£ car/tent £5.20-£7.80, car/caravan £5.20-£7.80,
motorhome £5.20-£7.80, motorbike/tent £5.20-£7.80,
children £1.50
《 MasterCard Visa
☎ 🔋 ⅋ 🐕
Last arrival time: 11:00
➡ From A285 follow signs for Graffham, site is 1½ to
2 miles on left.

PEVENSEY BAY East Sussex   5D4

Camping & Caravanning Club Site
Norman's Bay, Pevensey Bay BN24 6PR
☎ 01323 761190
Open end March-start November ▲ ⊕ ⇶
Size 12 acres, 200 touring pitches, 100 with electric
hookup, 15 ☂, 25 WCs, 2 CWPs
£ car/tent £5.60-£8.60, car/caravan £5.60-£8.60,
motorhome £5.60-£8.60, motorbike/tent £5.60-£8.60,
children £1.50
ℂℂ MasterCard Visa
⬚ ☎ GR ⚟ ⚹ ⋔
Last arrival time: 11:00
➜ From A295 follow signs for Eastbourne, over level
crossing, then turn left signed Beachland.

PICKERING North Yorkshire   11E2

Vale Of Pickering Caravan Park
Carr House Farm, Allerston, Pickering YO18 7PQ
☎ 01723-859280 Fax 01723-850060
Open 15 March-30 October ▲ ⊕ ⇶
Size 8 acres, 120 touring pitches, 100 with electric
hookup, 120 level pitches, 1 static caravans, 7 ☂, 12
WCs, 1 CWP
£ car/tent £5.70-£8.50, car/caravan £5.70-£8.50,
motorhome £5.70-£8.50, motorbike/tent £5.70-£8.50,
children £0.50
⬚ ⬚ ☎ ⚟ Calor Gaz ⚹ ⋔ WS
➜ Travel E from Pickering on A170. 1 mile past Wilton
turn S onto B1415. Site in 1 mile.

Wayside Caravan Park
Wrelton, Pickering YO18 8PG
☎ 01751-472608 Fax 01751-472608
Open Easter-early October ▲ ⊕ ⇶

*Quiet, south facing, sheltered park with country
views, with modern toilet facilites and cubicled wash
basins. Ideal centre for the North York Moors and the
coast.*

Size 10 acres, 72 touring pitches, 35 with electric
hookup, 72 level pitches, 10 ☂, 21 WCs, 1 CWP
£ car/tent £7, car/caravan £8, motorhome £7

⬚ ✕¼ ⬚ ☎ ⬚ Calor Gaz ⚹ ⋔
Last arrival time: 11:00
➜ 2½ miles W of Pickering off A170, signposted at
Wrelton.

PLYMOUTH Devon   2C4

Brixton Camping Site
Venn Farm, Brixton, Plymouth PL8 2AX
☎ 01752-880378
Size 2 acres, 43 touring pitches, 12 with electric
hookup, 12 ☂, 1 CWP

POLZEATH Cornwall   2B3

Southwinds Caravan & Camping Site
Polzeath PL27 6QU
☎ 01208-863267 Fax 01208-862080
Open Easter-October ▲ ⊕ ⇶
Size 6 acres, 50 touring pitches, 40 with electric
hookup, 50 level pitches, 8 ☂, 14 WCs, 1 CWP
£ car/tent £6, car/caravan £8, motorhome £6,
motorbike/tent £6
ℂℂ MasterCard Visa
⬚¼ ✕¼ ⬤ ⬤¼ ⬚ ☎ ⬚ ⚟ Calor Gaz ⚹ ⋔
Last arrival time: 11:00
➜ 7 miles N of Wadebridge on B3314. Follow signs
to Polzeath.

Tristram Camping & Caravan Park
Polzeath PL27 6SR
☎ 01208-862215 Fax 01208-862080
Open Easter-October ▲ ⊕ ⇶
Size 5 acres, 70 touring pitches, 65 with electric
hookup, 60 level pitches, 12 ☂, 18 WCs, 1 CWP
£ car/tent £8, car/caravan £10, motorhome £8,
motorbike/tent £8
ℂℂ MasterCard Visa
⬚ ⬚¼ ✕ ⬤ ⬚ ☎ ⬚ ⚟ Calor Gaz ⚹ ⋔
Last arrival time: 11:30
➜ A30 or A38 to Wadebridge, then take B3314 to
Polzeath, 7 miles from Wadebridge.

STUNNING LOCATIONS EXCELLENT FACILITIES

South Winds

Tristram

Polzeath Bay, North Cornwall

COLOUR BROCHURE ON REQUEST

Polzeath is probably one of the most spectacular beaches in Cornwall. Visitors keep coming back year after year to enjoy the beauty and safety of its golden sands and clear blue sea. Polzeath is ideal for families with young children as there are numerous rock pools where they can play and swim in safety. Polzeath also boasts one of the best surfing beaches in Cornwall for the professional as well as the beginner. There are numerous other attractions and activities in the immediate location. At nearby Rock there's sailing, water skiing and wind surfing all within the beautiful Camel estuary.

We have two sites at Polzeath as shown on the aerial picture. Tristram is positioned on the gently sloping cliff overlooking the beach with its own direct access to the beach. The site is fenced off so it is private and safe for children. It also has its own shop and cafe / take away on site. South Winds is very different, many families like the location because it is so quiet and peaceful with beautiful sea and panoramic rural views yet only half a mile from the beach. Both sites have modern toilets, showers and laundry facilities.

Tristram *and* **South Winds**

For further information please call us on:
01208 863267 (South Winds)
01208 862215 (Tristram)
Fax: 01208 862080

AA   RAC   Access   VISA

ULTIMATE CAMPING & CARAVAN HOLIDAY PARKS IN CORNWALL
South Winds, Polzeath, Cornwall PL27 6QU

POOLE Dorset   3F3

Beacon Hill Touring Park
Blandford Road North, Poole BH16 6AB
☎ 01202-631631
Open Easter-end September ▲ 🚐 🚉

A secluded, peaceful site, yet close to the main routes. An ideal touring base for Dorset, Bournemouth and the New Forest, and only three miles from the Poole ferry terminal. Fishing, tennis, bar (entertainment and take-away during the high season).

Size 30 acres, 170 touring pitches, 140 with electric hookup, 150 level pitches, 22 🚿, 25 WCs, 2 CWPs
£ car/tent £6.60-£15, car/caravan £7.40-£15, motorhome £6.60-£15, motorbike/tent £6.60-£13, children £1
⚁ ✗ ✗¼ 🛒 🔌 🔁 🔳 🔳 🔳 GR 🔍 TV 🛁 🔲 Calor Gaz ⚘ ⚓
Last arrival time: 11:00
➜ ¼ mile N of junction of A35 and A350 towards Blandford. 3 miles N of Poole.

Huntick Farm
Lytchett Matravers, Poole BH16 6BB
☎ 01202-622222
Open Easter-30 September ▲ 🚐 🚉

Small, quiet, level grass site for 30 pitches in wooded surroundings and well away from the nearest road. This site has hot and cold water, showers and flushing lavatories with hook-ups available. Reduction of 10% for O.A.P's.

Size 3 acres, 30 touring pitches, 23 with electric hookup, 30 level pitches, 4 🚿, 6 WCs, 1 CWP
£ car/tent £4.50-£6, car/caravan £4.50-£7, motorhome £4.50-£7, motorbike/tent £4-£5, children £0.50
⚁¼ ✗¼ ⚁¼ 🛒 🔌 🔲 🛁 Calor Gaz ⚓ WS
Last arrival time: 10:30
➜ Off the A350 Blandford to Poole road, turn right into Lytchett Matravers and take the Huntick road at the Rose and Crown pub. The site is situated ¾ mile on right.

Organford Manor Caravans & Holidays

Poole BH16 6ES

☎ 01202-622202

Open 15 March-31 October A 🚐 🚙

Quiet secluded site in wooded grounds of the manor house. Touring field is level, sheltered and well-drained with good amenities.

Size 3 acres, 75 touring pitches, 34 with electric hookup, 75 level pitches, 45 static caravans, 6 🚿, 8 WCs, 1 CWP

£ car/tent £7.50-£9, car/caravan £7.50-£9, motorhome £6-£7.50, motorbike/tent £6-£7.50

🔋 ⛽ 🗑 🔌 🗑 ⛰ Calor Gaz 🐾

➡ Take first turning off A35, Poole to Dorchester road after the junction with A315 to Wareham, W of Lychett Minster, from there it is signposted.

Pear Tree Touring Park

Organford, Poole BH16 6LA

☎ 01202-622434 **Fax** 01202-622434

Open April-October A 🚐 🚙

Size 7½ acres, 125 touring pitches, 110 with electric hookup, 125 level pitches, 10 🚿, 20 WCs, 2 CWPs

£ car/tent £6.50-£9, car/caravan £6.50-£9, motorhome £6.50-£9, motorbike/tent £6.50-£9, children £1.50

℃ MasterCard Visa

🔋 ✕¼ 🍴¼ 🗑 🔌 🗑 ⛰ Calor Gaz ♿ 🐾 WS

Last arrival time: 9:00

➡ Between A351 at Holton Heath and A35 at Lytchett Minster. Take A351 signposted to Wareham. At Holton Heath crossroads, turn right down road beside garage signposted Organford. About ½ mile down road on left is wide entrance to park.

Rockley Park

Napier Road, Hamworthy, Poole BH15 4LZ

☎ 01202-679393 **Fax** 01202-632129

Open March-October A 🚐 🚙

A family holiday park in a lovely location overlooking Poole Harbour. Indoor/outdoor heated pools, kids clubs, sailing and scuba diving included in the wide range of leisure facilities. Restaurants and bars, excellent cabaret entertainment. A 'British Holidays Park'.

Size 97 acres, 74 touring pitches, 58 with electric hookup, 16 level pitches, 1,077 static caravans, 20 🚿, 24 WCs, 1 CWP

£ car/tent £9-£20, car/caravan £9-£20, motorhome £13-£20, motorbike/tent £14, children £2

Rental 🚐 from £157

℃ MasterCard Visa

🔋 ✕ 🍴 🗑 🔌 🗑 🗑 🗑 🗑 🗑 GR 🗑 ⛰ 🗑 Calor 🐾

Last arrival time: 12:00

➡ Leave M27 for Poole and follow signs for Poole town centre. Once in town centre, Rockley Park is signposted.

Hints & Tips

In winter take your seat cushions home. Not only will they keep dry but thieves won't be able use or sell a caravan without upholstery

Sandford Park

Holton Heath, Poole BH16 6JZ

☎ 01202-631600 Fax 01202-625678

Open Easter-end October ▲ ⟐ ⟐

Size 60 acres, 505 touring pitches, 460 with electric hookup, 505 level pitches, 268 static caravans, 27 ℞, 60 WCs, 2 CWPs

£ car/tent £7.90-£13.40, car/caravan £7.90-£13.40, motorhome £7.90-£13.40, motorbike/tent £7.90-£12.40, children £1.50-£2.50

Rental ⟐ Chalet. £99-£476

《 MasterCard Visa

⚊ ✕ ➤ ▣ ▣ ⬛ ⬛ ⬛ GR ⬛ TV ⚠ Calor ⬛ WS

Last arrival time: 10:00

➡ 2½ miles NE of Wareham on A351 turn into Organford Road at Holton Heath crossroads. Site is 50 yards on left.

See advert on previous page

South Lytchett Manor Caravan Park

Lytchett Minster, Poole BH16 6JB

☎ 01202-622577

Open 4 April-11 October ▲ ⟐ ⟐

Size 11 acres, 150 touring pitches, 68 with electric hookup, 150 level pitches, 21 ℞, 26 WCs, 1 CWP

£ car/tent £6.60-£8.20, car/caravan £6.60-£8.20, motorhome £6.60-£8.20, motorbike/tent £6.60-£8.20, children £1-£1.30

《 MasterCard Visa

⚊ ✕¼ ➤¼ ▣ ⬛ TV ⚠ Calor Gaz ⬛ ✦ WS

Last arrival time: 10:00

➡ From junction of A35 and A350, travel S on A350 to Upton. Turn right onto B3067 for 1 mile and site is on right.

Burrowhayes Farm Camping & Caravan Site

West Luccombe, Porlock TA24 8HU

☎ 01645-862463

Open 15 March-31 October ▲ ⟐ ⟐

Ideally situated for walkers and riders in the glorious Horner Valley, part of the National Trust's Holnicote Estate, the site is surrounded by moors and woods and contains a stream.

Size 8 acres, 54 touring pitches, 40 with electric hookup, 40 level pitches, 19 static caravans, 8 ℞, 17 WCs, 2 CWPs

£ car/tent £5.50-£7.50, car/caravan £5.50-£7.50, motorhome £5.50-£7.50, motorbike/tent £5.50-£7.50, children £1

Rental ⟐ £90-£230

⚊ ▣ ⬛ ⬛ Calor Gaz ⬛ ✦

➡ Take M5 to Bridgwater, A39 to Minehead, then towards Porlock. 5 miles W of Minehead, take left toward West Luccombe. Site in ½ mile on right.

Porlock Caravan Park

Near Minehead, Porlock TA24 8NS

☎ 01643- 862269 **Fax** 01643-862269

Open April (Easter)-October **Å 🚐 🚚**

Size 5 acres, 40 touring pitches, 32 with electric
hookup, 40 level pitches, 55 static caravans, 6 🏚, 14
WCs, 2 CWPs

£ car/tent £5-£6.50, car/caravan £6-£6.50, motorhome
£5-£5.50, motorbike/tent £4-£5.50

Rental 🚐 Chalet. £164.50-£293.75

🛒 ✕¼ 🍴¼ 🔥 🔧 🗑 Calor Gaz ✝ WS

➜ Minehead to Porlock: take B3225 turning to right,
signed Porlock Weir. After 50 yards turn right signed
Porlock Caravan Park.

Sparkhayes Farm

Sparkhayes Lane, Porlock TA24 8NE

☎ 01643-862470

Open 1 April-October **Å 🚚**

*Three acres of level camping overlooking Bristol
Channel. 100 yards from village centre, pubs, shops
and restaurants. Near SW coast path. Children and
dogs welcome.*

Size 6 acres, 50 touring pitches, 50 level pitches, 4
🏚, 9 WCs, 1 CWP

£ car/tent £7-£8, motorhome £7-£8, motorbike/tent
£7-£8, children £1.50

🛒¼ ✕¼ 🍴¼ 🔥 🔧 🗑 ✝

➜ Signposted Sparkhayes Lane, N off A39 in village
centre. 6 miles W of Minehead.

PORTHTOWAN Cornwall   2A4

Rosehill Touring Park

Porthtowan TR4 8AR

☎ 01209-890802

Open April-October **Å 🚐 🚚**

*A quiet, sheltered site just four minutes from the
beach. Set on 3 acres with 40 level pitches.*

Size 3 acres, 40 touring pitches, 20 with electric
hookup, 40 level pitches, 4 🏚, 7 WCs, 2 CWPs

£ car/tent £7-£9.50, car/caravan £7-£9.50, motorhome
£7-£9.50, motorbike/tent £7-£9.50

Rental 🚐

🛒 🍴 🗑 🔥 Calor Gaz ✝

Last arrival time: 9:30

➜ From A30 take St Agnes road at Chiverton
roundabout. Follow Porthtowan signs from Shell
garage at Seven Milestone. Site is just past turning for
Beach Road at Porthtowan.

PORTSMOUTH & SOUTHSEA Hampshire   4B4

Southsea Leisure Park

Melville Road, Southsea PO4 9TB

☎ 01705-735070 **Fax** 01705-821302

Open all year **Å 🚐 🚚**

Size 12 acres, 188 touring pitches, 188 with electric
hookup, 188 level pitches, 45 static caravans, 16 🏚,
24 WCs, 4 CWPs

£ car/tent £8.50-£9, car/caravan £10-£15,
motorbike/tent £8.50-£9

Rental 🚐

㏄ MasterCard Visa

🛒 ✕ 🍴 🔥 🗑 ⅛ 🅿 GR 🔍 🍴 ⚠ 🔧 Gaz ♿ WS

Last arrival time: 2:00

➜ From M27 take A2030 S for 3 miles, then turn left
onto A288, following caravan signs, turn left into
Bransbury Road. Site on left, signed.

POULTON-LE-FYLDE Lancashire   10B3

Higher Compley Park
Garstang Road West, Poulton-le-Fylde FY6 8AR
☎ 01253-890831 Fax 01253-892832
Open 1 March-4 January ▲ ⊕ ⊞
Size 14 acres, 50 touring pitches, 50 with electric
hookup, 50 level pitches, 150 static caravans, 8 ⋒, 10
WCs, 1 CWP
£ car/tent £8.50-£10.50, car/caravan £8.50-£10.50,
motorhome £8.50-£10.50, motorbike/tent £8.50-
£10.50, children £1.50
Rental ⊕
🛒 ✗¼ ⛟¼ 🅾 🔋 🖉 ⚠ Calor ⛽
Last arrival time: 8:00
➜ From M55 turn right onto A585 to Fleetwood and
fork left at traffic lights. Follow Blackpool sign onto
A586, park on left.

READING Berkshire   4B2

Loddon Court Farm
Beech Hill Road, Spencers Wood, Reading RG7 1HT
☎ 01734-883153
▲ ⊕ ⊞
Size 4 acres, 30 touring pitches, 30 level pitches, 4
⋒, 8 WCs, 1 CWP
£ car/tent £6, car/caravan £6, motorhome £6,
motorbike/tent £6, children £1
🅾 🔋 Calor WS
Last arrival time: 10:00
➜ Signposted from M4 junction 11 and from Riseley
roundabout to A33. Both routes via Spencers Wood.

Wellington Country Park
Riseby, Reading R67 1SP
☎ 0118-932 6444 Fax 0118-932 6445
Open March-November ▲ ⊕ ⊞

Idyllic setting in 350 acres of woodland. Access to all
park attractions. Ideal base for London, Windsor,
Legoland, Portsmouth, Southampton and Winchester.

Size 350 acres, 58 touring pitches, 45 with electric
hookup, 6 ⋒, 16 WCs,
£ car/tent £7-£12, car/caravan £7-£12, motorhome £7-
£12, motorbike/tent £7-£12
⊂⊂ MasterCard Visa
🛒 ✗ 🅾 🔋 🖉 ⚠ ⛽
Last arrival time: 5:30
➜ Between Reading and Basingstoke off B3349.

REJERRAH Cornwall   2A4

Monkey Tree Farm Tourist Park
Newquay, Rejerrah TR8 5QL
☎ 01872-572032
Open Easter-October ▲ 🚐 🚏
Size 18 acres, 245 touring pitches, 84 with electric hookup, 245 level pitches, 18 ⛺, 34 WCs, 1 CWP
🅿 ✕ 🛒 🔋 ♿
➜ A3075 from Newquay to Perranporth. After 4 miles turn left, signposted Zelah. Site is 800 yards.

RICHMOND North Yorkshire   10C2

Brompton-on-Swale Caravan Park
Brompton, Richmond DL10 7EZ
☎ 01748-824629
Open March-31 October ▲ 🚐 🚏
Size 10 acres, 150 touring pitches, 140 with electric hookup, 150 level pitches, 22 static caravans, 15 ⛺, 23 WCs, 2 CWPs
£ car/tent £6.90-£9.65, car/caravan £6.90-£10.40, motorhome £6.90-£10.40, motorbike/tent £5.50, children £0.75-£1.50
Rental Chalet. £145-£220
🅿 📺 🔋 🍴 🔌 📺 🏧 Calor ♿ 🐾
Last arrival time: 10:00
➜ Exit A1 at Catterick onto A6136. Follow B6271 through Brompton-on-Swale towards Richmond. Park on left, 1½ SE of Richmond.

Swaleview Caravan Park
Reeth Road, Richmond DL10 4SF
☎ 01748-823106
Open March-October ▲ 🚐 🚏

Situated beside River Swale in a wooded valley in Yorkshire Dales National Park.

Size 12 acres, 25 touring pitches, 25 with electric hookup, 50 level pitches, 100 static caravans, 10 ⛺, 20 WCs, 1 CWP
£ car/tent £5.90-£6.90, car/caravan £6.90-£7.10, motorhome £6.50-£6.90, motorbike/tent £6.90, children £0.50-£0.90
Rental 🚐 £115-£185
🅿 📺 🔋 🍴 🔌 🏧 📺 Calor Gaz
Last arrival time: 9:00
➜ 3 miles W of Richmond on A6108. 7 miles from A1/A1M at Scotch Corner.

RINGWOOD Hampshire   4A4

Oakdene Forest Park
Ringwood BH24 2RZ
☎ 01590-642513 Fax 01590-645610
Open 1 March-3 January ▲ 🚐 🚏
Size 55 acres, 388 touring pitches, 255 with electric hookup, 388 level pitches, 207 static caravans, 39 ⛺, 80 WCs, 1 CWP
£ car/tent £4.75-£19, car/caravan £4.75-£19, motorhome £4.75-£19, motorbike/tent £4.75-£19
Rental 🚐 £150-£445 per week
CC MasterCard Visa
🅿 ✕ 🛒 📺 📞 🔋 🏧 📺 🔌 📺 🏧 Calor Gaz 🐾
Last arrival time: 10:00
➜ M27 W, A31 through Ringwood heading W. Park is on left in 3 miles.
See advert on next page

Red Shoot Camping Park
Linwood, Ringwood BH24 3QT
☎ 01425-473789 Fax 01425-471558
Open March-October ▲ 🚐 🚏

Beautifully situated in the New Forest. Ideal for walking, touring and the nature lover, yet only half an hour from the coast.

Size 4 acres, 105 touring pitches, 45 with electric hookup, 105 level pitches, 6 ⛺, 18 WCs, 1 CWP
£ car/tent £8-£10.80, car/caravan £8-£10.80, motorhome £8-£10.80, motorbike/tent £8-£10.80
🅿 ✕ 🛒 🍴 📺 🏧 🔌 Calor Gaz ♿ 🐾
Last arrival time: 8:30
➜ Off A338, 2 miles N of Ringwood, turn right and follow signs to Linwood. Site signed.

Don't forget to mention the guide
When booking, please remember to tell the site that you chose it from
RAC Camping & Caravanning 1998

Hints & Tips
Caravans are stolen from laybys and motorway service stations. Even if you are just stopping for a cup of tea or to stretch your legs make sure you secure your caravan.

Touring in the perfect location

Oakdene Forest Park will provide you with the perfect location for your touring holiday. There's all-weather fun and excitement for the kids and perfect relaxation for mum and dad. Set in 55 acres on the edge of the beautiful Avon Forest, Oakdene is only 9 miles from Bournemouth's sandy beaches, offering the following superb facilities:

- Indoor and outdoor pools
- 'Forest Edge' riding stables
- Children's adventure playground
- Licensed club with entertainment
- Sauna, solarium and mini-gym
- Cafeteria and takeaway
- General store and launderette
- Touring pitches (many with power)
- Rallies welcome

OAKDENE FOREST PARK
ST LEONARDS

 AA⊟
 ROSE AWARD 1998

Oakdene, St. Leonards, Ringwood,
Hants BH24 2RZ
e-mail: holidays@shorefield.co.uk
http://www.shorefield.co.uk
Oakdene is a member of the Shorefield Group

For a free brochure telephone

01590 642513
Fax: 01590 645610

Ref ORAC

Office open seven days a week

The New Forest

Superb Pool

Best of both worlds

LYTTON Lawn is the perfect location for a relaxing touring holiday. Only $2^1/_2$ miles from Shorefield Country Park, Lytton Lawn is set in beautiful natural parkland, close to Milford beach and the historic New Forest.
Caravans have individual pitches, with plenty of space for the car, caravan or tent, awning and barbecue.

Facilities include:
- Electricity hook up
- Showers and purpose-built laundrette
- 'Premier pitches' ● Children's area

Plus *FREE* membership of our exclusive Leisure Club:
- Indoor/Outdoor pools
- Dance studio
- Tennis courts
- Top class restaurant
- Sauna, Solarium and Spa bath
- Special facilities for children
- Nightly entertainment

For a free brochure telephone

01590 642513

Quoting ref: RAC

Office open seven days a week

SHOREFIELD
COUNTRY PARKS

WINNER 1990

BRITISH GRADED HOLIDAY PARKS

ROSE AWARD
CARAVAN HOLIDAY PARK
1998

Shorefield Country Parks, Shorefield Road,
Milford on Sea, Hampshire SO41 0LH

River Laver Holiday Park

Studley Road, Ripon HG4 2QR
📞 01765 690508 Fax 01748-811393
Open 1 March-31 December 🅰 ⊕ ⊞

A five acre park with 50 touring pitches, situated one mile from the city centre and ideally located for touring the Yorkshire Dales.

Size 5 acres, 50 touring pitches, 50 with electric hookup, 50 level pitches, 50 static caravans, 8 🚿, 10 WCs, 1 CWP
£ car/tent £8.50-£10.50, car/caravan £8.50-£10.50, motorhome £8.50-£10.50, motorbike/tent £10.50
Rental ⊕ £120-£395
CC MasterCard Visa
🛒 ✕¼ 🐶¼ 🔘 🔋 🎲 Calor Gaz ♿ 🐾 WS
Last arrival time: 9:00
➧ From A1 take A61 or B6265 to Ripon (following signs for Fountains Abbey). Park is situated off B6265, 1 mile from Ripon Centre.

Sleningford Watermill Caravan & Camping

North Stainley, Ripon HG4 3HQ
📞 01765-635201
Open 1 April-31 October 🅰 ⊕ ⊞
Size 14 acres, 65 touring pitches, 50 with electric hookup, 55 level pitches, 25 static caravans, 10 🚿, 18 WCs, 6 CWPs
£ car/tent £7-£10.50, car/caravan £6.50-£10.50, motorhome £6.50-£10.50, motorbike/tent £6.50-£10.50, children £0.50-£1
Rental Chalet. £140-£170
🛒 🔘 🔋 🖶 🎲 🇬🇷 🔲 🏔 Calor Gaz ♿ 🐾 WS
Last arrival time: 10:00
➧ 5 miles from Ripon on A6108.

Lordine Court Caravan Park

Ewhurst Green, Staplecross, Robertsbridge TN32 5TS
📞 01580-830209 Fax 01550-830091
Open Easter-31 October 🅰 ⊕ ⊞

An inland site with good access to the main coastal resorts. Close to Bodiam Castle and the pretty town of Battle. Shop, licensed bar, pay-phone, children's playground, outdoor pool, restaurant. All year storage.

Size 40 acres, 200 touring pitches, 50 with electric hookup, 60 level pitches, 120 static caravans, 17 🚿, 25 WCs, 2 CWPs
£ car/tent £5.50-£15, car/caravan £5.50-£15, motorhome £5.50-£15, motorbike/tent £5.50-£15
🛒 ✕ 🐶 🔘 🔋 🎲 🇬🇷 🏔 Calor Gaz 🐾 WS
Last arrival time: 10:00
➧ A21 from London, left at Flimwell to Hawkhurst. B2244 at Hawkhurst to Cripps Corner. Left onto B2165 (Northam direction).

Hollingworth Lake Caravan Park

Rakewood, Littleborough, Rochdale OL15 0AT
📞 01706-378661
Open all year 🅰 ⊕ ⊞
Size 7 acres, 45 touring pitches, 35 with electric hookup, 45 level pitches, 8 🚿, 8 WCs, 2 CWPs
£ car/tent £6-£8, car/caravan £6-£8, motorhome £5-£8, motorbike/tent £4-£6
Rental Chalet.
🛒 🔘 🔋 🖶 🎲 🏔 Calor Gaz ♿ 🐾 WS
Last arrival time: 8:00
➧ From M62 junction 21 take B6225 from Hollingworth Lake Country Park, at Fisherman's Inn. Take Rakenwood Road, then second on right.

Coquetdale Caravan Park

Whitton, Rothbury NE65 7RU
📞 01669-620549
Open Easter-31 October 🅰 ⊕ ⊞
Size 14 acres, 55 touring pitches, 30 with electric hookup, 30 level pitches, 180 static caravans, 10 🚿, 15 WCs, 2 CWPs
£ car/tent £8-£10, car/caravan £8-£10, motorhome £8-£10, motorbike/tent £8-£10
🔘 🔋 🖶 🏔 Calor Gaz 🐾 WS
➧ ½ mile SW of Rothbury on Newton road.

ROYDON Essex 5D2

Roydon Mill Leisure Park
Roydon, Harlow CM19 5EJ
📞 01279-792777 Fax 01279-792695
Open all year 🅰 ⛺ 🚐
Size 58 acres, 110 touring pitches, 72 with electric hookup, 110 level pitches, 106 static caravans, 8 🚿, 14 WCs, 2 CWPs
£ car/tent £9.50-£10.70, car/caravan £9.50-£10.70, motorhome £9.50-£10.70, motorbike/tent £9.50-£10.70, children £1.65
Rental 🚐 £150-£280
ℂℂ MasterCard Visa
🛒 🛒¼ ✗ ✗¼ 🍴 ▣ 🔌 ⊡ 🚩 🔧 ⊿ GR ▣ ⚠ 🍽 Calor Gaz ♿ WS
Last arrival time: 24 hrs
➡ From N via A1 or M1/M25/M11. From S take junction 7 off M11 and follow signs to Harlow, then A414 and B181 to Roydon. At end of High Street, just before level crossing.

RUGELEY Staffordshire 7F2

Camping & Caravanning Club Site
Old Youth Hostel, Wandon, Rugeley WS15 1QW
📞 01889-582166
Open end March-start November 🅰 ⛺ 🚐
Size 5 acres, 60 touring pitches, 36 with electric hookup, 7 🚿, 7 WCs, 1 CWP
£ car/tent £5.20-£7.80, car/caravan £5.20-£7.80, motorhome £5.20-£7.80, motorbike/tent £5.20-£7.80, children £1.50
ℂℂ MasterCard Visa
▣ 🔌 ♿ ♙
Last arrival time: 11:00
➡ From Cannock follow A460 and signs to Hednesford. At traffic lights turn right. After 1 mile turn left. Site is on left ½ mile from Hazelslade.

Silvertrees Caravan Park
Stafford Brook Road, Rugeley WS15 2TX
📞 01889-582185 Fax 01889-582185
Open 1 April-31 October 🚐 🚐

Located in the heart of Cannock Chase, Silvertrees is an idyllically peaceful park, set in 30 acres of natural woodlands, graded '4 ticks' and Rose Awarded by the ETB.

Size 30 acres, 50 touring pitches, 50 with electric hookup, 50 level pitches, 50 static caravans, 4 🚿, 9 WCs, 1 CWP
£ car/caravan £8-£10, motorhome £8-£10
Rental 🚐 £149-£350 (short breaks from £77)
ℂℂ MasterCard Visa
▣ 🔌 ⊡ 🚩 GR ▣ 📺 🍽 Calor ♙
➡ 2 miles W of Rugeley off A51 on unclassified road signposted Penkridge. Turn right at bottom of hill by white fence. Entrance 100 yards on left.

SALCOMBE Devon 2C4

Alston Farm Caravan Site
Salcombe TQ7 3BJ
📞 01548-561260 Fax 01548-561260
Open Easter-end October 🅰 ⛺ 🚐
Size 12 acres, 150 touring pitches, 50 with electric hookup, 150 level pitches, 40 static caravans, 18 🚿, 35 WCs, 1 CWP
£ car/tent £5-£6.50, car/caravan £6-£8, motorhome £5-£6.50, motorbike/tent £5-£6.50, children £0.50
🛒 ▣ 🔌 🍴 Calor Gaz ♿ ♙ WS
➡ Signposted on left on A381 Kingsbridge to Salcombe main road.

Bolberry House Farm Camping & Caravan
Bolberry, Malborough, Kingsbridge TQ7 3DY
📞 01548-561251
Open Easter-October 🅰 ⛺ 🚐

A friendly family run park in a peaceful setting on a farm which adjoins spectacular National Trust coastline, with superb sea views and cliff walks nearby. First class facilities on a well maintained park.

Size 5½ acres, 20 touring pitches, 36 with electric hookup, 50 level pitches, 10 static caravans, 8 🚿, 12 WCs, 1 CWP
£ car/caravan £6.50
Rental 🚐
🛒¼ ✗¼ ⛟¼ ▣ 🔌 ⚠ Calor Gaz ♙ WS
➡ Take A381 from Kingsbridge towards Salcombe. Turn sharp right, through village of Malborough and follow signs to Bolberry. Park is on right on outskirts of hamlet.

Higher Rew Caravan Park

Malborough, Kingsbridge, Salcombe TQ7 3DW

☎ 01548-842681

Open Easter-October Å 🚐 🚛

Quiet family park in area of outstanding natural beauty, adjoining National Trust land, only one mile from South Sands and Salcombe Estuary. Cliff walks are nearby.

Size 5 acres, 75 touring pitches, 40 with electric hookup, 75 level pitches, 8 ſ, 10 WCs, 1 CWP

£ car/tent £6-£8, car/caravan £6-£8, motorhome £6-£8, motorbike/tent £6-£8

🔲 🔳 🔲 GR 🔳 Calor Gaz 🛉

Last arrival time: 10:00

➧ From A381 at Malborough turn right and follow signs to Soar for 1 mile, then turn left at Rew Cross signpost to Higher Rew.

Sun Park Caravan & Camping Park

Soar Mill Cove, Malborough, Salcombe TQ7 3DS

☎ 01548-561378

Open Easter-31 October Å 🚐 🚛

Quality caravans and modern camping facilities on peaceful family run site surrounded by National Trust land. Walking distance of sandy cove. Where better to come and unwind.

Size 5 acres, 75 touring pitches, 18 with electric hookup, 75 level pitches, 34 static caravans, 8 ſ, 10 WCs, 1 CWP

£ car/tent £5-£9, car/caravan £5-£9, motorhome £5-£9, motorbike/tent £5-£9

Rental 🚐 £80-£275

🔲 🔳 🔲 GR TV 🔳 Calor Gaz 🛉

Last arrival time: 9:00

➧ From A38, turn left at Totnes and Kingsbridge sign. Bypass Kingsbridge by following signs to Salcombe. On entering village of Malborough turn sharp right signposted Soar. Pass through village and keep on road following signs to Soar Mill Cove and Sun Park. Site 1½ miles down this road on right.

Alderbury Caravan and Camping Park

Old Southampton Road, Whaddon, Salisbury

☎ 01722-710125

Open all year Å 🚐 🚛

Size 1½ acres, 39 touring pitches, 20 with electric hookup, 39 level pitches, 4 ſ, 6 WCs, 2 CWPs

£ car/tent £6.50, car/caravan £6.50, motorhome £6.50, motorbike/tent £6.50, children £1

🔳¼ ✕¼ 🔳¼ 🔳 ₺ 🛉

Last arrival time: 11:00

➧ From Salisbury take A36 Southampton road for 3 miles. Along dual carriageway take slip road marked Alderbury/Whaddon, turn right over flyover then left for site opposite Three Crowns pub.

Camping & Caravanning Club Site

Hudson's Field, Castle Road, Salisbury

☎ 01722-320713

Open end March-end September Å 🚐 🚛

Size 4½ acres, 100 touring pitches, 23 with electric hookup, 4 ſ, 12 WCs, 1 CWP

£ car/tent £5.20-£7.80, car/caravan £5.20-£7.80, motorhome £5.20-£7.80, motorbike/tent £5.20-£7.80, children £1.50

🔳 🛉

Last arrival time: 11:00

➧ From Amesbury take B342 to Salisbury, site is on right before town.

Coombe Touring Caravan Park

Race Plain, Netherhampton, Salisbury SP2 8PN

☎ 01722-328451

Open all year Å 🚐 🚛

Size 3 acres, 50 touring pitches, 48 with electric hookup, 50 level pitches, 6 ſ, 12 WCs, 2 CWPs

£ car/tent £5-£7.50, car/caravan £5-£7.50, motorhome £5-£7.50, motorbike/tent £5-£7.50, children £0.50-£1

🔳 🔲 🔳 🔲 ⚠ Calor Gaz ₺ 🛉

Last arrival time: 9:00

➧ A36 Salisbury to Warminster road. Turn onto A3094 at traffic lights. Cross on bend at top of hill. Take third left behind racecourse. Site is on right.

Hillcrest Camp Site

Southampton Road, Whiteparish, Salisbury SP5 2QW

☎ 01794-884471

Open all year Å 🚐 🚛

Size 2½ acres, 30 touring pitches, 12 with electric hookup, 15 level pitches, 3 ſ, 5 WCs, 1 CWP

£ car/tent £6.50-£7, car/caravan £6.50-£7, motorhome £6.50-£7, motorbike/tent £6.50-£7, children £1.50-£1.60

🔲 🔳 🔲 Calor Gaz 🛉

Last arrival time: 10:00

➜ The entrance is off A36, Southampton to Salisbury road, 1¼ miles SE of junction with A27. 8 miles from Salisbury, 13 miles from Southampton.

Stonehenge Touring Park

Orcheston, Salisbury SP3 4SH

☎ 01980-620304 Fax 01980-621121

Open all year ⚑ ⊕ ⛺

Size 2 acres, 30 touring pitches, 20 with electric hookup, 30 level pitches, 4 ₧, 5 WCs, 1 CWP

£ car/tent £7-£9, car/caravan £7-£9, motorhome £7-£9, motorbike/tent £7-£9, children £0.75-£1.50

⚡ ✕ ⛅ ⊟ ⛏ ⊟ ⚠ Calor Gaz ⚓

Last arrival time: 9:30

➜ Off A360 Salisbury to Devizes road.

Camping & Caravanning Club Site

The Sandringham Estate, Double Lodges, Sandringham PE35 6EA

☎ 01485-542555

Open end September-start December ⚑ ⊕ ⛺

Size 22 acres, 250 touring pitches, 152 with electric hookup, 22 ₧, 28 WCs, 2 CWPs

£ car/tent £5.60-£8.60, car/caravan £5.60-£8.60, motorhome £5.60-£8.60, motorbike/tent £5.60-£8.60, children £1.50

℃ MasterCard Visa

⚡¼ ⊟ ⛏ ⚠ ⚓

Last arrival time: 11:00

➜ From A42 turn right onto A149, 1 mile after Babingley turn right, right again at next crossroads. Site is on left.

Sandwich Leisure Park

Woodnesborough Road, Sandwich CT13 0AA

☎ 01227-771777 Fax 01227-273512

Open 17 March-31 October

Well maintained location adjoining open farmland, a few minutes walk from the town centre with a wealth of olde worlde pubs, restaurants and shops. Warm welcome awaits you.

Size 15 acres, 100 touring pitches, 100 with electric hookup, 200 level pitches, 100 static caravans, 8 ₧, 16 WCs, 2 CWPs

⚡ Calor Gaz WS

➜ A257 to Sandwich town centre, then on to Woodnesborough, over level crossing and take immediate right.

Marsh Farm Caravan Site

Sternfield, Saxmundham IP17 1HW

☎ 01728-602168

Open all year ⊕ ⛺

Size 20 acres, 45 touring pitches, 50 with electric hookup, 45 level pitches, 2 CWPs

£ car/caravan £6-£9

⚡ ⛏ ⊟ ⚓ WS

Last arrival time: 11:00

➜ Turn off A12 onto A1094 to Aldeburgh. After 1 mile turn left to Sternefield and in ½ mile caravan signs will direct you left for site.

Whitearch (Touring Caravan) Park

Main Road, Benhall, Saxmundham IP17 1NA

☎ 01728-604646 Fax 01728-604646

Open April-October ⚑ ⊕ ⛺

Set in Suffolk, with all its rural charm, on 14½ acres offering 30 pitches and close to Heritage Conservation land and Snape Concert Hall

Size 14½ acres, 30 touring pitches, 30 with electric hookup, 30 level pitches, 4 ₧, 6 WCs, 2 CWPs

£ car/tent £8.50, car/caravan £8.50, motorhome £8.50, motorbike/tent £8.50, children £0.50

⚡ ⛏ ⊟ ⊠ ⊟ ⚠ Calor Gaz ⚓

➜ From Ipswich on A12 towards Lowestoft turn off onto B1121 to Saxmundham. Entrance 20 yards on right.

SCARBOROUGH North Yorkshire   11E2

Cayton Village Caravan Park

D14 Mill Lane, Cayton Bay, Scarborough YO11 3NN

☎ 01723-583171

Open Easter-1 October ▲ ⊕ ⊞

A spacious, level, landscaped park sheltered by trees. Three miles south of Scarborough. Half a mile from beach. Adjoining village church, inns, fish shop and bus service.

Size 11 acres, 200 touring pitches, 170 with electric hookup, 200 level pitches, 18 ⋒, 34 WCs, 3 CWPs
£ car/tent £5-£8, car/caravan £5-£8, motorhome £5-£8, motorbike/tent £5-£8
⚑ ✕¼ ⚐¼ ▢ ⚫ ▯ ⚠ Calor Gaz ⅙ ⌁
Last arrival time: 8:00
➡ On A165 turn right at Cayton Bay traffic lights onto Mill Lane. The park is ½ mile on right hand side. On A64 take B1261 signposted Filey. At Cayton Village turn second left after Blacksmiths Arms onto Mill Lane. Park is on left in 500 yards.

Flower Of May Caravan Park

Lebberston Cliff, Scarborough YO11 3NU

☎ 01723-582324

Open Easter-end October ▲ ⊕ ⊞

Acclaimed privately owned park, constantly being updated to provide the most comprehensive facilities. Located on the coast between Scarborough and Filey. Fifty caravans for hire (own WCs). No single-sex groups.

Size 20 acres, 300 touring pitches, 270 with electric hookup, 300 level pitches, 184 static caravans, 36 ⋒, 36 WCs, 3 CWPs
£ car/tent £6.50-£10, car/caravan £6.50-£10, motorhome £6.50-£10, motorbike/tent £6.50-£10
Rental ⊕ £85-£305
⚑ ✕¼ ⚐ ▢ ⚫ ☒ ▣ ☒ ☒ GR TV ⚠ ⊟ Calor ⅙ WS
Last arrival time: dusk
➡ 2¼ miles NW of Filey, 5 miles SE of Scarborough on A165. Turn left, then NE to site.

Jacob's Mount Caravan Park

Stepney Road, Scarborough YO12 5NL

☎ 01723-361178 **Fax** 01723-361178

Open 1 March-31 October ▲ ⊕ ⊞

A small family run park with excellent on site facilities, surrounded by mature woodland yet only two miles from Scarborough on the A170. Highly Recommended.

Size 7 acres, 56 touring pitches, 44 with electric hookup, 12 level pitches, 44 static caravans, 4 ⋒, 14 WCs, 1 CWP
£ car/tent £6-£9, car/caravan £6-£9, motorhome £6-£9, motorbike/tent £6-£9
Rental ⊕ £110-£310.
⚑ ✕ ⚐ ▢ ⚫ ▯ GR TV ⚠ ⊟ Calor Gaz ⌁ WS
Last arrival time: 9:00
➡ Approximately 2 miles W of Scarborough on the A170 Scarborough to Thirsk road.

Lebberston Touring Caravan Park

Beckfield, Lebberston, Scarborough YO11 3PF

☎ 01723-582254

Open May-September 🚐 🚏

Size 7½ acres, 125 touring pitches, 125 with electric hookup, 100 level pitches, 8 🅿, 24 WCs, 2 CWPs

£ car/caravan £6.50, motorhome £6.50

🛇¼ ✗¼ ☔¼ 🔌 ⚠ Calor Gaz 🐕

Last arrival time: 9:00

➡ From A64 or A165, take B1261 to Lebberston. Site signposted.

Lowfield

Down Dale Road, Staintondale, Scarborough YO13 0EZ

☎ 01723-870574

Open all year 🅰 🚐 🚏

Size 2 acres, 33 touring pitches, 11 with electric hookup, 33 level pitches, 2 🅿, 5 WCs, 1 CWP

£ car/tent £5.50-£8, car/caravan £7, motorhome £5.50-£6.50, motorbike/tent £5, children £0.50

🛇 ✗¼ ☔¼ ▢ 🔌 ▯ ⚠ Calor Gaz ♿ 🐕

Last arrival time: 10:00

➡ A171 Whitby road to Cloughton, then Ravenscar road for 2 miles to site.

Merry Lees Caravan Park

Merry Lees, Staxton, Scarborough YO12 4NN

☎ 01944-710080 Fax 01944-710470

Open March-October 🅰 🚐 🚏

Ideally situated rural park in woodland based around a small lake, habitat of many birds. Central to moorland and coastal attractions; Flamingoland, Millenium, steam railway.

Size 8 acres, 50 touring pitches, 50 with electric hookup, 50 level pitches, 10 static caravans, 6 🅿, 7 WCs, 1 CWP

£ car/tent £5-£9.50, car/caravan £5-£9.50, motorhome £5-£9.50, motorbike/tent £5-£9.50

CC MasterCard Visa

🔌 Calor Gaz ♿ 🐕 WS

Last arrival time: 10:00

➡ On the A64, ½ mile past roundabout on left, 6 miles before Scarborough.

Scalby Close Camping Park

Burniston Road, Scarborough YO13 0DA

☎ 01723-365908

Open March-October 🅰 🚐 🚏

Size 2 acres, 42 touring pitches, 30 with electric hookup, 5 static caravans, 4 🅿, 10 WCs, 1 CWP

£ car/tent £4-£8.50, car/caravan £4-£8.50, motorhome £4-£8.50, motorbike/tent £4-£8.50

Rental 🚐 £115-£285

CC MasterCard Visa

🛇 ✗¼ ▢ 🔌 ▯ Calor Gaz 🐕 WS

Last arrival time: 10:00

➡ Site is on A165 2½ miles N of Scarborough.

Scalby Manor Caravan & Camping Site

Burniston Road., Scarborough

☎ 01723-366212

Open Easter-end October 🅰 🚐 🚏

Size 20 acres, 375 touring pitches, 150 with electric hookup, 230 level pitches, 25 🅿, 40 WCs, 2 CWPs

CC MasterCard Visa

🛇 ✗¼ ☔ ▢ 🔌 ⚠ Calor Gaz ♿ 🐕

Last arrival time: 7:00

➡ At 2¼ miles N of Scarborough on A165, follow signs for Burniston/Whitley.

Spring Willows Touring Caravan & Camping

Main Road, Staxton, Scarborough YO12 4SB

☎ 01723-891505 Fax 01723-891505

Open March-4 January 🅰 🚐 🚏

Size 12 acres, 184 touring pitches, 164 with electric hookup, 184 level pitches, 13 🅿, 29 WCs, 3 CWPs

🛇 ✗ ☔ ▢ 🔌 ▯ 🔲 🏧 GR 📺 ⚠ 🍴 Calor Gaz ♿ 🐕 WS

Last arrival time: 7:00

➡ A64 towards Scarborough. Right at Staxton onto A1039 to Filey. Site entrance on right.

SCOTCH CORNER North Yorkshire   11D2

Scotch Corner Caravan Park
Richmond, Scotch Corner DL10 6NS
☎ 01748 822530 Fax 01748-050370
Open April-October ⚊ 🚐 🚗

*Landscaped, level, grassed, well-spaced pitches.
Booking advisable July/August and bank holiday
weekends.*

Size 7 acres, 75 touring pitches, 43 with electric
hookup, 75 level pitches, 6 ⛺, 14 WCs, 1 CWP
£ car/tent £8-£10, car/caravan £8-£10, motorhome £8-
£10, motorbike/tent £7-£9, children £1
℄ MasterCard Visa
🛒 ✗¼ 🍴¼ 🚿 🍴 🚻 Calor Gaz ♿ 🐕 WS
Last arrival time: 10:30
➠ Leave A1 at Scotch Corner and take A6108
Richmond exit. Proceed 250 yards on dual
carriageway, then cross central reservation and return
200 yards to site entrance.

SELSEY West Sussex   4C4

Warner Farm Touring Park
Warner Lane, Selsey
☎ 01243-604499 Fax 01243-604499
Open 1 March-31 October ⚊ 🚐 🚗

*Situated in beautiful Sussex, with top family
entertainment and two swiming pools. Special offers
with great savings in June, July, September and
October.*

Size 10 acres, 200 touring pitches, 130 with electric
hookup, 180 level pitches, 20 ⛺, 30 WCs, 4 CWPs
£ car/tent £6.50-£16.50, car/caravan £6.50-£20.50,
motorhome £6.50-£20.50, motorbike/tent £6.50-£19
Rental 🚐
℄ MasterCard Visa
🛒 ✗ 🍴 🚿 🚻 🍴 🔲 🔳 🔲 🔲 🔲 🔲 GR 📺 🏧 ⛽ Calor Gaz ♿
🐕
Last arrival time: 8:00
➠ From Chichester A27 take B2145 to Selsey. At
Selsey turn right into School Lane and follow signs
for park.

SETTLE North Yorkshire   10C3

Knight Stainforth Hall Camping & Caravan
Little Stainforth, Settle BD24 ODP
☎ 01729-822200 Fax 01729-823387
Open March-October ⚊ 🚐 🚗

*Family run camping park catering mainly for
families. Situated in the Yorkshire Dales National
Park on the west bank of the River Ribble, near
waterfall and Pack-horse Bridge.*

Size 10 acres, 50 touring pitches, 50 with electric
hookup, 80 level pitches, 60 static caravans, 8 ⛺, 21

WCs, 1 CWP
£ car/tent £8, car/caravan £8, motorhome £8, motorbike/tent £8, children £1
℀ MasterCard Visa
⚡ ✕¼ ▣ 🛁 ▤ 🅖 🅠 📺 ⚠ Calor Gaz 🐕
Last arrival time: 9:30
➡ Take A65 Settle to Kendal. Turn off opposite Settle High School on Stackhouse Lane. Site is 2½ miles.

SEVENOAKS Kent   5D3

Camping & Caravanning Club Site
Styants Bottom, Seal, Sevenoaks TN15 0ET
📞 01732-762728
Open end March-early November 🅰 🚐 🚛
Size 4 acres, 60 touring pitches, 31 with electric hookup, 4 🚿, 7 WCs, 1 CWP
£ car/tent £5.20-£7.80, car/caravan £5.20-£7.80, motorhome £5.20-£7.80, motorbike/tent £5.20-£7.80, children £1.50
℀ MasterCard Visa
▣ 🔌 ⚠ ♿ 🐕
Last arrival time: 11:00
➡ On A25 from Sevenoaks turn right into Styants Bottom Road. Site is signposted just before Crown Point Inn.

SHEFFIELD South Yorkshire   8B1

Fox Hagg Farm Caravan Site
Lodge Lane, Rivelin, Sheffield S6 5SN
📞 0114-230-5589
Open 1 April-31 October 🅰 🚐 🚛
Size 2 acres, 10 touring pitches, 10 with electric hookup, 30 level pitches, 20 static caravans, 4 🚿, 6 WCs, 1 CWP
£ car/tent £4-£6, car/caravan £5-£6, motorhome £5-£6, motorbike/tent £4
⚡ ⚡¼ ✕¼ 🍴¼ ▣ ♿ 🐕 WS
Last arrival time: 12:00
➡ Take A57 to Lodge Lane. Site is 300 yards before Rivelin post office.

SHERIFF HUTTON North Yorkshire   11D3

Camping & Caravanning Club Site
Bracken Hill, Sheriff Hutton YO6 1QG
📞 01347-878660
Open end March-early November 🅰 🚐 🚛
Size 10 acres, 90 touring pitches, 42 with electric hookup, 6 🚿, 9 WCs, 1 CWP
£ car/tent £5.20-£7.80, car/caravan £5.20-£7.80, motorhome £5.20-£7.80, motorbike/tent £5.20-£7.80, children £1.50
℀ MasterCard Visa
▣ 🔌 ⚠ ♿ 🐕
Last arrival time: 11:00
➡ From York travel N on A64. Head towards village of West Lilling, turn left at T junction, site on left.

Beeston Regis
CARAVAN PARK

A lovely 44 acre clifftop park situated close to the town of Sheringham in an area of outstanding natural beauty. We welcome touring caravans, motorhomes and tents and have 56 electric hookups, two shower blocks, a small shop and access to a clean, sandy beach. Phone for brochure.

Cromer Road, Beeston Regis, West Runton, Norfolk NR27 9NG
Tel: 01263-823614

SHERINGHAM Norfolk   9E2

Beeston Regis Caravan & Camping Park
Cromer Road, West Runton, Sheringham NR27 9NG
📞 01263-823614
Open 24 March-October 🅰 🚐 🚛
Size 440 touring pitches, 56 with electric hookup, 120 static caravans, 16 🚿, 30 WCs, 2 CWPs
£ car/tent £8, car/caravan £9-£13, motorhome £9-£13, motorbike/tent £8
Rental 🚐 from £150-£349
℀ MasterCard Visa
⚡ ✕¼ 🍴¼ 🔌 ▣ 🛁 ▤ ⚠ ♿ 🐕 WS
➡ Take A148 to Sheringham and follow signs. At Sheringham roundabout turn right onto A149 coast road to Cromer, ½ mile on left hand side.

Woodlands Caravan Park
Holt Road, Sheringham NR26 8TU
📞 01263-823802
Open March-October 🚐 🚛

➡

← Woodlands Caravan Park

Quiet, secluded park surrounded by woodland and fields in a very pleasant area. No motorcycles. 28 days maximum stay. Open March-October.

Size 21 acres, 286 touring pitches, 216 with electric hookup, 250 level pitches, 133 static caravans, 28 ☂, 74 WCs, 4 CWPs

£ car/caravan £7.25-£11, motorhome £7.25-£11

⚑ ✕ ☞ ◙ ⬓ █ ☐ ⬓ ⊞ ▦ ☒ ⊞ ⚐ Calor Gaz ♿ ♞

Last arrival time: 12:00

➡ On N side of A148. 4 miles E of Holt.

SIDMOUTH Devon	3D3

Salcombe Regis Camping & Caravan Park
Salcombe Regis, Sidmouth EX10 0JH
📞 01395-514303 **Fax** 01395-514303
Open April-October ▲ ⛺ ⛟

Quiet family-run park, situated on the edge of the picturesque village of Salcombe Regis in an area of outstanding natural beauty. Ideal base for exploring east Devon. Colour brochure available on request.

Size 16 acres, 100 touring pitches, 60 with electric hookup, 60 level pitches, 10 static caravans, 14 ☂, 14 WCs, 2 CWPs

£ car/tent £6-£8.75, car/caravan £6-£8.75, motorhome £6-£8.75, motorbike/tent £6-£8.75

Rental ⛺ £99-£315

((MasterCard Visa

⚑ ⚑¼ ✕¼ ☞¼ ◙ █ ☐ ⚠ Calor Gaz ♿ ♞ WS

Last arrival time: 10:00

➡ Signposted off A3052 Exeter to Lyme Regis coast road, 1 mile E of Sidmouth.

SILLOTH Cumbria	10A1

Solway Holiday Village
Silloth CA5 4QQ
📞 016973-31236 **Fax** 016973-32553
Open all year ▲ ⛺ ⛟

Discover nearby Lake District and Borders. Quality accomodation and spacious touring area. Indoor pool, bowling alley, deer farm, bars, kiddies club. O.A.P. and Rally discounts.

Size 130 acres, 150 touring pitches, 90 with electric hookup, 150 level pitches, 200 static caravans, 5 ☂, 10 WCs, 1 CWP

£ car/tent £7-£11, car/caravan £7-£11, motorhome £7-£11, motorbike/tent £7-£11

Rental ⛺ Chalet. £90-£395 weekly (family of four)

((MasterCard Visa

⚑ ✕ ☞ ◙ █ ☐ ⬓ ☒ ▦ ▶ ☒ GR ⬓ TV ⚠ ⊞ ⚐ Calor Gaz ♿ ♞ WS

Last arrival time: 10:00

➡ From S: leave M6 junction 41. From N: leave A74 junction 44 - take B5305 to Silloth, turning right on reaching seafront towards Skinburness. The park is about a mile on right.

Stanwix Park Holiday Centre

Greenrow, Silloth CA5 4HH
☎ 016973-31671 Fax 016973-32555
⛺ 🚐 🚏

Large, well-run holiday site, with ballroom, disco, bar, play park and riding school. Ideal location for exploring Lake District, Roman wall, Gretna Green. Tennis court. Boating and golf nearby. 80 caravans and 28 chalets for hire (own WCs).

Size 20 acres, 121 touring pitches, 121 with electric hookup, 121 level pitches, 186 static caravans, 15 🚿, 20 WCs, 121 CWPs
£ car/tent £11-£14.50, car/caravan £11-£14.50, motorhome £11-£14.50, motorbike/tent £11-£14.50
Rental 🚐 Chalet. £155-£400
CC MasterCard Visa
🔋✕ 🛒 ▣ 🔌 ▣ 🔲 🔲 🔲 🔲 🔲 🔲 GR TV ⚠ 🔲 🔌
Calor Gaz ♿ 🐕 WS
Last arrival time: 10:00
➜ 1 mile S of Silloth on B5300.

Tanglewood Caravan Park

Causeway Head, Silloth CA5 4PE
☎ 016973-31253
Open March-October ⛺ 🚐 🚏

Natural, tree-sheltered, friendly park, ideal for touring the Lakes and the Borders. Large modern holiday homes for hire with colour TV.

Size 7 acres, 21 touring pitches, 21 with electric hookup, 21 level pitches, 56 static caravans, 4 🚿, 12 WCs, 2 CWPs
£ car/tent £6, car/caravan £6, motorhome £6, motorbike/tent £6, children £1-£2
Rental 🚐
▣ 🔌 🔲 GR TV ⚠ 🔌 Calor 🐕
Last arrival time: 11:00
➜ On B5302, 4 miles on from Abbeytown on left, or, on B5302, 1 mile from Silloth on right.

SILSDEN West Yorkshire   10C3

Dales Bank Holiday Park
Low Lane, Silsden BD20 9JH

☎ 01535-656523

Open April-October Å ⚏ ⚏

Size 5 acres, 52 touring pitches, 20 with electric hookup, 52 level pitches, 4 ⚏, 10 WCs, 1 CWP

£ car/tent £6, car/caravan £6, motorhome £6

⚏ ✕ ⚏ ⚏ GR ⚏ ⚏ Calor Gaz & ⚏ WS

Last arrival time: 11:00

➡ Follow signs from police station for 1½ miles.

SKEGNESS Lincolnshire   9D2

Butlins Funcoast World Touring Site
Skegness PE25 1NJ

☎ 01754 762311 **Fax** 01754 767833

Open March-October

Size 150 touring pitches

➡ Between Skegness and Mablethorpe

Hints & Tips
When braking it will take you an average of 20% more distance to stop. Always avoid violent braking

Richmond Holiday Centre
Richmond Drive, Skegness PE25 3TQ

☎ 01754-762097 **Fax** 01754-765631

Open 1 March-30 November ⚏ ⚏

Family owned park, with on-site facilities including a Post Office, arcade, launderette, hair salon, leisure complex and heated indoor pool. Live nightly entertainment subject to season.

Size 46 acres, 175 touring pitches, 107 with electric hookup, 175 level pitches, 550 static caravans, 24 ⚏, 100 WCs, 3 CWPs

£ car/caravan £8-£13.50, motorhome £8-£13.50

Rental ⚏ £100-£280

ɑ Visa

⚏ ⚏¼ ✕ ✕¼ ⚏ ⚏¼ ⚏ ⚏ ⚏ ⚏ ⚏ ⚏ ⚏ ⚏ GR TV ⚏ ⚏ ⚏ Calor Gaz & ⚏ WS

➡ Follow signs to bus station. Site is 400 yards beyond coach station on right.

SKIPSEA East Yorkshire   11F3

Far Grange Park
Windhook, Hornsea Road, Skipsea YO25 8SY
☎ 01262-468293 Fax 01262-468648
Open March-October ▲ ⛺ 🚐

Full facilities for touring caravans, tents and motorhomes. Luxury rose award holiday homes for hire. Holiday homes for sale. Leisure centre and indoor swimming pool.

Size 60 acres, 170 touring pitches, 170 with electric hookup, 170 level pitches, 327 static caravans, 20 🚻, 76 WCs, 4 CWPs
£ car/tent £9-£13, car/caravan £9-£13, motorhome £9-£13
Rental ⛺ £140-£310
CC MasterCard Visa
🧺 ✕ 🍽 🔲 📞 ⛽ 🍴 ✈ 🎱 ◧ 🔭 📻 GR 🔍 📺 ⛰ ✈ ⛳ Calor Gaz & 🐕
➡ Halfway between Skipsea and Hornsea on B1242.

SKIRLINGTON LEISURE PARK

Pleasantly situated between the east coast villages of Skipsea and Atwick. It is a family run business with a reputation for high standards.

6-8 Berth Caravans for Hire • Hook ups
Indoor Heated Swimming Pool • Jacuzzi • Sauna • Solarium
Snooker & Pool • 9 Hole Putting Green • Golf Driving Range
Fishing Lake • Children's Play Areas • Duck Pond • Animal Farm
Sandy Beach Nearby.

The Tow Bar Inn offers restaurant & bar meals, a children's room and live entertainment most evenings.

The park is ideally placed for trips to Bridlington, Scarborough, York, the North Yorkshire Moors and many other local attractions.

LOW SKIRLINGTON, SKIPSEA, DRIFFIELD, E. YORKSHIRE YO25 8SY
Tel: 01262 468213/468466

Skirlington Leisure Park
Low Skirlington, Skipsea YO25 8SY
☎ 01262-468213 Fax 01262-468105
Open 1 March-31 October ▲ ⛺ 🚐

Situated on the East Yorkshire coast, a family run business with a reputation for high standards and constant updating of all facilities. Call for a brochure.

Size 80 acres, 275 touring pitches, 275 with electric hookup, 275 level pitches, 465 static caravans, 45 🚻, 55 WCs, 5 CWPs
£ car/tent £8-£14, car/caravan £8-£14, motorhome £8-£14, motorbike/tent £8-£14
Rental ⛺ £90-£275
CC MasterCard Visa
🧺 ✕ 🍽 🔲 📞 ⛽ 📻 ▶ 🔭 🔭 🎿 GR 📺 ⛰ ⛳ Calor Gaz & 🐕 WS
➡ M62 signposted to Beverley, follow signs to Hornsea. Brown signposts direct to site once in Hornsea.

SLIMBRIDGE Gloucestershire   7E4

Tudor Caravan & Camping
Shepherds Patch, Slimbridge GL2 7BP
☎ 01453-890483
Open all year ▲ ⛺ 🚐

Behind a pub in farming country, this orchard site is bordered by the Gloucester to Sharpness canal, with the Wild Fowl Trust on the far bank.

Size 7½ acres, 75 touring pitches, 45 with electric hookup, 75 level pitches, 4 🚻, 12 WCs, 1 CWP
£ car/tent £6.75-£7, car/caravan £7-£7.50, motorhome £7-£7.50, motorbike/tent £6.75-£7, children £0.75
CC MasterCard
🧺 ✕¼ 🍽¼ 📞 ⛽ ⛳ Calor 🐕
➡ From junction of A4135 and A38, 11 miles SW of Gloucester, take road through Slimbridge towards Wild Fowl Trust for 1½ miles. On left immediately before canal bridge.

SLINGSBY North Yorkshire   11E3

Camping & Caravanning Club Site
Railway Street, Slingsby YO6 7AA
☎ 01653-628335
Open late March-early November **A ⏚ ⏛**
Size 3 acres, 60 touring pitches, 41 with electric
hookup, 4 ⏚, 9 WCs, 1 CWP
£ car/tent £4.60-£6.80, car/caravan £4.60-£6.80,
motorhome £4.60-£6.80, motorbike/tent £4.60-£6.80,
children £1.40
CC MasterCard Visa
⏚¼ ⏚ ⏚ ⏚ ⏛
Last arrival time: 11:00
➡ From A64 Scarborough to York road, take B1257 at
Maltby to Slingsby. Follow signs to site.

SNAINTON North Yorkshire   11E2

Jasmine Caravan Park
Cross Lane, Snainton YO13 9BE
☎ 01723-859240 Fax 01723-859240
Open March-January **A ⏚ ⏛**

*Well sheltered park in excellent area for walking and
cycling. Local attractions to suit all ages and tastes.
Several 'In Bloom' awards. Static and chalet for hire.*

Size 5 acres, 70 touring pitches, 70 with electric
hookup, 70 level pitches, 4 ⏚, 14 WCs, 1 CWP
£ car/tent £6-£8.50, car/caravan £6-£8.50, motorhome
£6-£8.50, motorbike/tent £6-£8.50, children £0.75
Rental ⏚ Chalet. £160-£250 per week
⏚ ⏚ ⏚ ⏚ Calor Gaz ⏚ ⏛ WS
➡ Turn off A170 in Snainton village opposite junior
school. After ¾ mile signposted. Midway between
Scarborough and Pickering.

Don't forget to mention the guide
When booking, please remember to tell
the site that you chose it from
RAC Camping & Caravanning 1998

SNETTISHAM Norfolk   9D2

Diglea Camping & Caravan Park
Beach Road, Snettisham, King's Lynn PE31 7RA
☎ 01485-541367
Open 1 April-31 October **A ⏚ ⏛**

*Attractive, level, quiet, family run park in a peaceful
rural setting, ½ mile from the beach. Ideally situated
for exploring the north Norfolk coast and the historic
town of King's Lynn.*

Size 15 acres, 200 touring pitches, 20 with electric
hookup, 200 level pitches, 150 static caravans, 14 ⏚,
30 WCs, 2 CWPs
£ car/tent £5.50-£8.50, car/caravan £5.50-£8.50,
motorhome £5.50-£8.50, motorbike/tent £5.50-£8.50
Rental ⏚ £145-£295
⏚¼ ⏚¼ ⏚¼ ⏚ ⏚ ⏚ ⏚ Calor Gaz ⏚ WS
Last arrival time: 10:00
➡ From King's Lynn take A149 King's
Lynn/Hunstanton road. After approximately 10½
miles turn left at sign marked Snettisham Beach. Park
is 1½ miles on left.

SOUTH BRENT Devon   2C3

Edeswell Farm Country Caravan Park
Rattery, South Brent TQ10 9LN
☎ 01364-72177 Fax 01364-72177
Open 1 April-31 October **A ⏚ ⏛**
Size 21 acres, 46 touring pitches, 22 with electric
hookup, 40 level pitches, 20 static caravans, 10 ⏚, 10
WCs, 1 CWP
£ car/tent £7.50-£9.50, car/caravan £7.50-£9.50,
motorhome £7.50-£9.50, motorbike/tent £7.50-£9.50,
children £1
⏚ ⏚ ⏚ ⏚ ⏚ ⏚ ⏚ ⏚ ⏚ ⏚ Calor Gaz ⏚ WS
Last arrival time: 8:30
➡ From A38 to Marley Head junction take A385 to
Paignton. Site ½ mile on right.

SOUTH MOLTON Devon   2C2

Black Cock Inn & Camping Park
Molland, South Molton EX36 3NW
☎ 01769-550297 Fax 01769-550297
Open March-November ⚑ ⌂ ⛟

A traditional stone-built inn on the edge of Exmoor, within easy reach of the North Devon coastline. Formerly a hotel, the inn once serviced the Taunton to Barnstaple railway.

Size 7 acres, 64 touring pitches, 24 with electric hookup, 48 level pitches, 2 static caravans, 8 ⌂, 15 WCs, 1 CWP
£ car/tent £5.50-£7.50, car/caravan £6.50-£9, motorhome £6.50-£8.50, motorbike/tent £5.50-£7.50
Rental ⌂ Chalet. from £25 per day.
℃ MasterCard Visa
⚑ ✕ ⛽ 🛢 🔋 🖪 🗵 💻 GR TV ♨ 🍴 Calor ♿ ✦ WS
Last arrival time: 11:00
➔ Signed from A361, 4 miles E of South Molton.

SOUTH SHIELDS Tyne & Wear   11D1

Lizard Lane Caravan & Camping Site
Marsden, South Shields NE34 7AB
☎ 0191-454 4982
Open 1 March-26 October ⚑ ⌂ ⛟
Size 4¼ acres, 45 touring pitches, 45 level pitches, 70 static caravans, 6 ⌂, 14 WCs, 1 CWP
£ car/tent £6.60-£7.60, car/caravan £6.60-£7.60, motorhome £6.60-£7.60, motorbike/tent £5.10-£5.90, children £1.50
⚑¼ ✕¼ ⛽¼ 🛢 🔋 🖪 📶 ✈ ♨ Calor Gaz ✦ WS
➔ 2 miles S of South Shields on A183.

Sandhaven Caravan Park
Sea Road, South Shields
☎ 0191-454 5594
Open 1 March-end October ⚑ ⌂ ⛟
Size 7 acres, 49 touring pitches, 49 with electric hookup, 49 level pitches, 51 static caravans, 6 ⌂, 14 WCs, 1 CWP
£ car/tent £8.60-£9.80, car/caravan £8.60-£9.80, motorhome £8.60-£9.80, motorbike/tent £7.60-£8.60
Rental ⌂
⚑¼ ✕¼ ⛽¼ 🛢 🔋 🖪 Calor Gaz ♿ ✦ WS
➔ Site ¾ mile E of town centre on coast road.

SOUTHAMPTON Hampshire   4B4

Dibles Park Caravan Site
Dibles Road, Warsash, Southampton SO3 9SA
☎ 01489-575232
Open 1 March-30 November ⚑ ⌂ ⛟
Size 5 acres, 15 touring pitches, 15 with electric hookup, 15 level pitches, 4 ⌂, 7 WCs, 1 CWP
£ car/tent £5-£6, car/caravan £6.70, motorhome £6.70
⚑¼ ✕¼ ⛽¼ 🛢 🔋 🖪 🗵 Calor ✦ WS
➔ Junction 8 M27 turn left A27 to Sarisbury Green. Right into Barnes Lane, right into Brook Lane, left at Warsash Village then the third turning on right.

Riverside Park
Satchells Lane, Hamble, Southampton SO31 4HR
☎ 01703-453220 Fax 01703-453611
Open 1 March-31 October ⚑ ⌂ ⛟

A quiet family park, set midway between Portsmouth, Winchester and the New Forest and overlooking the adjoining marina and river.

Size 6 acres, 45 touring pitches, 35 with electric hookup, 40 level pitches, 32 static caravans, 3 ⌂, 6 WCs, 1 CWP
£ Car/tent £8-£10, car/caravan £8-£10, motorhome £8-£10
℃ MasterCard Visa
⚑¼ ✕ 🔋 🖪 ♨ Calor WS
➔ M27 (junction 8) S to Hamble (B3397) for two miles. Park signed off Hamble Lane (B3397) 1 mile.

SOUTHPORT Lancashire   10B4

Leisure Lakes Caravan Park
Mere Brow, Tarleton, Southport PR4 JX
☎ 01772-813446 Fax 01772-816250
🅰 ⛺ 🚐

A 90 acre site with two lakes for fishing, windsurfing, canoeing and jet skis. Also mountain bike hire. Pub on site serving meals.

Size 90 acres, 87 touring pitches, 80 with electric hookup, 87 level pitches, 6 🚿, 11 WCs, 2 CWPs
£ car/tent £9.50, car/caravan £9.50, motorhome £9.50
🛒¼ ✗¼ 🍴 🗇 🔌 ☎ 🎣 🛝 ⚠ ⛽ Calor Gaz 🚹 🐕
Last arrival time: 9:00
➡ From Southport, take A565 N for 3½ miles, then turn right onto B5246 to Mere Brow village, site entrance is 500 yards on right.

SPALDING Lincolnshire   8C2

Lake Ross Caravan Park
Dozens Bank, West Pinchbeck, Spalding PE11 3NA
☎ 01775-761690
Open 1 April-31 October 🅰 ⛺ 🚐

Small family run business with a friendly atmosphere. This quiet caravan site is situated in the midst of open countryside providing an excellent base from which to tour the Fens. Within easy reach of Peterborough, King's Lynn, Boston and Grantham.

Size 2½ acres, 20 touring pitches, 12 with electric hookup, 20 level pitches, 4 static caravans, 2 🚿, 3 WCs, 1 CWP

£ car/tent £7.50, car/caravan £7.50, motorhome £7.50, motorbike/tent £7.50, children £0.50
Rental ⛺ £90-£160
🛒 🛒¼ ✗¼ 🍴¼ ☎ 🗇 🔌 📺 ⛽ Calor Gaz ♿ 🐕
Last arrival time: 11·30
➡ On A151 Spalding-Bourne road.

ST AGNES Cornwall   2A4

Beacon Cottage Farm
Beacon Drive, St Agnes TR5 0NU
☎ 01872-552347
Open May-October 🅰 ⛺ 🚐

Small secluded park on a working family farm set in six landscaped paddocks covering two acres. Ten minutes walk to the sandy beach. Beautiful scenery, lovely walks. Quiet and uncommercialised.

Size 4 acres, 50 touring pitches, 27 with electric hookup, 45 level pitches, 4 🚿, 9 WCs, 1 CWP
£ car/tent £5-£11, car/caravan £5-£11, motorhome £5-£11, motorbike/tent £5-£11, children £1.50-£2.50
🛒 🗇 ☎ 🗇 ⚠ Calor Gaz 🐕 WS
Last arrival time: 8:00
➡ Leave A30 at Chiverton roundabout and take B3277 to St Agnes. On reaching village, turn left, signposted The Beacon, and follow signs to park.

Trevarth Holiday Park
Blackwater, St Agnes TR4 8HR
☎ 01872-560266 Fax 01872-560266
Open Easter-mid October 🅰 ⛺ 🚐

Small family run park in rural area, conveniently situated for the north and south coast resorts.

Size 4½ acres, 30 touring pitches, 27 with electric hookup, 30 level pitches, 20 static caravans, 3 🚿, 4

WCs, 1 CWP
£ car/tent £5-£7.30, car/caravan £5-£7.30, motorhome £5-£7.30, motorbike/tent £5-£7.30, children £1
Rental A £90-£335
CC MasterCard Visa
♨¼ ✕¼ ♥¼ ▣ ▨ ▤ GR ⚠ Calor Gaz ★ WS
Last arrival time: 10:00
➠ 300 yards down Blackwater road, from Cliverton roundabout which is on A30, 4½ miles N of Redruth.

ST AUSTELL Cornwall   2B4

Croft Farm Touring Park
Luxulyan, Bodmin PL30 5EQ
☎ 01726-85028 **Fax** 01726-850498
Open April-October A ◑ ♨

Sheltered and secluded, Croft offers a peaceful, comfortable base for your stay whether spring, summer or autumn. Recently gained a silver 'David Bellamy Award'.

Size 6 acres, 46 touring pitches, 44 with electric hookup, 44 level pitches, 6 static caravans, 8 ♔, 12 WCs, 2 CWPs
£ car/tent £5.30-£9.60, car/caravan £5.30-£9.60, motorhome £5.30-£9.60, motorbike/tent £5.30-£9.60, children £1.05-£1.25
Rental ◑ Chalet. caravans £80-£230, cottages £160-£405
CC MasterCard Visa
♨ ♥ ▣ ▨ ⚠ Calor Gaz ♿
➠ From A30 Bodmin turn left at A391 to St Austell. Continue to Bugle, turn left at cross road (traffic lights) onto B3374 to Penwithick. Continue to Penwithick, turn left to Trethurgy/Luxulyan. At T-junction turn left. Park is on left hand side in ½ mile.

Trencreek Farm Holiday Park
Hewaswater, St Austell PL26 7JG
☎ 01726-882540
Open April-October
Size 56 acres, 196 touring pitches, 100 with electric hookup, 30 level pitches, 32 static caravans, 14 ♔, 25 WCs, 3 CWPs
CC MasterCard Visa
♨ ♥ ▣ ▨ ▦ ▨ GR ▨ TV ⚠ Calor Gaz ♿
Last arrival time: 24 hrs
➠ Off B3287 1 mile from junction with A390 to St Mawes and Tregony.

Trevor Farm Camping & Caravan Site
Gorran, St Austell PL26 6LW
☎ 01726-842387 **Fax** 01726-842387
Open 1 April-end October A ◑ ♨

Level meadow site on working farm. 50 pitches, including 20 electric hook-ups. 1 mile to coastal walks and beach.

Size 4 acres, 50 touring pitches, 24 with electric hookup, 50 level pitches, 4 ♔, 12 WCs, 1 CWP
£ car/tent £5-£11, car/caravan £5-£11, motorhome £5-£11, motorbike/tent £5-£11
▣ ▨ ▤ ▨ ⚠ ★
Last arrival time: 8:00
➠ From St Austell S on B3273, 3¼ miles past Pentewan, turn right signed Gorran. After 4½ miles bear right. After ¼ mile turn right to site.

Trewhiddle Holiday Estate
Trewhiddle, Pentewan Road, St Austell PL26 7AD
☎ 01726-67011 **Fax** 01726-67010
A ◑ ♨

A country park in the peaceful Pentewan Valley, with the sea nearby. 16 acre family site ideally situated for exploring Cornwall. Excellent facilities for family holidays.

Size 16 acres, 105 touring pitches, 50 with electric hookup, 50 static caravans, 9 ♔, 16 WCs, 1 CWP
£ car/tent £6-£10, car/caravan £6-£10, motorhome £6-£10, motorbike/tent £6-£10, children £1
Rental ◑ Chalet. £130-£360
CC MasterCard Visa
♨ ✕ ♥ ▣ ▨ ▦ GR ⚠ ▤ Calor Gaz ★
Last arrival time: 10:00
➠ From St Austell take B3273 to Mevagissey. Site entrance is ¾ mile on right from roundabout.

ST IVES Cornwall   2A

Ayr Holiday Park
Higher Ayr, St Ives TR26 1EJ
☎ 01736-795855 fax 01736-798797
Open 1 April-31 October **A** ⚘ ⚘
Size 4 acres, 40 touring pitches, 35 with electric hookup, 20 level pitches, 43 static caravans, 10 ⚑, 11 WCs, 1 CWP
£ car/tent £8.25-£14.50, car/caravan £9.25-£14.50, motorhome £8.50-£13.50, motorbike/tent £14.50, children £1-£1.75
Rental ⚘ Chalet. £140-£550
₵ MasterCard Visa
🛁¼ ✗¼ 🚽¼ ⊟ 🔌 ⊟ GR 🅰 Calor Gaz 🐕
Last arrival time: 8:00
➡ From the A30 follow the holiday route to St Ives joining B3311 and B3306. ½ mile from St Ives turn left at mini roundabout following signs to Ayr and Porthmeor Beach.

Hints & Tips
Caravans are stolen from laybys and motorway service stations. Even if you are just stopping for a cup of tea or to stretch your legs make sure you secure your caravan.

Balnoon Camp Site
Halsetown, St Ives TR26 3JA
☎ 01736-795431
Open Easter-31 October **A** ⚘ ⚘

Small, quiet, level sheltered site, pleasantly situated with tree and hedge screening, just 2 miles from St Ives town centre and beaches.

Size ¾ acre, 24 touring pitches, 24 level pitches, 2 ⚑, 4 WCs, 1 CWP
£ car/tent £5-£8, car/caravan £5-£8, motorhome £5-£8, motorbike/tent £5-£8, children £0.50-£1
🛁 ✗¼ ⊟ Calor Gaz 🐕
Last arrival time: 8:00
➡ Leave A30 W of Hayle at large roundabout and take A3074 for St Ives. At second mini roundabout take first left (signposted Holiday Route). Continue for 3 miles taking second right signposted Balnoon.

Polmanter Tourist Park

Halsetown, St Ives TR26 3LX
☎ 01736-795640 Fax 01736-795640
Open Easter-31 October Å ⊕ ⊕

Award winning park, with excellent facilities including a heated swimming pool, located within easy walking distance of St Ives and its glorious beaches, just one mile away.

Size 13 acres, 240 touring pitches, 188 with electric hookup, 34 ℞, 40 WCs, 4 CWPs
£ car/tent £7-£14, car/caravan £7-£14, motorhome £7-£14, motorbike/tent £7-£14, children £1.50-£1.75
CC MasterCard Visa
🛒 ✗ 🖵 🖩 📞 🚿 🔁 🔳 GR 🔍 ⚠ 🔌 Calor Gaz ⊀
Last arrival time: 9:00
➔ Off A30 to St Ives (A3074). First left at mini-roundabout. Take holiday route (HR) to St Ives (Halsetown). Right at Halsetown Inn, then first left.

Trevalgan Family Camping Park

St Ives TR26 3BJ
☎ 01736-796433 Fax 01736-796433
Open 1 May-30 September Å ⊕ ⊕
Size 5 acres, 120 touring pitches, 22 with electric hookup, 120 level pitches, 10 ℞, 15 WCs, 1 CWP
£ car/tent £6-£9.50, car/caravan £6-£9.50, motorhome £6-£9.50, motorbike/tent £6-£9.50, children £2-£4
CC MasterCard Visa
🛒 🖵 🖩 📞 🚿 🔁 GR 🔍 TV ⚠ Calor Gaz ⅋ ⊀ WS
➔ Take A30 to B3306 and follow signs for park.

ST LEONARDS Hampshire　　　　4A4

Camping International

229 Ringwood Road, St Leonards BH24 2SD
☎ 01202-872817 Fax 01202-861292
Open 1 March-October Å ⊕ ⊕
Size 9 acres, 205 touring pitches, 165 with electric hookup, 205 level pitches, 16 ℞, 22 WCs, 2 CWPs
£ car/tent £7.70-£11.30, car/caravan £7.70-£11.30, motorhome £7.70-£11.30, motorbike/tent £7.70-£11.30, children £1.50-£1.70
CC MasterCard Visa
🛒 ✗ 🖵 🖩 📞 🚿 🔁 GR 🔍 TV ⚠ 🔌 Calor Gaz ⅋ ⊀ WS
Last arrival time: 10:00
➔ On main A31 2½ miles W of Ringwood. Entrance in Boundary Lane.

ST MAWES Cornwall   2B4

Trethem Mill Touring Park

St Just-in-Roseland, St Mawes TR2 5JF

📞 01872-580504 Fax 018/2-580968

Open 1 April-31 October ⚠ ⏏ ⏖

Discover the beautiful Roseland, staying on our exclusive, peaceful park, offering immaculate facilties in tranquil countryside setting. Ideal for beaches, walking, watersports, gardens and touring Cornwall.

Size 11 acres, 84 touring pitches, 37 with electric hookup, 40 level pitches, 8 🚿, 16 WCs, 1 CWP
£ car/tent £6-£9, car/caravan £6-£9, motorhome £6-£9, motorbike/tent £6-£9, children £1-£2
CC MasterCard Visa
🛒 🗑 🔌 GR TV ⚠ Calor Gaz 🚻 🐕
➡ From Tregony follow A3078 to St Mawes. 2 miles after passing through Trewithian look for sign.

ST NEOTS Cambridgeshire   8C4

Camping & Caravanning Club Site

Rush Meadow, St Neots PE19 2UD

📞 01480-474404

Open end March-early November ⚠ ⏏ ⏖
Size 10 acres, 180 touring pitches, 53 with electric hookup, 12 🚿, 18 WCs, 2 CWPs
£ car/tent £5.60-£8.60, car/caravan £5.60-£8.60, motorhome £5.60-£8.60, motorbike/tent £5.60-£8.60, children £1.50
CC Visa
🗑 🔌 🚻 🐕
Last arrival time: 11:00
➡ Site signposted from B1043 in St Neots.

STAMFORD Lincolnshire   8C3

Tallington Lakes

Barholm Road, Tallington, Stamford PE9 4RT

📞 01778-347000 Fax 01778-346213

Open all year ⚠ ⏏ ⏖
Size 100 touring pitches, 60 with electric hookup, 100 level pitches, 3 🚿, 5 WCs, 1 CWP
£ car/tent £7.50, car/caravan £8.50, motorhome £8.50, motorbike/tent £7.50
Rental ⏏
🛒¼ ✕ 🔌 🗑 📱 🔌 🔲 🗑 🔲 ⚠ 🐕 WS
Last arrival time: 8:00

STANDLAKE Oxfordshire   4B2

Hardwick Parks

Downs Road, Off Witney Road, Standlake OX8 7PZ

📞 01865-300501 Fax 01865-300037

Open 1 April-31 October ⚠ ⏏ ⏖
Size 180 acres, 250 touring pitches, 76 with electric hookup, 250 level pitches, 117 static caravans, 20 🚿, 18 WCs, 1 CWP
£ car/tent £7.75-£9.75, car/caravan £7.75-£9.75, motorhome £7.75-£9.75, motorbike/tent £4.50-£5
CC MasterCard Visa
🛒 ✕ 🔌 🗑 🔌 🔲 🔌 Calor Gaz 🚻 🐕 WS
Last arrival time: 8:00
➡ Signposted from A415, 4½ miles S of Witney.

STOURPORT-ON-SEVERN Worcestershire   7E3

Redstone Caravan Park

The Rough, Stourport-on-Severn DY13 0LD

📞 01299-823872 Fax 01299-828026

Open 1 February-31 December ⏏ ⏖
Size 12 acres, 36 touring pitches, 28 with electric hookup, 36 level pitches, 290 static caravans, 8 🚿, 24 WCs, 2 CWPs
£ car/caravan £8-£11, motorhome £8-£11
🛒 ✕¼ 🔌 🗑 🔌 ⚠ 🔌 Calor Gaz 🚻 🐕
Last arrival time: 9:00
➡ A451 from Kidderminster, over bridge, second left into The Rough.

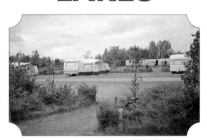

STRATFORD-UPON-AVON Warwickshire   7F3

Dodwell Park

Evesham Road, Stratford-upon-Avon CV37 9ST
📞 01789-204957 Fax 01926-336476
Open all year ▲ 🚐 🚛

Set in beautiful countryside two miles from Stratford-upon-Avon this is an ideal site for visiting the Cotswolds and Warwick Castle.

Size 17 acres, 50 touring pitches, 50 with electric hookup, 40 level pitches, 6 🚿, 7 WCs, 1 CWP
£ car/tent £8-£9, car/caravan £8-£9, motorhome £8-£9, motorbike/tent £6-£7, children £0.70
CC MasterCard Visa
🛒 🗑 📞 🚰 Calor Gaz 🗼 🗼
Last arrival time: 9:30
➡ From Stratford-upon-Avon take B439 to Bidford for 2 miles. Park lies on left (not racecourse site).

Island Meadow Caravan Park

The Mill House, Aston Cantlow B95 6JP
📞 01789-488273 Fax 01789-488273
Open 1 March-31 October ▲ 🚐 🚛

Quiet, peaceful, secluded riverside park beside picturesque and historic village. Ideal centre for Shakespeare's country, only six miles from Stratford-upon-Avon. English Tourist Board grading four ticks.

Size 7 acres, 24 touring pitches, 24 with electric hookup, 24 level pitches, 56 static caravans, 4 🚿, 11 WCs, 1 CWP
£ car/tent £6.50, car/caravan £8.50, motorhome £8.50, motorbike/tent £6.50, children £0.80
Rental 🚐 £160 (low season)-£270 (high season)
🛒 ✗¼ 🗑 📞 🚰 📋 Calor Gaz 🗼 🗼
Last arrival time: 9:00
➡ From A46 Stratford to Alcester, or from A3400 Stratford to Henley-in-Arden, follow signs for Aston Cantlow Village.

SWANAGE Dorset   3F3

Ulwell Cottage Caravan Park

Swanage
📞 **01929-422823 Fax 01929-421500**
Open 1 March-7 January Å ⊿ ⇝

Friendly "Village Inn", heated indoor pool, shop. 1 mile from the beach. Ideal for families, walkers, golfers and all watersports. Some "all service" hard standing pitches. Luxury caravans some with heating throughout.

Size 13 acres, 77 touring pitches, 60 with electric hookup, 40 level pitches, 140 static caravans, 24 ﬁ, 22 WCs, 4 CWPs
£ car/tent £10-£18, car/caravan £10-£18, motorhome £10-£18
Rental ⊿ Chalet. £120-£450
ⓒ MasterCard Visa
🔌 ✕ 🍴 ▣ 📞 🖭 🎿 ⚠ ⊞ Calor Gaz 🛒
Last arrival time: 10:00
➡ Take A351 to Swanage and on seafront turn left. Follow this road towards Studland for 1½ miles and turn left just before telephone kiosk on left.

TAMWORTH Staffordshire   7F2

Camping & Caravanning Club Site

Kingsbury Water Park, Bodymoor Heath, Sutton Coldfield
📞 **01827-874101**
Open end March-start November Å ⊿ ⇝
Size 18 acres, 60 touring pitches, 35 with electric hookup, 8 ﬁ, 12 WCs, 1 CWP
£ car/tent £4.60-£6.80, car/caravan £4.60-£6.80, motorhome £4.60-£6.80, motorbike/tent £4.60-£6.80
ⓒ MasterCard Visa
▣ 📞 ⚅ 🛒
Last arrival time: 11:00
➡ Off A4097 or A4091 take unclassified road and follow Water Park signs.

Drayton Manor Park

Fazeley, Tamworth B78 3TW
📞 **01827-287979 Fax 01827-288916**
Open Easter-end October Å ⊿ ⇝
Size 4 acres acres, 75 touring pitches, 37 level pitches, 12 ﬁ, 15 WCs, 2 CWPs
£ car/tent £9, car/caravan £11
ⓒ MasterCard Visa
🔌 🔌¼ ✕ ✕¼ 🍴 🍴¼ 📞 ▣ ⊞ Gaz ⚅ 🛒
➡ From M42 junction 9 or 10 take A5404 or A446 onto A4091.

TAUNTON Somerset   3D2

Ashe Farm Camping & Caravan Site

Thornfalcon, Taunton TA3 5NW
📞 **01823-442567 Fax 01823-443372**
Open 1 April-31 October Å ⊿ ⇝

Peaceful, family run site with lovely views of the hills. Central for touring and within easy reach of the coast, hills and Somerset Levels.

Size 7 acres, 30 touring pitches, 30 with electric hookup, 30 level pitches, 3 static caravans, 6 ﬁ, 10 WCs, 2 CWPs
£ car/tent £6, car/caravan £6-£7.50, motorhome £6-£7.50, motorbike/tent £6, children £1
Rental ⊿ £110-£140 week.
🔌 ✕¼ 🍴¼ 📞 ▣ 🔄 ⒼⓇ 🔲 ⚠ Calor Gaz ⚅ 🛒 WS
Last arrival time: 12:00
➡ Leave M5 at junction 25. Take A358 Chard road for 2½ miles. Along dual carriageway, turn right at Nags Head pub. Site ¼ mile on right.

Holly Bush Park
Culmhead, Taunton TA3 7EA
☎ 01823-421515 Fax 01823-421885
🅰 ⛺ 🚐

A beautiful, quiet, family run site in an area of outstanding natural beauty. Numerous places of interest are within easy reach, including National Trust properties.

Size 2 acres, 40 touring pitches, 26 with electric hookup, 40 level pitches, 6 ⛶, 9 WCs, 1 CWP
£ car/tent £6-£7, car/caravan £6-£7, motorhome £6-£7, motorbike/tent £6-£7, children £1.25
Rental 🅰 & equipment £10 daily.
🛁 ✕¼ 🍽¼ 🖭 📞 🖬 Calor Gaz ⚹ ⛎ WS
Last arrival time: 10:00
➡ Take Jn25 of M5, follow signs for Taunton, Corfe and the racecourse. 3½ miles after Corfe, turn right at cross roads. After 500 yards, turn right at give way sign. Site is 150 yards on the left past Holman Clavel Pub.

TAVISTOCK Devon   2C3

Harford Bridge Holiday Park
Peter Tavy, Tavistock PL19 9LS
☎ 01822-810349 Fax 01822-810028
Open mid March-mid November 🅰 ⛺ 🚐

Beautiful family run park in Dartmoor National Park offering glorious views. Level and sheltered with many trees and shrubs. Ideal for walking or touring.

Size 16 acres, 120 touring pitches, 40 with electric hookup, 120 level pitches, 16 static caravans, 12 ⛶, 14 WCs, 1 CWP

£ car/tent £6-£9, car/caravan £6-£9, motorhome £6-£9, motorbike/tent £6-£9, children £1-£1.50
Rental ⛺ Chalet. £100-£285
℃ MasterCard Visa
🛁 🖭 📞 🖬 📠 🖬 📺 📠 Calor Gaz ⛎ WS
Last arrival time: 9:00
➡ Off A386 Tavistock to Okehampton road. 2 miles N of Tavistock, take the Peter Tavy turn.

Higher Longford Farm
Moorshop, Tavistock PL19 9JY
☎ 01822-613 360 Fax 01822-618 722
Open all year 🅰 ⛺ 🚐
Size 6 acres, 52 touring pitches, 40 with electric hookup, 52 level pitches, 10 ⛶, 14 WCs, 2 CWPs
£ car/tent £7.50-£8.50, car/caravan £7.50-£8.50, motorhome £7.50-£8.50, motorbike/tent £5.50-£6.50, children £0.50-£0.75
Rental Chalet. £90-£160
🛁 ✕ 🍽 🖭 📞 🖬 📠 🍴 Calor Gaz ⚹ ⛎ WS
➡ Take B3357 Tavistock to Princetown. The road is 2½ miles from Tavistock on right before Park Hill.

Langstone Manor Camping & Caravan Park
Moortown, Tavistock PL19 9TZ
☎ 01822-613371
Open 15 March-15 November 🅰 ⛺ 🚐
Size 5½ acres, 40 touring pitches, 14 with electric hookup, 40 level pitches, 25 static caravans, 6 ⛶, 7 WCs, 1 CWP
£ car/tent £6-£7, car/caravan £6-£7, motorhome £6-£7, motorbike/tent £6-£7, children £1
Rental ⛺ Chalet.
🛁 ✕ 📞 🖬 📠 📠 🍴 Calor Gaz ⚹
Last arrival time: 11:00
➡ Take B3357 from Tavistock to Princetown. After 2 miles, turn right at crossroads. Pass over cattle grid and turn left. Follow signs to site ½ mile on right.

TEBAY Cumbria   10B2

Tebay Caravan Park
Tebay CA10 3SB
☎ 015396-24511 Fax 015396-24511
Open mid March-31 October 🅰 ⛺ 🚐
Size 4 acres, 70 touring pitches, 60 with electric hookup, 70 level pitches, 2 static caravans, 6 ⛶, 10 WCs,
£ car/tent £6.95-£8.70, car/caravan £6.95-£8.70, motorhome £6.95-£8.70, motorbike/tent £6.95-£8.70
🛁 ✕ 🍽 🍴 Calor ⚹ WS
➡ Leave M6 1 mile N of jct 38 signed Westmorland Services. Access also from southbound services.

Don't forget to mention the guide
When booking, please remember to tell the site that you chose it from
RAC Camping & Caravanning 1998

TELFORD Shropshire   7E2

THE IRONBRIDGE GORGE MUSEUM

The Ironbridge Gorge in Shropshire is ideal for a short break in stunning scenery with marvellous Museums and Heritage.

IRONBRIDGE GORGE MUSEUMS
Open Daily 10.00-17.00
Tel: 01952 433522/432166 Fax: 01952 432204

Camping & Caravanning Club Site
Stelford, Haughton, Telford TF6 6BU
☎ 01743-709334
Open end March-start November Å ⚏ ⚏
Size 18 acres, 160 touring pitches, 18 with electric hookup, 2 CWPs
£ car/tent £3.20-£4.80, car/caravan £3.20-£4.80, motorhome £3.20-£4.80, motorbike/tent £3.20-£4.80, children £1
CC MasterCard Visa
☎ ⚏ ⚏ ⚏
Last arrival time: 11:00
➡ Take A53 for 1½ miles passing Upper Astley, turn right and continue for about 1 mile.

Severn Gorge Caravan Park
Bridgnorth Road, Tweedale, Telford TF7 4JB
☎ 01952-684789 Fax 01952-684789
Open all year Å ⚏ ⚏

Set amongst woodland. This well organised site provides a perfect base for exploring Ironbridge and the rest of Shropshire. Open all year. Brochures available on request.

Size 16 acres, 84 touring pitches, 66 with electric hookup, 84 level pitches, 6 ⚏, 11 WCs, 1 CWP
£ car/tent £8.50-£11, car/caravan £8.50-£11, motorhome £8.50-£11, children £1
⚏ ⚏¼ ✕¼ ⚏¼ ⚏ ⚏ ⚏ ⚏ Calor Gaz & ⚏ WS

Last arrival time: 11:45
➡ From M54 junction 4 follow signs for A442 Kidderminster, then take A442 and follow signs for Tweedale. At Cuckoo Oak roundabout take third exit. Site 300 yards on right.

TENTERDEN Kent   5E3

Woodlands Caravan Park
Tenterden Road, Biddenden, Tenterden TN27 8BT
☎ 01580-291216 Fax 01580-291216
Open 1 March-31 October Å ⚏ ⚏

In the heart of the beautiful Kent countryside, Woodlands offers a perfect base for visiting all tourist attractions. Located in a picturesque and tranquil location. The Channel Tunnel is only 35 minutes drive. Please call for our brochure.

Size 24 acres, 100 touring pitches, 36 with electric hookup, 100 level pitches, 13 static caravans, 8 ⚏, 16 WCs, 1 CWP
£ car/tent £8.50-£10, car/caravan £8.50-£10, motorhome £8.50-£10, motorbike/tent £6.50-£8, children £2-£2.50
⚏ ⚏¼ ⚏ ⚏ ⚏ ⚏ ⚏ ⚏ Calor Gaz & ⚏ WS
➡ Situated on A262 3 miles N of Tenterden, 1½ miles S of Biddenden.

TEWKESBURY Gloucestershire   7E4

Brooklands Farm Touring Caravan Park
Alderton, Tewkesbury GL20 8NX
☎ 01242-620259
Open 16 March-16 January Å ⚏ ⚏

Set around a small lake in 20 acres of farm land, the Cotswolds and surrounding area of natural beauty are on the doorstep.

Size 10 acres, 80 touring pitches, 70 with electric hookup, 80 level pitches, 8 ℞, 14 WCs, 3 CWPs
£ car/tent £7-£10, car/caravan £7-£10, motorhome £7-£10, motorbike/tent £7-£10, children £1-£1.25
🔋 ✕¼ 🅿¼ 🔲 🔌 🔲 🔲 ⒼⓇ 🔲 🔲 ⚠ Calor ⛏ WS
➡ From M5 junction 9, take A46 Evesham road to Teddington roundabout. At roundabout take B4077 to Stow-on-the-Wold, site 3 miles on right.

THIRSK North Yorkshire   11D2

York House Caravan Park
Balk, Thirsk YO7 2AQ
📞 01845-597495
Open 1 April-31 October
Size 12 acres, 80 touring pitches, 30 with electric hookup, 60 level pitches, 200 static caravans, 10 ℞, 22 WCs, 1 CWP
🔋 ✕ 🔲
➡ From Thirsk, travel E on A170 for 2 miles, turn S for 1 mile, left to site on left in ½ mile.

THRAPSTON Northamptonshire   8C3

Mill Marina Caravan Park
Midland Road, Thrapston NN14 4JR
📞 01832-732850
Open 1 April-31 October 🏕 🚐 🚉
Size 10 acres, 45 touring pitches, 20 with electric hookup, 45 level pitches, 6 static caravans, 4 ℞, 5 WCs, 1 CWP
£ car/tent £6.80-£7.80, car/caravan £8.80-£9.80, motorhome £7.80-£8.80, motorbike/tent £6.80-£7.80, children £1.50
Rental 🚐 £110-£160
🔲 🔌 🔲 🔲 🔲 Calor Gaz ⛏
Last arrival time: 9:00
➡ Take junction 13 on A14 and/or Thrapston exit from A605. Follow camping signs.

TILSHEAD Wiltshire   4A3

Brades Acre Caravan Site
Near Salisbury, Tilshead SP3 4RX
📞 01980-620402
🏕 🚐 🚉
Size 1½ acres, 26 touring pitches, 21 with electric hookup, 26 level pitches, 2 ℞, 4 WCs, 1 CWP
£ car/tent £6-£7, car/caravan £6-£7, motorhome £6-£7, motorbike/tent £6-£7, children £0.75
ⓒ Visa
🔋¼ ✕¼ 🅿¼ 🔲 🔌 🔲 🔲 Calor ⛏ WS
Last arrival time: 9:00
➡ 14 miles from Salisbury on A360 to Devizes.

YORK HOUSE
Caravan Park

At the foot of the Hambleton Hills in the heart of Herriot country York House provides an ideal centre for quiet family holidays or walking enthusiasts. Fourteen acres of land, a trout stream and play area further enhance the site's appeal.

BALK, THIRSK,
NORTH YORKSHIRE YO7 2AQ
Tel: 01845-597495

TINTAGEL Cornwall   2B3

Headland
Atlantic Road, Tintagel PL34 0DE
📞 01840-770239 **fax** 01840-770239
Open Easter-31 October 🏕 🚐 🚉

A quiet, family run park in King Arthur's Tintagel. Overlooking cliffs, close to coast path, beaches, shops, pubs etc. Ideal for walking & touring.

Size 5 acres, 60 touring pitches, 18 with electric hookup, 20 level pitches, 30 static caravans, 7 ℞, 11 WCs, 3 CWPs
£ car/tent £6.50-£9, car/caravan £7-£10, motorhome £6-£8, motorbike/tent £6.50-£9, children £0.50-£1
Rental 🚐 £110-£325
ⓒ MasterCard Visa
🔋 ✕¼ 🅿¼ 🔲 🔌 🔲 ⚠ Calor Gaz ♿ ⛏
Last arrival time: 9:00
➡ Signposted from B3263 through village to Headlands.

TIVERTON Devon   3D2

Minnows Camping & Caravan Park
Sampford Peverell, Tiverton EX16 7EN
☎ 01884-821770
Open March-January A ⊕ ⊞
Size 41 touring pitches, 31 with electric hookup, 41 level pitches, 4 ☂, 6 WCs, 1 CWP
£ car/tent £6-£9, car/caravan £6-£9, motorhome £6-£9, motorbike/tent £6-£9, children £1-£1.10
CC MasterCard Visa
⬥¼ ✗¼ ☂¼ ☖ ☐ ⊡ ⚠ Calor Gaz ⅙ ☆
Last arrival time: 8:00
➡ From M5 junction 27 onto A361 exit after 600 yards. Signed "Sampford Peverell", right at roundabout over bridge - site ahead

TORPOINT Cornwall   2C4

Whitsand Bay Holiday Park
Millbrook, Torpoint PL10 1JZ
☎ 01752-822597
Open April-end October A ⊕ ⊞

Whitsand Bay Holiday Park in Cornwall, yet only 6 miles from Plymouth. The only quality park on the Rame Peninsula. With stunning views from the terraced pitches overlooking the Tamar estuary and Plymouth against a backdrop of the moors. First class facilities in a first class family park.

Size 27 acres, 120 touring pitches, 68 with electric hookup, 68 level pitches, 90 static caravans, 12 ☂, 12 WCs, 2 CWPs
£ car/tent £5-£13, car/caravan £5-£13, motorhome £5-£13, motorbike/tent £5-£13
Rental ⊕ Chalet. from £60-£380
CC MasterCard Visa
⬥ ✗ ☂ ☖ ☐ ⊡ ⚐ ⚑ ☒ ⚞ ⚟ ☊ ⚠ ⊟ Calor Gaz ⅙ ☆ WS
Last arrival time: 12:00
➡ At Antony (A374), S onto B3247 for 1¼ miles. At T-junction, turn left for ¼ mile, then right onto Cliff Road. Site 2 miles.

TORQUAY Devon   3D3

Widdicombe Farm Caravan Park
Marldon, Torquay TQ3 1ST
☎ 01803-558325 **Fax** 01803-558325
Open Easter-5 November A ⊕ ⊞
Size 30 acres, 200 touring pitches, 170 with electric hookup, 170 level pitches, 3 static caravans, 18 ☂, 20 WCs, 3 CWPs
£ car/tent £6-£10, car/caravan £6-£10, motorhome £6-£10, motorbike/tent £6-£10
Rental ⊕ £90-£250 weekly.
⬥ ✗ ☂ ☖ ☐ ⊡ ☒ ⚠ ⊟ Calor Gaz ⅙ ☆ WS
➡ On A380 Torquay to Paignton/Brixham ring road.

TORRINGTON Devon   2C2

Greenways Valley
Great Torrington EX38 7EW
☎ 01805-622153 **Fax** 01805-622320
Open March-October A ⊕ ⊞
Size 8 acres, 8 touring pitches, 8 with electric hookup, 8 level pitches, 5 static caravans, 2 ☂, 5 WCs, 1 CWP
£ car/tent £4-£8, car/caravan £4-£8, motorhome £4-£8, motorbike/tent £4-£8, children £1-£3
Rental ⊕ Chalet. £90-£280 weekly.
CC MasterCard Visa
⬥ ☖ ☐ ⊡ ☒ ⚠ Calor Gaz ☆
➡ B3227 towards South Moulton and turn right at Borough Road. Take third left onto Cadwell Lane. Site is ½ mile on the right.

TRURO Cornwall — 2B4

Camping & Caravanning Club Site
Tretheake Manor, Veryan, Truro TR2 5PP
☎ 01872-501658
Open late March-late September ▲ 🚐 🚙
Size 120 touring pitches, 75 with electric hookup, 8 ⓘ, 20 WCs
£ car/tent £5.20-£7.80, car/caravan £5.20-£7.80, motorhome £5.20-£7.80, motorbike/tent £5.20-£7.80, children £1.50
ⓒ MasterCard Visa
🏊 🗑 🛒 ⚠ ★
Last arrival time: 11:00
➡ From A390 follow A3078 through Tregony. At filling station turn right towards Portloe, site is 2½ miles.

Carnon Downs Caravan & Camping Park
Carnon Downs, Truro TR3 6JJ
☎ 01872-862283 Fax 01872-862800
Open 1 April-31 October ▲ 🚐 🚙
Size 14 acres, 150 touring pitches, 100 with electric hookup, 150 level pitches, 8 ⓘ, 17 WCs, 2 CWPs
£ car/tent £6.50-£10.50, car/caravan £6.50-£10.50, motorhome £6.50-£10.50, motorbike/tent £6.50-£10.50, children £1.50
ⓒ MasterCard Visa
🏊 🗑 🛒 🚿 📺 Calor Gaz ★ WS
➡ On A39 2½ miles W of Truro. Left side of Truro to Falmouth road.

Cosawes Caravan Park
Truro, Perranarworthal TR3 7QS
☎ 01872-863724 Fax 01872-870268
▲ 🚐 🚙
Size 100 acres, 40 touring pitches, 24 with electric hookup, 100 static caravans, 4 ⓘ, 6 WCs, 1 CWP
£ car/tent £6-£7, car/caravan £7-£7.50, motorhome £6.50, motorbike/tent £6
Rental 🚐 £60
🏊¼ 🗑 🛒 🚿 🖨 Calor Gaz ♿ ★ WS
➡ 6 miles W of Truro on A39.

Leverton Place Caravan & Camping Park
Green Bottom, Truro TR4 8QW
☎ 01872-560462 Fax 01872-560668
▲ 🚐 🚙

Explore Cornwall from this family run park. Excellent, modern, clean toilet block, heated in winter. Small enclosure separated by sheltering hedges. Heated swimming pool.

Size 10 acres, 107 touring pitches, 100 with electric hookup, 97 level pitches, 15 static caravans, 25 ⓘ, 38 WCs, 2 CWPs
£ car/tent £7.50-£16.50, car/caravan £7.50-£16.50, motorhome £7.50-£16.50, motorbike/tent £15.50, children £1.10-£1.20
Rental 🚐 Chalet. £100-£370
ⓒ MasterCard Visa
🏊 ✕ 🍴 🛒 🚿 📶 GR 🔍 📺 ⚠ 🚰 Calor Gaz ♿ ★ WS
Last arrival time: 10:00
➡ 3 miles W of Truro, from A30 take A390 to Truro. At first roundabout take the road to Chacewater, right at mini-roundabout. Leverton Place is on right.

Liskey Touring Park
Greenbottom, Truro TR4 8QN
☎ 01872-560274 Fax 01872-560274
Open 1 April-20 September ▲ 🚐 🚙

Quiet family park appealing to the discerning. Excellent touring centre. Spotlessly clean facilities including bathrooms, ladies cubicles, serviced pitches, hardstandings, adventure playground, playbarn, pub 600 yds.

Size 8 acres, 65 touring pitches, 46 with electric hookup, 44 level pitches, 8 ⓘ, 9 WCs, 1 CWP
£ car/tent £6-£9.50, car/caravan £6-£9.50, motorhome £6-£9.50, motorbike/tent £6-£9.50, children £1.20-£1.50
🏊¼ ✕¼ 🍴¼ 🗑 🛒 🚿 🔍 📺 ⚠ Calor Gaz ★ WS
Last arrival time: 9:00
➡ From A30 Bodmin-Redruth road turn left onto A390 towards Truro. In 2 miles turn right at the roundabout and then immediately right. At mini-roundabout the site is on right in 600 yards.

Hints & Tips
Tiredness can kill. If you are planning a long journey make sure you plan some breaks.

Ringwell Valley Holiday Park

Bissoe Road, Carnon Downs, Truro TR3 6LQ

☎ 01872-862194 Fax 01872-864343

Open April-October ⚑ ⚐ ⚐

Situated between Truro and Falmouth. Relax on a small picturesque family park overlooking country views. New luxury caravans. Bar, restaurant and swimming pool. All the facilities without the crowds.

Size 12 acres, 35 touring pitches, 25 with electric hookup, 25 level pitches, 38 static caravans, 7 ℞, 17 WCs, 1 CWP

£ car/tent £7-£11, car/caravan £7-£11, motorhome £6-£10, motorbike/tent £7-£11

Rental ⚐ £100-£450

⊂⊂ MasterCard Visa

⚐ ✕ ⚐ ⚐ ⚐ ⚐ ⚐ ⚐ ⚐ ⚐ ⚐ Calor Gaz ⚐ WS

Last arrival time: 9:30

➡ From Truro take A39 Falmouth road to roundabout in 2 miles. Follow signs to Carnon Downs, then turn right into Bissoe Road to site ¾ mile on right.

Summer Valley Touring Park

Shortlanesend, Truro TR4 9DW

☎ 01872-277878

Open 1 April-31 October ⚑ ⚐ ⚐

An award-winning park, centrally located for Cornwall's beaches, gardens and historic houses. Ideal for visiting in the spring for the gardens, and in the autumn for quieter moments.

Size 3 acres, 60 touring pitches, 26 with electric hookup, 30 level pitches, 6 ℞, 9 WCs, 1 CWP

£ car/tent £6-£8, car/caravan £6-£8, motorhome £6-£8, motorbike/tent £6-£8, children £0.75

⚐ ✕¼ ⚐¼ ⚐ ⚐ ⚐ ⚐ Calor Gaz ⚐

Last arrival time: 9:00

➡ From A30 turn left onto B3284 Truro road and site is 1½ miles. Or take B3284 from Truro, site is 2½ miles.

TUXFORD Nottinghamshire   8B1

Greenacres Touring Park

Lincoln Road, Tuxford NG22 0JN

☎ 01777 870264 Fax 01777 872512

Open 15 March-31 October ⚑ ⚐ ⚐

Size 4 acres, 69 touring pitches, 60 with electric hookup, 60 level pitches, 19 static caravans, 4 ℞, 11 WCs, 1 CWP

£ car/tent £6.75, car/caravan £6.75, motorhome £6.75, motorbike/tent £6.75, children £0.50

Rental ⚐ £75-£150

⚐ ⚐¼ ✕¼ ⚐¼ ⚐ ⚐ ⚐ ⚐ Calor Gaz ⚐ ⚐ WS

➡ From A1 follow signs. Site is on A6075, 300 yards on left after Fountain pub.

ULLSWATER Cumbria   10B2

Cove Caravan & Camping Park

Watermillock, Penrith CA11 0LS

☎ 017684-86549

Open 1 March-31 October ⚑ ⚐ ⚐

Size 5 acres, 50 touring pitches, 17 with electric hookup, 25 level pitches, 39 static caravans, 4 ℞, 8 WCs, 1 CWP

£ car/tent £6.40-£6.80, car/caravan £8-£8.50, motorhome £6.40-£6.80, motorbike/tent £6.40-£6.80

Rental ⚐ £190-£225

⚐¼ ⚐ ⚐ ⚐ ⚐ Calor Gaz ⚐ ⚐

➡ From M6 junction 40 take A66 to Keswick and at next roundabout take A592 to Ullswater. At 'T' junction turn right. At Brackenrigs Inn turn right and park is 1½ miles on left.

Hillcroft Park

Pooley Bridge, Ullswater CA10 2LT
☎ 01768-486363 Fax 01768-486010
Open 6 March-14 November ▲ ⏴ ⛺
Size 21 acres, 25 touring pitches, 6 with electric
hookup, 6 level pitches, 200 static caravans, 20 ⬙, 36
WCs, 3 CWPs
£ car/tent £8-£11, car/caravan £11, motorhome £8-
£11, motorbike/tent £8-£11, children £1.50
⚡ ✕¼ ☕¼ ◙ ◖ ☐ ⚠ Calor Gaz 㫪 ㅐ
➔ From M6 junction 40 take A66 towards Keswick,
then A592 to Ullswater. At the head of the lake turn
left, go through Pooley Bridge and bear right at
church. Head straight through crossroads to site on left.

Park Foot Caravan & Camping Park

Howtown Road, Pooley Bridge, Ullswater CA10 2NA
☎ 01768-486309 Fax 01768-486041
Open 15 March-31 October ▲ ⏴ ⛺

*A family park set in the magnificent Lakeland Fells.
With access to Lake Ullswater for boat launching and
car parking. Children's playground, graded excellent
by the Tourist Board.*

Size 20 acres, 110 touring pitches, 70 with electric
hookup, 200 level pitches, 129 static caravans, 24 ⬙,
50 WCs, 2 CWPs
£ car/tent £7-£10.50, car/caravan £12-£15,
motorhome £7-£10.50, motorbike/tent £7-£10.50,
children £1
Rental Houses/log cabins - £45 night, £180-£480 week.
⚡ ✕ ☕ ◙ ◖ ☐ ⬙ ☒ ▯ GR ◙ ☐ TV ⚠ ⬚ Calor Gaz 㫪 ㅐ
Last arrival time: 11:00
➔ From M6 junction 40 take A66 Keswick road. Take
A592 to Ullswater. At 'T' junction turn left. At Pooley
Bridge turn right and right again at crossroads. Site is
1 mile down Howtown road on left.

Quiet Site

Watermillock, Ullswater CA11 0LS
☎ 01768-486337 Fax 01768-486610
Open 1 March-14 November ▲ ⏴ ⛺
Size 6 acres, 60 touring pitches, 47 with electric
hookup, 53 level pitches, 23 static caravans, 8 ⬙, 15
WCs, 1 CWP
£ car/tent £8-£10, car/caravan £9-£11, motorhome £8-
£10, motorbike/tent £7-£9, children £1
Rental ▲ ⏴
⚡ ◖ ☐ GR ◙ ☐ TV ⚠ ⬚ Calor Gaz ㅐ WS
Last arrival time: 9:00
➔ From M6 junction 40 take A66 to Keswick. After ¾

mile turn left onto A592 (signed Ullswater). After 4
miles turn right at T-junction. After 1½ miles turn
right at Bracherigg Hotel. Site on right after 1½ miles

Ullswater Caravan Camping Site

Watermillock, Ullswater CA11 0LR
☎ 01768-486666 Fax 01768-486095
Open 1 March-14 November ▲ ⏴ ⛺

*Situated in scenic countryside with its own lake
access and ½ mile from Lake Ullswater. Ideal for
touring the Lake District.*

Size 14 acres, 40 touring pitches, 40 with electric
hookup, 40 level pitches, 55 static caravans, 20 ⬙, 35
WCs, 2 CWPs
£ car/tent £9, car/caravan £10, motorhome £9,
motorbike/tent £8, children £1
Rental ⏴ Chalet. £150-£350
⚡ ☕ ◙ ◖ ☐ GR TV ⚠ ⬚ Calor Gaz 㫪 ㅐ
Last arrival time: 9:00
➔ From M6 junction 40 take A592 to Ullswater, turn
right at telephone kiosk, signposted Longthwaite and
Watermillock church.

Waterfoot Caravan Park

Pooley Bridge, Ullswater CA11 0JF
☎ 01768-486302
Open March-October ⏴ ⛺

*22 acres with level and sloping pitches. Sheltered
quiet country park. Touring vans only. 5 mins walk
to lake, good access to Lakeland Fells for walking.*

Size 22 acres, 57 touring pitches, 57 with electric
hookup, 36 level pitches, 123 static caravans, 6 ⬙, 10
WCs, 1 CWP
£ car/caravan £11.50-£13, motorhome £11.50-£13
⚡ ☕ ◙ ◖ ☐ ⚠ ⬚ Calor Gaz 㫪 ㅐ
Last arrival time: dusk
➔ From jn 40 of M6 take A66 for 1 mile and then
A592 to Ullswater. Park is on right 6 miles from M6.

UMBERLEIGH Devon   2C2

Camping & Caravanning Club Site

Over Weir, Umberleigh EX37 9DU

📞 01769-560009

Open late March-early November ▲ ⊞ ⊞
Size 60 touring pitches, 33 with electric hookup, 6
🕭, 9 WCs, 1 CWP
£ car/tent £5.20-£7.80, car/caravan £5.20-£7.80,
motorhome £5.20-£7.80, motorbike/tent £5.20-£7.80,
children £1.50
⊂⊂ MasterCard Visa
🕭 📵 GR ⚠ ☂
Last arrival time: 11:00
➡ S from Barnstaple on A377. Turn right at
Umberleigh sign. Turn right again and follow club
sign.

WADEBRIDGE Cornwall   2B3

Dinham Farm Caravan & Camping Park

St Minver, Wadebridge PL27 6RH

📞 01208-812878

Open April-October ▲ ⊞ ⊞

*Lovely, secluded, family park overlooking the River
Camel, surrounded by trees and shrubs, offering
super pitch hookups and heated pool. Near Rock,
Polzeath and Daymer Bay.*

Size 2½ acres, 40 touring pitches, 15 with electric
hookup, 20 level pitches, 20 static caravans, 4 🕭, 12
WCs, 1 CWP
£ car/tent £6, car/caravan £6, motorhome £5-£6,
motorbike/tent £6, children £0.75-£1
Rental ⊞
📵 GR ⚠ Calor Gaz ☂
➡ From Wadebridge travel on B3314 for 3 miles. Site
on left.

Gunvenna Touring Caravan & Camping Park

St Minver, Polzeath

📞 01208-862405

Open Easter-November

*Gunvenna Camping and Caravanning Park. Open
Easter - November. 10 acres. 75 pitches. Electric hook-
ups. Beautiful views. Indoor heated pool. From £7.50-
£12 per pitch.*

Size 10 acres, 200 touring pitches, 24 with electric
hookup, 75 level pitches, 6 🕭, 20 WCs, 3 CWPs
⚄ ✕ ⊡ 📵 GR ⚠ ⊞ Calor
➡ From Wadebridge, travel N on B3314 for 4½ miles
to site on right.

Laurels

Whitecross, Wadebridge PL27 7JQ

📞 01208-813341

Open March (Easter) ▲ ⊞ ⊞

*Designated area of outstanding natural beauty.
Views to Camel Estuary. Near to Bodmin Moor,
Padstow and beautiful beaches. Ideal for walking,
cycling and touring area. New owners.*

Size 3 acres, 30 touring pitches, 20 with electric
hookup, 30 level pitches, 4 🕭, 8 WCs, 1 CWP
£ car/tent £7, car/caravan £7, motorhome £7,
motorbike/tent £7, children £0.50
⚄¼ ✕¼ ⊞¼ 📵 GR ⚠ ♿ ☂ WS
Last arrival time: 10:00
➡ ½ mile S of Whitecross at A39/A389 junction.

Little Bodieve Holiday Park

Bodieve, Wadebridge PL27 6EG

📞 01208-812323

Open 1 April-31 October ▲ ⊞ ⊞
Size 22 acres, 195 touring pitches, 60 with electric
hookup, 195 level pitches, 76 static caravans, 24 🕭,
20 WCs, 5 CWPs

£ car/tent £6-£9, car/caravan £6-£9, motorhome £6-£9, motorbike/tent £6-£9, children £1.50-£2.20
Rental ⚑ £100-£410
CC MasterCard Visa
⚒ ✗ ⛴ ▣ ◧ GR ⚒ ⊟ Calor Gaz ⚤ ⚲ WS
Last arrival time: 8:00
➜ 1 mile N of Wadebridge, just off A39. Take B3314 toward Rock and Port Isaac.

Trewince Holiday Park
St Issey, Wadebridge PL27 7RL
📞 **01280-812830**
Open 17 April-31 October
Size 125 touring pitches, 42 with electric hookup, 22 static caravans, 11 ☗, 12 WCs, 3 CWPs
CC Visa
⚒ ◧ Calor Gaz WS
➜ Take A39 to Wadebridge, then A389 to Padstow. The site is signposted and is on left.

Nostell Priory Holiday Park
Nostell, Wakefield WF4 1QD
📞 **01924-863938 Fax 01924-862226**
Open April-September ▲ ⚑ ☗
Size 35 acres, 60 touring pitches, 60 with electric hookup, 60 level pitches, 80 static caravans, 8 ☗, 12 WCs, 1 CWP
£ car/tent £8-£9, car/caravan £8-£9, motorhome £8-£9, children £0.50
▣ ▣ ⊟ ⚒ Calor Gaz ⚲ WS
Last arrival time: 9:00
➜ From A38 Wakefield to Doncaster road turn left at Foulby.

Bridge Villa International C & C Site
Crowmarsh Gifford, Wallingford OX10 8HB
📞 **01491-836860 Fax 01491-839103**
Open 1 February-31 December ▲ ⚑ ☗
Size 4 acres, 111 touring pitches, 111 with electric hookup
£ car/tent £6, car/caravan £6, motorhome £6, motorbike/tent £5, children £0.50
⚒ ⚒¼ ✗¼ ⛴¼ ⚒ ⊟ Calor Gaz ⚤ ⚲ WS
➜ Site located off A4130.

Riverside Park
Crowmarsh, Wallingford OX10 8EB
📞 **01491-835232**
Open 1 May-30 September ▲ ⚑ ☗
Size 1 acre, 28 touring pitches, 28 level pitches, 6 ☗, 6 WCs
£ car/tent £7-£9, car/caravan £7-£9, motorhome £7-£9, motorbike/tent £7-£9, children £0.25
⚒¼ ✗¼ ⛴ ⚒ ⊟ ▣ ▣ Gaz ⚤
Last arrival time: 8:00
➜ A34 to Didcot, then follow sign to Wallingford. Go over main road bridge, then take first left.

Camping & Caravanning Club Site
Theobalds Park, Bulls Cross Ride, Waltham Abbey
📞 **01992-620604**
Open late March-early November ▲ ⚑ ☗
Size 14 acres, 150 touring pitches, 12 with electric hookup, 4 ☗, 6 WCs, 1 CWP
£ car/tent £4.60-£6.80, car/caravan £4.60-£6.80, motorhome £4.60-£6.80, motorbike/tent £4.60-£6.80, children £1.40
CC MasterCard Visa
▣ GR ⚒ ⚲ WS
➜ Leave M25 (jn 25), get in right hand lane, go under motorway, then right at traffic lights. Follow signs for Crews Hill, then Bulls Cross to site on right.

Birchwood Tourist Park
Bere Road, Coldharbour, Wareham BH20 7PA
📞 **01929-554763**
Open March-October ▲ ⚑ ☗
Size 46 acres, 175 touring pitches, 118 with electric hookup, 175 level pitches, 14 ☗, 20 WCs, 2 CWPs
£ car/tent £6, car/caravan £6, motorhome £6, motorbike/tent £6, children £0.50-£1
CC MasterCard Visa
⚒ ⛴ ▣ ⚒ ⊟ ▣ ▣ ▣ ▣ GR ▣ ⚒ Calor Gaz ⚤ ⚲
Last arrival time: 10:00
➜ From A35 E of Bere Regis follow signs to Wareham. Second touring park on left.

Lookout Holiday Park

Stoborough, Wareham BH20 5AZ

☎ **01929-552546 Fax 01929-552546**

Open February-November ▲ 🚐 🚏

A quiet, family park, ideally situated for exploring the Purbecks. Touring pitches available on hardstandings or grass. Fully equipped caravans with colour TV for hire.

Size 15 acres, 150 touring pitches, 107 with electric hookup, 150 level pitches, 90 static caravans, 10 ⚲, 17 WCs, 2 CWPs

£ car/tent £9-£11, car/caravan £9-£11, motorhome £9-£11, motorbike/tent £9-£11

Rental 🚐 £95-£350

℄ MasterCard Visa

🛠 🚿 ⊡ ℄ ⎙ GR ◙ ⚠ Calor Gaz WS

Last arrival time: 10:00

➜ From centre of Wareham proceed S to Swanage. Cross over River Frome, pass through village of Stoborough. Park on left of main road.

Manor Farm Caravan Park

East Stoke, Wareham BH20 6AW

☎ **01929-462870**

Open April-September ▲ 🚐 🚏

Size 2½ acres, 40 touring pitches, 30 with electric hookup, 40 level pitches, 4 ⚲, 8 WCs, 1 CWP

£ car/tent £6.50-£8.50, car/caravan £6.50-£8.50, motorhome £6.50-£8.50, motorbike/tent £6.50-£8.50

🛠 ℄ ⊡ ⚠ Calor Gaz 🐕

Last arrival time: 10:00

➜ Off A352 between Wareham and Wool. Turn off at redundant church in East Stoke.

WARRINGTON Cheshire 7E1

Hollybank Caravan Park

Warburton Bridge Road, Rixton, Warrington WA3 6HU

☎ **0161-775 2842**

Open all year ▲ 🚐 🚏

Size 9 acres, 75 touring pitches, 60 with electric hookup, 60 level pitches, 7 ⚲, 10 WCs, 2 CWPs

£ car/tent £8.50-£10, car/caravan £9.50-£11, motorhome £9.50-£11, motorbike/tent £8.50-£10, children £1

🛠 🛠¼ ✗¼ 🍴¼ ⊡ ℄ ⊡ GR ◙ ⚠ Calor Gaz ♿ 🐕 WS

Last arrival time: 9:00

➜ 2 miles E of M6 junction 21 on A57 (Irlam). Turn right at lights into Warburton Bridge Road and site is on left.

WASHINGTON West Sussex 4C4

Washington Caravan and Camping Park

London Road, Washington RH20 4AJ

☎ **01903-892869 Fax 01903-893252**

Open all year ▲ 🚐 🚏

Size 4½ acres, 100 touring pitches, 20 with electric hookup, 4 ⚲, 10 WCs, 1 CWP

£ car/tent £8.50, car/caravan £7.50, motorhome £7.50, motorbike/tent £8.50, children £3

℄ MasterCard Visa

🛠 🛠¼ ✗¼ ⊡ ℄ Calor Gaz ♿ 🐕

➜ N of Washington on A283. E of roundabout with A24, signposted South Downs Way. Site is below Chanctonbury Ring.

WATCHET Somerset 3D2

Warren Bay Caravan & Camping Park

Watchet TA23 0JR

☎ **01984-631460 Fax 01984-633999**

▲ 🚐 🚏

Size 22 acres, 180 touring pitches, 30 with electric hookup, 15 level pitches, 155 static caravans, 12 ⚲, 27 WCs, 2 CWPs

£ car/tent £3.50-£4, car/caravan £3.50-£6, motorhome £3.50-£4.50, motorbike/tent £4, children £1

Rental 🚐 £129-£205

℄ MasterCard Visa

🛠 ⊡ ℄ ⊡ ⑤ Calor Gaz 🐕 WS

➜ From M5 junction 23 take A39 for 17 miles. Then B3191 at Watchet and follow sign for Blue Anchor.

WELLS Somerset 3E2

Homestead Park

Wookey Hole, Wells BA5 1BW

☎ **01749-673022**

Open 1 April-31 October ▲ 🚐 🚏

Size 4½ acres, 50 touring pitches, 6 with electric hookup, 50 level pitches, 2 ⚲, 14 WCs, 1 CWP

£ car/tent £8.80, car/caravan £8.60, motorhome £8, motorbike/tent £7, children £1-£2

🛠¼ ✗¼ 🍴¼ ℄ ⊡ Calor Gaz 🐕

➜ Leave Wells by A371 towards Cheddar. Turn right for Wookey Hole. Site 1¼ miles on left in village.

Mendip Heights Caravan & Camping Park

Priddy, Wells BA5 3BP

☎ **01749-870241 Fax 01749-870241**

Open 1 March-15 November ▲ 🚐 🚏

Size 4¼ acres, 90 touring pitches, 21 with electric hookup, 40 level pitches, 4 ⚲, 11 WCs, 1 CWP

£ car/tent £6.40-£7, car/caravan £6.40-£7, motorhome £6.40-£7, motorbike/tent £6.40-£7, children £1.50

🛠 ✗¼ ⊡ ℄ ⊡ ◙ ⚠ Calor Gaz 🐕 WS

Last arrival time: 10:30
➜ From Wells take A39 towards Bristol for 3 miles. Turn left at Green Ore traffic lights onto B3135 for 5 miles, then turn left at camp site sign.

WEM Shropshire   7D2

Lower Lacon Caravan Park
Lerdene, Crabtree Lane, Wemsbrook Road, Wem SY4 5RP
📞 01939-232376 Fax 01939-233606
Open all year Ⓐ ⊕ ⊞
Size 48 acres, 270 touring pitches, 120 with electric hookup, 270 level pitches, 50 static caravans, 12 ⚲, 25 WCs, 3 CWPs
£ car/tent £9-£9.50, car/caravan £9-£9.50, motorhome £9-£9.50, motorbike/tent £9-£9.50, children £0.75
Rental ⊕ holiday homes £80-£260
CC MasterCard Visa
⚑ ✗ ➾ ⊡ � ⊟ 🔲 GR TV ⋀ 🔌 Calor Gaz ᬭ ★ WS
Last arrival time: 24 hrs
➜ From A49 take B506 to Wem. Go over level crossing onto B5065 Market Drayton road. Park is 1 mile on left.

WEST WITTERING West Sussex   4C4

Scotts Farm Camping Site
West Wittering PO20 8ED
📞 01243-671720 Fax 01243-513669
Open March-October Ⓐ ⊕ ⊞

Spacious family run site set in 30 acres of level grassland. Village and beach within easy walking distance, lovely country walks, play area, super pitches available.

Size 25 acres, 330 touring pitches, 130 with electric hookup, 330 level pitches, 33 ⚲, 48 WCs, 4 CWPs
£ car/tent £8-£9, car/caravan £8-£9, motorhome £8-£9, motorbike/tent £8-£9
⚑¼ ✗¼ ➾¼ ⊡ � ⊟ ⋀ Calor Gaz ᬭ ★
Last arrival time: 11:30
➜ A286 from A27 to Chichester. After 4 miles turn left to East Wittering/Bracklesham Bay just past self service station on right. Carry on for 1 mile, turn right past Lively Lady pub. Go past East Wittering village and site on right.

WESTON-SUPER-MARE Somerset   3E1

Airport View Caravan Park
Moor Lane, Worle, Weston-super-Mare BS24 7LA
📞 01934-622168 Fax 01934-628245
Open 1 March-31 October Ⓐ ⊕ ⊞
Size 10 acres, 200 touring pitches, 40 static caravans, 10 ⚲, 15 WCs, 1 CWP
£ car/tent £5-£7.50, car/caravan £5-£7.50, motorhome £5-£7.50, children £0.50
Rental ⊕
CC MasterCard Visa
✗ ➾ ⊡ � GR ⋀ 🔌 Calor Gaz ᬭ ★ WS
Last arrival time: 9:00
➜ (A371) turn into Moor Lane. Site 100 yards.

Country View Caravan & Touring Park
Sand Road, Sand Bay, Weston-super-Mare BS22 9UJ
📞 01934-627595 Fax 01934-627595
Open March-October Ⓐ ⊕ ⊞
Size 120 touring pitches, 82 with electric hookup, 120 level pitches, 65 static caravans, 8 ⚲, 12 WCs, 1 CWP
£ car/tent £4-£12, car/caravan £6.50-£12, motorhome £6.50-£12, motorbike/tent £4-£12
Rental ⊕ £90-£295
CC MasterCard Visa
⚑ ✗¼ ➾¼ ⊡ � 🔲 GR ⋀ 🔌 Calor Gaz ᬭ ★ WS
Last arrival time: 10:00
➜ From M5 (jn 21) follow signs to Weston-super-Mare, and then 100 yards bear left to Kewstoke/Sand Bay. Turn right at Homebase DIY store and go straight over three roundabouts. Turn right into Sand Road and site on right.

Dulhorn Farm Camping Site

Weston Road, Lympsham, Weston-super-Mare BS24 0JQ

☎ 01943-750298 Fax 01934-750913

Open March-October ▲ 🚐 🚍

Size 2 acres, 42 touring pitches, 28 with electric hookup, 42 level pitches, 3 static caravans, 2 ℞, 5 WCs, 1 CWP

£ car/tent £4.50-£7, car/caravan £4.50-£7, motorhome £4.50-£7, motorbike/tent £4.50-£7

Rental 🚐 Chalet. £80-£230

✗¼ 🍴¼ 🄰 Calor Gaz 🐕 WS

Last arrival time: 8:00

➡ From A38 take A370 to Weston-super-Mare. Site is ¼ mile on left.

Purn International Holiday Park

Bridgwater Road (A370), Bleadon, Weston-super-Mare BS24 0AN

☎ 01934-812342 Fax 01934-812342

Open 1 March-7 November ▲ 🚐 🚍

Size 11 acres, 60 touring pitches, 40 with electric hookup, 60 level pitches, 110 static caravans, 6 ℞, 12 WCs, 2 CWPs

£ car/tent £5.50-£9.50, car/caravan £6.50-£9.50, motorhome £6-£9, motorbike/tent £5-£8

Rental 🚐 £115-£285

🛒 ✗ 🍴 🎮 🄲 🈁 📺 🖻 GR 🄰 🔌 Calor Gaz ♿ 🐕 WS

Last arrival time: 12:00

➡ From junction 21 take signs for Western & Hospital. Turn left at hospital roundabout onto A370. Site 1 mile on right after Anchor Inn pub.

West End Farm Touring Park

Locking, Weston-super-Mare BS24 8RH

☎ 01934-822529

Open all year

Size 10 acres, 75 touring pitches, 75 with electric hookup, 75 level pitches, 4 ℞, 15 WCs, 1 CWP

🛒 🍴 🄲 ♿

➡ 2½ miles W of junction 21 of M5, or 2 miles E of Weston-super-Mare on A370, turn S by Heron Hotel on A371 for 1 mile, turn right, follow signs. Or follow signs to International Helicopter Museum. Park is 20 yards away.

Weston Gateway Tourist Park

West Wick, Weston-super-Mare BS24 7TF

☎ 01934-510344

Open March-November ▲ 🚐 🚍

Amenities on this level, grassy site include a club with bar, restaurant and TV lounge, and children's play area. Swimming pool three miles. Families and couples only.

Size 15 acres, 180 touring pitches, 105 with electric hookup, 180 level pitches, 14 ℞, 59 WCs, 1 CWP

£ car/tent £4.50-£9, car/caravan £4.50-£9, motorhome £4.50-£9, motorbike/tent £4.50-£9

🛒 🍴 🄲 🈁 📺 🄰 🔌 Calor Gaz ♿ 🐕 WS

Last arrival time: 11:30

➡ Leave M5 junction 21 to Weston-super-Mare. Branch left for West Wick. Park is on right after 500 yards.

Bagwell Farm Touring Park

Chickerell, Weymouth DT3 4EA

☎ 01305-782575

Open March-October ▲ 🚐 🚍

Size 14 acres, 320 touring pitches, 174 with electric hookup, 320 level pitches, 12 ℞, 38 WCs, 1 CWP

£ car/tent £3.50-£8.50, car/caravan £5.50-£9.50, motorhome £5.50-£9.50, motorbike/tent £3.50-£6.75

🛒 ✗¼ 🍴 🄲 🈁 GR 🄰 Calor Gaz ♿ WS

Last arrival time: 11:00

➡ 4 miles W of Weymouth on B3157, 500 yards past Victoria Inn.

East Fleet Farm Touring Park

Chickerell, Weymouth DT3 4DW

☎ 01305-785768

Open 15 March-15 January 🛆 ⛺ ⛺

Peaceful and spacious park on the shores of the Fleet overlooking Chesil Bank and the sea. In an area of outstanding natural beauty.

Size 20 acres, 150 touring pitches, 80 with electric hookup, 150 level pitches, 17 ⛁, 42 WCs, 2 CWPs
£ car/tent £4.50-£9.50, car/caravan £4.50-£9.50, motorhome £4.50-£9.50, motorbike/tent £4.50-£9.50, children £0.25

🖳 🖳¼ 🗇 🔌 🗇 🗛 Calor Gaz 🕭 🛨
➜ Off B3157, left at Chickerell TA camp.

Pebble Bank Caravan Park

Camp Road, Wyke Regis, Weymouth DT4 9HF

☎ 01305-774844 **Fax** 01305-774844

Open 1 April-early October 🛆 ⛺ ⛺

Quiet family park in a picturesque situation close to Weymouth centre, with superb views.

Size 8 acres, 45 touring pitches, 40 with electric hookup, 40 level pitches, 95 static caravans, 5 ⛁, 10 WCs, 1 CWP
£ car/tent £5-£9, car/caravan £6-£12, motorhome £5-£9, motorbike/tent £5-£9, children £1
Rental ⛺ £125-£325

🖳¼ ✗¼ 🗑¼ 🗇 🔌 🗇 🗛 🗄 Calor Gaz 🛨
Last arrival time: 10:00
➜ From harbour roundabout at Weymouth continue up hill to mini roundabout opposite Rodwell pub. Turn right onto Wyke Road. Camp Road is 1 mile further on at apex of sharp right hand bend at bottom of hill.

WHATSTANDWELL Derbyshire 7F1

Merebrook Caravan Park

Matlock Road, Whatstandwell DE4 5HH

☎ 01773-852154

Open all year 🛆 ⛺ ⛺

Size 11 acres, 50 touring pitches, 28 with electric hookup, 50 level pitches, 116 static caravans, 12 ⛁, 24 WCs, 4 CWPs
£ car/tent £7, car/caravan £7, motorhome £7-£8, motorbike/tent £1-£3

🗇 🔌 🗇 🗒 Calor Gaz 🕭 🛨
Last arrival time: 11:00
➜ Entrance on A6 600 yards from river bridge at Whatstandwell. 15 miles from Derby and 5 miles from Matlock.

WHITBY North Yorkshire 11E2

Hollins Farm

Glaisdale, Whitby YO21 2PZ

☎ 01947-897516

Open Easter 🛆

Size 1 acre, 2 ⛁, 2 WCs
£ car/tent £3, motorbike/tent £3, children £0.75

🗇 🛨
➜ From A171 take road to Glaisdale for 4 miles. In Glaisdale, opposite phone box, road leads up round church. Come up that road for 1½ miles, to site on left, 100 yards down a tarmac drive.

Middlewood Farm Holiday Park

Fylingthorpe, Robin Hood's Bay, Whitby YO22 4UF

☎ 01947-880414 **Fax** 01947-880414

Open Easter-31 October 🛆 ⛺ ⛺

Size 6 acres, 20 touring pitches, 20 with electric hookup, 120 level pitches, 30 static caravans, 8 ⛁, 18 WCs, 1 CWP
£ car/tent £6.50-£8.50, car/caravan £6.50-£8.50, motorhome £6.50-£7.50, motorbike/tent £6.50-£7.50, children £0.50
Rental ⛺

🖳¼ ✗¼ 🗑¼ 🗇 🔌 🗇 🗛 Calor Gaz 🛨
Last arrival time: 11:00
➜ 2½ miles S of Whitby on A171 turn E on B1447. After 1½ miles turn right to Fylingthorpe. At village crossroads continue straight ahead to park on Middlewood Lane.

Hints & Tips

Hill starts need more throttle than normal to get going and you will need delicate clutch control to avoid stalling

Northcliffe Holiday Park

High Hawsker, Whitby YO22 4LL

☎ 01947-880477 Fax 01947-880972

Open 15 March-31 October ⚠ 🚐 🚎

A secluded family park situated on the beautiful, unspoilt Heritage Coast, between Whitby and Robin Hood's Bay, with panoramic sea views.

Size 26 acres, 30 touring pitches, 30 with electric hookup, 16 level pitches, 161 static caravans, 6 🚿, 10 WCs, 1 CWP

£ car/tent £6-£10, car/caravan £6-£10, motorhome £6-£10, motorbike/tent £4-£8

Rental 🚐

ℂℂ MasterCard Visa

🛒 🛱 🗑 🔌 GR ⚠ Calor Gaz &

Last arrival time: 9:00

➡ 3 miles S of Whitby on the A171 turn left onto B1447 (High Hawkser-Robin Hoods Bay). Through village and at top of hill turn left into a private lane for ½ mile.

Partridge Nest Farm

Eskdaleside, Sleights, Whitby YO22 5ES

☎ 01947-810450 Fax 01947-811413

Open March-October

Size 40 acres, 6 with electric hookup, 6 static caravans, 6 🚿, 6 WCs

Rental 🚐 £135-£250 pw, £19-£35 pn

🎣 Calor 🐕

Last arrival time: 8:00

➡ 1 mile from Sleights on Grosmont Road.

Sandfield House Farm Caravan Park

Sandsend Road, Whitby YO21 3SR

☎ 01947-602660

Open March-October 🚐 🚎

Quiet, clean park set in beautiful undulating countryside in National Park. Quarter of a mile from long sandy beach. One mile to Whitby centre. Lovely walks and sea views.

Size 12 acres, 50 with electric hookup, 50 level pitches, 16 🚿, 22 WCs, 1 CWP

£ car/caravan £6.50-£8.50, motorhome £6.50-£8.50

🛒¼ ✗¼ 🛱¼ 🗑 🔌 🔲 Calor Gaz 🐕

Last arrival time: 9:00

➡ 1 mile N of Whitby on A174 coast road to Sandsend, opposite golf course.

York House Caravan Park

High Hawsker, Whitby YO22 4LW

☎ 01947-880354

Open 21 March-31 October ⚠ 🚐 🚎

Size 4 acres, 59 touring pitches, 59 with electric hookup, 20 level pitches, 41 static caravans, 8 🚿, 13 WCs, 1 CWP

£ car/tent £6.50-£7.50, car/caravan £6.50-£7.50, motorhome £6.50-£7.50, motorbike/tent £5-£7.50, children £0.50

🛒 🛒¼ ✗¼ 🛱¼ 🗑 🔌 🗑 ⚠ Calor Gaz 🐕 WS

Last arrival time: 10:00

➡ 3 miles S of Whitby on A171.

Limberlost Camping Site

Church Lane, Seasalter, Whitstable CT5 4BU

☎ 01227-272270

Open all year ⚠ 🚐 🚎

Size 2½ acres, 77 touring pitches, 40 with electric hookup, 77 level pitches, 6 🚿, 1 CWP

£ car/tent £6, car/caravan £8, motorhome £8

🛒¼ ✗¼ 🛱¼ 🔌 🗑 GR 🎣 📺 ⚠ 🍴 & 🐕

Last arrival time: 10:00

➡ From junction of M2, A2 and A299, travel on A299 towards Whitstable. After 4½ miles, turn left into Church Lane to site on right.

Camping & Caravanning Club Site

Sutton Hill, Woodlands, Wimborne Minster BH21 6LF

☎ 01202-822763

Open late March-early November ⚠ 🚐 🚎

Size 12¾ acres, 150 touring pitches, 84 with electric hookup, 7 🚿, 16 WCs, 1 CWP

£ car/tent £5.60-£8.60, car/caravan £5.60-£8.60, motorhome £5.60-£8.60, motorbike/tent £5.60-£8.60, children £1.50

ℂℂ MasterCard Visa

🗑 🔌 GR ⚠ & 🐕

Last arrival time: 11:00

➡ From Ringwood take B3081 through Verwood. Site is 1½ miles on right after Verwood.

Charris Camping & Caravan Park

Candy's Lane, Corfe Mullen, Wimborne Minster BH21 3EF

☎ **01202-885970**

Open 1 March-30 October **A ⚐ ⚑**

Size 3 acres, 45 touring pitches, 45 with electric hookup, 22 level pitches, 4 ☗, 8 WCs, 1 CWP

£ car/tent £6-£7, car/caravan £6-£7, motorhome £6-£7, motorbike/tent £6-£7, children £1

⚑ ✕¼ ⚑¼ ☗ ☐ Calor Gaz ⚑ WS

Last arrival time: 11:00

➜ From Wimbourne take A31 to Dorchester. Turn left after Wimbourne Caravans, Little Chef and Esso Garage.

Merley Court Touring Park

Merley, Wimborne Minster BH21 3AA

☎ **01202-881488 Fax 01202-881484**

Open 1 March-7 January **A ⚐ ⚑**

The first ever English Tourist Board 'Caravan Park of the Year'. Also, Practical Caravan magazine 'Best Family Park' 1993 and 1997. Ideally placed for Bournemouth, Poole and the New Forest.

Size 15 acres, 160 touring pitches, 160 with electric hookup, 160 level pitches, 19 ☗, 37 WCs, 3 CWPs

£ car/tent £6-£11.50, car/caravan £6-£11.50, motorhome £6-£11.50, motorbike/tent £6-£11.50, children £1.30-£1.70

⚏ MasterCard Visa

⚑ ✕ ⚑ ☐ ☗ ☐ ⊡ ☒ GR ☒ ⚍ ☐ Calor Gaz ⚑ ⚑

Last arrival time: 10:00

➜ Adjacent to Merley Bird Gardens and clearly signposted off A31 Wimborne bypass and A349 Poole junction.

Springfield Touring Park

Candy's Lane, Corfe Mullen, Wimborne Minster BH21 3EF

☎ **01202-881719**

Open mid March-October **A ⚐ ⚑**

Highly commended in Practical Caravan 1996 - 100 Best U.K. Parks. Set in Dorset overlooking the Stour Valley and close to Poole, Bournemouth, the New Forest. Modern facilities, free showers, awnings.

Size 3½ acres, 45 touring pitches, 45 with electric hookup, 35 level pitches, 6 ☗, 8 WCs, 1 CWP

£ car/tent £6-£8, car/caravan £7-£8, motorhome £7-£8, motorbike/tent £5, children £1.25

⚑ ✕¼ ⚑¼ ☐ ☗ ☐ ⚍ Calor Gaz ⚑ ⚑

Last arrival time: 10:00

➜ Turn left off A31 (Ringwood to Dorchester) at roundabout at western end of Wimborne by-pass into road signpost Corfe Mullen, south ¼ mile Candy's Lane on right, park entrance 300 yards past farm.

Wilksworth Farm Caravan Park

Cranborne Road, Wimborne Minster BH21 4HW

☎ **01202-885467**

Open 1 March-30 October **A ⚐ ⚑**

Country park with excellent facilities in a peaceful setting. Tennis courts, games room, heated swimming pool and children's play area are on site. New coffee shop/takeaway.

Size 12 acres, 85 touring pitches, 70 with electric hookup, 75 level pitches, 77 static caravans, 10 ☗, 19 WCs, 1 CWP

£ car/tent £6-£11, car/caravan £6-£11, motorhome £6-£11, motorbike/tent £6, children £1

Rental ⚐

⚑ ✕ ✕¼ ⚑ ☐ ☗ ☐ ⊡ ☒ GR ☒ ⚍ Calor Gaz ⚑ ⚑

Last arrival time: 9:30

➜ From A31 to Wimborne town centre, then B3078 N to Cranborne. Park is on left.

WINCANTON Somerset   3F2

Wincanton Racecourse

Wincanton BA9 8BJ

☎ 01963-34276

Open end April-mid September ▲ ⏏ ⇆

A peaceful rural site, 1 mile from Wincanton. Surrounded by numerous places to visit, i.e. the beautiful Stourhead Gardens. Golf course, pay and play.

Size 2 acres, 50 touring pitches, 18 with electric hookup, 50 level pitches, 4 ſ, 7 WCs, 1 CWP
£ car/tent £6.50, car/caravan £5-£8, motorhome £5-£8, motorbike/tent £5, children £1
ℂℂ MasterCard Visa
🛒¼ ✗¼ ⛟¼ 🔧 🅿 📺 Calor ⛏
Last arrival time: 8:00
➡ From A303 follow signs to Racecourse, then take B3081 Bruton Road.

WINCHESTER Hampshire   4B3

Balldown Camping & Caravan Park

Stockbridge Road, Sparsholt, Winchester SO21 2NA

☎ 01962-776619

WINDERMERE Cumbria   10B2

Park Cliffe Camping & Caravan Estate

Birks Road, Tower Wood, Windermere LA23 3PG

☎ 015395-31344 Fax 015395-31971

Open March-October ▲ ⏏ ⇆

Flat and gently sloping, grass and hardstanding, rural site with magnificent views over surrounding countryside. Highest tent pitches have commanding views over Lake Windermere and Langdale.

Size 25 acres, 45 touring pitches, 50 with electric hookup, 45 level pitches, 50 static caravans, 10 ſ, 19 WCs, 1 CWP
£ car/tent £9.20-£11.60, car/caravan £11-£11.60, motorhome £11-£11.60, motorbike/tent £9.20-£11.60, children £1-£1.50
Rental ▲
ℂℂ MasterCard Visa
🛒 ✗ ⛟ ⊙ 🔧 ⊡ ⚠ 🔌 Calor Gaz ⛏ WS
Last arrival time: 10:00
➡ M6 junction 36 take A590 to Newby Bridge. Turn right onto A592, go 4 miles and turn right into Birks Road. The park is third of a mile on right.

White Cross Bay Caravan Park

Ambleside Road, Windermere LA23 1LF

☎ 015394-43937 Fax 015394-88704

Open March-14 November ⏏ ⇆
Size 72 acres, 125 touring pitches, 25 with electric hookup, 125 level pitches, 250 static caravans, 45 ſ, 80 WCs, 2 CWPs
£ car/caravan £10.50-£14, motorhome £10.50-£14
Rental ⏏ Chalet. £140-£560
ℂℂ MasterCard Visa
🛒 ✗ ⛟ 🔧 🔌 ▣ GR ⚠ 🔌 Calor ⛏ WS
Last arrival time: 11:00
➡ 2 miles N of Windermere and 3 miles S of Ambleside. Site on W of A591.

WINSFORD Somerset   3D2

Halse Farm

Near Minehead, Winsford TA24 7JL

☎ 0164-851259 Fax 0164-851259

Open mid March-October ▲ ⏏ ⇆

Exmoor National Park, small, peaceful, glorious views. Quality heated toilet block. Launderette, pay phone. Disabled facilities. 1 mile from thatched pub, shop.

Size 3 acres, 44 touring pitches, 21 with electric hookup, 44 level pitches, 4 ſ, 8 WCs, 1 CWP
£ car/tent £5.50-£7.50, car/caravan £5.50-£7.50, motorhome £5.50-£7.50, children £0.50-£1

▣ ▤ ▯ ◿ Calor Gaz ⚒ ✝
Last arrival time: 11:00
➜ Turn off A396 for Winsford. In village turn left in front of Royal Oak, then follow lane for 1 mile. Entrance is immediately on left after cattle grid.

WISBECH Cambridgeshire 9D3

Orchard View Caravan & Camping Park
Sutton St Edmund, Spalding, Wisbech PE12 0LT
☎ 01945-700482
Open 31 March-31 October ▲ 🚐 🚛
Size 6 acres, 35 touring pitches, 14 with electric hookup, 35 level pitches, 2 static caravans, 2 ⚿, 9 WCs, 1 CWP
🛁 ⚡ ◿ ⚄ Calor ⚒ WS
➜ N off A47 onto B1187 ½ mile before bridge over River Nene. After 4 miles turn right to Broadgate, signed Sutton St Edmund (second turning over bridge). Site on right in ¾ mile.

WISBOROUGH GREEN West Sussex 4C3

Bat and Ball
New Pound, Wisborough Green RH14 0EH
☎ 01403-700313
Open all year ▲ 🚐 🚛
Size 3 acres, 26 touring pitches, 26 level pitches, 2 ⚿, 4 WCs, 1 CWP
£ car/tent £4.50, car/caravan £4.50, motorhome £4.50, motorbike/tent £4.50
✕ ⚡ ▤ ▯ GR ◿ ⚄ Calor ✝
➜ Off A272 on B2133 from S to N.

WITTON-LE-WEAR Co. Durham 13F4

Witton Castle Caravan Site
Bishop Auckland, Witton-le-Wear DL14 0DE
☎ 01388-488230 Fax 01388-488008
Open 1 March-31 October ▲ 🚐 🚛
Size 150 acres, 186 touring pitches, 50 with electric hookup, 100 level pitches, 298 static caravans, 9 ⚿, 50 WCs, 1 CWP
£ car/tent £6.50-£14.25, car/caravan £6.50-£14.25, motorhome £6.50-£14.25, motorbike/tent £6.50-£14.25, children £0.50
🛁 ✕ ⚡ ▣ ▤ ▥ ▨ GR TV ◿ ⚄ Calor Gaz ✝ WS
➜ Signposted on E side of A68 between Toft Hill and Witton-le-Wear. 4 miles W of Bishop Auckland.

WOKINGHAM Berkshire 4C2

California Chalet & Touring Park
Nine Mile Ride, Finchampstead, Wokingham RG11 3NY
☎ 01734-733928
Open 1 March-30 October ▲ 🚐 🚛

Pretty wooded family run park set alongside a lake with fishing available. Close to London, Windsor and Thorpe Park.

Size 5½ acres, 29 touring pitches, 24 with electric hookup, 29 level pitches, 3 ⚿, 4 WCs, 1 CWP
£ car/tent £9-£10.75, car/caravan £9-£10.75, motorhome £9-£10.75, motorbike/tent £9-£10.75, children £0.50
🛁 ✕¼ ⚡¼ ▣ ▤ ▯ ▨ ▧ ◿ ⚒ ✝
Last arrival time: 10:00
➜ From M3 junction 3 onto A322 towards Bracknell, turn left onto B3430 towards Finchampstead. Site is on right in 6 miles.

WOODBRIDGE Suffolk 9F4

Forest Camping
Tangham Campsite, Butley, Woodbridge IP12 3NF
☎ 01394-450707
Open 1 April-10 January ▲ 🚐

A spacious, level, well-drained site in the middle of forestry land. Good for walking and cycling.

Size 7 acres, 90 touring pitches, 66 with electric hookup, 90 level pitches, 6 ⚿, 12 WCs, 3 CWPs
£ car/tent £7-£8.50, car/caravan £7-£8.50, motorhome £7-£8.50, motorbike/tent £7-£8.50, children £1-£2
🛁 ▣ ▤ ▯ ◿ Calor Gaz ✝
Last arrival time: 9:00
➜ Take A1152 off A12 at Woodbridge and then left on B1084 to Orford. After 4 miles turn right into forest.

Moon & Sixpence

Newbourn Road, Waldringfield, Woodbridge IP12 4PP

📞 **01473-736650 Fax 01473-736270**

Open 1 April-31 October ▲ 🚐 🚏

Tranquil picturesque location with excellent facilities. Sandy beach, lake, fishing in September and October. Neighbouring golf course, nearby rollerskating, ten pin bowling, indoor bowls, cinemas, water sports.

Size 85 acres, 90 touring pitches, 90 with electric hookup, 90 level pitches, 150 static caravans, 12 🚿, 24 WCs, 1 CWP

£ car/tent £10-£14, car/caravan £10-£14, motorhome £10-£14, motorbike/tent £10-£14

CC MasterCard Visa

🛒 ✕ 🍴 🛇 🔋 🎣 🚻 GR 🔍 ⛽ 🚮 Calor Gaz 🐕

Last arrival time: 9:00

➜ Turn E off A12 Ipswich Eastern by-pass onto minor road signposted Newbourn and follow signs.

St Margaret's House Caravan Site

Shottisham, Woodbridge IP12 3HD

📞 **01394-411247**

Open 1 April-31 October ▲ 🚐 🚏

Size 2½ acres, 30 touring pitches, 16 with electric hookup, 30 level pitches, 2 🚿, 4 WCs, 1 CWP

£ car/tent £5, car/caravan £5-£6.50, motorhome £5-£6.50, motorbike/tent £5, children £0.25

🛒¼ ✕¼ 🍴¼ 🔋 🛇 Calor Gaz 🐕

Last arrival time: 10:00

➜ Turn right off A12 onto A1152 signposted Bawdsey/Orford. After 1½ miles fork right onto B1083 signposted Bawdsey. 4 miles to T junction, turn left into Shottisham, the site is on left, 100 yards past Sorrel Horse pub.

WOODHALL SPA Lincolnshire   8C2

Bainland Country Park

Horncastle Road, Woodhall Spa LN10 6UX

📞 **01526-352903 Fax 01526-353730**

Open all year ▲ 🚐 🚏

Size 50 acres, 150 touring pitches, 150 with electric hookup, 150 level pitches, 10 static caravans, 13 🚿, 16 WCs, 53 CWPs

£ car/tent £8-£24, car/caravan £8-£24, motorhome £8-£24, motorbike/tent £8-£24

Rental 🚐 Chalet. £160-£570

CC MasterCard Visa

🛒 ✕ 🍴 🛇 🔋 🎣 📺 🚻 🎣 🚮 GR 🔍 📺 🚮 🚮 Calor Gaz 👤
🐕 WS

Last arrival time: 9:00

➜ On B1191, 6 miles from Horncastle, on left just past Burmah petrol station. 1½ miles from Woodhall Spa.

Camping & Caravanning Club Site

Wellsyke Lane, Kirkby-on-Bain LN10 6YU

📞 **01526-352911**

Open late March-early November ▲ 🚐 🚏

Size 6 acres, 100 touring pitches, 66 with electric hookup, 6 🚿, 9 WCs, 1 CWP

£ car/tent £5.20-£7.80, car/caravan £5.50-£7.80, motorhome £5.20-£7.80, motorbike/tent £5.20-£7.80, children £1.50

CC MasterCard Visa

🛇 🔋 👤 🐕

Last arrival time: 11:00

➜ Take A153 to Horncastle and then B1191 to Woodhall Spa. Turn left and go down Kirkby Lane for 1¾ miles to site.

WOOL Dorset   3F3

Whitemead Caravan Park

East Burton Road, Wool BH20 6HG

📞 **01929-462241 Fax 01929-426641**

Open March-October ▲ 🚐 🚏

Size 5 acres, 95 touring pitches, 54 with electric hookup, 95 level pitches, 6 🚿, 13 WCs, 1 CWP

£ car/tent £5.50-£9.50, car/caravan £5.50-£9.50, motorhome £5.50-£9.50, motorbike/tent £5.50-£9.50, children £0.75

Rental Lodge £120-£210

🛒 ✕¼ 🍴 🛇 🔋 🚮 Calor Gaz 👤 🐕 WS

Last arrival time: 11:00

➜ Off A352 Wareham to Weymouth & Dorchester road (East Burton Road).

WOOLACOMBE Devon   2C2

Twitchen Park

Mortehoe, Woolacombe EX34 7ES

📞 **01271-870476 Fax 01271-870498**

Open Easter-end October ▲ 🚐 🚏

Popular family park, close to Woolacombe's glorious sandy beach and coastal walks. A licensed club is on site, with seasonal entertainment, free swimming lessons and more.

Size 45 acres, 51 touring pitches, 51 with electric hookup, 295 static caravans, 24 🚿, 46 WCs, 2 CWPs
£ car/tent £6-£16, car/caravan £7.50-£19, motorhome £7.50-£19
Rental 🚐
CC MasterCard Visa
🏪✕🍴🔌🛒🎣📶📺🏧 🔧 Calor Gaz
Last arrival time: 9:00
➜ From A361 10 miles N of Barnstaple take B3343 left for 1¾ miles to Woolacombe. Take right turn signed Mortehoe. Park entrance is 1½ miles on left.

Warcombe Farm Camping Park
Station Road, Mortehoe, Woolacombe EX34 7EJ
☎ 01271-870690 **Fax** 01271-871070
Open 15 March-31 October **A** 🚐 🚍
Size 19 acres, 25 touring pitches, 22 with electric hookup, 140 level pitches, 6 🚿, 12 WCs, 1 CWP
£ car/tent £3.50-£6.95, car/caravan £5.50-£9.50, motorhome £4.50-£8.50, motorbike/tent £6.95
🏪✕¼ 🍴¼ 🔌🛒📶🏧 Calor Gaz 🐕
➜ Turn left off A361 onto B3343. After 2 miles turn right onto road to Mortehoe. Site on right under 1 mile.

Mill House Caravan & Camping Site
Hawford, Worcester WR3 7SE
☎ 01905-451283 **Fax** 01905-754143
Open April-October **A** 🚐 🚍
Size 8 acres, 150 touring pitches, 20 with electric hookup, 150 level pitches, 15 static caravans, 4 🚿, 9 WCs, 1 CWP
£ car/tent £5.50, car/caravan £5.50, motorhome £5.50, motorbike/tent £5.50
🏪🍴🔌🏧 Calor Gaz 🔧 🐕
➜ Site is 3 miles N of Worcester, on E of A449.

Camping & Caravanning Club Site
The Walled Garden, Clumber Park, Worksop S80 3BD
☎ 01909-482303
Open end March-start November **A** 🚐 🚍
Size 2½ acres, 55 touring pitches, 17 with electric hookup, 2 🚿, 8 WCs, 1 CWP
£ car/tent £4.60-£6.80, car/caravan £4.60-£6.80, motorhome £4.60-£6.80, motorbike/tent £4.60-£6.80
CC MasterCard Visa
🏪🏧🔧 🐕
➜ From A841 follow Clumber Park signs. After 2½ miles left at crossroads and follow signs for Estate Office. Right at office, site on left.

Greensprings Touring Park
Rockley Abbey, Worsbrough S75 3DS
☎ 01226-288298 **Fax** 01226-288298
Open 1 April-31 October **A** 🚐 🚍

Quiet secluded rural setting with pleasant walks. Ideal location for a relaxing break on journeys north and south and as a base for exploring Yorkshire and Derbyshire.

Size 4 acres, 60 touring pitches, 32 with electric hookup, 50 level pitches, 6 🚿, 9 WCs, 2 CWPs
£ car/tent £6, car/caravan £6, motorhome £6, motorbike/tent £6
Calor Gaz 🐕
Last arrival time: 9:00
➜ From M1 junction 36, take A61 towards Barnsley. Turn left after ¼ mile onto 'B' road signed Pilley. Follow road for ¾ mile. Site entrance is on left.

Bureside Holiday Park
Boundary Farm, Oby, Great Yarmouth NR29 3BW
☎ 01493-369233
Open Whitsun-mid September **A** 🚐 🚍

Explore peaceful country lanes and river banks or go fishing in the carp and tench lake. Also river frontage, slipway, heated swimming and kiddies pools.

Size 12 acres, 170 touring pitches, 57 with electric hookup, 120 level pitches, 45 static caravans, 8 🚿, 26 WCs, 3 CWPs
£ car/tent £7.50, car/caravan £7.50, motorhome £7.50, motorbike/tent £7.50
🏪🔌🎣📶🏧 Calor Gaz 🐕
Last arrival time: 8:00
➜ From junction A47/A1064 W of Acle, take A1064 N to Billockby. Keep left on B1152 for 1½ miles, then left at crossroads along unclassified road (signed Oby) for 1 mile. Take second left, then go ¼ mile and turn right to site.

Grange Touring Park

Ormesby St Margaret, Great Yarmouth NR29 3QG

☎ 01493-730023 Fax 01493-730188

Open Easter-mid October ⚐ 🚐 🚏

Size 3½ acres, 70 touring pitches, 60 with electric hookup, 70 level pitches, 10 🚿, 15 WCs, 1 CWP

£ car/tent £6-£10, car/caravan £6-£10, motorhome £6-£10, motorbike/tent £6-£10

℅ Visa

🏊 ✕ 🍴¼ 🛢 🔌 🛒 🗊 🎣 ⚠ 🐕 Calor Gaz 🚹 🐕

Last arrival time: 9:00

➔ At junction of A149 and B1159, 3 miles N of Caister.

Liffens Holiday Park

Burgh Castle, Great Yarmouth NR31 9QB

☎ 01493-780357 Fax 01493-782383

Open 1 April-30 October ⚐ 🚐 🚏

A friendly family holiday park, set in lovely Broadland countryside but only ten minutes from Great Yarmouth.

Size 22 acres, 100 touring pitches, 100 with electric hookup, 150 level pitches, 130 static caravans, 16 🚿, 28 WCs, 2 CWPs

£ car/tent £8-£12, car/caravan £8-£12, motorhome £8-£12

Rental 🚐 Chalet. £80-£375, 6 berth luxury caravans.

℅ MasterCard Visa

🏊 ✕ 🍴 🛢 🔌 🛒 🗊 🛒 GR 🛒 TV ⚠ 🎣 🍴 Calor Gaz 🚹 🐕 WS

Last arrival time: 11:00

➔ From Great Yarmouth take A12 over bridge and after two roundabouts watch for left turn to Burgh Castle. Follow two miles to T junction, turn right and follow signs to Liffens.

Long Beach Estate

Hemsby, Great Yarmouth NR29 4JD

☎ 01493-730023 Fax 01493-730188

Open 22 March-21 October ⚐ 🚐 🚏

Size 30 acres, 30 touring pitches, 30 with electric hookup, 130 level pitches, 120 static caravans, 10 🚿, 25 WCs, 2 CWPs

£ car/tent £5-£11, car/caravan £7-£11, motorhome £7-£11, motorbike/tent £5-£7

Rental 🚐 Chalet.

🏊 ✕ ✕¼ 🍴 🍴¼ 🛢 🔌 🛢 GR TV ⚠ 🎣 Calor Gaz 🚹 🐕 WS

Last arrival time: 11:00

➔ From B1159 at Hemsby, turn right on Beach Road, then second left (signposted Longbeach).

Willowcroft Camping & Caravan Park

Staithe Road, Repps-with-Bastwick, Great Yarmouth NR29 5JU

☎ 01692-670380 Fax 01692-670380

⚐ 🚐 🚏

Size 2 acres, 40 touring pitches, 20 with electric hookup, 40 level pitches, 2 🚿, 5 WCs, 1 CWP

£ car/tent £7-£8, car/caravan £7-£8, motorhome £7-£8, motorbike/tent £7-£8, children £1

🏊¼ ✕¼ 🍴¼ 🔌 🛢 Calor Gaz 🐕 WS

Last arrival time: 10:00

➔ In Repps-with-Bastwick (A149) take Ashby/Thurne road. In ½ mile turn into Staithe Road. Site ½ mile on right.

YEOVIL Devon   3E2

Long Hazel Camping Caravan Park

High Street, Sparkford, Yeovil

☎ 01963-440002

Open March-31 December ⚐ 🚐 🚏

Size 3½ acres, 76 touring pitches, 24 with electric hookup, 3 static caravans, 5 🚿, 8 WCs, 2 CWPs

£ car/tent £8-£10, car/caravan £8-£10, motorbike/tent £8-£10

➔ On the A359 off Hazelgrove roundabout at junction of A359 and A303.

YORK North Yorkshire   11D3

Castle Howard Caravan Site

Coneysthorpe, Castle Howard YO6 7DD
☎ 01653-648444 Fax 01653-648462
Open 1 March-31 October ▲ ⊕ ⊞
Size 17 acres, 70 touring pitches, 34 with electric hookup, 70 level pitches, 120 static caravans, 6 ♠, 15 WCs, 2 CWPs
£ car/tent £6.80-£7, car/caravan £6.80-£7, motorhome £6.80-£7, motorbike/tent £6.80-£7
♠ ♠¼ ◻ ◻ ◻ ◻ Calor ☊
Last arrival time: 9:00
➡ 15 miles NE of York off A64 (on York-Scarborough road).

Cawood Holiday Park

Ryther Road, Cawood, York YO8 OTT
☎ 01757-268450 Fax 01757-268537
Open 1 March-31 January ▲ ⊕ ⊞

A country site ideal for York and the Dales, and one hour from coast. Fishing, lakeside bar with family entertainment. Disabled bungalows, five caravans and nine chalets for hire (own WCs). No single-sex groups.

Size 8 acres, 60 touring pitches, 60 with electric hookup, 60 level pitches, 10 static caravans, 10 ♠, 12 WCs, 1 CWP
£ car/tent £8.50-£10.50, car/caravan £8.50-£10.50, motorhome £8.50-£10.50, motorbike/tent £8.50-£10.50, children £1
Rental ⊕ Chalet. bungalow £195-£395, caravans £175-£375
₵₵ MasterCard Visa
♠ ✕ ◻ ◻ ◻ ◻ ◻ ◻ ◻ ◻ ◻ ◻ Calor Gaz ⅋ ☊
Last arrival time: 11:00
➡ From A1 or York, take B1222 to Cawood and turn right at traffic lights onto B1223 for 1 mile towards Tadcaster. Site is on left.

Don't forget to mention the guide
When booking, please remember to tell the site that you chose it from
RAC Camping & Caravanning 1998

Mount Pleasant Caravan Village

Acaster Malbis, York YO2 1UW
☎ 01904-707078 Fax 01904-707078
Open 1 March-30 November ▲ ⊕ ⊞

Rural park set in the countryside, yet only four miles from the centre of York. Level mown grass for tourers and tents. The camp has its own bus service to York throughout the day.

Size 18 acres, 60 touring pitches, 40 with electric hookup, 60 level pitches, 165 static caravans, 12 ♠, 45 WCs, 2 CWPs
£ car/tent £5.75, car/caravan £5.99, motorhome £5.99, motorbike/tent £5.75
Rental ⊕ £33 per night
♠ ✕¼ ◻¼ ◻ ◻ ◻ Calor Gaz ⅋ ☊
➡ Turn off A64, follow signs to Bishopthorpe, then for Acaster Airfield (disused). Follow signs for site.

Naburn Lock Caravan Site
Naburn, York YO1 4RU
☎ 01904-728697 Fax 01904-728697
Open March-6 November **Å ⊿ ⬚**

Small rural site, with nearby facilities for fishing and horse riding. Restaurant ½ mile, swimming pool four miles.

Size 8 acres, 100 touring pitches, 84 with electric hookup, 100 level pitches, 8 ☊, 12 WCs, 2 CWPs
£ car/tent £8-£9.50, car/caravan £9.50, motorhome £9.50, motorbike/tent £8, children £1.25
🚿 ✕¼ 🔧 🔲 🚮 Calor Gaz ♿ ⼂
Last arrival time: 9:00
➜ 4 miles S of York. From A19 turn onto B1222. Site is 2½ miles on left.

Poplar Farm Caravan Park
Acaster Malbis, York YO2 1UH
☎ 01904-706548
Open April-October **Å ⊿ ⬚**
Size 8 acres, 50 touring pitches, 45 with electric hookup, 50 level pitches, 80 static caravans, 10 ☊, 20 WCs
Rental Å
🚿 ✕ 🔧 ⊟ 🔲 🚮 ⼁ Calor Gaz ♿ ⼂ WS
➜ S off A64 at Copmanthorpe. Site 2¼ miles.
See advert on previous page

Rawcliffe Manor Caravan Site
Manor Lane, Shipton Road, York YO3 6TZ
☎ 01904-624422
Open all year **Å ⊿ ⬚**

Well located near to York, with a daily bus service to the city from the site and next to a large shopping/leisure complex. Superb facilities for the disabled.

Size 5 acres, 120 touring pitches, 120 with electric hookup, 120 level pitches, 14 ☊, 24 WCs, 2 CWPs
£ car/tent £8.20-£11, car/caravan £7.50-£11, motorhome £7-£11, motorbike/tent £7.60-£8.60, children £1-£1.20
⊂⊂ MasterCard Visa
🚿¼ ✕ 🍺 ⊟ 🔧 ⊟ 🔲 GR TV ⼀ ⼁ Calor Gaz ♿ ⼂
Last arrival time: 11:00
➜ ½ mile off A19 Thirsk road on York side of junction with A1237 (York bypass).
See advert on previous page

Scotland

Top: Glen Nevis Caravan &
Camping Park, Fort William

Right: Trossachs Holiday Park,
Aberfoyle

Below: Seton Sands Holiday Park,
Longniddry

Aberfeldy Caravan Park

Dunkeld Road, Aberfeldy PH15 2AQ

📞 **01738-639911** Fax **01738-441690**

Open late March-late October 🅰 🚐 🚐

Size 5½ acres, 102 touring pitches, 132 with electric hookup, 132 level pitches, 30 static caravans, 18 🚾, 36 WCs, 1 CWP

£ car/tent £7, car/caravan £7-£8.90, motorhome £7-£8.90, motorbike/tent £6, children £1

CC MasterCard Visa

🛁¼ ✗¼ 🚱¼ ⚠ 🚻 ⊀ WS

➥ 9 miles W of A9 (Ballinluig junction) on A827 to Killin.

Trossachs Holiday Park

Gartmore, Aberfoyle FK8 3SA

📞 **01877-382614** Fax **01877-382732**

Open 15 March-31 October 🅰 🚐 🚐

A small exclusive enviromental caravan park, 1997 winner - Best park in Scotland. 45 landscaped touring pitches, tents welcome, Thistle award caravans and mountain bikes for hire.

Size 40 acres, 45 touring pitches, 45 with electric hookup, 45 level pitches, 60 static caravans, 4 🚾, 9 WCs, 1 CWP

£ car/tent £8.50-£10.50, car/caravan £8.50-£10.50, motorhome £8.50-£10.50, motorbike/tent £8.50-£10.50

Rental 🚐 £129-£425

CC MasterCard Visa

🛁 ✗¼ 🚱¼ 🅾 🗞 🖤 ℗ 🄶🅁 ⚠ Calor Gaz ⊀ WS

Last arrival time: 9:00

➥ On E side of A81, 3 miles S of Aberfoyle.

Queensberry Bay Caravan Park

Powfoot, Annan DG12 5PU

📞 **01461-700205**

Open April-October 🅰 🚐 🚐

Size 11 acres, 60 touring pitches, 60 with electric hookup, 60 level pitches, 70 static caravans, 8 🚾, 13 WCs, 1 CWP

£ car/tent £8, car/caravan £8, motorhome £8, motorbike/tent £8

🛁 🅾 📞 Calor Gaz 🚻 ⊀

Last arrival time: 9:00

➥ W of Annan on B724, turn S to Powfoot.

Applecross Camp Site

via Loch Carron, Wester Ross, Applecross IV54 8ND

📞 **01520-744268** Fax **01520-744268**

Open Easter-September 🅰 🚐 🚐

Size 6 acres, 60 touring pitches, 10 with electric hookup, 60 level pitches, 3 static caravans, 8 🚾, 12 WCs, 1 CWP

CC Visa

🛁 ✗ 🚱 Calor Gaz

➥ From A896 turn left after Kishorn to Applecross - 11 miles. Caravans continue on A896 towards Shielding. After 7½ miles turn left to Applecross - 24 miles.

Red Lion Caravan Park

Dundee Road, Arbroath

📞 **01241-872038** Fax **01241-430324**

Open March-October 🚐 🚐

Size 20 acres, 31 touring pitches, 31 with electric hookup, 31 level pitches, 239 static caravans, 6 🚾, 12 WCs, 1 CWP

£ car/caravan £8.50, motorhome £8.50

Rental ⚡

CC MasterCard Visa

⚡ ✕ 🚿 🗑 🔌 🏧 Calor ♿ ⚓

Last arrival time: 8:00

➜ Site on left of A92 on entering Arbroath.

Gorten Sands Caravan Site

Gorten Farm, Arisaig PH39 4NS

📞 01687-450283

Open Easter-30 September ⛺ ⚡ 🚐

A peaceful, family run hill and coastal farm site in a historic scenic area with safe sandy beaches. The unspoilt location offers views to Skye and the isles.

Size 6 acres, 42 touring pitches, 20 with electric hookup, 42 level pitches, 3 static caravans, 6 🚿, 10 WCs, 1 CWP

£ car/tent £7-£8.50, car/caravan £8.50, motorhome £7-£8, motorbike/tent £7, children £0.75

Rental ⚡ £200-£300

⚡¼ ✕¼ 🚿¼ 🗑 🔌 🗄 Calor Gaz ⚓

Last arrival time: 11:00

➜ A830 to point 2 miles W of Arisaig. Turn left at signpost "Back of Keppoch", continue ¾ mile to road end across cattle grid.

Aviemore Mountain Resort Caravan Park

Aviemore PH22 1PF

📞 01479-810751 Fax 01479-810862

Open 1 December-31 October

Size 6 acres, 90 touring pitches, 72 with electric hookup, 90 level pitches, 4 🚿, 18 WCs, 1 CWP

£ car/tent £6.50-£7.50, car/caravan £7-£8, motorhome £7-£8, children £1

CC MasterCard Visa

⚡¼ ✕¼ 🚿¼ 🗄 ⚓

Last arrival time: 10:00

➜ Off A9 in Aviemore village.

High Range Touring Caravan Park

Grampian Road, Aviemore PH22 1PT

📞 01479-810636 Fax 01479-811322

Open December-October ⛺ ⚡ 🚐

A small and select touring park situated in woodland grounds, 500 yards from the Aviemore centre. A launderette, playground, continental restaurant and bar, and motel and 'family' rooms are available.

Size 2 acres, 36 touring pitches, 36 with electric hookup, 36 level pitches, 4 🚿, 5 WCs, 1 CWP

£ car/tent £6-£8.50, car/caravan £6-£8.50, motorhome £6-£8.50, motorbike/tent £6-£8.50, children £8.50

Rental Chalet

CC MasterCard Visa

⚡¼ ✕ ✕¼ 🚿¼ 🗑 🔌 🗄 🏧 ⚓

Last arrival time: 8:00

➜ From main A9 take B9152. Park is in complex at S end of Aviemore.

Middlemuir Holiday Park

Tarbolton, Mauchline, Ayr KA5 5NR
☎ 01292-541647 Fax 01292-541649
Open 1 March-31 October 🅰 ⛺ 🚐
Size 18 acres, 35 touring pitches, 18 with electric
hookup, 64 static caravans, 4 🚿, 8 WCs, 1 CWP
£ car/tent £5-£9, car/caravan £7-£13.50, motorhome
£7-£13.50, motorbike/tent £9
Rental ⛺ £140-£300
🔟 ☎ 🔟 GR Gaz ⚲
➜ 5 miles E of Ayr on B743 Mauchline road.

Sundrum Castle Holiday Park

Coylton, Ayr KA6 6HX
☎ 01292-570057
Open 26 March-31 October 🅰 ⛺ 🚐

Well-organised site with games room, adventure
playground, nightclub. Suitable for families. 103
caravans for hire (own WCs). All-male or female
parties with management's prior consent.

Size 23 acres, 52 touring pitches, 30 with electric
hookup, 52 level pitches, 252 static caravans, 8 🚿, 16
WCs, 1 CWP
£ car/tent £10-£16, car/caravan £10-£16, motorhome
£10-£16, motorbike/tent £10-£16
Rental ⛺
((MasterCard Visa
🔟 ✕ 🍴 🔟 ☎ 🔟 🔟 🔟 🔟 GR 🔟 🔟 Calor ⚲ ⚲
Last arrival time: 12:00
➜ 4 miles E of Ayr A70, turn N, site signed.

Reraig Caravan Site

Kyle of Lochalsh, Balmacara IV40 8DH
☎ 01599-566215
Open 1 May-30 September 🅰 ⛺ 🚐
Size 2 acres, 45 touring pitches, 36 with electric
hookup, 40 level pitches, 4 🚿, 9 WCs, 1 CWP
£ car/tent £6.80, car/caravan £6.80, motorhome £6.80
((MasterCard Visa
🔟¼ ✕¼ ⚲

Last arrival time: 10:00
➜ Adjacent to Balmacara Hotel on A87, 1¾ miles W
on junction with A890.

Wester Bonnyton Farm Site

Gamrie, Banff AB45 3EP
☎ 01261-832470
Open March-October 🅰 ⛺ 🚐
Size 3 acres, 30 touring pitches, 8 with electric
hookup, 10 level pitches, 18 static caravans, 4 🚿, 4
WCs, 1 CWP
£ car/tent £5-£6, car/caravan £6-£7, motorhome £6-
£7, motorbike/tent £5-£6
Rental ⛺ Chalet. caravans £150-£160
🔟 ☎ GR 🔟 🔟 🔟 Calor ⚲ ⚲ WS

Blair Castle Caravan Park

Blair Atholl, Pitlochry PH18 5SR
☎ 01796-481263 Fax 01796-481587
Open 1 April-26 October 🅰 ⛺ 🚐
Size 35 acres, 283 touring pitches, 175 with electric
hookup, 112 static caravans, 28 🚿, 97 WCs, 3 CWPs
£ car/tent £7.50-£9.50, car/caravan £7.50-£9.50,
motorhome £7.50-£9.50, children £0.50
((Visa
🔟 ✕ 🍴 GR 🔟 Calor Gaz ⚲
Last arrival time: 9.30
➜ Turn off A9, 6 miles N of Pitlochry. Follow signs to
Blair Atholl.

The River Tilt Park

Bridge of Tilt, Blair Atholl PH18 5TE
☎ 01796-481467 Fax 01796-481511
Open March-November ▲ ⟑ ⟱

Situated on the banks of the River Tilt, next to the golf course and overlooking the castle entrance. Panoramic views over the river.

Size 14 acres, 35 touring pitches, 35 with electric hookup, 35 level pitches, 45 static caravans, 4 ℟, 6 WCs, 1 CWP
£ car/tent £6-£9, car/caravan £9-£14, motorhome £9-£13, motorbike/tent £6-£7
Rental ⟑ Chalet. caravans £265-£325, chalets £225-£510.
℀ MasterCard Visa
⊉¼ ✕ 💧 🗑 🔌 🖥 🗊 🏓 🎱 🏓 🍴 🗑 ⟑ 🏓 Calor Gaz 🐾 WS
Last arrival time: 11:00
➡ A9 N of Pitlochry onto B8079 signed Blair Atholl. On entering village turn left before hotel and follow sign.

Nether Craig Caravan Park

Alyth, Blairgowrie PH11 8HN
☎ 01575-560204 Fax 01575-560315
Open mid March-end October ▲ ⟑ ⟱

Enjoy the peace of rural Angus at this award winning, family run touring park, convenient for country pursuits and near much of historic interest.

Size 4 acres, 40 touring pitches, 40 with electric hookup, 40 level pitches, 5 ℟, 7 WCs, 1 CWP
£ car/tent £5, car/caravan £7.50-£9.50, motorhome £7.50-£9.50, motorbike/tent £5, children £0.85
⊉ 🗑 🔌 🗊 🗑 ⟑ Calor Gaz ⟟ 🐾 WS
Last arrival time: 9:00
➡ At roundabout S of Alyth join B954 signposted Glenisla. Follow caravan signs for 4 miles. Do not go into Alyth.

Boat of Garten Caravan & Camping Park

Boat of Garten PH24 3BN
☎ 01479-831652 Fax 01479-831652
▲ ⟑ ⟱

Size 11 acres, 37 touring pitches, 37 with electric hookup, 37 level pitches, 30 static caravans, 8 ℟, 15 WCs, 1 CWP
£ car/tent £5-£8.50, car/caravan £6.50-£11, motorhome £6.50-£11, motorbike/tent £8
Rental ⟑ £169-£365
℀ MasterCard Visa
⊉ ✕¼ 💧¼ 🗑 🔌 🗊 ⟑ Calor Gaz ⟟ 🐾 WS
Last arrival time: 10:00
➡ From A9 take A95 towards Grantown-on-Spey, then follow signs for Boat of Garten. Park is situated in centre of village. Signposted.

Croft Na-Carn Caravan Park

Loch Garten, Boat of Garten
☎ 01309-672051 Fax 01343-830880
Open all year ⚠ 🚐 🚚

*Located on the 'Road to the Ospreys' and surrounded
by beautiful scenery; fishing, golf, a whisky trail and
walking are just some of the attractions.*

Size 4½ acres, 15 touring pitches, 10 with electric
hookup, 15 level pitches, 10 static caravans, 2 🐾, 4
WCs, 1 CWP
£ car/tent £4.50-£7.50, car/caravan £6.50-£7.50,
motorhome £6.50-£7.50, motorbike/tent £4.50-£7.50,
children £1
Rental 🚐 Chalet. £70-£350
◫ 🔌 Calor Gaz ♿ ⊮ WS
Last arrival time: 8:30
➡ Leave A9 immediately N of Aviemore onto A95
heading for Grantown on Spey, turn right for Boat of
Garten. Through village, cross River Spey at road
junction of B970, turn left towards Nethybridge. In ½
mile turn right for Loch Garten, the park is 100 yards
on the left. Alternatively follow RSPB roadsigns for
osprey.

BRIDGE OF CALLY Perthshire   15E4

Corriefodly Holiday Park

Bridge of Cally PH10 7JG
☎ 01250-886236
Open December-October ⚠ 🚐 🚚

*Situated in central Perthshire six miles north of
Blairgowrie, the site is an ideal touring base. Open
December-October, 17 acres, 55 tourers, apartments
for hire.*

Size 17 acres, 55 touring pitches, 55 with electric
hookup, 35 level pitches, 57 static caravans, 4 🐾, 12
WCs, 1 CWP
£ car/tent £5-£7, car/caravan £7.50-£9, motorhome
£7.50-£9, motorbike/tent £5-£7
Rental £135-£260 - self catering apartments
🛒¼ ✗¼ ◫ 🔌 🍴 🗒 GR 🔲 ⚠ 🐕 Calor ♿ ⊮
Last arrival time: 11:00
➡ A93 N from Blairgowrie for 6 miles. At junction of
A93 and A924 fork onto A924. Site is 300 yards on
left.

CALLANDER Perthshire   12C1

Keltie Bridge Caravan Park

Keltie Bridge, Callander FK17 8LQ
☎ 01877-330811 Fax 01877-330075
Open 1 April-31 October ⚠ 🚐 🚚
Size 12 acres, 40 touring pitches, 30 with electric
hookup, 40 level pitches, 40 static caravans, 5 🐾, 7
WCs, 1 CWP
£ car/tent £7.50-£9, car/caravan £7.50-£9, motorhome
£7.50-£9, motorbike/tent £5.50-£7.50
◫ 🔌 ♿ ⊮ WS
➡ Signposted from A84 between Doune and
Callander.

CAMPBELTOWN Argyll   12B3

Camping & Caravanning Club Site

East Trodigal, Machrihanish, Campbeltown
☎ 01586-810366
Open end March-end September ⚠ 🚐 🚚
Size 10 acres, 90 touring pitches, 42 with electric
hookup, 4 🐾, 12 WCs, 1 CWP
£ car/tent £4.60-£6.80, car/caravan £4.60-£6.80,
motorhome £4.60-£6.80, motorbike/tent £4.60-£6.80,
children £1.40
⊂⊂ MasterCard Visa
🔌 ♿ ⊮
Last arrival time: 11:00
➡ A82 from Glasgow to Tarbet. Then A83 to
Campbeltown. From town take B843 (to
Machrihanish). Site is on N side of road, ½ mile
before Machrihanish.

CANNICH Inverness-shire   14C3

Cannich Caravan Park

Cannich by Beauly
☎ 01456-415364 Fax 01456-415263
Open Easter-31 October ⚠ 🚐 🚚
Size 8 acres, 50 touring pitches, 20 with electric
hookup, 50 level pitches, 9 static caravans, 8 🐾, 10
WCs, 1 CWP

£ car/tent £5.50-£8.50, car/caravan £5.50-£8.50, motorhome £5.50-£8.50, motorbike/tent £3.50-£5.50
Rental ☎ £140-£190
☎¼ ✗¼ ♥¼ ▣ █ ❂ ▣ ⒢ ⊺ⱽ ⚠ Calor Gaz ♿ ⊁ WS
Last arrival time: 11:00
➜ 100 yards off A831.

CARNOUSTIE Angus 13E1

Woodlands Caravan Park
Newton Road, Carnoustie DD7 6HR
☎ 01241-853246 Fax 01307-461889
Open March-October ▲ ☎ ⊞

In grounds of former Carnoustie House, a wooded site with a children's play area. Open from Easter to October.

Size 4½ acres, 108 touring pitches, 64 with electric hookup, 108 level pitches, 12 static caravans, 8 ⓕ, 12 WCs, 1 CWP
☎¼ ✗¼ ♥¼ ▣ █ ⒢ ⚠ Calor ♿ ⊁
➜ From A92 Dundee-Arbroath follow caravan signs "Carnoustie" 1½ miles.

CARRADALE Argyll 12B3

Carradale Bay Caravan Site
Kintyre, Carradale PA28 6QG
☎ 01583-431665
Open Easter-30 September ▲ ☎ ⊞

On safe sandy bay, beside the River Carra. Adjacent fishing, forest walks, golf course and all village amenities.

Size 12 acres, 56 touring pitches, 40 with electric hookup, 40 level pitches, 3 static caravans, 8 ⓕ, 16 WCs, 1 CWP
£ car/tent £7-£12.80, car/caravan £7-£12.80, motorhome £7-£12.80, motorbike/tent £7-£12.80, children £1.10-£1.20
Rental Chalet. £95-£325
☎¼ ✗¼ ♥¼ ▣ █ ❂ ▣ ⊁ WS
Last arrival time: 10:00
➜ From Tarbert take A83 to Campbeltown, then B842 to Carradale. After 14 miles at T-junction, turn right onto B879 (signposted Carradale). After ½ mile turn right at Carwen Park sign and follow track to site.

CASTLE DOUGLAS Kirkcudbrightshire 12C4

Loch Ken Holiday Park
Parton, Castle Douglas DG7 3NE
☎ 0164-470282 Fax 01644-470297
Size 6 acres, 50 touring pitches, 35 with electric hookup, 30 level pitches, 33 static caravans, 7 ⓕ, 10 WCs, 1 CWP
☎ Calor Gaz ♿ WS
➜ 7 miles from A75 at Castle Douglas on the A713 beside the A713.

Lochside Caravan Park
Castle Douglas DG7 1EZ
☎ 01556-502949 Fax 01556-502521
Open Easter-October ▲ ☎ ⊞
Size 6 acres, 160 touring pitches, 97 with electric hookup, 161 level pitches, 16 ⓕ, 29 WCs, 3 CWPs
£ car/tent £7.10-£8.70, car/caravan £7.10-£8.70, motorhome £7.10-£8.70, motorbike/tent £7.10-£8.70
☎¼ ✗¼ ♥¼ █ ❂ ▣ ⚠ ♿ ⊁
➜ Off A75 in Castle Douglas by Carlingwark Loch.

COMRIE Fife 12C1

West Lodge Caravan Park
Comrie PH6 2LS
☎ 01764-670354
Open 1 April-31 October ▲ ☎ ⊞
Size 3 acres, 20 touring pitches, 20 with electric hookup, 20 level pitches, 36 static caravans, 6 ⓕ, 10 WCs, 1 CWP
£ car/tent £7, car/caravan £9, motorhome £9, children £0.50
Rental ☎ £19-£29 nightly. £99-£190 weekly.
☎ ✗¼ ♥¼ ▣ █ ❂ Calor Gaz ⊁ WS
Last arrival time: 10:00
➜ On A85, 1 mile E of Comrie.

CONNEL Argyll   12B1

Camping & Caravanning Club Site
Barcaldine, Connel PA37 1SG
☎ 01631-720348
Open end March-start November ▲ 🚐 🚎
Size 4 acres, 75 touring pitches, 40 with electric
hookup, 4 level pitches, 6 🚿, 14 WCs, 2 CWPs
£ car/tent £5.20-£7.80, car/caravan £5.20-£7.80,
motorhome £5.20-£7.80, motorbike/tent £5.20-£7.80,
children £1.50
℃ MasterCard Visa
🛒 🖸 🔧 ⨹ ⚠ ✝
Last arrival time: 11:00
➡ A828 Oban to Fort William road for 6 miles to N of
Connel Bridge. Site is on right, just before Barcaldine
village sign.

CONTIN Ross-shire   14C3

Riverside Chalets & Caravan Park
Strathteffer, Contin IV14 9ES
☎ 01997-421351
Open all year ▲ 🚐 🚎
Size 2 acres, 15 touring pitches, 12 with electric
hookup, 15 level pitches, 3 static caravans, 2 🚿, 5
WCs, 1 CWP
£ car/caravan £2.50
Rental Chalet.
🛒 ✗ 🛍 🖸 🖸 Calor Gaz ✝ WS
➡ On A835 between Inverness and Ullapool at
Strathpeffer Junction.

CRAIGELLACHIE Banffshire   15E3

Aberlour Gardens Caravan Park
Aberlour-on-Spey, Craigellachie AB38 9LP
☎ 01340-871586
Open April-October ▲ 🚐 🚎

*Attractive five acre wooded site within an historic
walled garden. Close to River Spey, Speyside Way and
Malt Whisky Trail.*

Size 5 acres, 20 touring pitches, 18 with electric
hookup, 14 level pitches, 26 static caravans, 5 🚿, 8
WCs, 1 CWP
£ car/tent £6-£6.50, car/caravan £7-£7.50, motorhome
£7-£7.50, motorbike/tent £6-£6.50
🛒 🖸 🔧 ⚠ Calor Gaz ᴴ ✝ WS
Last arrival time: 10:00
➡ Midway between Aberlour and Craigellachie off
A95.

Camping & Caravanning Club Site
Speyside, Elchies, Craigellachie
☎ 01340-810414
Open late March-early November ▲ 🚐 🚎
Size 75 touring pitches, 35 with electric hookup, 8
🚿, 8 WCs, 1 CWP
£ car/tent £8.75-£11.55, car/caravan £8.75-£11.55,
motorhome £8.75-£11.55, motorbike/tent £8.75-
£11.55, children £1.40
℃ MasterCard Visa
🖸 🔧 ⚠ ⨹ ✝
Last arrival time: 11:00
➡ Situated on B9102, 2½ miles from junction with
A941 Elgin to Craigellachie road.

CROCKETFORD Kirkcudbrightshire   13D4

Park of Brandedleys
Crocketford, Near Dumfries DG2 8RG
☎ 01556-690250 **Fax** 01556-690681
Open 1 March-31 October ▲ 🚐 🚎

*Easily accessible landscaped park with fine views to
the loch and hills. Top quality toilets with ensuite
units, bath and baby/ hair care room.*

Size 16 acres, 80 touring pitches, 80 with electric
hookup, 50 level pitches, 28 static caravans, 13 🚿, 25
WCs, 2 CWPs
£ car/tent £9-£14, car/caravan £9-£14, motorhome £9-
£14, motorbike/tent £9-£14, children £2
Rental 🚐 Chalet. £140-£500
℃ MasterCard Visa
🛒 🛒¼ ✗ ✗¼ 🛍 🖸 🔧 🍴 🍴 ⬛ ⬛ 🔲 ⨹ 🔲 ⚠ 🍺 Calor
Gaz ᴴ ✝ WS
Last arrival time: 10:00
➡ Fork left off A75 Dumfries to Stranraer in
Crocketford at park sign. Site on right in 160 yards.

CUPAR Fife 13E1

Clayton Caravan Park
St Andrew KY16 9YA
☎ 01334-870242 Fax 01334-870057
Open Easter-October ▲ ⏺ ⏺
Size 25 acres, 26 touring pitches, 26 with electric hookup, 26 level pitches, 170 static caravans, 5 ⏺, 10 WCs, 1 CWP
£ car/tent £7-£8, car/caravan £9.50-£11, motorhome £8.50-£10, motorbike/tent £7-£8
⫌ Visa
⏺ ✕ ⏺ ⏺ ⏺ ⏺ ⏺ GR ⏺ ⏺ Calor Gaz ⏺ ⏺ WS
Last arrival time: 10:30
➜ 4½ miles W of St Andrews on A91, between Dairsie and Guardbridge.

DALBEATTIE Kirkudbrightshire 13D4

Castle Point Caravan Park
Rockcliffe, Dalbeattie DG5 4QL
☎ 01556-630248
Open April-October ▲ ⏺ ⏺

A small quiet coastal site near Rockcliffe Village in Galloway. The site and walks nearby have some of the best views along the Solway coast.

Size 3 acres, 29 touring pitches, 29 with electric hookup, 29 level pitches, 7 static caravans, 4 ⏺, 10 WCs, 1 CWP
£ car/tent £7.50-£9.50, car/caravan £7.50-£9.50, motorhome £7.50-£9.50, motorbike/tent £7.50-£9.50, children £0.85-£1.25
Rental ⏺ £135-£230
⏺ Calor Gaz ⏺ ⏺
Last arrival time: 9:30
➜ From Dalbeattie travel S along the A710 coastal road. After 5 miles turn right to Rockcliffe (1 mile). At brow of hill just after entering Rockcliffe turn left down signposted road to site.

Islecroft Caravan & Camping Site
Dalbeattie DG5 4HE
☎ 01556-610012 Fax 01556-502521
Open Easter-September ▲ ⏺ ⏺
Size 3½ acres, 74 touring pitches, 10 with electric hookup, 4 ⏺, 10 WCs, 1 CWP
£ car/tent £5.55-£6.60, car/caravan £5.55-£6.60, motorhome £5.55-£6.60, motorbike/tent £5.55-£6.60
⏺¼ ✕¼ ⏺¼ ⏺ ⏺ ⏺ ⏺
➜ In Dalbeattie, off Mill Street and adjacent to Colliston Park.

DALKEITH Midlothian 13D2

Fordel Cravan & Camping Park
Lauder Road, Dalkeith EH22 2PH
☎ 0131-660 3921 Fax 0131-663 8891
Open March-October ▲ ⏺ ⏺
Size 4 acres, 45 touring pitches, 12 with electric hookup, 45 level pitches, 7 ⏺, 6 WCs, 2 CWPs
£ car/tent £7-£8, car/caravan £8.50-£12.50, motorhome £8.50-£12.50, motorbike/tent £6.50-£7.50
⏺ ✕ ⏺ ⏺ ⏺ ⏺ ⏺ Calor Gaz ⏺ ⏺ WS
➜ 8 miles SE Edinburgh on main Edinburgh to Newcastle route, A68.

DINGWALL Ross-shire 15D3

Camping & Caravanning Club Site
Jubilee Park Road, Dingwall IV15 9QZ
☎ 01349-862236
Open end March-start November ▲ ⏺ ⏺
Size 10 acres, 90 touring pitches, 52 with electric hookup, 6 ⏺, 13 WCs, 1 CWP
£ car/tent £5.60-£8.60, car/caravan £5.60-£8.60, motorhome £5.60-£8.60, motorbike/tent £5.60-£8.60
⫌ MasterCard Visa
⏺ ⏺ ⏺ ⏺
Last arrival time: 11:00
➜ In Dingwall, coming from S, take by-pass and follow signs. First right down Hill Street, then right at junction, left over railway bridge, then first left.

DRYMEN Stirlingshire 12C2

Camping & Caravanning Club Site
Milarrochy Bay, Balmaha, Drymen
☎ 01360-870236
Open end March-start November ▲ ⏺ ⏺
Size 12 acres, 140 touring pitches, 40 with electric hookup, 6 ⏺, 11 WCs, 1 CWP
£ car/tent £5.60-£8.60, car/caravan £5.60-£8.60, motorhome £5.60-£8.60, motorbike/tent £5.60-£8.60, children £1.50
⫌ MasterCard Visa
⏺ ⏺ ⏺ ⏺ ⏺ ⏺ ⏺ WS
Last arrival time: 11:00
➜ From Dumbarton head N on A82, then follow A811 to Drymen. In Drymen, turn N for Balmaha on B837. Site on left after Balmaha.

DUMFRIES Dumfriesshire   13D4

Southerness Holiday Village
Southerness, Dumfries DG2 8AZ.
☎ 01387-880256 Fax 01387-880429
Open 1 March-31 October A 🚐 🚏
Size 8 acres, 150 touring pitches, 110 with electric hookup, 150 level pitches, 350 static caravans, 35 ⛺, 35 WCs
£ car/tent £6.50-£8, car/caravan £6.50-£9, motorhome £6.50-£9, motorbike/tent £6.50-£8
Rental 🚐
CC MasterCard Visa
🦮 ✕ 🍴 🅿 🔌 🚿 🔥 GR 🍳 TV ⚠ 🔋 Calor Gaz 🦮 WS
➡ Take A710 from Dumfries for 16 miles, signposted from Kirkbean.

DUNBAR East Lothian   13E2

Belhaven Bay Caravan Park
Spott Road, Dunbar EH42 1RS
☎ 01620-893348 Fax 01620-895623

Camping & Caravanning Club Site
Barns Ness, Dunbar EH42 1QP
☎ 01368-863536
Open March-early November A 🚐 🚏
Size 10 acres, 80 touring pitches, 42 with electric hookup, 80 level pitches, 4 ⛺, 9 WCs, 1 CWP
£ car/tent £4.60-£6.80, car/caravan £4.60-£6.80, motorhome £4.60-£6.80, motorbike/tent £4.60-£6.80, children £1.40
CC MasterCard Visa
🅿 🍴 ⚠ 🦮 WS
Last arrival time: 11:00
➡ Look for signpost East Barns, 20 miles N of Berwick-on-Tweed on A1. Turn at junction signposted to site.

DUNBEATH Caithness-shire   15E1

Inver Guest House
Inver, Dunbeath KW6 6EH
☎ 01593-731252
Open April-October A 🚐 🚏

Flat, grassy, sheltered site, near to the sea on the rocky coastline. A good access point for bird watchers,

archeologists and Niel M. Gunn enthusiasts. Forty miles south of John O' Groats.

Size 8 acres, 15 touring pitches, 15 level pitches, 2 ⛺, 4 WCs, 1 CWP
£ car/tent £2-£2.50, car/caravan £2-£2.50, motorhome £2-£2.50, motorbike/tent £2-£2.50, children £1
🦮¼ ✕¼ 🅿¼ 🍴 🅿 🔌 🦮
➡ Follow the A9 N. Bypass Dunbeth village, over the bridge for ½ mile. The site is directly behind Inver Guest House on left.

DUNOON Argyll   12B2

Stratheck Caravan Park
Loch Eck, Dunoon PA23 8SG
☎ 01369-840472 Fax 01369-840472
Open March-December A 🚐 🚏
Size 13 acres, 70 touring pitches, 45 with electric hookup, 70 level pitches, 80 static caravans, 8 ⛺, 18 WCs, 1 CWP
£ car/tent £5-£7, car/caravan £6.50-£8.50, motorhome £6.50-£8.50, motorbike/tent £5-£7
Rental 🚐 £140-£290
🦮 🍴 🅿 🔥 GR ⚠ 🍳 Calor Gaz ♿ 🦮 WS
Last arrival time: 8:00
➡ 7 miles N of Dunoon on A815. 500 yards past Younger Botanic Gardens

DURNESS Sutherland   14C1

Sango Sands Camping & Caravan Site
Sangomore, Durness IV27 4PP
☎ 01971-511262 Fax 01971-511205
Open 1 April-15 October A 🚐 🚏
Size 10 acres, 82 touring pitches, 20 with electric hookup, 60 level pitches, 12 ⛺, 18 WCs, 2 CWPs
£ car/tent £7, car/caravan £7, motorhome £7, motorbike/tent £7, children £1.75
🦮 🦮¼ ✕ 🍴 🅿 🔌 🅿 🍳 Calor Gaz 🦮
Last arrival time: 6:00
➡ On A838 in centre of Durness village, overlooking Sango Bay.

EDINBURGH   13D2

Mortonhall Caravan Park
36 Mortonhall Gate, Frogston Road East, Edinburgh EH16 6TJ
☎ 0131-664 1533 Fax 0131-6645387
Open 27 March-31 October A 🚐 🚏
Size 200 acres, 250 touring pitches, 50 with electric hookup, 18 static caravans, 2 CWPs
CC Visa
🦮 ✕ 🍴 🔍 ♿
➡ From N or S, leave city bypass at Lothianburn or Straiton junctions and follow signs for Mortonhall Caravan Park. From city centre, take main road S from either E or W end of Princes Street.

ELGIN Morayshire   15E3

Red Craig Hotel & Caravan Park
Elgin IV30 2XX
☎ 01343-835663 Fax 01343-835663
Open 1 April-31 October ▲ ⚙ ⛺

A family run hotel and caravan park with every facility on site. Excellent food and carryouts. Weekend entertainment. Panoramic views. Well positioned for the castle and whisky trails.

Size 4 acres, 30 touring pitches, 10 with electric hookup, 10 level pitches, 8 static caravans, 4 ⚐, 6 WCs, 1 CWP
£ car/tent £5.50-£8, car/caravan £8-£9, motorhome £8-£9, motorbike/tent £6-£7
CC MasterCard Visa
🛁¼ ✗ ➍ ⓪ ❶ ⒤ ▣ ⚠ ⬟ Calor ♿ ⭥ WS
Last arrival time: 10:30
➥ Take the signposted road off A96 to Burghead onto B9013, just before entering Burghead turn onto signposted B9040 Hopeman Road. Site is 300 yards on left.

ETTRICK Selkirkshire   13D3

Angecroft Caravan Park
Ettrick TD7 5HY
☎ 01750-62310 Fax 01721-730627
Open all year ▲ ⚙ ⛺

Overlooking water and surrounded by woodland, Angecroft is the ideal place to get away and enjoy the peace and quiet of the Scottish Borders.

Size 5 acres, 10 touring pitches, 10 with electric hookup, 10 level pitches, 30 static caravans, 4 ⚐, 8 WCs, 1 CWP
£ car/tent £5-£7, car/caravan £7-£8.70, motorhome £7-£8.70, motorbike/tent £5-£7
Rental ⚙ Chalet. £90-£230
🛁 ✗¼ ⓪ ❶ ⓪ ▣ ▢ Calor Gaz ♿ ⭥ WS
Last arrival time: 11:00
➥ From A74/M74 enter Lockerbie and take B723 through Borland to Eskdalemuir. Turn left onto B709 and park is on left 11 miles N of Eskdalemuir. From A7 at Langholm take B709 to park (23 miles). From A7 at Hawick take B711. Park is 4 miles W of Tushielaw on B709.

FOCHABERS Morayshire   15E3

Burnside Caravan Site
The Nurseries, Fochabers IV32 7ES
☎ 01343-820362
Open 1 April-30 October ▲ ⚙ ⛺
Size 11 acres, 110 touring pitches, 40 with electric hookup, 110 level pitches, 8 ⚐, 24 WCs, 2 CWPs
£ car/tent £7, car/caravan £7, motorhome £7
🛁¼ ✗¼ ➍¼ ⓪ ❶ ⒤ GR ▣ ⚠ ⭥ WS
➥ From junction on A96 and A98 travel S on A96 for ½ mile. Site on right.

FORFAR Angus   13E1

Drumshademuir Caravan Park
Roundyhill, Forfar DD8 1QT
☎ 01575-573284
Open mid March-end October ▲ ⚙ ⛺
Size 7½ acres, 80 touring pitches, 50 with electric hookup, 80 level pitches, 30 static caravans, 8 ⚐, 12 WCs, 2 CWPs
£ car/tent £5.50-£6.50, car/caravan £8-£9, motorhome £8-£9, motorbike/tent £5-£6.50
Rental Chalet.
🛁 ✗ ➍ ⓪ ❶ ⓪ ⚠ ⬟ Calor Gaz ♿ ⭥ WS
Last arrival time: 11:00
➥ Take A928 from A94 at Glamis for Kirriemuir, 3 miles N of Glamis Castle on Kirriemuir road.

Hints & Tips
Watch your speed.
With a load on your back, acceleration will be slower. You will need more time and space for overtaking. Your combination is longer and wider than your car alone so you will need to take this into consideration before pulling out. Stopping distances will be longer so allow more space between the car in front as your speed increases.

Glen Nevis
Caravan & Camping Park

Beautifully situated in one of Scotland's most famous glens, close to the mighty Ben Nevis, the highest mountain in Britain, yet only 2½ miles from the historic town of Fort William. The park has separate spacious areas for tourers and tents and offers modern, clean, well equipped facilities. Many pitches are fully serviced with electricity, water and drainage. Showers, laundry, scullery, well stocked shop, gas and play areas, are all situated on park and our spacious restaurant and lounge is only a few minutes walk.

**FORT WILLIAM,
INVERNESS-SHIRE PH33 6SX
TEL: 01397 702191**

FORT WILLIAM Inverness-shire   14C4

Glen Nevis Caravan & Camping Park
Glen Nevis, Fort William PH33 6SX
☎ 01397-702191 Fax 01397-703904
Open 15 March-31 October Å 🚐 🚍

Spacious park with seperate screened areas for caravans, motor caravans and tents. Good standard of facilities and 24 hour supervision in season. Magnificient location with outstanding scenery.

Size 30 acres, 380 touring pitches, 180 with electric hookup, 280 level pitches, 34 🐕, 73 WCs, 3 CWPs
£ car/tent £7.40-£10, car/caravan £7.80-£10.20, motorhome £7.40-£10, motorbike/tent £6.80-£9.30, children £0.95-£1.40
℃ MasterCard Visa
🛒 ✕ 🍽 🚿 ☎ 🎣 ♿ 🛒 Calor Gaz ♿ ☂
Last arrival time: 11:00
➡ A82 to mini roundabout at N outskirts of Fort William. Exit for Glen Nevis Park. Site is 2½ miles on right.

Linnhe Caravan & Chalet Park
Corpach, Fort William PH33 7NL
☎ 01397-772376 Fax 01397-772007
Open 15 December-31 October Å 🚐 🚍

Beautifully landscaped with magnificent views over Loch Eil. Enjoy a host of outdoor activities or simply relax in well tended surroundings. Graded "Excellent". Private beach.

Size 13½ acres, 64 touring pitches, 61 with electric hookup, 64 level pitches, 77 static caravans, 8 🐕, 15 WCs, 1 CWP
£ car/tent £6.50-£8, car/caravan £8-£12.50, motorhome £8-£12.50, motorbike/tent £6.50-£8, children £0.50
Rental 🚐 Chalet. caravans £155-£405, chalets £350-£525
℃ MasterCard Visa
🛒 🍽 🚿 ☎ 🎣 ⚠ 🔲 Calor Gaz ☂ WS
Last arrival time: 9:00
➡ On A830, 1½ miles W of Corpach village, signposted, 5 miles from Fort William.

FORTROSE Ross-shire   15D3

Camping & Caravanning Club Site
Well Road, Rosemarkie, Fortrose
☎ 01380-621117
Open end March-end September Å 🚐 🚍
Size 5 acres, 60 touring pitches, 5 🐕, 16 WCs, 2 CWPs
£ car/tent £4.60-£6.80, car/caravan £4.60-£6.80, motorhome £4.60-£6.80, motorbike/tent £4.60-£6.80, children £1.40
℃ MasterCard Visa
🍽 ☎ ♿ ☂
Last arrival time: 11:00
➡ Follow A9 over Kessock Bridge, turn right at Tore roundabout on A832 signposted Fortrose and Cromarty. In Fortrose turn right.

GAIRLOCH Ross-shire   14B2

Gruinard Bay Caravan Park
Laide, Gairloch IV22 2ND
☎ 01445-731225 Fax 01445-731225
Open 1 April-31 October Å 🚐 🚍

Level, grassy site adjacent to a sandy beach. Quiet and restful with superb views over Gruinard Bay to the islands and mountains.

Size 3½ acres, 34 touring pitches, 18 with electric hookup, 18 level pitches, 14 static caravans, 4 ⋒, 9 WCs, 1 CWP
£ car/tent £8, car/caravan £8, motorhome £8, motorbike/tent £8, children £1.25
Rental ⊞ £130-£215
⅃ ⅃¼ ✕¼ ⬤¼ ⊡ ⬛ ⊟ Calor Gaz ⊁
Last arrival time: 10:00
➡ From A835(T) Inverness to Ullapool road, at Braemore junction (near Corrieshalloch Falls), turn left onto A832 signposted to Gairloch. Park is on right.

Sands Holiday Centre
Gairloch IV21 2DL
☎ 01445-712152 Fax 01445-712518
Open 1 April-15 October ⋀ ⊞ ⊞

Positioned beside a sandy beach with views westward. Ideally located for walking, fishing, watersports and touring.

Size 50 acres, 300 touring pitches, 60 with electric hookup, 20 static caravans, 22 ⋒, 54 WCs, 1 CWP
£ car/tent £7-£9, car/caravan £7-£12, motorhome £7-£9, motorbike/tent £6.50-£9
Rental ⊞
ℂℂ MasterCard Visa
⅃ ⊡ ⬛ ⊟ ⋔ Calor Gaz ⊁
Last arrival time: 10:00
➡ Follow A382 to Gairloch. At Gairloch take B8021 to Melvaig, 4 miles along this road will bring you to park.

GLASGOW   12C2

Craigendmuir Park
3 Campsie View, Stepps, Glasgow G33 6AF
☎ 0141-779 4159 Fax 0141-779 4057
Open all year ⋀ ⊞ ⊞
Size 2½ acres, 20 touring pitches, 12 with electric hookup, 20 static caravans, 10 ⋒, 10 WCs, 2 CWPs
£ car/tent £6.50, car/caravan £6.50, motorhome £6.50, motorbike/tent £6.50
Rental ⊞ Chalet. from £150
ℂℂ MasterCard Visa
⅃ ✕ ⊡ ⬛ ⊟ Calor ᪥ ⊁
➡ From junction 11 on M8 follow A80 to Cumberland/Stirling. From N on A80 to Stepps.

Strathclyde Country Park
366 Hamilton Road, Motherwell ML1 3ED
☎ 01698-266155 Fax 01698-252925
Open April-October ⋀ ⊞ ⊞

➡

← Strathclyde Country Park

One of Scotlands leading centres for outdoor recreation, with a wide range of activities including, land and water sports, sandy beaches, play areas and a programme of special events.

Size 14 acres, 250 touring pitches, 100 with electric hookup, 100 level pitches, 32 ⚲, 24 WCs, 4 CWPs
£ car/tent £6.45, car/caravan £7.50, motorhome £7.50, motorbike/tent £6.45
⚑ ✗¼ ⬤¼ ⎙ ⬛ ⟁ Calor ♿ ↟ WS
➜ From M74 junction 5 take A725 (Belshill). Park signed off roundabout, also off motorway.

GLENCOE Argyll   14C4

Invercoe Caravans
Invercoe, Glencoe PA39 4HP
☎ 01855-811210 Fax 01855-811210
Open 1 April-31 October ▲ 🚐 🚏
Size 5 acres, 60 touring pitches, 40 with electric hookup, 55 level pitches, 5 static caravans, 9 ⚲, 14 WCs, 3 CWPs
£ car/tent £8-£9, car/caravan £9-£10, motorhome £9-£10, motorbike/tent £8-£9, children £0.50
Rental 🚐 £170-£265
⚑ ✗¼ ⬤¼ ⎙ ⬛ ⬛ ⟁ ⊞   Calor Gaz ♿ ↟
Last arrival time: 11:00
➜ From Glasgow follow A82 to Glencoe. At Glencoe Hotel turn right onto B863 for ¼ mile.

GLENLUCE Wigtownshire   12B4

Glenluce Caravan and Camping
Glenluce DG8 0QR
☎ 01581-300412
Open mid March-mid October ▲ 🚐 🚏

Peaceful, secluded, family run sun trap park. Close to the village, beach, golfing, bowling, pony trekking, fishing and superb walks.

Size 5 acres, 18 touring pitches, 12 with electric hookup, 18 level pitches, 30 static caravans, 4 ⚲, 7 WCs, 1 CWP
£ car/tent £6.50-£8, car/caravan £7.50-£9, motorhome £7.50-£9, motorbike/tent £6.50-£8
Rental 🚐 £120-£295
⚑¼ ✗¼ ⬤¼ ⎙ ⬛ ⎙ ⟁ Calor Gaz ↟ WS

Last arrival time: 11:00
➜ Exit A75 to Glenluce village. Park entrance is opposite Inglenook restaurant in centre of village.

GRETNA Dumfriesshire   13D4

Braids Caravan Park
Annan Road, Gretna DG16 5DQ
☎ 01461-337409 Fax 01461-337409
Open all year ▲ 🚐 🚏

Family run full facility park in an ideal touring centre. Touring advice. Open all year. Rallies welcome. Nicely placed away from motorway. B&B in owners bungalow.

Size 4 acres, 84 touring pitches, 58 with electric hookup, 50 level pitches, 5 static caravans, 8 ⚲, 10 WCs, 3 CWPs
£ car/tent £6-£7, car/caravan £6.75-£7.75, motorhome £6.75-£7.75, motorbike/tent £6
⚑ ✗¼ ⬤ ⎙ ⬛ ⎙ ⟁ Calor Gaz ♿ ↟ WS
Last arrival time: 12:00
➜ A74 N, A75, second left into Gretna.

HADDINGTON East Lothian   13E2

Monks' Muir
Haddington EH41 3SB
☎ 01620-860340 Fax 01620-860340
Open all year ▲ 🚐 🚏

A multi-award winning, friendly, sheltered site with glorious views and excellent facilities in an area of great beauty. Only 15 minutes from the fringes of Edinburgh, surrounded by fine beaches, golf courses and farmland.

Size 8 acres, 43 touring pitches, 35 with electric hookup, 43 level pitches, 25 static caravans, 6 ⌂, 18 WCs, 2 CWPs
£ car/tent £8-£8.60, car/caravan £8.40-£11, motorhome £8.40-£11, motorbike/tent £8
Rental ⌂
⚡ ✕ ⬤ 🔲 🔳 🗄 ⚠ ⬛ Calor Gaz ✕ WS
Last arrival time: 12:00
➥ Directly on main A1 road, north side, equidistant from Haddington and East Linton.

HAWICK Roxburghshire   13E3

Bonchester Bridge Caravan Park
Bonchester Bridge, Hawick TD9 8JN
☎ 01450-860676
Open 1 April-31 October ⛺ ⌂ 🚐
Size 2 acres, 20 touring pitches, 20 with electric hookup, 20 level pitches, 1 static caravans, 4 ⌂, 10 WCs, 1 CWP
£ car/tent £5-£6.50, car/caravan £6-£7, motorhome £5-£6.50, motorbike/tent £5-£7.50, children £1.50-£3
Rental ⌂ £110
⚡ ⚡¼ ✕ ✕¼ ⬤ 🔲 🗄 🔳 Calor Gaz ✕ ✕
Last arrival time: 9:00
➥ Off A68 and A7.

INCHTURE Perthshire   13D1

Inchmartine Caravan Park & Nurseries
Inchture
☎ 01821-670212 Fax 01821-670266
Open end March-end October ⛺ ⌂ 🚐
Size 4 acres, 45 touring pitches, 36 with electric hookup, 36 level pitches, 3 ⌂, 10 WCs
£ car/tent £8, car/caravan £8, motorhome £8, motorbike/tent £8
⚡¼ ✕¼ ⬤¼ Calor Gaz ✕ WS
Last arrival time: 8:00
➥ Site signed from A85 Perth/Dundee road, 1½ miles from Perth.

INVERARAY Argyll   12B1

Argyll Caravan & Camping Park
Inveraray PA32 8XT
☎ 01499-302285 Fax 01499-302421
Open 1 April-31 October ⛺ ⌂ 🚐

Attractively situated on the shores of Loch Fyne. 2½ miles south of Inveraray on A83. All normal modern amenities including shop, lounge bar, recreation hall and laundrette.

Size 8 acres, 60 touring pitches, 40 with electric hookup, 60 level pitches, 200 static caravans, 16 ⌂, 80 WCs, 2 CWPs
£ car/tent £6.50-£8.20, car/caravan £8-£9.50, motorhome £8-£9.50, motorbike/tent £6.50-£8.20
⟨⟨ MasterCard Visa
⚡ ✕ ⬤ 🔲 🔳 🗄 ▶ GR 🔳 ⚠ ⬛ Calor Gaz 👤 ✕ WS
➥ 2 miles SW of Inveraray on A83.

INVERGARRY Inverness-shire   14C4

Faichem Park
Ardgarry Farm, Faichem, Invergarry PH35 4HG
☎ 01809-501226
Open April-October ⛺ ⌂ 🚐

A quiet, family run park, spotlessly clean and well maintained. Set amidst mountains and pines. A perfect location for touring the Western Highlands. B.G.H.P. graded excellent. Award for excellence in sanitation facilities and attractive environment.

Size 2 acres, 30 touring pitches, 14 with electric hookup, 11 level pitches, 2 ⌂, 6 WCs, 1 CWP
£ car/tent £6.50-£7, car/caravan £6.50-£7, motorhome £6.50-£7, motorbike/tent £6.50-£7, children £0.25
Rental ⌂ Chalet. £80-£405
🔲 🗄 Calor Gaz ✕
Last arrival time: 10:00
➥ From A82 at Invergarry take A87. Continue for 1 mile and turn right at Faichem signpost. Bear left up hill and entrance is first on right.

Hints & Tips
In winter take your seat cushions home. Not only will they keep dry but thieves won't be able use or sell a caravan without upholstery

Faichemard Farm Camping & Caravanning

Faichem, Invergarry PH35 4HG
☎ 01809-501314
Open April-October Å 🚐 🚎

A unique ten acre site, 40 pitches each with its own picnic table and magnificent view.

Size 10 acres, 40 touring pitches, 12 with electric hookup, 25 level pitches, 4 🚿, 8 WCs, 1 CWP
£ car/tent £6, car/caravan £6, motorhome £6, motorbike/tent £6
Rental Chalet.
🗄 🔌 🖱 🛅
Last arrival time: 10:00
➔ One mile W of Invergarry on A87, turn right and go past Ardgarry Farm and Faichem Park campsite. Turn right at sign for A & D Grant.

INVERNESS Inverness-shire   15D3

Auchnahillin Caravan Park

Daviot East, Inverness IV1 2XQ
☎ 01463-772286 Fax 01463-772286
Open Easter-mid October Å 🚐 🚎

Highly commended park with excellent amenities. Set amid splendid Highland scenery and nestling in a peaceful valley with views of the surrounding forests and mountains, Auchnahillin is the ideal base for touring or enjoying the multitude of activities in this lovely area.

Size 12 acres, 65 touring pitches, 35 with electric hookup, 65 level pitches, 22 static caravans, 6 🚿, 18 WCs, 1 CWP

£ car/tent £5.50-£8, car/caravan £7.50-£9, motorhome £7.50-£9, motorbike/tent £4.50-£6.50, children £0.50
Rental 🚐 Chalet. £135-£295
🗄 ✕ 🗄 🔌 🖱 🔳 🧺 🖱 🛅 Calor Gaz 🚻 🛅 WS
Last arrival time: 10:00
➔ Turn off A9 S of Inverness onto Moy/Daviot East road (B9154). The park is just N of Moy.

Bunchrew Caravan Park

Bunchrew, Inverness IV3 6TD
☎ 01463-237802 Fax 01463-225803
Open April-December Å 🚐 🚎

Situated on the shore of the Beauly Firth with wonderful views of the water and hills. A perfect base for touring the Highlands.

Size 15 acres, 100 touring pitches, 50 with electric hookup, 100 level pitches, 14 static caravans, 8 🚿, 18 WCs, 1 CWP
£ car/tent £7.50-£8, car/caravan £7.50-£8, motorhome £7.50-£8, motorbike/tent £6-£6.50, children £1
Rental 🚐 £140-£225
🗄 ✕¼ 🗄 🔌 🖱 🧺 Calor Gaz 🚻 WS
➔ Leave Inverness on A862, site is 3 miles W of town.

Coulmore Bay Site

North Kessock, Inverness
☎ 01463-731322
Open April-November Å 🚐 🚎

Level farm site beside shingle/rock beach and next to a water sports centre. Small shop open June-August, others 3 miles.

Size 5 acres, 30 touring pitches, 8 with electric hookup, 30 level pitches, 80 static caravans, 6 ♠, 6 WCs, 2 CWPs
£ car/tent £6, car/caravan £8, motorhome £8, motorbike/tent £6
CC MasterCard
✕ ♥ 🗗 🗐 🛗 ⊟ ♿ ⚓ WS
Last arrival time: 10:30
➡ 3 miles W of North Kessock, along shore road.

Scaniport Camping & Caravanning Park
Scaniport, Inverness IV1 2DL
📞 **01463-751351**
Open Easter-September ▲ ⚏ ⊞
Size 2 acres, 30 touring pitches, 30 level pitches, 2 ♠, 6 WCs, 1 CWP
£ car/tent £4.50, car/caravan £5.50-£6.50, motorhome £5.50-£6.50, motorbike/tent £4.50, children £0.75
🗐 ⊟ Calor Gaz ♿ ⚓
➡ From Inverness take B862 towards Dores, 5 miles on site is opposite telephone box at Scaniport.

IRVINE Ayrshire   **12C3**

Cunninghamhead Estate Caravan Park
Irvine, Kilmarnock KA3 2PE
📞 **01294-850238**
Open 1 April-30 September ▲ ⚏ ⊞
Size 10 acres, 60 touring pitches, 18 with electric hookup, 60 level pitches, 50 static caravans, 4 ♠, 14 WCs, 1 CWP
£ car/tent £6.50-£8, car/caravan £6.50-£8, motorhome £6.50-£8, motorbike/tent £6-£7
Rental ⚏ £125-£235
🗐 🗗 ⊟ 🗐 🗐 🗐 🛗 ⊟ Gaz ⚓ WS
Last arrival time: 10:00
➡ From S take A78 to Irvine by-pass. From Newhouse interchange take A736 Glasgow Road (Long Drive) through Oldhall roundabout and Newmoor roundabout until you reach Stanecastle roundabout. Turn right onto B769 Stewarton Road. The park is 2½ miles on left.

ISLE OF ARRAN   **12B2**

Middleton Caravan & Camping Park
Lamlash KA27 8NN
📞 **01770-600251**
Open mid April-mid October ▲ ⚏ ⊞
Size 7 acres, 30 touring pitches, 40 level pitches, 49 static caravans, 4 ♠, 9 WCs, 1 CWP
£ car/tent £7-£9, car/caravan £7.50-£9.50, motorhome £7-£9, motorbike/tent £6.50-£7.50, children £1.25
🍴¼ ✕¼ 🗗 Calor Gaz ♿ ⚓
Last arrival time: 10:00
➡ From Brodick ferry turn left 3 miles to Lamlash. Past Police Station on left, over bridge, first left and then first right.

JEDBURGH Roxburghshire   **13E3**

Camping & Caravanning Club Site
Elliot Park, Jedburgh TD8 6EF
📞 **01835-863393**
Open end March-start September ▲ ⚏ ⊞
Size 3 acres, 60 touring pitches, 25 with electric hookup, 8 ♠, 6 WCs, 1 CWP
£ car/tent £4.60-£6.80, car/caravan £4.60-£6.80, motorhome £4.60-£6.80, motorbike/tent £4.60-£6.80, children £1.40
CC MasterCard Visa
🗗 🗐 ♿ ⚓
Last arrival time: 11:00
➡ From S on A68 keep to main road. First turn after bridges. Site is on northern outskirts of Jedburgh.

JOHN O'GROATS Caithness   **15E1**

John O'Groats Caravan Site
John O'Groats KW1 4YS
📞 **01955-611329**
Open April-October ▲ ⚏ ⊞

On the sea front overlooking Pentland Firth and the Orkney islands. Day trips available. Magnificent cliff scenery 1½ miles from site. Snack bar, restaurant, harbour, museum, craft shops 200 yards. Wild life cruises. Seal colony three miles.

Size 4 acres, 90 touring pitches, 28 with electric hookup, 70 level pitches, 8 ♠, 10 WCs, 2 CWPs
£ car/tent £6.50-£7.50, car/caravan £6.50-£7.50, motorhome £6.50-£7.50, motorbike/tent £5-£5.50, children £0.50
🍴¼ ✕¼ ♥¼ 🗐 🗗 ⊟ Calor Gaz ♿ ⚓
Last arrival time: 10:00
➡ Entrance on right at N end of A9 on seafront beside last house in Scotland.

Don't forget to mention the guide
When booking, please remember to tell the site that you chose it from
RAC Camping & Caravanning 1998

KELSO Roxburghshire   13E3

Springwood Caravan Park
Springwood Estate, Kelso TD5 8LS
☎ 01573-224596 **Fax** 01573-224033
Open April-October **Å 🚐 🚙**

*Situated in wooded parkland adjacent to River Teviot,
only one mile from market town of Kelso. Riverside
walks adjacent to park, short grass and clean
facilities.*

Size 30 acres, 46 touring pitches, 46 with electric
hookup, 15 level pitches, 230 static caravans, 8 🚿, 30
WCs, 1 CWP
£ car/caravan £8-£9, motorhome £8-£9, children
£0.50
⊂⊂ MasterCard Visa
◻ ⚟ ◻ GR ◻ ⚠ Calor ♿ ⊬
Last arrival time: 10:00
➡ A699 from Kelso to Selkirk. Site in 1 mile.

KENMORE Perthshire   12C1

Kenmore Caravan & Camping Park
Kenmore, Aberfeldy PH15 2HN
☎ 01887-830226 **Fax** 01887-830211
Open mid March-mid October **Å 🚐 🚙**

*A well located site by the River and Loch Tay in
magnificent Highland Perthshire. First class facilities
available, including bar, restaurant and golf course.*

Size 14 acres, 160 touring pitches, 140 with electric
hookup, 60 level pitches, 60 static caravans, 14 🚿, 45
WCs, 4 CWPs
£ car/tent £7-£8, car/caravan £8-£9, motorhome £8-
£9, motorbike/tent £6-£7, children £0.50

Rental Chalet.

℃ MasterCard Visa

🛒 ✕ ☕ 🅿 🔌 🍴 ▶ ⚡ 🔳 GR TV ⚠ 🔌 Calor Gaz ♿ 🐕 WS

Last arrival time: 10:00

➡ A9 N to Ballinluig. A837 W to Kenmore. Through village over bridge on right.

Pettycur Bay Caravan Park

Kinghorn Road, Kinghorn KY3 9YE

📞 01592-890321 **Fax** 01592-891420

Open 1 March-31 October 🏕 🚐 🚏

Size 42 acres, 50 touring pitches, 45 with electric hookup, 34 level pitches, 450 static caravans, 12 🚿, 20 WCs, 2 CWPs

£ car/tent £8-£12, car/caravan £8-£12, motorhome £8-£12, motorbike/tent £122

Rental 🚐 £95-£369

℃ MasterCard Visa

🛒 ✕ ☕ 🅿 🔌 🍴 TV ⚠ 🔌 Calor 🐕 WS

Last arrival time: 10:00

➡ From Forth Road Bridge take junction 1 A921 - Park located between Burntisland and Kinghorn.

Kilvrecht Camping & Caravan Site

Tay District Forestry Commission, Inver Park, Dunkeld PH8 0JR

📞 01350-727284 **Fax** 01350-728635

Open 26 March-25 October 🏕 🚐 🚏

Size 3 hectares, 60 touring pitches, 60 level pitches, 4 WCs, 1 CWP

£ car/tent £5, car/caravan £5, motorhome £5, motorbike/tent £3

⚠ 🐕

➡ From Kinloch Rannoch take South Loch Rannoch road for 3½ miles to the site which is set in Birch Woods, ¾ mile from southern shore of Loch Rannoch.

Silvercraigs Caravan & Camping Site

Kirkcudbright DG6 4BT

📞 01557-330123 **Fax** 01556-502521

Open Easter-October 🏕 🚐 🚏

Size 5 acres, 50 touring pitches, 49 with electric hookup, 40 level pitches, 4 🚿, 8 WCs, 1 CWP

£ car/tent £6.60-£8.15, car/caravan £6.60-£8.15, motorhome £6.60-£8.15, motorbike/tent £6.60-£8.15

🛒¼ ✕¼ 🛒¼ 🔌 ☕ ⚠ 🐕

➡ In Kirkcudbright off Silvercraigs Road, overlooking own.

Dunroamin Caravan Park

Main Street, Lairg IV27 4AR

📞 01549-402447 **Fax** 01549-402447

Open 1 April-31 October 🏕 🚐 🚏

Situated in the village of Lairg on the south side of the A839, 300 yards from the village centre. Holiday caravans for rent. Tents, caravans and motorhomes all welcome.

Size 4 acres, 50 touring pitches, 16 with electric hookup, 50 level pitches, 10 static caravans, 2 🚿, 5 WCs, 1 CWP

£ car/tent £5-£6.50, car/caravan £5.50-£7.50, motorhome £5.50-£7.50, motorbike/tent £5-£6.50, children £0.50

℃ MasterCard Visa

🛒¼ ✕ 🛒 ☕ 🔌 ☕ 🔌 Calor Gaz 🐕

Last arrival time: 10:00

➡ S side of A839, 300 yards from Lairg village centre and Loch Shin. Adjacent to Crofters restaurant.

Hints & Tips

Watch your speed.
With a load on your back, acceleration will be slower. You will need more time and space for overtaking. Your combination is longer and wider than your car alone so you will need to take this into consideration before pulling out. Stopping distances will be longer so allow more space between the car in front as your speed increases.

Woodend Caravan & Camping Park

Achnairn, Lairg IV27 4DN

📞 01549-402248

Open 1 April-30 September A 🚐 🏕

Quiet craft site with beautiful views of Loch Shin, woodlands and hills. Ideal touring centre for all of northwest Sutherland, with many forest walks.

Size 4 acres, 55 touring pitches, 22 with electric hookup, 5 static caravans, 4 🚿, 9 WCs, 1 CWP
£ car/tent £5.50, car/caravan £5.50-£6.50, motorhome £5.50-£6.50, motorbike/tent £5.50
Rental 🚐 £130 weekly, £18 nightly.
🛒 🗑 📞 🗄 🅰 Calor Gaz 🐕
Last arrival time: 11:00
➡ From Lairg take A836 for 3 miles. Then take A838 and follow site signs.

Clyde Valley Caravan Park

Kirkfieldbank, Lanark ML11 9JW

📞 01555-663951

Open 1 April-31 October A 🚐 🏕

Set in the orchards of the Clyde Valley, with two fishing rivers running by, and a children's play area. Restaurant and shop adjacent.

Size 10 acres, 50 touring pitches
🔲
➡ ½ mile W of Lanark on A73 turn left A72, at ½ mile on, turn right just before River Clyde bridge.

Crossburn Caravan Park

Douglas, Lanark ML11 0QA

📞 01555-851029

Open all year A 🚐 🏕
Size 4 acres, 50 touring pitches, 50 with electric hookup, 50 level pitches, 6 🚿, 14 WCs, 1 CWP
£ car/tent £5.50, car/caravan £6.50, motorhome £6.50, motorbike/tent £5.50
ℂℂ MasterCard Visa
🛒¼ ✗¼ 🔌 Calor 🐕
➡ 2 miles W of M74 on Edinburgh to Ayr road, then A70 to village of Douglas.

Thirlestane Castle Caravan & Camping

Lauder TD2 6RU

📞 01578-722254 **Fax** 01578-718749

Open 1 April-1 October A 🚐 🏕
Size 4 acres, 50 touring pitches, 18 with electric hookup, 30 level pitches, 8 🚿, 10 WCs, 1 CWP
£ car/tent £7, car/caravan £7, motorhome £7, 🗑 📞 🔲
♿ 🐕 WS
➡ Signed off A68 and A697, ½ mile S of Lauder.

Dovecot Caravan Park

Northwaterbridge, Laurencekirk AB30 1QL

📞 01674-840630 **Fax** 01674-840630

Open 1 April-31 October A 🚐 🏕
Size 6 acres, 25 touring pitches, 25 with electric hookup, 25 level pitches, 40 static caravans, 6 🚿, 9 WCs, 1 CWP

£ car/tent £6.75-£7.75, car/caravan £6.75-£7.75, motorhome £6.75-£7.75, motorbike/tent £5.50-£6.50

Rental ⊕

⚑ ▣ ⚑ ▢ Calor **&** ⚑ WS

Last arrival time: 8:00

➡ Turn off A90 at signpost for RAF base. Site is 500 yards on left.

LEVEN Fife   13E1

Woodland Gardens Caravan & Camping Site

Lundin Links, Leven KY8 5QG

☎ 01333-360319

Open March-October **⚑ ⊕ ⚑**

Size 1 acre, 20 touring pitches, 20 with electric hookup, 20 level pitches, 5 static caravans, 2 ⏚, 7 WCs, 1 CWP

£ car/tent £6.60, car/caravan £6.60, motorhome £6.60, motorbike/tent £6.60, children £1.10

Rental ⊕ £95-£240

⚑ ▣ ⚑ ▢ GR TV ⚠ Calor Gaz ⚑ WS

Last arrival time: 10:00

➡ Turn N off A915 at E end of Lundin Links. Site is signposted on A915 and is ½ mile from main road.

LOCKERBIE Dumfriesshire   13D4

Halleaths Touring Camping & Caravan Park

Lochmaben, Lockerbie DG11 1NA

☎ 01387-810630 Fax 01387-810630

Open mid March-16 November **⚑ ⊕ ⚑**

Size 8 acres, 70 touring pitches, 60 with electric hookup, 70 level pitches, 9 static caravans, 8 ⏚, 12 WCs, 1 CWP

£ car/tent £5, car/caravan £7, motorhome £7, motorbike/tent £5, children £0.50

Rental ⊕ £10 ppn

⚑ ⚑¼ ▣ ⚑ ▢ ⚠ Calor **&** ⚑ WS

➡ From M74 Lockerbie take A709 following signs to Lochmaben and Dumfries. Site on right 3 miles W of Lockerbie

Hoddom Castle Caravan Park

Hoddom, Lockerbie DG11 1AS

☎ 01576-300251 Fax 01576-300757

Open Easter-October **⚑ ⊕ ⚑**

Size 24 acres, 170 touring pitches, 140 with electric hookup, 170 level pitches, 30 static caravans, 15 ⏚, 60 WCs, 1 CWP

£ car/tent £6-£11, car/caravan £6-£11, motorhome £6-£11, motorbike/tent £5.50-£11

CC MasterCard Visa

⚑ ✕ ▰ ⚑ ⚑ ▢ ▢ ⚑ ⚑ GR ⚑ ⚠ ⚑ Calor Gaz **&** ⚑ WS

➡ Turn off A74 at Ecclefechan. Turn left at roundabout towards village. At church turn right onto B725 to Dalton. Entrance is 2½ miles on right.

LONGNIDDRY East Lothian   13E2

Seton Sands Holiday Park

Longniddry EH32 0QF

☎ 01875-813333

Open March-October **⚑ ⚑**

A family holiday park with beautiful beaches nearby and only 12 miles from the capital of Scotland - Edinburgh, the park boasts a new indoor pool, kids club and a wide range of leisure facilities, restaurants and bars, excellent cabaret entertainment. A 'British Holidays Park'.

Size 60 touring pitches, 32 with electric hookup, 620 static caravans, 6 ⏚, 11 WCs, 1 CWP

£ car/caravan £10-£14, motorhome £10-£14

CC MasterCard Visa

Rental ⊕

⚑ ⚑¼ ✕ ✕¼ ▰ ▰¼ ▣ ⚑ ⚑ ⚑ ⚑ GR ⚑ ⚠ ⚑ Calor **& ⚑**

➡ From Trament roundabout turn on B6371 for Cockenzie, then right on B1348. Site 1 mile on right.

LOSSIEMOUTH Morayshire   15E2

Silver Sands Leisure Park
Covesea, West Beach, Lossiemouth IV31 6SP
☎ 01343-813262 fax 01343-815205
Open March-October A 🚐 🚛
Size 70 acres, 140 touring pitches, 74 with electric hookup, 66 level pitches, 230 static caravans, 13 🚿, 21 WCs, 1 CWP
£ car/tent £7.25-£10.75, car/caravan £7.25-£10.75, motorhome £7.25-£10.75, motorbike/tent £7.25-£10.75
Rental 🚐
ℂℂ MasterCard Visa
🖂 ✗ 🍴 🗑 🔋 🛱 🔌 GR 🔍 ⚠ 🔥 Gaz 🐕 🐾 WS
Last arrival time: 10:30
➡ Follow A96 from Inverness-Aberdeen until you reach Elgin, then follow A941 to Lossiemouth. We are situated beneath the Covesea lighthouse.

LUSS Dunbartonshire   12C2

Camping & Caravanning Club Site
Luss, Loch Lomond, Glasgow
☎ 01436-860658
Open end March-start November A 🚐 🚛
Size 10 acres, 90 touring pitches, 16 with electric hookup, 7 🚿, 8 WCs, 1 CWP
£ car/tent £5.60-£8.60, car/caravan £5.60-£8.60, motorhome £5.60-£8.60, motorbike/tent £5.60-£8.60, children £1.50
ℂℂ MasterCard Visa
🔋 🚿 ⚠ 🐾
Last arrival time: 11:00
➡ Site is on lochside ¼ mile N of Luss on A82 Glasgow to Fort William road. It lies between road and Loch Lomond.

MAYBOLE Ayrshire   12C3

Camping & Caravanning Club Site
Culzean Castle, Maybole KA19 8JX
☎ 01655-760627
Open end March-start November A 🚐 🚛
Size 10 acres, 90 touring pitches, 60 with electric hookup, 8 🚿, 9 WCs, 1 CWP
£ car/tent £5.20-£7.80, car/caravan £5.20-£7.80, motorhome £5.20-£7.80, motorbike/tent £5.20-£7.80, children £1.50
ℂℂ MasterCard Visa
🗑 🔋 ⚠ & 🐾
Last arrival time: 11:00
➡ Entrance to Culzean Castle and site S from Ayr on A719, signposted.

MOFFAT Dumfriesshire   13D3

Camping & Caravanning Club Site
Hammerland's Farm, Moffat DG10 9QL
☎ 01683-220436

Open end March-start November A 🚐 🚛
Size 14 acres, 200 touring pitches, 89 with electric hookup, 8 🚿, 20 WCs, 1 CWP
£ car/tent £5.60-£8.60, car/caravan £5.60-£8.60, motorhome £5.60-£8.60, motorbike/tent £5.60-£8.60, children £1.50
ℂℂ MasterCard Visa
🔋¼ 🗑 🔋 ⚠ & 🐾 WS
Last arrival time: 11:00
➡ Take A708 NE from Moffat. Site approach is on right before Caspers Inn. Turn left at cadet hut, then left over bridge, follow signs.

MUIR OF ORD Ross-shire   15D3

Druimorrin Caravan & Camping Park
Orrin Bridge, Urray, Muir Of Ord IV6 7UL
☎ 01997-433252
Open Easter-end September A 🚐 🚛
Size 5½ acres, 60 touring pitches, 24 with electric hookup, 60 level pitches, 4 🚿, 13 WCs, 1 CWP
£ car/tent £5-£7, car/caravan £6-£7, motorhome £5.50-£6.50, motorbike/tent £4.50-£5.50
🔋 🗑 🔋 🔌 Calor Gaz 🐾 WS
Last arrival time: 12:00
➡ From Inverness take A9 N to Tore roundabout. A832 signposted Muir of Ord, pass through village and continue W on A832 for 2½ miles, site is on right.

MUSSELBURGH Midlothian   13D2

Drum Mohr Caravan Park
Levenhall, Musselburgh EH21 8JS
☎ 01316-656867 Fax 01316-536859
Open 1 March-31 October A 🚐 🚛

Family run and set in beautiful surroundings with easy access to Edinburgh. Situated between the B1361 and B1348.
Size 10 acres, 120 touring pitches, 100 with electric hookup, 120 level pitches, 12 🚿, 20 WCs, 2 CWPs
£ car/tent £8-£9, car/caravan £8-£9, motorhome £8-£9, motorbike/tent £8-£9, children £1
🔋 🗑 🔋 ⚠ Calor Gaz & 🐾
Last arrival time: 10:00
➡ From the A1 follow park signs situated between the B1348 and B1361 above the mining museum.

Spindrift Caravan Park

Little Kildrummie, Nairn IV12 5QU
☎ 01667-453992
Open 1 April-31 October ⚠ 🚐 🚙

Small, secluded family run park, overlooking the River Nairn. Winner of an Environmental Award 1996 and an ideal base from which to explore the Highlands.

Size 3 acres, 40 touring pitches, 28 with electric hookup, 40 level pitches, 4 🏠, 8 WCs, 2 CWPs
£ car/tent £5.50-£8.50, car/caravan £5.50-£8.50, motorhome £5.50-£8.50, motorbike/tent £5.50-£8.50
🛁¼ ✕¼ 🚿¼ 🍴 🔌 🍳 Calor Gaz ♿ ﹖
Last arrival time: 10:00
➡ From Nairn take B9090 Cawdor road S for 1½ miles. Turn right at sharp left hand bend onto unclassified road signposted Little Kidrummie. The entrance is 400 yards on left.

Cock Inn Caravan Park

Auchenmalg, Glenluce, Newton Stewart DG8 0JH
☎ 01581-500227
Open 1 March-31 October ⚠ 🚐 🚙

Quiet family park overlooking Luce Bay offering a full range of facilities including a shop, sauna, sunbed, laundry room, free showers and holiday caravans. Ideal for fishing, golf and hillwalking. Tourers welcome.

Size 7 acres, 30 touring pitches, 20 with electric hookup, 13 level pitches, 60 static caravans, 5 🏠, 12 WCs, 3 CWPs

£ car/tent £6.50-£8, car/caravan £6.50-£11, motorhome £6.50-£11, motorbike/tent £6-£8
Rental 🚐 Chalet. £130-£235
🛁 ✕ 🍴 🔌 🍳 🖼 🅿 Calor Gaz ♿ ﹖ WS
Last arrival time: 10:30
➡ From A75 Newton Stewart/Stranraer road take A747 to Port William for 5 miles to Auchenmalg.

Three Lochs Caravan Park

Balminnoch, Kirkcowan, Newton Stewart DG8 0EP
☎ 01671-830304 **Fax** 01671-830335
⚠ 🚐 🚙

Set opposite beautiful Loch Heron, with newly refurbished shower block. We are now AA four pennant and have been upgraded to Four ticks Thistle commended.

Size 22 acres, 45 touring pitches, 29 with electric hookup, 75 level pitches, 100 static caravans, 6 🏠, 7 WCs, 1 CWP
£ car/tent £8-£9, car/caravan £8-£9, motorhome £8-£9, motorbike/tent £8-£9
Rental 🚐 £120-£285 weekly, £26 nightly.
🛁 🛒 🔌 🍴 🅂 🅁 🅹 🅶🆁 🔲 🅿 Calor Gaz ♿ ﹖ WS
Last arrival time: 10:00
➡ 7 miles W of Newton Stewart on A75 heading towards Stranraer turn right at crossroads signed Dirnow/Three Lochs. Then follow signs for park.

Tantallon Caravan Park

Dunbar Road, North Berwick EH39 5NJ
☎ 01620-893348 **Fax** 01620-895623

Ganavan Sands Touring Caravan Park

Ganavan, Oban PA34 5TU
☎ 01631-562179
Open April-October ⚠ 🚐 🚙
Size 76 touring pitches, 68 with electric hookup, 62 level pitches, 6 🏠, 10 WCs, 1 CWP
£ car/tent £7-£8, car/caravan £7-£8, motorhome £7-£8, motorbike/tent £7-£8
🛁 🛒 🍴 🔌 🅿 🔲 ♿
➡ From town centre follow Esplanade coast road keeping sea immediately adjacent on left for 2 miles.

Oban Caravan & Camping Park
Gallachmore Farm, Oban
☎ 01631-562425 Fax 01631-566624
Open Easter-October Å ⊕ ⇄
Size 15 acres, 150 touring pitches, 73 with electric hookup, 15 static caravans, 8 ⏃, 16 WCs, 1 CWP
£ car/tent £7-£8, car/caravan £7-£8, motorhome £7-£8, motorbike/tent £7-£8
Rental ⊕ Chalet. £160-£300
⏚ ▣ ☏ ⎙ ⎗ GR TV ⋀ Calor Gaz ☂
Last arrival time: 11:00
� From Oban town centre follow signs to Gallanach, sea on right 2½ miles from town, site beside sea.

OLDSHOREMORE Sutherland   14C1

Oldshoremore
by Lairg, Oldshoremore
☎ 0197182-281
Open April-September Å ⊕ ⇄

A one acre site, part grass, part hard standing. Ten minutes walk from a mile long golden sandy beach. Ideal for hill climbing, fishing, beautiful scenery.

Size 1 acre, 13 touring pitches, 3 with electric hookup, 13 level pitches, 2 static caravans, 1 ⏃, 4 WCs, 1 CWP
£ car/tent £6.30-£6.80, car/caravan £6.70-£7.20, motorhome £6.80-£7.20, motorbike/tent £6.30, children £0.60-£0.85
Rental ⊕ £60-£150
▣ ⎙ ☂
Last arrival time: 11:00
� Take A838 to Rhiconich, there join B801 in Kinlochbervie 4 miles. Then take unclassified road to Oldshoremore - 2 miles.

ORKNEY ISLANDS   15F1

Pickaquoy Caravan & Camp Site
Pickaquoy Road, Kirkwall KW15 1RR
☎ 01856-873535 Fax 01856-876327
Open May-September Å ⊕ ⇄
Size 30 touring pitches, 6 with electric hookup, 1 CWP
£ car/tent £3.25-£4.35, car/caravan £4.85-£7.70, motorhome £4.85-£7.70, motorbike/tent £3.25-£4.35
⏚¼ ✗¼ ⊕¼ ▣ ☏

� Just off main A965 road from Stromness to Kirkwall, 150 yards SW of foot of hill coming down into Kirkwall.

Point of Ness Caravan & Camping Site
Ness Road, Stromness KW16 3DN
☎ 01856-873535 Fax 01856-876327
Open May-September Å ⊕ ⇄
Size 30 touring pitches, 6 with electric hookup, 1 CWP
£ car/tent £3.25-£4.35, car/caravan £4.85-£7.70, motorhome £4.85-£7.70, motorbike/tent £3.25-£4.35
⏚¼ ✗¼ ⊕¼ ▣ ☏ ⅙ ☂
� 1 mile W of Pierhead.

PEEBLES Peeblesshire   13D2

Crossburn Caravan Park
Edinburgh Road, Peebles EH45 8ED
☎ 01721-720501 Fax 01721-720501
Open April-October Å ⊕ ⇄
Size 6 acres, 40 touring pitches, 30 with electric hookup, 40 level pitches, 90 static caravans, 10 ⏃, 16 WCs, 2 CWPs
£ car/tent £8, car/caravan £9, motorhome £8.50, motorbike/tent £5
Rental ⊕ from £240
℄ MasterCard Visa
⏚ ▣ ☏ ⎙ GR ⋀ Calor Gaz ⅙ ☂ WS
Last arrival time: 11:00
� ½ mile N of Peebles on A703.

Rosetta Caravan Park
Rosetta Road, Peebles EH45 8PG
☎ 01721-720770
Open 1 April-31 October Å ⊕ ⇄

A beautiful, family owned, wooded park, graded 5 ticks excellent. The 1990 Calor Award Winner 'Best Park in Scotland'; finalist in 1993. Licensed bar, adjacent golf course, fishing arranged.

Size 24 acres, 130 touring pitches, 130 with electric hookup, 130 level pitches, 28 static caravans, 12 ⏃, 27 WCs, 3 CWPs
£ car/tent £6.50-£7.50, car/caravan £8.75-£9.25, motorhome £8.75-£9.25, motorbike/tent £6.50-£7.50
Rental ⊕ £160-£190
⏚ ✗¼ ⊕¼ ☏ ⎙ ⎗ ⊞ TV ⋀ ⊟ Calor Gaz ☂
� Signposted on main roads into Peebles.

PENPONT Dumfriesshire   13D3

Penpont (Floors) Caravan Park
Thornhill, Penpont DG3 4BH
☎ 01848-330470
Open April-October ▲ ⊕ ⊞
Size 1½ acres, 20 touring pitches, 8 with electric hookup, 10 level pitches, 6 ⚲, 7 WCs, 1 CWP
£ car/tent £6.50-£7.50, car/caravan £7.50, motorhome £7.50, motorbike/tent £7.50
Rental ⊕
⚑¼ ✗¼ ⊡ ⚑ ⊟ Calor Gaz ⚲ WS
Last arrival time: 11:00
➡ 2 miles W of Thornhill, on left approaching Penpont village

PERTH Perthshire   13D1

Camping & Caravanning Club Site
Scone Palace Caravan Park, Old Scone, Perth PH2 6BB
☎ 01738-552323
Open end March-early November ▲ ⊕ ⊞
Size 12 acres, 150 touring pitches, 85 with electric hookup, 8 ⚲, 28 WCs, 1 CWP
£ car/tent £5.60-£8.60, car/caravan £5.60-£8.60, motorhome £5.60-£8.60, motorbike/tent £5.60-£8.60, children £1.50
CC MasterCard Visa
⊡ ⚑ ⒢⍰ ⌂ ⚲ ⚲
Last arrival time: 11:00
➡ Site lies 2 miles N of Perth, adjacent to the racecourse. Signposted.

Cleeve Caravan Park
3/5 High Street, Perth PH1 5JJ
☎ 01738-475211 **Fax** 01738-441690
Open end March-end October ▲ ⊕ ⊞

Quiet, well screened, wooded site with a high standard of facilities and a good reputation. Children's play area. Easy access to the centre of Perth. Off-season discount for OAPs.

Size 5 acres, 100 touring pitches, 80 with electric hookup, 80 level pitches, 11 ⚲, 20 WCs, 4 CWPs
£ car/tent £6.80-£7, car/caravan £7.80-£8.90, , motorbike/tent £6, children £1
CC MasterCard Visa
⚑ ✗¼ ⚑ ⌂ Calor Gaz ⚲ ⚲
Last arrival time: 8:00
➡ ½ mile E of A9/M90, on W side of Perth (A93).

PITLOCHRY Perthshire   15D4

Faskally Home Farm Caravan Site
Pitlochry PH16 5LA
☎ 01796-472007
Open 15 March-31 October ▲ ⊕ ⊞

Level grassy site. Children's play area. Fishing on Loch Faskally and rivers Tummel and Garry. Forty caravans for hire (own WCs). Open from the 15 March to 31 October.

Size 23 acres, 250 touring pitches, 20 with electric hookup, 60 static caravans, 18 ⚲, 78 WCs,
⚑ ✗ ⒢ ⍰ ⚑ ⚲
➡ 2 miles N of Pitlochry on A924 (A9).

Milton Of Fonab Caravan Site
Pitlochry PH16 5NA
☎ 01796-472882 **Fax** 01796-474363
Open Easter-October ▲ ⊕ ⊞

A quiet family run site on the banks of the River Tummel. Spectacular scenery. Mountain bike hire and free trout fishing. Static caravans for hire.

Size 15 acres, 154 touring pitches, 130 with electric hookup, 130 level pitches, 36 static caravans, 9 ⚲, 4 WCs, 1 CWP
£ car/tent £9-£9.50, car/caravan £9-£9.50, motorhome £9-£9.50, children £0.50
Rental ⊕ from £41 nightly, from £230 weekly.
⚑ ⚑¼ ✗¼ ⚑¼ ⊡ ⚑ ⊟ ⊡ Calor Gaz ⚲ WS
Last arrival time: 9:30
➡ ½ mile S of Pitlochry opposite Bells Distillery.

POOLEWE Ross-shire   14B2

Camping & Caravanning Club Site
Inverewe Gardens, Poolewe, Achnasheen
☎ 01445-781249
Open end March-start November **A 🚐 🚍**
Size 3 acres, 55 touring pitches, 18 with electric
hookup, 8 🚿, 10 WCs, 1 CWP
£ car/tent £5.20-£7.80, car/caravan £5.20-£7.80,
motorhome £5.20-£7.80, motorbike/tent £5.20-£7.80,
children £1.50
CC MasterCard Visa
🛒¼ ✕¼ 🖀 🔌 🕭 🐕
Last arrival time: 11:00
➡ Site is on A832, just N of Poolewe.

PORTPATRICK Wigtownshire   12B4

Castle Bay Caravan Park
Portpatrick DG9 9AA
☎ 01776-810462
Open March-October **A 🚐 🚍**
Size 22½ acres, 26 touring pitches, 26 with electric
hookup, 20 level pitches, 96 static caravans, 2 🚿, 5
WCs, 1 CWP
£ car/tent £5, car/caravan £7, motorhome £7,
motorbike/tent £5
Rental 🚐 £140-£215
🛒 ✕¼ 🍺¼ 🖀 🔌 🖥 🄶 🛆 Calor Gaz 🕭 🐕 WS
Last arrival time: 11:30
➡ Into Portpatrick on A77, left opposite Old Mill
Restaurant. Continue for ¾ mile, under railway bridge,
site on right.

Galloway Point Holiday Park
Portpatrick, Stranraer DG9 9AA
☎ 01776-810561 **Fax** 01776-810561
Open Easter-mid October **A 🚐 🚍**
Size 18 acres, 40 touring pitches, 40 with electric
hookup, 15 level pitches, 60 static caravans, 7 🚿, 20
WCs, 1 CWP
£ car/tent £7-£10, car/caravan £10, motorhome £8-
£10, motorbike/tent £7-£8
Rental 🚐 £175-£275
🛒¼ ✕ 🍺 🖀 🔌 🖥 🛆 🄳 Calor Gaz 🐕 WS
Last arrival time: 11:00
➡ A75 from Dumfries, A77 from Glasgow, first left
opposite Old Mill, park is on right opposite Barn Inn.

Sunnymeade Caravan Park
Portpatrick, Stranraer DG9 8LN
☎ 01776-810293
Open mid March-end October **A 🚐 🚍**
Size 8 acres, 15 touring pitches, 14 with electric
hookup, 60 static caravans, 4 🚿, 9 WCs, 1 CWP
£ car/tent £7-£9, car/caravan £7-£9, motorhome £7-
£9, motorbike/tent £7
Rental 🚐 from £115
🛒¼ ✕¼ 🍺¼ 🖀 🔌 🖥 🄳 Calor 🐕 WS
➡ Take A75 to Portpatrick and turn left on entering
town. Site is ¼ mile on left.

PRESTWICK Ayrshire   12C3

Prestwick Holiday Park
Prestwick KA9 1TH
☎ 01292-479261
Open March-October
Size 12 acres, 40 touring pitches, 40 with electric
hookup, 40 level pitches, 168 static caravans, 4 🚿, 10
WCs, 1 CWP🛒 ✕¼ 🍺 🔌 🖀 🖥 🄶 📺 🛆 🄳 🕭
Last arrival time: flexible
➡ 1 mile N of Prestwick on A79, turn W opposite
Prestwick Airport, for ½ mile.

SANDHEAD Wigtownshire   12B4

Sandhead Caravan Park
Sandhead DG9 9JN
☎ 01776-830296
Open April-October **A 🚐 🚍**
Size 10 acres, 30 touring pitches, 20 with electric
hookup, 30 level pitches, 80 static caravans, 5 🚿, 15
WCs, 2 CWPs
£ car/tent £7-£8, car/caravan £7-£8, motorhome
£6.50-£7.50, motorbike/tent £5-£7
Rental 🚐 £200-£220
🛒 🖀 🔌 🄳 Calor Gaz 🕭 🐕
Last arrival time: 10:00
➡ From A75 turn S on A716 towards Drummore, site
on left approaching Sandhead village.

Sands Of Luce Caravan Park
Sandhead, Stranraer DG9 9JR
☎ 01776-830456 **Fax** 01776-830456
Open 1 April-31 October **A 🚐 🚍**

*Peaceful, friendly park extending onto beautiful
sandy beach and large dune area. Touring pitches
beside the beach. New toilet blocks provide excellent
facilities. A warm welcome awaits all our visitors.*

Size 12 acres, 36 touring pitches, 36 with electric
hookup, 36 level pitches, 34 static caravans, 8 🚿, 16
WCs, 1 CWP
£ car/tent £6.50-£8, car/caravan £6.50-£8, motorhome
£6-£7.50, motorbike/tent £5.70-£7.20, children £0.40
Rental 🚐 £135-£275

🔣 🔣 🔣 🔣 🔣 ⚠ Calor Gaz ♿ 🐕 WS

Last arrival time: 10:00

➜ From Stranraer follow A77 to turn off to Portpatrick. Keep on A716 signposted to Dummore (do not turn right to Portpatrick). Entrance to caravan park is 1 mile past village of Stoneykirk at A716/ B7084 junction.

SELKIRK Selkirkshire   13E3

Victoria Park Caravan Site
Victoria Park, Buccleugh Road, Selkirk TD7 5DN
📞 01750-20987 Fax 01896-757003
Open 1 April-31 October 🏕 🚐 🚠
Size 3 acres, 60 touring pitches, 26 with electric hookup, 60 level pitches, 6 🚿, 11 WCs, 1 CWP
£ car/tent £6-£7, car/caravan £6-£7, motorhome £6-£7, motorbike/tent £6-£7
🔣¼ ✗¼ 🔣¼ 🔣 🔣 🔣 🔣 🔣 🔣 ⚠ 🔣 Calor ♿ 🐕

Last arrival time: 9:00

➜ A7 N follow signs from Selkirk market place. A7 S turn at town entrance signposted A72 Peebles then A708 Moffat.

SKELMORLIE Ayrshire   12B2

Mains Camping & Caravan Park
Skelmorlie PA17 5EU
📞 01475-520794 Fax 01475-520794
Open March-October 🏕 🚐 🚠

Quiet peaceful family run park with outstanding views of the Firth of Clyde and Islands. Ideal base for touring the west of Scotland.

Size 4 acres, 20 touring pitches, 20 with electric hookup, 20 level pitches, 70 static caravans, 13 🚿, 23 WCs, 1 CWP
£ car/tent £5-£6, car/caravan £7-£9, motorhome £6, motorbike/tent £5-£6
Rental 🚐 Chalet. £175-£340
🔣 🔣 🔣 🔣 🔣 📺 Calor Gaz 🐕 WS
Last arrival time: 12:00

➜ Signposted off A78, 4 miles N of Largs.

SPEAN BRIDGE Inverness-shire   14C4

Stronaba Caravan Site
Spean Bridge PH34 4DX
📞 01397-712259
Open April-October 🏕 🚐 🚠

Stronaba Caravan and Camping Site, 2½ miles north of Spean Bridge. Entrance on main A82 road Fort William - Inverness. Central location for touring the Highlands, Loch Ness and Skye. Caledonian Canal and all outdoor activities in surrounding area.

Size 4 acres, 20 touring pitches, 4 with electric hookup, 18 level pitches, 4 🚿, 6 WCs, 1 CWP
£ car/tent £6-£7, car/caravan £6-£7, motorhome £6-£7, motorbike/tent £6-£7, children £0.50-£1
🔣 🐕
Last arrival time: 10:00

➜ 2½ miles N of Spean Bridge on A82, gateway signposted.

ST CYRUS Kincardineshire   15F4

East Bowstrips Caravan Park

St Cyrus, Montrose DD10 0DE
☎ 01674-850328 Fax 01674-850328
Open 1 April-31 October 🏕 🚐 🚑

Quiet family park by the coast with excellent facilities, and a particular welcome for disabled visitors. Only one mile from the glorious sandy St Cyrus beach and nature reserve.

Size 4 acres, 30 touring pitches, 27 with electric hookup, 26 level pitches, 18 static caravans, 4 🚿, 7 WCs, 1 CWP
£ car/tent £5.50-£6.50, car/caravan £6.50-£7.50, motorhome £6.50-£7.50, motorbike/tent £5.50-£6.50

Rental 🚐 £99-£199
🚿 🚿¼ ✗¼ 🍴¼ 🔲 🛒 🗑 🛢 Calor 🐕 ⚓
Last arrival time: 10:00
➡ Travelling N on A92 coast road enter village of St Cyrus. Pass hotel on left, then first left, second right (signposted).

ST FILLANS Perthshire   12C1

Loch Earn Caravan Park

South Shore Road, St Fillans
☎ 01764-685270 Fax 01764-685270
Open end March-end October 🏕 🚐 🚑
Size 2 acres, 40 touring pitches, 30 with electric hookup, 30 level pitches, 200 static caravans, 8 🚿, 19 WCs,
£ car/tent £8.50, car/caravan £8.50, motorhome £8.50
🚿 ✗ 🛒 🗑 🔲 🛢 🗑 🆖 🔲 🛢 🆕 Calor ⚓
Last arrival time: 8:00
➡ Travelling W on A85 from Crieff turn left onto South Loch Earn Road, just before St Fillans. Continue to site in 1 mile at lochside.

STIRLING Stirlingshire   12C2

Auchenbowie Caravan Site

Auchenbowie, Stirling FK7 8HE
☎ 01324-82211 Fax 01324-822950
Open April-October 🚐 🚑

A peaceful site in rural surroundings, centrally located and ideal for touring. A wide range of activities are available locally.

Size 3½ acres, 60 touring pitches, 40 with electric hookup, 60 level pitches, 7 static caravans, 6 🚿, 12 WCs, 2 CWPs
£ car/tent £7, car/caravan £7, motorhome £7, motorbike/tent £5.50
℅ MasterCard Visa
🔲 🛢 ⚓ WS
➡ Leave M9/M80 at junction 9 and head S on A872 for ½ mile, turn right for further ½ mile.

Mains Farm Camping

Thornhill, Stirling FK8 3QR

☎ 01786-850605 Fax 01786-850605

Open 1 April-31 October Å ⊞ ⊞

Family-run farm site near Thornhill Village, offering panoramic views to the Flintry Hills. Ideal centre for historic Stirling, Loch Lomond and the Trossachs.

Size 5 acres, 35 touring pitches, 20 with electric hookup, 35 level pitches, 3 �ℝ, 11 WCs, 1 CWP
£ car/tent £6, car/caravan £6-£8.50, motorhome £6-£7.50, motorbike/tent £6, children £0.50
Rental ⊞ £135-£175
🛁¼ ✗¼ 🍴¼ ⚠ Calor Gaz ᕒ ⚲ WS
Last arrival time: 10:00
➔ From Stirling/M9 junction 10 and follow A84 for 5 miles. Bear left onto A873 and at crossroads in Thornhill turn left onto B822. Site 150 yards.

STRANRAER Wigtownshire 12B4

Cairnryan Caravan & Chalet Park

Stranraer DG9 8QX

☎ 01581-200231 Fax 01581-200207

Open 1 March-31 October Å ⊞ ⊞

Overlooks Loch Ryan and the ferry terminal. Six caravans and ten chalets for hire (own WCs).

Size 7½ acres, 10 touring pitches, 9 with electric hookup, 10 level pitches, 82 static caravans, 6 ℝ, 8 WCs, 1 CWP
£ car/tent £4, car/caravan £8, motorhome £8, motorbike/tent £4
Rental ⊞ Chalet. apartments £90-£175, caravans £80-£225
🛁¼ ✗¼ 🖥 🍴 🖪 🖬 🄶🄰 ⚠ ⚲ Calor ᕒ ⚲
Last arrival time: 11:00
➔ 5 miles N of Stranraer on A77 in village of Cairnryan, directly opposite ferry terminal for Ireland.

TAIN Ross-shire 15D2

Meikle Ferry Caravan Park

Meikle Ferry, Tain IV19 1JX

☎ 01862-892292

Open 15 January-15 December Å ⊞ ⊞

Size 3½ acres, 30 touring pitches, 20 with electric hookup, 30 level pitches, 15 static caravans, 4 ℝ, 8 WCs, 1 CWP
£ car/tent £4.50-£7, car/caravan £6-£8, motorhome £6-£8, motorbike/tent £4.50-£5.50, children £0.50
Rental ⊞ £90-£210
🛁 ✗¼ 🖥 🍴 🖪 ⚠ ⚲ WS
Last arrival time: 11:00
➔ 2 miles N of Tain on A9, straight on at roundabout for new Dornoch bridge. Park access is 300 yards on right.

TARBERT, LOCH FYNE Argyll 12B2

Point Sands Caravan Park

Tayinloan, Tarbert PA29 6XG

☎ 01583-441263 Fax 01583-441216

Open 1 April-31 October Å ⊞ ⊞

Size 69 static caravans, 7 ℝ, 17 WCs, 2 CWPs
£ car/tent £8-£10, car/caravan £9-£12, motorhome £8-£12, motorbike/tent £5-£9
Rental ⊞ £125-£295
Ⅽ Visa
🛁 🛁¼ 🖥 🍴 🖪 ⚠ Calor Gaz ᕒ ⚲ WS
➔ From Tarbert travel S on A83 for 17 miles, then right to site (in ½ mile)

Hints & Tips

Tyres are your only contact with the road. Look after them and you will improve the safety and behaviour of your unit. Never mix cross ply and radials on the same axis.

Loch Lomond Holiday Park
Inveruglas, Tarbet G83 7DW
☎ 01301-704224 **Fax** 01301-704206
Open March-October,December-January ⊕ ⊞

Beautiful lochside location, ideally situated for touring, hill walking, water sports etc..

Size 13 acres, 18 touring pitches, 18 with electric hookup, 18 level pitches, 72 static caravans, 5 ☂, 7 WCs, 2 CWPs
£ car/caravan £6.50-£12, motorhome £6.50-£12
Rental ⊕ Chalet. caravans £130-£300, chalets £190-£575
℃ MasterCard Visa
⚒ ✗¼ ◙ ☎ ⊞ ⊟ ⒢⒭ ⓣⓥ ⚠ Calor Gaz ♿ ☈
Last arrival time: 9:00
➡ 3 miles N of Tarbet on A82.

ULLAPOOL Ross-shire	14C2

Ardmair Point Caravan Site
Ullapool IV26 2TN
☎ 01854-612054 **Fax** 01854-612757
Open Easter-September ⚐ ⊕ ⊞

Beautiful quiet location with pitches having outstanding views over the Summer Isles, some sheltered pitches. Award winning facilities, boat rental, fishing all available on site.

Size 9 acres, 54 touring pitches, 54 with electric hookup, 54 level pitches, 12 ☂, 22 WCs, 1 CWP
£ car/tent £8, car/caravan £8, motorhome £8, motorbike/tent £8

Rental Chalet. from £170 p.w., £100 3 nights
℃ MasterCard Visa
⚒ ✗ ⚑ ⊟ ⚑ Calor Gaz ♿ ☈
Last arrival time: 10:00
➡ 3½ miles N of Ullapool on A835, enter park at beach telephone box.

Broomfield Holiday Park
Shore Street, Ullapool IV26 2SX
☎ 01854-612020
Open April-September
Size 11 acres, 140 touring pitches, 60 with electric hookup, 140 level pitches, 12 ☂, 40 WCs, 2 CWPs⚒¼ ✗¼ ⚑¼ ⚠ Calor Gaz ♿
Last arrival time: flexible
➡ Drive along Shore Street, second right past harbour.

Wales

Top: Whitewell Caravan Park,
Tenby

Right: Cei Bach Country Club,
New Quay

Below: Fishguard Bay
Caravan Park, Fishguard

Aeron Coast Caravan Park

North Road, Aberaeron SA46 0JF

☎ 01545-570349

Open Easter-end October ▲ ⊕ ⊞

Size 22 acres, 50 touring pitches, 50 with electric hookup, 50 level pitches, 150 static caravans, 8 ⌂, 36 WCs, 2 CWPs

£ car/tent £6.50-£9.50, car/caravan £7-£10, motorhome £6.50-£9.50, children £0.50

⚏ ⚏¼ ✕¼ ☮ ⚏¼ ▣ ☒ ☐ ☒ ☒ GR ▣ ⊤ ⚠ ⚏

Calor Gaz ⌁

Last arrival time: 11:00

➜ Main coastal road A487 on northern edge of Aberaeron. Filling station at entrance.

Henllys Farm

Abergele

☎ 01745-351208 Fax 01745-351208

Open 1 April-15 October ▲ ⊕ ⊞

A family run park overlooking open farmland, and near to the attractions of the town and Rhyl. Ideally located for touring North Wales.

Size 11 acres, 280 touring pitches, 280 with electric hookup, 280 level pitches, 19 ⌂, 50 WCs, 1 CWP

£ car/tent £8-£9, car/caravan £8.50-£11

⚏¼ ▣ ☒ ☐ ⚠   Calor Gaz ⚅ ⌁

Last arrival time: 9:00

➜ Turn off A55 at Towyn, follow signs to crossroads and village. Turn off just past church.

Llety Caravan Park

Tresaith, Aberporth, Cardigan SA43 2ED

☎ 01239-810354 Fax 01239-810354

Open 1 March-31 October ▲ ⊕ ⊞

This family run park is only five minutes walk from the beach, shop, restaurant and local inn. An ideal location with panoramic views of Cardigan Bay.

Size 12 acres, 20 touring pitches, 20 with electric hookup, 10 level pitches, 80 static caravans, 5 ⌂, 18 WCs, 1 CWP

£ car/tent £6.50-£8.75, car/caravan £6.50-£8.75, motorhome £6.50-£8.75, motorbike/tent £6.50-£8.75

⚏¼ ✕¼ ⚏¼ ▣ ☒ ☐ Calor Gaz ⌁ WS

Last arrival time: 9:00

➜ Turn off A487 towards Aberporth along B4333. Take coastal road towards Tresaith where park is situated ½ mile on left.

Bryn Cethin Bach Caravan Park

Lon Garmon, Abersoch LL53 7UL

☎ 01758-712719

Open March-October ⊕ ⊞

Size 22 acres, 15 touring pitches, 15 with electric hookup, 14 level pitches, 53 static caravans, 6 ⌂, 7 WCs, 1 CWP

£ car/caravan £9-£10, motorhome £9-£10

✕¼ ⚏¼ ▣ ☒ ☐ ☑ Calor ⌁

Last arrival time: 6:00

➜ A499 to Abersoch. At Land & Sea Garage fork right - Bryn Cethin Bach ½ mile up hill on right.

Sea View Camping & Caravan Park

Sarn Bach, Abersoch LL53 7ET

☎ 01758-712052 Fax 01758-713243

Open April-October ▲ ⊕ ⊞

Family site with magnificent views overlooking Abersoch harbour. Short walk down to quiet beach. Hook ups. Open April to October.

Size 4 acres, 60 touring pitches, 20 with electric hookup, 40 level pitches, 6 ᴿ, 10 WCs, 1 CWP
£ car/tent £6-£7.50, car/caravan £7.50-£9, motorhome £7.50-£9, motorbike/tent £6-£7.50
⬛ 🔌 🚻 🕭 WS
➡ 1 mile from Abersoch towards Sarn Bach. Turn left at crossroads in Sarn Bach. Site is 250 yards on right.

ABERYSTWYTH Ceredigion   6B3

Glan y Mor Leisure Park
Clarach Bay, Aberystwyth SY23 3DT
☎ 01970-828900 **Fax** 01970-828890
Open 1 March-1 November

Beach front location, surrounded by wooded hillsides. Ten-pin bowling alley, indoor swimming pool, jacuzzi, sauna, sunbeds, steam room and fitness gym. Children's play areas and organised activities. Easy access to Aberystwyth and Mid Wales resorts and attractions.

Size 12 acres, 100 touring pitches, 40 with electric hookup, 75 level pitches, 160 static caravans, 14 ᴿ, 14 WCs, 2 CWPs
£ car/caravan £6-£10
℀ MasterCard Visa
🦞 ✕ ⬤ 🔌 🔲 GR ◀ ⚠ 🔥 Calor Gaz ♿ WS
Last arrival time: 12:00
➡ Leave A487 at Bow Street where Clarach Bay is signposted. Follow signs for North Beach for 2 miles. Site entrance is at beach front.

Midfield Caravan Park
Southgate, Aberystwyth SY23 4DX
☎ 01970-612542
Open April-October 🅰 🚐 🏕
Size 6 acres, 75 touring pitches, 28 with electric hookup, 40 level pitches, 57 static caravans, 14 ᴿ, 12 WCs, 1 CWP
£ car/tent £8.20-£9, car/caravan £8.20-£9, motorhome £8.20-£9, motorbike/tent £8.20-£9, children £0.60
🦞¼ ✕¼ ⬤¼ 🔌 🚻 ⚠ Calor Gaz ♿ 🕭
Last arrival time: 10:00
➡ 1½ miles SE of Aberystwyth on A4120 and 200 yards from junction with A4817.

Pengarreg Caravan Park
Llanrhystyd, Aberystwyth SY23 5JD
☎ 01974-202247
Open 1 March-31 October 🅰 🚐 🏕

Pleasantly situated on the seafront overlooking Cardigan Bay, 9 miles south of Aberystwyth. Amenities include free showers, shop, laundry, electric hook-ups, boating ramp, restaurant/club. 9 and 18 hole golf course within 1 mile. Excellent rates, SAE for details.

Size 75 touring pitches, 20 with electric hookup, 75 level pitches, 10 ᴿ, 20 WCs, 1 CWP
£ car/tent £4.50-£6.50, car/caravan £4.50-£6.50, motorhome £4.50-£6.50, motorbike/tent £4.50-£6.50
🦞 ✕ ⬤ 🚻 🕭 📁 GR ⚠ Calor Gaz ♿ 🕭 WS
➡ At S end of Llanrhystyd on A487, turn W opposite Lloyd Motor garage. Site signposted.

TOURING & CAMPING PARK

Llangynog Road, Bala, Gwynedd LL23 7PH
Tel: 01678-520549 Fax: 01678-520006

THIS SMALL FAMILY RUN, PEACEFUL, PICTURESQUE, LANDSCAPED TOURING AND CAMPING PARK IN UNSPOILT SURROUNDINGS 100 YARDS FROM BALA LAKE IS PROUD TO LIST THE FOLLOWING

TOP 10 *FOR YOUR ENJOYMENT . . . . . .*

(1) **FREE, NEW** Hot Showers of **CONTINENTAL** Standard

(2) **NEAREST** Park to Bala Town (a gentle 10 minute walk)

(3) **FREE, NEW** Spacious Private **VANITY** Cubicles with Individual Lights, Mirrors and Shaving Points.

(4) **FREE, NEW** Disabled Room and **FREE, NEW** Baby Room

(5) **CLOSEST** Park to Bala Sailing Club & Small Gauge Railway

(6) **NEW** Laundry with Washer, Dryer, Iron and Deep Sink

(7) **CALOR GAS** and Provisions in Well Stocked **SHOP**

(8) **DOGS** Welcome on our Park and Country Lane Dog Walk Area

(9) **NEW** All Electric **FLAT HARD STANDING** Pitches

(10) **MODERN UNDERCOVER** Dishwashing & Food Prep Area

For Brochure or Advance Bookings, please phone **01678 520549**
or Fax us on **01678 520006**

Camping & Caravanning Club Site

Crynierth Caravan Park, Cefn-Ddwysarn, Bala LL23 7LN

☎ 01678-530324

Open end March-end October **Å ⚑ ♞**
Size 50 touring pitches, 47 with electric hookup, **6** ↖, 9 WCs, 1 CWP
£ car/tent £5.20-£7.80, car/caravan £5.20-£7.80, motorhome £5.20-£7.80, motorbike/tent £5.20-£7.80, children £1.50
⊂⊂ MasterCard Visa
▨ ⚃ ⚏ ♿ ♞
Last arrival time: 11:00
➡ 3 miles to E of Bala, ½ mile from A494 between Bala and Corwen. Leave A5 at Druid.

Pen-y-Bont Touring & Camping Park

Llangynog Road, Bala LL23 7PH

☎ 01678-520549 **Fax** 01678-520006

Open 1 April-31 October **Å ⚑ ♞**
Size 5 acres, 35 touring pitches, 35 with electric hookup, 30 level pitches, 9 ↖, 11 WCs, 1 CWP
£ car/tent £6.35-£7.55, car/caravan £7.45-£8.75, motorhome £7.55-£8.25, motorbike/tent £6.35-£7.55
⊂⊂ MasterCard Visa
⚃ ⚃¼ ✕ ✕¼ ⚍ ⚍¼ ▨ ⚃ ⚏ Calor ♿ ♞ WS
Last arrival time: 12:00
➡ From main Bala road (A494), turn onto B4391. Site ¾ mile on right.

Pen-Y-Garth Caravan & Camping Park

Rhos-y-Gwaliau, Bala LL23 7ES

☎ 01678-520485 **Fax** 01678-520485

Open 1 March-31 October **Å ⚑ ♞**

Generous pitches, acres of space and a quiet, peaceful atmosphere in beautiful surroundings. Nine acres of recreation/picnic areas overlooking lake and town. In easy reach of numerous tourist attractions, Snowden, coast etc. Modern WC/shower blocks, games room, Dragon Award holiday homes for hire. Bar meals.

Size 20 acres, 35 touring pitches, 35 with electric hookup, 55 level pitches, 54 static caravans, 9 ↖, 12 WCs, 1 CWP
£ car/tent £6.95-£8.25, car/caravan £6.95-£8.25, motorhome £6.95-£8.25, motorbike/tent £6.95-£8.25, children £1.50
Rental ⚑ £120-£275 weekly

⚃ ✕ ▨ ⚃ ⚏ ⌷ ⚍ ⚏ ⚄ Calor Gaz ♿ ♞
Last arrival time: 10:30
➡ Take B4391 Bala to Llangynog road. 1½ mile from Bala fork right at signpost to Lake Vyrnwy and Rhos-y-Gwalian. Site entrance 600 yards on right.

Treborth Hall Farm Camping & Caravan

Trebroth Road, Bangor LL57 2RX

☎ 01248-364399 **Fax** 01248-364333

Å ⚑ ♞

Beautiful setting located between the Britannia Bridge and the Menai Suspension Bridge. Close to the Menai Straits. Touring site contained in old walled orchard.

Size 4 acres, 25 touring pitches, 25 with electric hookup, 100 level pitches, 4 static caravans, 8 ↖, 10 WCs, 2 CWPs
£ car/tent £4-£7, car/caravan £7, motorhome £7
Rental ⚑
⚃¼ ✕¼ ⚍¼ ⚃ ⌷ ⚍ ⚃ ⚏ ♿ ♞ WS
➡ Turn off A55 dual carriageway just before crossing Britannia Bridge onto Anglesey. Turn onto A487 for Bangor, ¾ mile on left towards Bangor. Entrance to site signposted.

Hendre Mynach Touring Caravan & Camping

Llanaber Road, Barmouth LL42 1YR

☎ 01341-280262 **Fax** 01341-280586

Open 1 March-30 November **Å ⚑ ♞**

← Hendre Mynach Touring Caravan & Camping

Only 100 yards from a safe sandy beach, 15 minutes walk to the town centre, many mountain walks, courtesy bus to the local pub, games room, children's room.

Size 10 acres, 60 touring pitches, 60 with electric hookup, 60 level pitches, 22, 22 WCs, 2 CWPs
£ car/tent £6-£8, car/caravan £7-£11, motorhome £6-£10, motorbike/tent £6-£9, children £1
Calor Gaz
Last arrival time: 10:30
➔ ½ mile N of Barmouth on A496 Barmouth to Harlech road on seaward side.

BARRY Vale of Glamorgan 3D1

Vale Touring Caravan Park
Port Road (West), Barry
01446-719311
Open 1 April-1 October
Size 3 acres, 40 touring pitches, 15 with electric hookup, 40 level pitches, 4, 6 WCs, 1 CWP
£ car/caravan £6-£7, motorhome £6-£7, children £1-£1.50
¼ ¼ Calor
➔ Follow A4226 Barry to St Athan. The park is on left 1½ miles out of Barry.

BENLLECH BAY Anglesey 6B1

Plas Uchaf Caravan & Camping Park
Benllech Bay, Benllech LL74 8NU
01407-763012
Open March-October
Size 9 acres, 88 touring pitches, 75 with electric hookup, 75 level pitches, 25 static caravans, 6, 16 WCs, 2 CWPs
£ car/tent £6-£7, car/caravan £6-£7, motorhome £6-£7
¼ ¼ ¼ Calor WS
Last arrival time: 10:00
➔ From A5025 take B5108. Site is signposted and is ½ mile from Benllech.

BETWS-YN-RHOS Denbighshire 6C1

Hunters Hamlet Touring Caravan Park
Sirior Goch Farm, Betws-yn-Rhos LL22 8PL
01745-832237 Fax 01745-832237
Open 21 March-31 October

A small, family-run country site with superior facilities, including family bathroom. Top grading.

Size 2½ acres, 23 touring pitches, 23 with electric hookup, 23 level pitches, 3, 11 WCs, 1 CWP
£ car/caravan £8-£11, motorhome £7-£10
CC MasterCard Visa
Calor WS
Last arrival time: 10:00
➔ From A55 take Abergele turn off A547 to traffic lights. Straight through then take first left onto A548 by George & Dragon pub. 2¾ miles to first crossroads. Turn right onto B5381 and site is first on the left.

BODORGAN Anglesey 6B1

Pen-y-Bont Touring Site
Malltraeth, Bodorgan LL62 5BA
01407-840209
Open April

Friendly site on two hundred acre working farm with magnificent views of Snowdonia and Newborough Forest. Excellent modern facilities. Large children's play area. Ideal location for bird watchers and lovers of watersports. Separate paddocks for tents. Dogs welcome. Luxury static caravan for hire.

Size 4 acres, 25 touring pitches, 20 with electric hookup, 25 level pitches, 1 static caravans, 4 �, 6 WCs, 1 CWP
£ car/tent £4-£6, car/caravan £6-£8.50, motorhome £6, motorbike/tent £4-£6
Rental 🚐
⚡¼ ✗¼ 🚿¼ 🖼 🖻 /ɪ\ Calor Gaz ⅙ ✯ WS
Last arrival time: 11:00
➜ On approaching Anglesey over Brittania Bridge on A5, take left road, A4080 to Brynsigncyn. Follow A4080 to Newborough through forestry, before village of Malltraeth site is on right.

BORTH Ceredigion   6C3

Cambrian Coast Holiday Park
Ynyslas, Borth SY24 5JU
☎ 01970-871233 **Fax** 01970-871124
Open March-November

An 'Excellence' graded park close to a sandy 'Blue Flag' beach. The site offers a club with family entertainment, and children's activities, go-karts and bouncy castle. Concessionary use of indoor swimming pool.

Size 12 acres, 75 touring pitches, 48 with electric hookup, 75 level pitches, 144 static caravans, 9 �, 9 WCs, 1 CWP
£ car/tent £6-£10, car/caravan £6-£10
Rental 🚐 from £95-£399
✗ MasterCard Visa

⚡ ✗ 🚿 🗐 🖼 🖻 🖾 /ɪ\ ⊟ Calor Gaz ⅙ WS
Last arrival time: 12:00
➜ From A487 N of Aberystwyth to Borth. Park entrance is on seafront road, 1 mile N of Borth village.

Glanlerry Caravan Park
Borth
☎ 01970-871413
Open Easter-October ⅄ 🚐 🏕

A small family-owned site, well sheltered with level pitches. The site is within easy walking distance of Borth, with its 3 miles of unspoilt sand.

Size 40 with electric hookup, 40 level pitches, 6 �, 11 WCs, 1 CWP
£ car/tent £6.50-£6.75, car/caravan £6.75-£9, motorhome £6.50-£8
⚡¼ ✗¼ 🚿¼ 🗐 🖻 /ɪ\ Calor Gaz ✯ WS
➜ 5 miles NE of Aberystwyth (A487), turn N on B4353. Site 2 miles.

Mill House Caravan & Camping Park

Dol-y-Bont, Borth SY24 5LX
📞 01970-871481
Open Easter-mid October ▲ ⚑ ⊞

Select sheltered site beside a trout stream, with modern amenities. One mile from the seaside village of Borth, with sandy beaches, safe bathing and rock pools.

Size 8 acres, 16 touring pitches, 16 with electric hookup, 16 level pitches, 15 static caravans, 2 ⊮, 5 WCs, 1 CWP
£ car/tent £8, car/caravan £8, motorhome £8
⬛ ⬛ Calor Gaz ⟲ WS
Last arrival time: 8:00
➡ From Borth to Aberyswyth B4353, 1 mile from Borth fork left by railway bridge and white railings into Doly-Bont village and follow signs.

Brynich Caravan Park

Brecon LD3 7SH
📞 01874-623325 Fax 01874-623325
Open Easter-October ▲ ⚑ ⊞

With panoramic views and a friendly atmosphere to greet you, this quiet, immaculate site offers a wide range of facilities, including free hot water and disabled and baby rooms. Cleanliness is a priority.

Size 20 acres, 130 touring pitches, 106 with electric hookup, 120 level pitches, 18 ⊮, 24 WCs, 3 CWPs
£ car/tent £7.50-£8.50, car/caravan £7.50-£8.50, motorhome £7.50-£8.50, motorbike/tent £7.50-£8.50, children £1
⬛ ⬛ ⬛ ⬛ ⬛ Calor Gaz ♿ ⟲ WS
➡ 1 mile E of Brecon on A470 (Builth Wells), 200 yards from roundabout with A40 (Abergavenny).

Llynfi Holiday Park

Llangorse Lake, Llangorse, Brecon LD3 7TR
📞 01874-658283 Fax 01874-658575
Open April-October ▲ ⚑ ⊞
Size 17 acres, 60 touring pitches, 40 with electric hookup, 60 level pitches, 100 static caravans, 8 ⊮, 12 WCs, 2 CWPs
£ car/tent £7-£9, car/caravan £7-£9, motorhome £7-£9, motorbike/tent £7-£9, children £1.50-£2
⬛¼ ✗¼ ⬛ ⬛ ⬛ ⬛ GR ⬛ ⬛ TV ⬛ ⬛ Calor Gaz ⟲ WS
Last arrival time: 11:00
➡ Follow A40 via Bwlch to Llangorse Lake via B4560. From A438 via Talgarth on B4560.

Anchorage Caravan Park

Bronllys, near Brecon LD3 0LD
📞 01874-711246
Open all year ▲ ⚑ ⊞

A park with high standards and panoramic views of the Brecon National Park. Ideally situated for touring and walking in south and mid Wales.

Size 13 acres, 60 touring pitches, 40 with electric hookup, 25 level pitches, 8 ⌂, 20 WCs, 1 CWP
£ car/tent £7, car/caravan £7, motorhome £7, motorbike/tent £7
⚑¼ ✕¼ ⚑¼ ▢ ▣ ▤ ▥ ⚠ Calor Gaz ৬ ⚲ WS
Last arrival time: 11:00
➡ On A438, 8 miles N of Brecon on the W side of Bronllys village.

Riverside International C & C Site
Talgarth, Near Brecon, Bronllys LD3 0HL
☎ **01874-711320**
Open Easter-October ⚑ ⚘ ⛺

Well maintained, clean and friendly family run site, situated in the heart of Wales with panoramic views of the Black Mountains. Warm welcome assured.

Size 10 acres, 84 touring pitches, 78 with electric hookup, 84 level pitches, 12 ⌂, 32 WCs, 2 CWPs
£ car/tent £8-£9, car/caravan £8-£9, motorhome £8-£9, motorbike/tent £8-£9, children £1-£1.20
⚑¼ ✕ ⚑ ▢ ▣ ▤ ▥ ▦ ▧ ▨ ▩ GR ▦ ▥ ▤ ⚠ ▦ ⚐ Calor Gaz ৬ WS
➡ Situated on A479 between Bronllys and Talgarth, directly opposite Bronllys Castle.

BRYNSIENCYN Anglesey 6B1

Fron Caravan & Camping Site
Brynsiencyn, Llanfairpwllgwyngyll LL61 6TX
☎ **01248-430310**
Open Easter-end September ⚑ ⚘ ⛺
Size 5 acres, 70 touring pitches, 41 with electric hookup, 60 level pitches, 8 ⌂, 9 WCs, 1 CWP
£ car/tent £7.50, car/caravan £7.50, motorhome £7.50, motorbike/tent £7
⚑ ▢ ▣ ▤ ▥ GR ▦ ⚠ Calor Gaz ⚲
Last arrival time: 11:00
➡ Leave Brittania Bridge at first sliproad signed A4080 Llanfairpwllgwynn, after 400 yards turn left again signed Brynsiencyn. Site is ½ mile on right after village.

Ad Astra Caravan Park
Brynteg, Nr Benllech LL78 7JH
☎ **01248-853283**
Open 1 March-31 October ⚑ ⚘ ⛺

Quiet, secluded family run park with first class facilities. Best park in Wales runner up. Tourist board grade 5. Ideal for a quiet and peaceful holiday.

Size 3½ acres, 12 touring pitches, 12 with electric hookup, 12 level pitches, 38 static caravans, 4 ⌂, 8 WCs, 1 CWP
£ car/tent £6, car/caravan £7.50-£9, motorhome £7.50-£9, motorbike/tent £6
Rental ⚘ £150-£220
⚑¼ ✕¼ ▢ ▣ ▤ ▥ ⚠ Calor ৬ ⚲ WS
➡ 2 miles W of Benllech off B5108 (Brynteg), on B5110 (Llangefni) road.

Nant Newydd Caravan Park
Brynteg LL78 8JH
☎ **01248-852842**
Open 1 March-31 October

Small select country site, very quiet, well landscaped with waterfalls and fountains. 5 star quality, voted runners up to best park in Wales for 2 years.

Size 30 touring pitches, 30 with electric hookup, 30 level pitches, 83 static caravans, 8 ⌂, 14 WCs, 3 CWPs
⚑ ▣ Calor Gaz ৬ WS
➡ After leaving Britannia Bridge take A5025 Amlwch-Benllech. Turn left at square, take B5108 towards Llangefni for 2 miles. At crossroads turn left on to B5110. Site 1 mile on right.

Hints & Tips
Make sure your mirrors are adjusted correctly before moving off.

FForest Fields Caravan & Camping Park

Hundred House, Builth Wells LD1 5RT
☎ 01982-570406 Fax 01982-570406
Open Easter-October Å ⊞ ⊡

*A beautiful, tranquil, family run site with no
clubhouse or statics. Immaculately maintained
facilities. Hill and farm walks direct from the site.
Graded 4 ticks. Award for environmental excellence.
'A rare gem of a site'.*

Size 7 acres, 60 touring pitches, 40 with electric
hookup, 40 level pitches, 6 ⋔, 8 WCs, 1 CWP
£ car/tent £5-£6.50, car/caravan £7.50, motorhome
£6.50, motorbike/tent £5.50-£6.50
▣ ☏ ☐ ◪ Calor Gaz ⋔ WS
➜ 4 miles E of Builth Wells on A481.

Llewelyn Leisure Park

Cilmery, Builth Wells LD2 3NU
☎ 01982-552838 Fax 01982-552838
Open Easter-31 October Å ⊞ ⊡

*Customer comments - 'treated like royalty', 'friendly
and relaxed atmosphere', 'comfortable and clean',
'peaceful with wonderful views'. Nearby fishing, golf,
and theatre. Adjacent inn with meals. Bus and train
services 200 yards.*

Size 2.16 acres, 25 touring pitches, 18 with electric
hookup, 10 level pitches, 30 static caravans, 2 ⋔, 3
WCs, 2 CWPs
£ car/tent £6-£8, car/caravan £6-£9, motorhome £6-
£9, motorbike/tent £4-£8
Rental ⊞ Chalet. £49-£299.
㏄ MasterCard Visa
☏ ✕¼ ▣ ☏ ☐ ▨ GR ◪ ▥ Calor Gaz ⅙ ⋔ WS
Last arrival time: 10:30
➜ 2 miles W of Builth Wells on south side of A483 in
Cilmery Village, adjacent to Prince Llewelyn inn.

Bryn Gloch Caravan & Camping Park

Betws Garmon, Caernarfon LL54 7YY
☎ 01286-650216 Fax 01286-650216
Open all year Å ⊞ ⊡

*Clean and quiet award-winning site, just in
Snowdonia National Park and on the banks of the
River Gwyrcai. Splendid facilities in the area
overlooked by the Snowdonia mountain ranges.*

Size 12 acres, 150 touring pitches, 110 with electric
hookup, 100 level pitches, 15 static caravans, 14 ⋔,
20 WCs, 3 CWPs
£ car/tent £6.50-£8, car/caravan £6.50-£8, motorhome
£6.50-£8, motorbike/tent £6.50-£8, children £1.50
Rental ⊞ £100-£260
☏ ✕ ▼ ▣ ☏ GR ◪ ▥ ⊞ Calor Gaz ⅙ ⋔
➜ On A4085 Caernarfon to Beddgelert road, 7 miles
from Beddgelert on left, 5 miles from Caernarfon on
right. Site entrance on main road.

GLAN GWNA
HOLIDAY PARK

Welcomes you to Snowdonia

Glan Gwna is an enchanting holiday village hidden amongst the woods and meadows of an old country estate. Within easy reach of historic castles, golden beaches, lakes, and breath-taking mountain walks.

Glan Gwna has many amenities including excellent Coarse and Game fishing on four lakes and the river Seiont, horse-riding on site, tennis court, heated (outdoor) swimming pool, clubhouse with live entertainment, and poolside bar with meals and takeaway.

SHOP • HAIRDRESSING SALON • LAUNDERETTE • GAMES ARCADE • COACH EXCURSIONS.

Excellent touring facilities for caravans, tents and motor homes, full time warden on site – dogs welcome.
Super pitches available.

BOOKING ESSENTIAL BANK HOLIDAYS AND SUMMER MONTHS.

Directions to site:
1½ miles from Caernarfon on A4085.

For brochure and bookings phone or fax
CAEATHRO, NR. CAERNARFON, GWYNEDD, NORTH WALES LL55 2SG
Tel/Fax: Caernarfon (01286) 673456   Site Wardens: 676402

Cadnant Valley Camping & Caravan Park

Llanberis Road, Caernarfon LL55 2DF

☎ 01286-673196

Open 14 March-31 October ▲ 🚐 �"

Set in a peaceful, sheltered valley with an attractive stream, an easy stroll from all Caernarfon amenities. A well-maintained, clean site.

Size 4½ acres, 70 touring pitches, 34 with electric hookup, 70 level pitches, 8 🚿, 12 WCs, 1 CWP
£ car/tent £6.50-£8, car/caravan £6.50-£8, motorhome £6.50-£8, motorbike/tent £6.50-£7.30, children £1
🚿¼ ✗¼ 🚰¼ 🔥 ⚠ Calor Gaz 🐾
Last arrival time: 10:00
➡ Situated on A4086 only ½ mile from Caernarfon Castle. From town, follow Llanberis signs. Entance on left just before fire station.

Dinlle Caravan Park

Dinas Dinlle, Caernarfon LL54 5TW

☎ 01286-830324 Fax 01286-831526

Open 1 March-31 October ▲ 🚐 �"

With extremely good and well maintained facilities and touring pitches, particularly well spaced out on large areas of open grassland, this is an ideal site for discerning tourers.

Size 22 acres, 250 touring pitches, 150 with electric hookup, 250 level pitches, 138 static caravans, 25 🚿, 50 WCs, 2 CWPs
£ car/tent £5-£11, car/caravan £5-£11, motorhome £5-£11, motorbike/tent £5-£11
Rental 🚐 £100-£500
⊂⊂ MasterCard Visa
🚿 🚰 🔥 ⚠ GR ⚠ ⚁ Calor Gaz ⚙ WS
Last arrival time: 10:00
➡ A499 out of Caernarfon towards Pwhelli (4 miles), right for Dinas Dinlle & Caernarfon airport. Park on right.

Glan Gwna Holiday Park

Caeathro, Caernarfon LL55 2SG

☎ 01286-673456 Fax 01286-673456

Open Easter-September ▲ 🚐 �"
Size 200 acres, 100 touring pitches, 80 with electric hookup, 120 static caravans, 7 🚿, 15 WCs, 1 CWP
£ car/tent £7-£14, car/caravan £7-£14, motorhome £7-£14, motorbike/tent £7
Rental 🚐 Chalet.
🚿 ✗ 🚰 🔥 ⚠ GR ⚠ ⚁ TV ⚠ ⚁ Calor 🐾
Last arrival time: 11:00
➡ 1½ miles S of Caernarfon, off A4085.
See advert on previous page

Llyn-Y-Gele Farm Caravan Park

Pontllyfni, Caernarfon LL54 5EL

☎ 01286-660283

Open Easter-31 October ▲ 🚐 �"
Size 5 acres, 24 touring pitches, 6 with electric hookup, 6 level pitches, 24 static caravans, 2 🚿, 7 WCs, 2 CWPs
£ car/tent £5-£6.50, car/caravan £6.50-£7.50, motorhome £5-£7.50, motorbike/tent £5-£6.50, children £1
🚿¼ ⚁ ⚠ Calor 🐾 WS
➡ On A449, 7½ miles SW of Caernarfon.

Plas Gwyn Caravan Site

Llanrug, Caernarfon LL55 2AQ

☎ 01286-672619 Fax 01286-672619

Open Easter-end October
Size 4 acres, 30 touring pitches, 20 with electric hookup, 20 level pitches, 18 static caravans, 4 🚿, 6 WCs, 1 CWP
🚿 ✗¼ 🚰¼ 🔥 Calor Gaz ⚙
Last arrival time: 10:00
➡ From Caernarfon take A4086 for 3 miles, site on right. From Llanberis take A4086 for 3 miles. Site is on left.

Riverside Camping

Caer Glyddyn, Pontrug, Caernarfon LL5 2BB

☎ 01286-678781 Fax 01286-677223

Open Easter-October ▲ 🚐 �"
Size 4½ acres, 60 touring pitches, 8 with electric hookup, 60 level pitches, 4 🚿, 8 WCs, 1 CWP
£ car/tent £5-£7, car/caravan £8, motorhome £7, motorbike/tent £5
🚿¼ ✗¼ 🔥 ⚁ ⚠ Gaz ⚙ 🐾
➡ 2 miles E of Caernarfon on right side of Llanberis road A4086.

Tyn-yr-Onnen Mountain Farm C&C Park

Waunfawr, Caernarfon LL55 4AX

☎ 01286-650281 Fax 01286-650281

Open April-October ▲ 🚐 �"
Size 4 acres, 30 touring pitches, 30 with electric hookup, 20 level pitches, 3 static caravans, 6 🚿, 6 WCs, 1 CWP
£ car/tent £7-£8, car/caravan £8-£9, motorhome £7-£8, motorbike/tent £6, children £1
Rental 🚐 Chalet.
⊂⊂ MasterCard Visa

⟟ ⟟¼ ✗¼ ⬛¼ ⬛ ⬛ ⬛ ⬛ ⬛ ⬛ GR ⬛ TV ⟰ Calor Gaz
♿ ♀ WS
Last arrival time: 10:00
➜ 4 miles from Caernarfon on A4085 turn left at Fish
& Chips shop/Church. Site is signposted from there.

CARDIFF   3D1

Pontcanna Caravan Site

Pontcanna Fields, Cardiff CF1 9JL
☎ 01222-398362
Open March-October ⛺ ⛟ ⛢
Size 20 acres, 43 touring pitches, 43 with electric
hookup, 43 level pitches, 8 ⛉, 10 WCs, 2 CWPs
£ car/tent £11.25, car/caravan £13.75
⬛ ⬛ Calor Gaz ♿ ♀
➜ W of Cardiff city centre. Entrance on E side of
A4119 Cathedral Road, via Sophia Close.

CARDIGAN Ceredigion   6B4

Bron Gwyn Mawr Farm Caravan & Camping

Penparc, Cardigan SA43 1SA
☎ 01239-613644 **Fax** 01239-613644
Open March-October ⛺ ⛟ ⛢

*Small, select park, peacefully secluded in unspoilt
countryside near the beautiful sandy beaches of Mwnt
and Aberporth, and the quaint old market town of
Cardigan. Ideal for walking, fishing, sight-seeing or
relaxing.*

Size 3 acres, 20 touring pitches, 15 with electric
hookup, 20 level pitches, 3 static caravans, 1 ⛉, 4
WCs, 1 CWP
£ car/tent £5-£8, car/caravan £5-£8, motorhome £5-
£8, motorbike/tent £5-£8
Rental ⛟ Chalet. £100-£275
⬛¼ ✗¼ ⬛ ⬛ ⬛ GR ⬛ ⟰ ♀
Last arrival time: 10:00
➜ From Cardigan take A487 towards Aberystwyth for
½ miles. Turn left at crossroads in Penparc village
signed Ferwig & Mwnt. Carry on over crossroads.
Entrance is on right about ½ mile from main road.

CARMARTHEN Carmarthenshire   6B4

Pendine Sands Holiday Park

Carmarthen SA33 4NZ
☎ 01994-453371
Open March-October

*A family run park adjacent to the famous Pendine
beach, boasting a heated indoor pool and kids clubs
in the wide range of leisure facilities. Restaurant and
bar, excellent cabaret entertainment. A 'British
Holidays Park'.*

Size 30 touring pitches, 10 with electric hookup, 550
static caravans, 6 ⛉, 16 WCs, 2 CWPs
℃ MasterCard Visa
⟟ ⬛ ⬛ ⬛ ⬛ ⬛ ⟰ ⬛ Gaz ♀
Last arrival time: 9:00
➜ Take A40 trunk road from Carmarthen to St Clears.
Pendine/Pentywyn is signposted to left along A4066,
8 miles from junction with A40. Pass through village
of Laugharne and park reception is 5 miles further
on right.

CLYNNOG-FAWR Gwynedd   6B1

Aberafon Gyrn Goch

Clynnog-Fawr LL54 5PN
☎ 01286-660295 **Fax** 01286-660582
Open all year ⛺ ⛟ ⛢
Size 15 acres, 150 touring pitches, 22 with electric
hookup, 100 level pitches, 16 ⛉, 14 WCs, 5 CWPs
£ car/tent £5-£5.50, car/caravan £5-£5.50, motorhome
£5-£5.50, motorbike/tent £5-£5.50, children £1.50-
£1.75
Rental Chalet. price on application
⟟ ⬛ ⬛ ⬛ ⬛ ⬛ TV Calor Gaz ♀
➜ 1 mile S of Clynnog-Fawr on A499 towards
Pwllheli.

Bron-Y-Wendon Caravan Park

Wern Road, Llanddulas, Colwyn Bay LL22 8HG
☎ 01492-512903
Open 21 March-30 October 🚐 🚊

*An award winning park with truly outstanding
facilities. Easily reached from the A55. All pitches
have sea views. Awarded Welsh Tourist Board
'Daffodil Award' for facilities and 'Welcome Host
Gold Award' for excellence in customer care.*

Size 8 acres, 130 touring pitches, 125 with electric
hookup, 100 level pitches, 13 🚿, 31 WCs, 2 CWPs
£ car/caravan £8-£9, motorhome £8-£9, children
£0.50
℃ Visa
🛁¼ ✕¼ 🍴¼ 🗑 🔌 GR 🔍 TV Calor ᴋ ★
➡ Follow the A55 into North Wales and take the
Llanddulas junction (A547). Then follow the tourist
information signs to the park.

Conwy Touring Park

Trefriw Road, Conwy LL32 8UX
☎ 01492-592856 Fax 01492-580024
Open Easter-October 🛖 🚐 🚊

*Set in spectacular scenery, the perfect location for
touring Snowdonia and coastal resorts. Pitches from
£4.85 per night. Special offers available.*

Size 70 acres, 319 touring pitches, 270 with electric
hookup, 300 level pitches, 50 🚿, 72 WCs, 7 CWPs
£ car/tent £4-£10.25, car/caravan £4.85-£10.25,
motorhome £4.85-£10.25, motorbike/tent £4-£10.25
℃ MasterCard Visa
🛁 🍴¼ 🗑 🔌 GR 🔥 🔌 Calor Gaz ᴋ ★
Last arrival time: 7:30
➡ Follow A55 to Conwy. Turn left at mini
roundabout in front of Conwy Castle. Follow B5106
for 1½ miles. Look for sign on left.

Tyn Terfyn Caravan Park

Tal-y-Bont, Conwy LL32 8YX
☎ 01492-660525
Open 14 March-31 October 🛖 🚐 🚊
Size 2 acres, 15 touring pitches, 12 with electric
hookup, 15 level pitches, 2 🚿, 3 WCs, 1 CWP
£ car/tent £3, car/caravan £4.50, motorhome £4.50
🛁¼ ✕¼ 🍴¼ 🗑 Calor Gaz ★
Last arrival time: 10:00
➡ 5 miles S of Conwy on B5106. First house on left
after road sign 'Tal y Bont'.

Hendwr Caravan Park

Llandrillo, Corwen LL21 0SN
☎ 01490-440210
Open 1 April-31 October 🛖 🚐 🚊

*A delightful, select level park with easy access,
situated on a family farm beside a stream and
offering clean, modern facilities.*

Size 10 acres, 40 touring pitches, 40 with electric
hookup, 40 level pitches, 80 static caravans, 8 🚿, 10
WCs, 2 CWPs
£ car/tent £4-£7, car/caravan £7, motorhome £7,
motorbike/tent £4-£7, children £1.50
Rental Chalet.
🛁 🗑 🔌 🗑 📗 Calor Gaz ★ WS
Last arrival time: 10:30
➡ From Corwen take A5 turning onto B4401 for 4
miles. At sign for Hendwr turn right down a wooded
driveway for ¼ mile. Site is on right.

CRICCIETH Gwynedd   6B2   DYFFRYN ARDUDWY Gwynedd   6B2

Camping & Caravanning Club Site
Tyddyn Sianel, Llanystumdwy, Criccieth
☎ 01766-522855
Open end March-start November Å ⊕ ⊞
Size 4 acres, 70 touring pitches, 45 with electric
hookup, 6 ⋔, 9 WCs, 1 CWP
£ car/tent £5.60-£8.60, car/caravan £5.60-£8.60,
motorhome £5.60-£8.60, motorbike/tent £5.60-£8.60,
children £1.50
ℂℂ MasterCard Visa
▣ ☖ ⅋ ⋔
Last arrival time: 11:00
➡ The site is signposted from Criccieth on A497
between Pwllheli and Porthmadog.

Llwyn Bugeilydd Farm
Criccieth LL52 0PN
☎ 01766-522235
Open March-31 October Å ⊕ ⊞
Size 6 acres, 20 touring pitches, 20 with electric
hookup, 20 level pitches, 2 ⋔, 6 WCs, 1 CWP
£ car/tent £5-£6.50, car/caravan £6.50-£8, motorhome
£6-£8, motorbike/tent £5-£6.50
⅋ ☖ ⚠ Calor Gaz ⋔
➡ From A55 take A487 through Caernarfon, then just
after Bryncir turn right onto B4411. Site 3½ miles on
left. From Porthmadog along A497, turn right in
Criccieth onto B4411, site 1 mile on right.

Murmur-Yr-Afon Touring
Dyffryn Ardudwy LL44 2BE
☎ 01341-247353 Fax 01341-247353
Open March-October Å ⊕ ⊞

*Family run park set in tranquil surroundings,
bordered by a trout stream and 20 minutes from the
beach. Ideal base to explore the National Park. Most
improved park in Wales 1997.*

Size 4 acres, 37 touring pitches, 31 with electric
hookup, 30 level pitches, 4 ⋔, 6 WCs, 1 CWP
£ car/tent £5.50-£8.50, car/caravan £5.50-£8.50,
motorhome £5.50-£8.50
⅋¼ ✗¼ ⬤¼ ☖ ⅋ ⅃ ⚠ Calor ⅋ ⋔
Last arrival time: 10:00
➡ Take the A496 coast road from Barmouth-Harlech.
Site is in Dyrffyn Village on right.

CROSSKEYS Caerphilly   3E1   FISHGUARD Pembrokeshire   6A4

Cwmcarn Forest Drive Campsite
Nant Carn Valley, Cwmcarn, Crosskeys NP1 7FA
☎ 01495-272001
Open March-November Å ⊕ ⊞

*Nestling on the banks of a stream and at the foot of a
seven mile scenic drive, stands this picturesque
campsite. Only 15 minutes from the M4*

Size 3 acres, 40 touring pitches, 30 with electric
hookup, 30 level pitches, 6 ⋔, 8 WCs, 1 CWP
£ car/tent £4-£6.50, car/caravan £6.40-£9.50,
motorhome £6.40-£9.50
☖ ⅋ ⅃ ⋔
Last arrival time: 6:00

Fishguard Bay Caravan Park
Dinas Cross, Fishguard SA42 0YD
☎ 01348-811415 Fax 01348-811425
Open 1 March-10 January Å ⊕ ⊞

*Beautiful views and walks available from this
secluded park on Pembrokeshire's Heritage Coast.
Modern caravans equipped to a high standard.*
Size 6 acres, 20 touring pitches, 20 with electric
hookup, 20 level pitches, 50 static caravans, 4 ⋔, 10
WCs, 1 CWP
£ car/tent £6.75-£8.75, car/caravan £7.75-£9.75,
motorhome £7.75-£9.75
Rental ⊕ £125-£320
℃℃ MasterCard Visa
⅋ ☖ ⅋ ☖ ㏿ ⎁ ⚠ Calor Gaz ⋔ WS
➡ Take A487 out of Fishguard towards Cardigan,
turning on your left. Signpost on right, about 3 miles.

Barcdy Caravan & Camping Park
Talsarnau, near Harlech LL47 6YG
☎ 01766-770736
Open Easter-31 October Å ⊕ ⌷

A quiet, friendly family park in beautiful natural surroundings, with facilities of a high standard. Ideally situated for touring this spectacular part of Wales.

Size 40 acres, 68 touring pitches, 44 with electric hookup, 44 level pitches, 30 static caravans, 10 ⋒, 14 WCs, 2 CWPs
£ car/tent £7-£9, car/caravan £7-£9, motorhome £7-£9, motorbike/tent £7-£9, children £1-£1.50
Rental ⊕ Chalet. £160-£270
⌷ ⌷ ⌷ ⌷ Calor Gaz
➨ Travelling S via Trawsfynydd take left turning at Maentwrog onto A496. Site is 4 miles along on left.

Brandy Brook Caravan Site
Haycastle, Haverfordwest SA62 5PT
☎ 01348-840272
Open Easter-end September Å ⊕ ⌷
Size 9 acres, 46 touring pitches, 10 level pitches, 30 static caravans, 2 ⋒, 5 WCs, 1 CWP
£ car/tent £3.50-£4.50, car/caravan £4.50-£6.25
⌷ ⌷ ⌷ Calor Gaz ⌷ WS
➨ 7 miles NW from Haverfordwest, at Roch (A487), right on to minor road for 1½ miles. Fork left for ½ mile. Site signed 1¼ miles.

South Cockett Caravan & Camping Park
Broadway, Little Haven, Haverfordwest SA62 3TU
☎ 01437-781296 Fax 01437-781296
Open Easter-October Å ⊕ ⌷
Size 6 acres, 70 touring pitches, 60 with electric hookup, 70 level pitches, 1 static caravans, 6 ⋒, 12 WCs, 3 CWPs
£ car/tent £4.75-£5.50, car/caravan £5.20-£6.95, motorhome £4.70-£6.45, motorbike/tent £4.50-£5.50
Rental ⊕ price on application
⌷ ⌷ ⌷ Calor Gaz ⌷ WS
Last arrival time: 11:00
➨ From Haverfordwest take B4341 signed Broad Haven for 4¼ miles, then left signposted Milford Haven to site after 300 yards.

Ants Hill Caravan & Camping Park
Laugharne SA33 4QN
☎ 01994-427293 Fax 01994-427293
Open Easter-31 October Å ⊕ ⌷

Situated in Dylan Thomas country and ideal for inland and coastal touring. Near the famous Pendine sands.

Size 9 acres, 60 touring pitches, 50 with electric hookup, 60 level pitches, 60 static caravans, 8 ⋒, 20 WCs, 1 CWP
£ car/tent £5.50-£7.50, car/caravan £7-£15, motorhome £7-£11, motorbike/tent £5.50-£7.50
Rental ⊕ £120-£300
⌷ ⌷¼ ✕¼ ⌷ ⌷¼ ⌷ ⌷ ⌷ ⌷ GR ⌷ ⌷ Calor WS
Last arrival time: 10:30
➨ M4 to Carmarthen, A40 towards St Clears. A4066 for Laugharne. Take first left turning before signpost of Laugharne.

Ty Newydd Caravan Park & Country Club
Llanbedrgoch LL76 8TZ
☎ 01248-450677 Fax 01248-450711
Open March-October Å ⊕ ⌷

Family run park on edge of small village in open country. Excellent toilet facilities, health & fitness centre, swimming pools and a licensed bar. Tourers and campers are made to feel very welcome.

Size 9 acres, 40 touring pitches, 40 with electric hookup, 40 level pitches, 61 static caravans, 4 ⋒, 8 WCs, 1 CWP

£ car/tent £7-£18, car/caravan £7-£18, motorhome £7-£18, motorbike/tent £7-£18
Rental 🚐 £180-£300
CC MasterCard Visa
🔋✖🍽🍴🔲🛢🗟🎣📻GR🔌⚠🚬 Calor Gaz 👦🐕 WS
Last arrival time: 12:00
➡ Take A5025 from Pentraeth. After ½ mile turn left at layby. Site is 1 mile on right.

LLANBEDROG Gwynedd   6B2

Refail Caravan & Camping Site
Refail, Llanbedrog LL53 7NP
📞 01258-740511
Open Easter-October A 🚐 🚙
Size 2 acres, 33 touring pitches, 27 with electric hookup, 27 level pitches, 6 🚿, 6 WCs, 1 CWP
£ car/tent £7-£8,050, car/caravan £7-£8.50, motorhome £7-£8.50, motorbike/tent £7-£8.50
🔋¼✖¼🍴¼🛢🔋🍴 Calor Gaz 👦 WS
➡ Take A499 from Pwllheli. Turn right in Llanbedrog onto B4413 (signposted Llanbedrog Village & Aberdaron). Park is 200 yards on right.

LLANDOVERY Carmarthenshire   6C4

Camping & Caravanning Club Site
Rhandirmwyn, Llandovery
📞 01550-760257
Open end March-early November A 🚐 🚙
Size 11 acres, 90 touring pitches, 48 with electric hookup, 6 🚿, 9 WCs, 1 CWP
£ car/tent £5.60-£8.60, car/caravan £5.60-£8.60, motorhome £5.60-£8.60, motorbike/tent £5.60-£8.60, children £1.50
CC MasterCard Visa
🛢🔋🍴⚠🚬 🐕 👦
Last arrival time: 11:00
➡ From A483 in Llandovery take road signed Rhandirmwyn for 7 miles. Turn left at Post Office in Rhandirmwyn. Site is signposted.

Erwlon Caravan & Camping Park
Llandovery SA20 0RD
📞 01550-720330
Open all year A 🚐 🚙

Family run park beautifully located alongside a babbling brook at the foothills of the Brecon Beacons. The site provides the ideal base for a touring holiday.

Size 8 acres, 40 touring pitches, 15 with electric hookup, 40 level pitches, 4 static caravans, 6 🚿, 14 WCs, 2 CWPs
£ car/tent £5-£9, car/caravan £5-£9, motorhome £5-£9, motorbike/tent £5-£9
🔋¼✖¼🍽¼🛢🍴⚠ Calor 👦 WS
Last arrival time: 11:30
➡ Beside A40 between Brecon and Llandovery, ½ mile from Llandovery.

LLANDRINDOD WELLS Powys   6C3

Disserth Caravan Park
Disserth, Howey, Llandrindod Wells LD1 6NL
📞 01597-860277 Fax 01597-860277
Open March-October A 🚐 🚙
Size 3 acres, 47 touring pitches, 40 with electric hookup, 47 level pitches, 19 static caravans, 6 🚿, 8 WCs, 1 CWP
£ car/tent £6.25-£7.50, car/caravan £6.25-£7.50, motorhome £6.25-£7.50, motorbike/tent £6.25-£7.50, children £0.90
Rental 🚐 £95-£275
CC MasterCard Visa
🔋✖🛢🔋🍴🚬 Calor Gaz 👦 WS
Last arrival time: 10:30
➡ Just 1 mile off A483 (Llandrindod Wells-Builth Wells road), follow signs for Disserth. Park alongside 13th century church and River Ithon.

Park Motel Caravan & Camping Park
Rhayader Road, Crossgates, Llandrindod Wells LD1 6RF
📞 01597-851201 Fax 01597-851201
Open 1 March-31 October A 🚐 🚙
Size 3 acres, 15 touring pitches, 5 with electric hookup, 15 level pitches, 15 static caravans, 2 🚿, 4 WCs, 1 CWP
£ car/tent £6-£6.75, car/caravan £6-£6.75, motorhome £6-£6.75, motorbike/tent £6.75, children £1
Rental 🚐 Chalet.
🔋✖🍽🔋🛢🗟GR⚠🚬 Calor Gaz 👦 WS
Last arrival time: 10:00
➡ Situated on A44, ½ mile W of Crossgates (Rhayader) roundabout towards Rhayader, 3 miles N of Llandrindod Wells (A483).

LLANDYSUL Carmarthenshire   6B4

Camping & Caravanning Club Site
Llwynhelyg, Cross Inn, Llandysul SA44 6LW
📞 01545-560029
Open 6 March-start November A 🚐 🚙
Size 13½ acres, 90 touring pitches, 56 with electric hookup, 6 🚿, 10 WCs, 1 CWP
£ car/tent £5.20-£7.80, car/caravan £5.20-£7.80, motorhome £5.20-£7.80, motorbike/tent £5.20-£7.80
CC MasterCard Visa
🔋✖🍽🛢🔋⚠🐕👦
Last arrival time: 11:00
➡ Turn left from A487 Cardigan-Aberystwyth. After 2 miles in village of Cross Inn turn left at Pub. Site is ¾ miles on right.

Rhydygalfe Caravan Park

Pontwelli, Llandysul SA44 5AP

☎ 01559-362738

Open all year **A** 🚐 🚎

Size 3 acres, 30 touring pitches, 18 with electric hookup, 30 level pitches, 15 static caravans, 8 🚿, 6 WCs, 1 CWP

£ car/tent £4, car/caravan £5, motorhome £5, motorbike/tent £4

Rental 🚐

🛁¼ ✗¼ 🚱¼ 🗑 🔥 🖥 🎮 🏧 Calor ☛ WS

➡ On right of A486 (from Llandysul to Cardigan). ¼ mile S of Llandysul.

Abermarlais Caravan Park

Llangadog SA19 9NG

☎ 01550-777868

Open 15 March-1 November **A** 🚐 🚎

Size 16 acres, 88 touring pitches, 43 with electric hookup, 80 level pitches, 8 🚿, 14 WCs, 1 CWP

£ car/tent £7, car/caravan £7, motorhome £7, motorbike/tent £6.50, children £1

🛁 🔥 🖥 🏧 Calor Gaz ♿ ☛ WS

Last arrival time: 11:00

➡ 7 miles W of Llandovery on A40 - site on right, or 7 miles E of Llandfield on A40 - site on left.

Cross Inn & Black Mountain Caravan Park

Llanddeusant, Llangadog SA19 9YG

☎ 01550-740621

Open all year **A** 🚐 🚎

Small family site set in the beautiful Brecon Beacons National Park with glorious views. Great walking, fishing. Lots of history and wildlife.

Size 9 acres, 30 touring pitches, 22 with electric hookup, 10 static caravans, 2 🚿, 5 WCs, 1 CWP

£ car/tent £4-£6, car/caravan £4, motorhome £6, motorbike/tent £6, children £4

Rental 🚐 £120-£255 weekly. Short stays available.

ℂℂ MasterCard Visa

🛁 ✗ 🚱 🗑 🔥 🏧 🔌 Calor Gaz ☛

➡ Take A40 from Brecon towards Llandovery. At Trecastle turn left and carry on over open countryside for 9 miles to site on the left.

Lakeside Caravan Park

Llangorse Lake, Llangorse LD3 7TR

☎ 0187484-226

Open April-October

Size 14 acres, 50 touring pitches, 19 with electric hookup, 50 level pitches, 80 static caravans, 10 🚿, 19 WCs, 2 CWPs

£ car/tent £6.60-£8.50, car/caravan £6.50-£8.50, motorhome £6.50-£8.50, motorbike/tent £6.50-£8.50, children £2

Rental 🚐 £135-£185 per week

ℂℂ MasterCard Visa

🛁 ✗ 🚱 🗑 🔥 🖥 🏧 🔌 Calor Gaz ☛

Last arrival time: 9:00

➡ B4560 from A40 from S, B4560 from A438 from N.

Bodnant Caravan Park

Nebo Road, Llanrwst LL26 0SD

☎ 01492-640248

Open 1 March-31 October **A** 🚐 🚎

A small quiet landscaped site for touring caravans and tents, and a winner of "Wales in Bloom" for 23 years. Centrally situated, near Llanrwst, for exploring the mountains and beaches of North Wales.

Size 4 acres, 60 touring pitches, 47 with electric hookup, 2 static caravans, 6 🚿, 9 WCs, 1 CWP

£ car/tent £7-£8, car/caravan £7-£8, motorhome £7-£8, motorbike/tent £7-£8, children £0.50

Rental 🚐 £160-£230, cottage £160-£230

🛁¼ ✗¼ 🚱¼ 🔥 🏧 Calor Gaz ♿ ☛

Last arrival time: 9:30

➡ S of Llanrwst turn off A470 opposite Birmingham garage onto B5427, signposted Nebo. Site is 30 yards past sign.

Maenan Abbey Caravan Park

Maenan, Llanrwst

☎ 01492-660630

Open 1 March-31 October 🚐 🚎

Plenty of trees and shrubs at this pleasant site, children's play area. 7 chalets for hire (own WCs). Good touring centre within easy reach of all attractions. No motorcycles.

Size 7 acres, 36 touring pitches, 25 with electric hookup, 36 level pitches, 71 static caravans, 4 ⚲, 7 WCs, 1 CWP

£ car/caravan £4.50-£9, motorhome £4.50-£9

Rental Chalet. from £100-£250

◼ ⑤ Calor

Last arrival time: 10:00

➜ 3 miles N of Llanrwst on A470, by Maenan Abbey Hotel.

Plas Meirion Caravan Park

Gower Road, Trefriw LL27 0RZ

📞 01492-640247 **Fax** 01492-640247

Open April-October ⚑ ⚏

Size 2 acres, 5 touring pitches, 5 with electric hookup, 5 level pitches, 26 static caravans, 2 ⚲, 5 WCs, 1 CWP

£ car/caravan £6.50-£9.50, motorhome £6.50-£9.50

Rental ⚑ £100-£260

⚑¼ ✕¼ ⚑¼ ◻ ◼ WS

Last arrival time: 10:30

➜ Site is in Trefriw, 1½ miles from Llanrwst on B5106. Turn right directly oposite Trefriw woollen mill down Gower Road. Site is 100 yards on left.

Tyddyn Isaf Camping & Caravan Site

Dulas, Lligwy Bay LL70 9PQ

📞 01248-410203 **Fax** 01248-410667

Open March-October ▲ ⚑ ⚏

Size 16 acres, 80 touring pitches, 50 static caravans, 8 ⚲, 14 WCs, 1 CWP

£ car/tent £5-£9, car/caravan £10-£11.50, motorhome £8-£10, children £0.80

Rental ⚑ £100-£270

⚑ ✕ ⚑ ◻ ◼ ◻ ⊞ ⚏ ⊞ Calor Gaz ⚑ WS

Last arrival time: 10:00

➜ Travel over Brittannia Bridge onto Isle of Anglesey and take A5025 to Moelfre. Left at roundabout onto A5025 for 2 miles. At phonebox/craft shop at Brynrefail turn right and site is ½ mile on right.

Tudor Glen Caravan Park

Jameston, Manorbier SA70 7SS

📞 01834-871417 **Fax** 01834-871832

Open March-October ▲ ⚑ ⚏

A family run site in the Pembrokeshire National Park, midway between Tenby and Pembroke. Manorbier Beach is less than 1 away.

Size 6 acres, 30 touring pitches, 30 with electric hookup, 30 level pitches, 20 static caravans, 7 ⚲, 14 WCs, 1 CWP

£ car/tent £4-£7, car/caravan £5-£8.50, motorhome £5-£8.50, motorbike/tent £4-£7, children £1-£1.25

Rental ⚑ £60-£365

⚑ ✕¼ ⚑¼ ◻ ◼ ◻ ⑤ GR ⚏ Calor WS

Last arrival time: 9:00

➜ Off Tenby to Pembroke road (A4239). Entrance is as you enter village of Jameston on right side from Tenby direction.

Grawen Farm Camping & Caravan Site

Cwm Taff, Cefn Coed, Merthyr Tydfil CF48 2HS

📞 01685-723740

Open April-October ▲ ⚑ ⚏

Size 4 acres, 50 touring pitches, 8 with electric hookup, 30 level pitches, 3 ⚲, 7 WCs, 1 CWP

£ car/tent £5-£6, car/caravan £6-£7, motorhome £5-£6, motorbike/tent £5-£6, children £0.50

CC MasterCard Visa

⚑ ◻ ◼ ◻ Calor ⚑ WS

Last arrival time: 12:00

➜ Site on A470, ½ mile from village of Cefen Coed y-Cymmer.

Trefach Caravan Park
Clynderwen, Crymmych SA66 7RU
☎ 01994-419225 Fax 01994-419225
Open March-October ▲ ⊞ ⊞
Size 18 acres, 20 touring pitches, 10 with electric
hookup, 6 level pitches, 45 static caravans, 4 ⛅, 13
WCs, 2 CWPs
£ car/tent £6-£10, car/caravan £6-£10, motorhome £6-
£10, motorbike/tent £6-£10
Rental ⊞ £95-£230
⚱ ✕ ◗ ▣ ▣ ▣ ▣ ▣ ▣ ▣ ▣ ⚠ ⊟ Calor Gaz ᕕ ⊁
WS
Last arrival time: 12:00
➜ 1½ miles off Cardigan-Tenby road (A478).
See advert on previous page

Allensbank Holiday Park
Narberth SA67 8RF
☎ 01834-860243 Fax 01834-861622
Open Easter-October ⊞ ⊞
Size 5 acres, 10 touring pitches, 10 with electric
hookup, 19 static caravans, 4 ⛅, 4 WCs, 1 CWP
£ car/tent £6-£12, car/caravan £6-£12, motorhome £6-
£12, motorbike/tent £6-£12, children £0.25
Rental ⊞ Chalet. £100-£350
▣ ▣ ▣ ▣ ▣ ▣ ▣ ⚠ ⊟ ⊁
Last arrival time: 10:30
➜ 1 mile S of Narberth on A478 towards Tenby.

Noble Court Caravan Park
Redstone Road, Narberth SA67 7ES
☎ 01834-861191 Fax 01834-861484
Open March-November ▲ ⊞ ⊞

*A small, friendly site with touring, motorhomes and
tent pitches, with electric hookup. Ideal touring centre
- 6 miles from beaches and mountains, 4 miles from
Oakwood Park.*

Size 8 acres, 92 touring pitches, 92 with electric
hookup, 62 level pitches, 60 static caravans, 12 ⛅, 15
WCs, 2 CWPs
£ car/tent £6-£8, car/caravan £6-£13.50, motorhome
£8-£13.50, motorbike/tent £8-£13.50
℄ MasterCard Visa
⚱¼ ✕ ◗ ▣ ▣ ▣ ▣ ▣ �𝕋 ⚠ ⊟ Calor Gaz ᕕ ⊁ WS
➜ ½ mile off A40 trunk road on B4313, within ½ mile
of Narbeth.

Cei Bach Country Club
New Quay SA45 9SL
☎ 01545-580237 Fax 01545-580237
Open Easter-end September ▲ ⊞ ⊞

*Award winning site set in Cei Bach Bay. All modern
facilities including bar, take-away, games room, ball
and play park, launderette and shop (100 yards).
New Quay 1½ miles.*

Size 60 touring pitches, 50 with electric hookup, 20
level pitches, 1 static caravans, 6 ⛅, 12 WCs, 1 CWP
£ car/tent £6-£12, car/caravan £6-£12, motorhome £6-
£12, motorbike/tent £6-£12
℄ MasterCard Visa
⚱¼ ✕¼ ◗ ▣ ▣ ▣ ▣ ⚠ ⊟ Calor Gaz ⊁
Last arrival time: 10:00
➜ From Aberystwyth S on A487 for 25 miles, then
right onto B4342 signed New Quay. Turn right at
Cambrian Hotel and follow signs.

Afon Teifi Caravan & Camping Park
Pentre Cagal, Newcastle Emlyn SA38 9HT
☎ 01559-370532
Open all year ▲ ⊞ ⊞
Size 23 acres, 110 touring pitches, 95 with electric
hookup, 110 level pitches, 9 ⛅, 16 WCs, 1 CWP
£ car/tent £6-£7, car/caravan £6-£7, motorhome £6-
£7, motorbike/tent £5-£6
⚱¼ ✕¼ ◗¼ ▣ ▣ ▣ ▣ ▣ ▣ ⚠ Calor Gaz ᕕ ⊁ WS
➜ On A484 Carmarthen to Cardigan road, 2 miles E of
Newcastle Emlyn. From M4 take A484.

Cenarth Falls Holiday Park
Cenarth, Newcastle Emlyn SA38 9JS.
☎ 01239-710345 Fax 01239-710345
Open March-November ▲ ⊞ ⊞

A friendly, family run park offering luxury caravan accommodation and touring/camping facilities of the highest standard. An ideal base for exploring West Wales.

Size 12 acres, 30 touring pitches, 26 with electric hookup, 30 level pitches, 89 static caravans, 4 🚿, 7 WCs, 1 CWP

£ car/tent £7.75-£12.75, car/caravan £7.75-£12.75, motorhome £7.75-£12.75, motorbike/tent £12.75

Rental 🚐 from £110-£423 pw

℃ MasterCard Visa

🏪 ✗ 🛝 🔲 🛒 🗑 🔲 GR TV ⚠ 🔌 Calor Gaz ᴆ 🐴

Last arrival time: 10:00

➡ Turn right at signs, ¼ mile after crossing Cenarth Bridge on A484.

Llwyngwair Manor Holiday Park

Newport SA42 0LX

📞 **01239-820498**

Open April-October Ⓐ 🚐 🚛

Set in 55 acres of beautiful parkland bounded by the River Nevern, renowned for fishing, in Pembrokeshire National Park. One mile from the Coastal Path.

Size 55 acres, 80 touring pitches, 54 with electric hookup, 80 level pitches, 100 static caravans, 6 🚿, 10 WCs, 1 CWP

£ car/tent £8-£10, car/caravan £8-£12, motorhome £8-£12, motorbike/tent £8-£10

Rental 🚐 Chalet. caravans £90-£230, chalet £120-£260

℃ MasterCard Visa

🏪 ✗ 🛝 🔲 🛒 🗑 🔲 GR 🔲 TV ⚠ 🔌 Calor ᴆ 🐴 WS

Last arrival time: 10:00

➡ On main A487 coast road between Fishguard and Cardigan; 1 mile N of Newport.

Cringoed Caravan and Camping Park

Llanbrynmair, Newtown SY19 7DR

📞 **01650-521237**

Open 1st April-31 October Ⓐ 🚐 🚛

Cringoed is a quiet site on the river with beautiful views of the soft mid Wales countryside. Ideal for walks, bird-watching, lakes and coasts.

Size 21 acres, 50 touring pitches, 30 with electric hookup, 20 static caravans, 4 🚿, 6 WCs, 1 CWP

£ car/tent £6, car/caravan £6, motorhome £6, motorbike/tent £6, children £0.50

Rental 🚐

🗑 🛒 Calor ᴆ 🐴 WS

➡ Turn off A470 at Llanbrynmair on B4518 for 1 mile.

Llwyn Celyn Holiday Park

Adfa, Newtown SY16 3DG

📞 **01938-810720**

Open 1 March-1 January Ⓐ 🚐 🚛

Size 10 acres, 16 touring pitches, 11 with electric hookup, 6 level pitches, 55 static caravans, 3 🚿, 4 WCs, 1 CWP

£ car/tent £5-£8, car/caravan £8, motorhome £8, motorbike/tent £5-£8

🏪¼ 🛝 🗑 🛒 🗑 GR ⚠ Calor ᴆ 🐴 WS

➡ Off B4390 leading from A483. Follow signs, W of New Mills.

Tynycwm Camping Site

Aberhafesp, Newtown SY16 3JF

📞 **01686-688651**

Open May-October Ⓐ 🚐 🚛

Size 3 acres, 50 touring pitches, 50 level pitches, 8 static caravans, 2 🚿, 3 WCs, 1 CWP

£ car/tent £5, car/caravan £5

ᴆ 🐴

➡ Follow A489 to Caersws, turn right onto B4569 to Aberhafesp. At first crossroads go straight over B4568 ignoring sign for Aberhafesp. At next crossroads turn left at Bwlch-y-Garreg signpost. Farm and site 1 mile on right.

Pen-y-fan Caravan & Leisure Park

Manmoel Road, Oakdale NP2 0HY
☎ 01495-226636 Fax 01495-227778
Open all year 🚐

A quiet level park with magnificent views of the surrounding countryside. An ideal base to visit the Welsh coastline, Brecon Beacons and Cardiff. All facilities of a very high standard. Warm welcome guaranteed.

Size 42 acres, 50 touring pitches, 50 with electric hookup, 50 level pitches, 10 static caravans, 8 🚿, 14 WCs, 2 CWPs
£ car/tent £7, car/caravan £7, motorhome £7, motorbike/tent £7, children £2
℃ MasterCard Visa
🛁 ✕ 🛒 🗑 🔌 🚻 📺 ⚠ 🚪 ⚓ 🐕 WS
➡ Leave M4 at junction 28 and take A467 to Crumlin, where left at traffic lights onto B4251 towards Oakdale. In 1¼ miles turn right and follow signs to Penyfan Pond. Fork left to site. This site is signposted.

Three Cliffs Bay Holiday Park

North Hills Farm, Penmaen SA3 2HB
☎ 01792-371218
Open 1 April-31 October ▲ 🚐 🚐

Site overlooks Three Cliffs Bay.
Size 5 acres, 95 touring pitches, 20 with electric hookup, 5 🚿, 13 WCs, 1 CWP
£ car/tent £8, car/caravan £9, motorhome £8.50, motorbike/tent £8
🛁 ✕¼ 🛒¼ 🗑 🔌 Calor Gaz 🐕
Last arrival time: flexible
➡ In Penmaen village, off A4118.

Woodlands Camping Park

Pendyffrin Hall, Penmaenmawr LL34 6UF
☎ 01492-623219
Open Easter-end October ▲ 🚐 🚐
Size 96 acres, 100 touring pitches, 40 with electric hookup, 100 level pitches, 16 WCs, 1 CWP
£ car/tent £6-£9, car/caravan £6-£11, motorhome £6-£9
🛁¼ ✕¼ 🛒¼ 🗑 🔌 🚪
Last arrival time: 9:00
➡ Off A55 between Conway-Penmaenmawr. Bypass Conway under river tunnel - approx. 1½ miles further on A55 pass through another road tunnel, 100yds after the tunnel take first turn left, entrance fourth on left, signposted.

Rhos Caravan Park

Pentraeth LL75 8DZ
☎ 01248-450214 Fax 01248-450214
Open March-October ▲ 🚐 🚐
Size 15 acres, 92 touring pitches, 70 with electric hookup, 92 level pitches, 66 static caravans, 12 🚿, 24 WCs, 2 CWPs
£ car/tent £5.50, car/caravan £6, motorhome £5.50, motorbike/tent £5.50, children £0.50
Rental 🚐
🛁 ✕¼ 🛒¼ 🗑 🔌 🗑 ⚠ Calor Gaz 🚪 🐕
➡ 1 mile N of Penraeth on A5025 - pass Bull Hotel, park on left.

Carreglwyd Camping & Caravan Park

Port Eynon, Swansea SA3 1NN
☎ 01792-390795 Fax 01792-390796
Open March-December ▲ 🚐 🚐

Beautifully situated alongside the sandy bay of Port Eynon, and an ideal base for exploring the magnificent Gower peninsula. Particularly suitable for families with young children.

Size 20 acres, 180 touring pitches, 16 with electric hookup, 100 level pitches, 16 🚿, 24 WCs, 1 CWP

£ car/tent £9, car/caravan £13, motorhome £9,
motorbike/tent £9, children £0.50
((Visa
⚑ ✕¼ ⬤¼ ⬛ ⬛ ⬛ Calor Gaz ⬥ ⚑
Last arrival time: 10:00
➜ Follow A4118 from Swansea to village of Port-
Eynon (16 miles). Drive through car park to entrance.

Newpark Holiday Park
Port Eynon SA3 1NL
☎ 01792-390292 Fax 01792-391245
Open April-October ⚑ ⬤ ⬛

*Striking scenic views overlooking the Bristol Channel.
Camping on level plateaux, luxury bungalows for six
with superb views.*

Size 14 acres, 112 touring pitches, 112 with electric
hookup, 80 level pitches, 10 ⬛, 20 WCs, 2 CWPs
£ car/tent £7.50-£10.50, car/caravan £8-£15
Rental Chalet. £140-£270 weekly
((MasterCard Visa
⚑ ✕¼ ⬤¼ ⬛ ⬛ ⬛ ⬛ ⬛ ⬛ Calor Gaz ⬥ ⚑ WS
➜ From Swansea take A4118 for 14 miles. Down hill
into Port Eynon. Large splayed entrance to site on left.

Happy Valley Caravan Park
Wigfach, Porthcawl CF32 0NG
☎ 01656-782144 Fax 01656-782146
Open 1 April-30 September ⚑ ⬤ ⬛

*Licensed club with entertainment/shops. All facilities.
Electric hook-ups for tourers. Situated on the Heritage
Coast overlooking Newton Bay and Ogmore by sea
with panoramic views of the Bristol Channel Coastline.*

Size 100 touring pitches, 30 with electric hookup, 50
level pitches, 8 ⬛, 16 WCs, 1 CWP
£ car/tent £5.50-£6.50, car/caravan £5.50-£6.50,
motorhome £5.50-£6.50, motorbike/tent £5.50-£6.50
Rental ⬛
((MasterCard Visa
⚑ ✕ ⬤ ⬛ ⬛ ⬛ ⬛ ⬛ ⬛ Calor Gaz ⬥ ⚑ WS
Last arrival time: 9:00
➜ From A48 take A4106 Bridgend/Porthcawl road 1
mile to Wigfach, turning immediately on right.

Black Rock Touring & Camping Park
Morfa Bychan, Porthmadog LL53 9LD
☎ **01766-513919**
Open March-October ▲ 🚐 🚛

An ideal family park situated behind the dunes of Black Rock beach. The site offers high class facilities including showers and toilets.

Size 9 acres, 150 touring pitches, 40 with electric hookup, 150 level pitches, 18 🚿, 16 WCs, 1 CWP
£ car/tent £9, car/caravan £11, motorhome £9, motorbike/tent £9
⅕¼ ✗¼ 🚱¼ 🗑 🔌 🖫 ⚠ Calor Gaz ♒
Last arrival time: 10:30
➡ Cross tollgate at Porthmadog, turn left at Woolworths in High Street, and follow Morfa Bychan road to end. At beach entrance bear right to park.

Greenacres Holiday Park
Blackrock Sands, Morfa Bychan, Porthmadog LL49 9YB
☎ **01766-512781 Fax 01766-512084**
Open March-October 🚐 🚛

A family holiday park with direct access to a lovely sandy beach, indoor pool, kids clubs, great live entertainment, bars and hot food. A 'British Holidays Park'.

Size 80 acres, 71 touring pitches, 61 with electric hookup, 71 level pitches, 180 static caravans, 10 🚿, 8 WCs, 1 CWP
£ car/caravan £6.50-£17, motorhome £6.50-£17, children £1.50

Rental 🚐
CC MasterCard Visa
⅕ ✗ 🚱 🗑 🔌 🖫 🔲 🗑 🖩 GR 🔍 ⚠ 🔌 Calor ♒
Last arrival time: 11:00
➡ After arriving at toll bridge at Porthmadog, go along High Street and turn between Post Office and Woolworths towards Black Rock Sands, Greenacres is on road, the other side of small village of Morfa Bychan.

Tyddyn Llwyn Caravan Park & Camp Site
Morfa Bychan Road, Porthmadog LL49 9UR
☎ **01766-512205 Fax 01766-512205**
Open Easter-31 October ▲ 🚐 🚛

Situated in a delightful saucer-shaped valley with beautiful views across rural countryside. Within twenty minutes walk from town and close to beach, golf club and water sports.

Size 12 acres, 153 touring pitches, 65 with electric hookup, 50 level pitches, 53 static caravans, 12 🚿, 24 WCs, 3 CWPs
£ car/tent £8-£10, car/caravan £8-£12, motorhome £8-£12, motorbike/tent £6-£8, children £1
⅕ ✗ 🚱¼ 🗑 🔌 🖫 🖩 GR 🔍 📺 ⚠ 🔌 Calor Gaz ♒
Last arrival time: 11:00
➡ From Porthmadog High Street turn by Woolworths towards Morfa Bychan. After passing sign to Borth-y-Gest only, signs for site on roadside at bottom of hill. Drive for park on right immediately opposite signs.

Nant Mill Touring Caravan Park
Nant Mill Farm, Prestatyn LL199L4
☎ **01745-852360**
Open 1 April-15 October
Size 5 acres, 150 touring pitches, 92 with electric hookup, 150 level pitches, 4 🚿, 15 WCs, 1 CWP
£ car/tent £8.50-£10.50, car/caravan £8.50-£10.50, motorhome £8.50-£10.50, motorbike/tent £8.50, children £0.30
⅕¼ ✗¼ 🚱¼ 🔌 🖫 ⚠ Calor Gaz ♿ ♒
Last arrival time: 10:30
➡ ½ mile E of Prestatyn on A548 coast road. Site is close to junction with A547.

Tyddyn Llwyn Caravan Park

Situated in a delightful rural setting close to both town, sea and mountains. An ideal centre from which to tour Snowdonia/North Wales with superb local attractions. A Country Hotel and restaurant is situated within the park.

Morfa Bychan Road, Porthmadog, Gwynedd LL49 9UR
Tel/Fax: (01766) 512205

Pitton Cross Caravan Park
Swansea SA3 1PH
📞 01792-390593 Fax 01792-391010
Open 1 April-31 October 🛆 🚐 🚛

Personally supervised by its owners, this is a level site with several small paddocks overlooking the sea and close to surfing beaches. An ideal base for walking, bird watching and hang-gliding.

Size 6 acres, 100 touring pitches, 50 with electric hookup, 100 level pitches, 8 🚿, 12 WCs, 2 CWPs
£ car/tent £7.50, car/caravan £8-£10, motorhome £8-£9, motorbike/tent £7-£7.50
✗ MasterCard Visa
🛒 🖻 📞 🗑 /Λ Calor Gaz ♿ 🐕 WS
Last arrival time: 9:00
➡ From A4118 turn right at Scurlage (from Swansea 16 miles) onto B4247 signposted Rhossilli. Park is 2 miles on left.

Moreton Farm Leisure Park
Moreton, Saundersfoot SA69 9EA
📞 01834-812016 Fax 01834-811890
Open March-December 🛆 🚐 🚛

Set in secluded valley 15-20 minutes walk from Saundersfoot. Heated toilet/shower block, access for disabled, covered dish washing and laundry facilities. Lodges and cottages available.

Size 60 touring pitches, 14 with electric hookup, 12 level pitches, 12 static caravans, 6 🚿, 6 WCs, 2 CWPs
£ car/tent £5-£6, car/caravan £8-£11.50, motorhome £7-£10.50, motorbike/tent £5-£6
Rental Chalet. £170-£350
🛒 ✗¼ 🖻 📞 🗑 📛 /Λ Calor
➡ A477 from St Clears, A478 towards Tenby, 1½ miles, park is on left, opposite chapel.

TRETIO
CARAVAN & CAMPING PARK

A small family park with beautiful views close to St Davids, Whitesands, Abereiddy and the coastal path. Children's play area, 9-hole Pitch and Putt. First class facilities including disabled. Free showers and hot water. 2 Holiday Caravans available. 'Welcome Host.'

For details of this delightful park contact Bryn or Phil Rees.

ST. DAVIDS, PEMBROKESHIRE, WEST WALES SA62 6DE
Tel: (01437) 781359/720270
Mobile: (0374) 815598

Caerfai Bay Caravan & Tent Park

Caerfai Bay, St David's SA62 6QT
☎ 01437-720274 Fax 01437-720274
Open 1 April-31 October Å 🚐 🏕

A quiet family run park, uniquely situated within the Pembrokeshire Coast National Park and just 200 yards of the sandy Caerfai Bay bathing beach. The site offers unsurpassed panoramic sea views of coastal scenery and St Davids with its magnificent cathedral is only ¾ mile away.

Size 10 acres, 85 touring pitches, 46 with electric hookup, 40 level pitches, 32 static caravans, 7 🛁, 17 WCs, 2 CWPs
£ car/tent £4.50-£6, car/caravan £4.50-£10, motorhome £4.50-£6, motorbike/tent £4.50-£6, children £1
Rental 🚐 £100-£300
🔋¼ ✗¼ 🍴¼ 🔲 🔌 🔳 Calor Gaz 🐕
Last arrival time: 8:00
➡ Turn off A487 near Marine Life Centre and follow signs to Caerfai Bay. Entrance to park is at end of road on right.

Camping & Caravanning Club Site

Dwr Cwmdig, St David's SA62 6DW
☎ 01348-831376
Open end March-end September Å 🚐 🏕
Size 4 acres, 40 touring pitches, 24 with electric hookup, 4 🛁, 7 WCs, 1 CWP
£ car/tent £8.20-£10.40, car/caravan £8.20-£10.40, motorhome £8.20-£10.40, motorbike/tent £8.20-£10.40, children £1.30
₡ MasterCard Visa
🔲 🔌 🐕
Last arrival time: 11:00
➡ 4 miles N of St Davids, off the coast road (A487) signposted to Fishguard.

Rhos-Y-Cribed

St David's SA62 6RR
☎ 01437-720336
Open all year Å 🚐 🏕
Size 6 acres, 5 touring pitches, 2 🛁, 4 WCs, 1 CWP
£ car/tent £3.50, car/caravan £5.50, motorhome £4, motorbike/tent £3, children £1.50
🔌 🐕
Last arrival time: 10:30
➡ Follow Porthclais road from St David's via Porthclais Harbour. Site signed.

Tretio Caravan & Camping Park

St David's SA62 6DE
☎ 01437-781359 Fax 01437-781600
Open Easter-end October Å 🚐 🏕
Size 5 acres, 40 touring pitches, 25 with electric hookup, 40 level pitches, 16 static caravans, 4 🛁, 8 WCs, 1 CWP
£ car/tent £4.25-£6.75, car/caravan £4.75-£7.25, motorhome £4.25-£6.75, motorbike/tent £4.25-£6.75
Rental 🚐 6 berth holiday homes £105-£230
🔋 🔌 🔲 🔳 ⚠ Calor Gaz ♿ 🐕 WS
➡ On leaving St David's keep left at RFC and carry on for 3 miles until sign. Park on right.
See advert on previous page

SWANSEA   2C1

Riverside Caravan Park

Ynysforgan Farm, Morriston, Swansea SA6 6QL
☎ 01792-775587
Open all year Å 🚐 🏕

Flat, level, grassy site with hardstandings, alongside the River Tawe. Ideal base for touring all of Gower, the Mumbles, Swansea and the attractions of the Vale of Neath.

Size 7 acres, 120 touring pitches, 100 with electric hookup, 120 level pitches, 13 🛁, 15 WCs, 1 CWP
₡ MasterCard Visa
🔋 ✗ 🍴 🔲 🔌 🔲 🔳 📻 🔳 GR ⚠ 🔌 Calor Gaz ♿ 🐕 WS
Last arrival time: 10:00
➡ 200 yards from junction 45 of M4 motorway.

TENBY Pembrokeshire   2B1

Buttyland Touring Caravan & Tent Park

Manorbier, Tenby SA70 7SN
☎ 01834-871278
Open Easter-October Å 🚐 🏕
Size 10 acres, 30 touring pitches, 30 with electric hookup, 30 level pitches, 6 🛁, 16 WCs, 2 CWPs
£ car/tent £3-£5, car/caravan £3.40-£5.50, motorhome £3.40-£5.50, motorbike/tent £3-£5
🔋 🍴 ⚠ 🐕
➡ Site is signed from main road 400 yards on right, first entrance past school.

Kiln Park Holiday Park

Marsh Road, Tenby SA70 7RB
📞 01834-844121 Fax 01834-845159
Open March-October ⚠ 🚐 🚲

A family holiday park set amidst the beauty of the Pembrokeshire Coast National Park. Indoor/outdoor heated pools, kids clubs, tennis and bowling included in the wide range of leisure facilities, restaurants and bars, excellent cabaret entertainment. A 'British Holidays Park'.

Size 95 acres, 490 touring pitches, 115 with electric hookup, 490 level pitches, 620 static caravans, 20 🏠, 47 WCs, 2 CWPs
£ car/tent £7-£10.50, car/caravan £7-£14, motorhome £7-£14
Rental 🚐
ℂ MasterCard Visa
🚻 🚻¼ ✕ ✕¼ 🚿 🚿¼ 🔲 🔃 🔘 🔲 🔲 🔲 GR 🔲 TV ⚠ 🔲 Calor Gaz ♿ 🐕
Last arrival time: 10:00
➡ Approaching Tenby, arrive at Kilgetty roundabout and follow A478 to Tenby for 6 miles. Follow signs to Penally/Pembrune. The park is ½ mile on left.

Stone Pitt Camping Site

Begelly, Kilgetty SA68 OXE
📞 01834-811086
Open March-January ⚠ 🚐 🚲

This peaceful friendly site is set in a rural village near Tenby, ideal for exploring Pembrokeshire, which has everything for an enjoyable holiday.

Size 3 acres, 30 touring pitches, 30 with electric hookup, 15 level pitches, 5 🏠, 7 WCs, 1 CWP
car/tent £6-£7, car/caravan £6-£7, motorhome £6-7, motorbike/tent £6-£7, children £1
Rental Cottages £105-£250
🚿¼ 🔲 🔃 🔲 ⚠ Calor Gaz 🐕 WS
Last arrival time: 9:30

Trefalun Park

Devonshire Drive, Florence, Tenby SA70 8RH
📞 01646-651514 Fax 01646-651746
Open March-October ⚠ 🚐 🚲
Size 11 acres, 60 touring pitches, 40 with electric hookup, 60 level pitches, 10 static caravans, 6 🏠, 9 WCs, 1 CWP
£ car/tent £5-£8, car/caravan £6-£10, motorhome £6-£10, motorbike/tent £5-£8, children £0.50
Rental 🚐 £100-£330
ℂ MasterCard Visa
🔲 ⚠ Calor Gaz 🐕
Last arrival time: 8:00
➡ A477 Kilgetty to Sageston, turn left onto B4318. After 2 miles turn left opposite wildlife park, Trefalun second entrance on left.

Well Park

Tenby SA70 8TL
📞 01834-842179
Open 1 March-31 October ⚠ 🚐 🚲
Size 11 acres, 80 touring pitches, 50 with electric hookup, 80 level pitches, 42 static caravans, 10 🏠, 20 WCs, 1 CWP
£ car/tent £5-£9, car/caravan £6-£10, motorhome £6-£10, motorbike/tent £5-£9
Rental 🚐 Chalet. £95-£350
🚻 ✕¼ 🚿¼ 🔲 🔃 🔲 GR 🔲 TV ⚠ Calor Gaz 🐕
Last arrival time: 10:30
➡ 1 mile before Tenby, on right side of A478.

Whitewell Caravan Park
Near Lydstep Beach, Tenby SA70 7RY
☎ **01834-842200**
Open Easter-September

Small country site, half a mile from Lystep beach. Free hot water showers, and electric hookups available.

Size 10 acres, 20 touring pitches, 25 with electric hookup, 40 level pitches, 50 static caravans, 6 ⚲, 25 WCs, 1 CWP
🗶 🖃 GR 🍴 ⛟
➤ Take A4139 W of Tenby past Penall village to Lydstep beach.

Wood Park Caravans
New Hedges, Tenby SA70 8TL
☎ **01834-843414**
Open April-September A 🚐 🚐
Size 10 acres, 60 touring pitches, 30 with electric hookup, 24 level pitches, 90 static caravans, 6 ⚲, 14 WCs, 1 CWP
£ car/tent £4-£8.50, car/caravan £5-£10, motorhome £5-£10, motorbike/tent £4-£8.50
Rental 🚐 £100-£340
🗶 ✗¼ 🖃 🗶 🖃 GR 🅰 Calor Gaz ♿
Last arrival time: 10:00
➤ At roundabout 2 miles N of Tenby follow A478 towards Tenby. Take second right and right again.

Bryn Bach Park
Merthyr Road, Tredegar NP2 3AY
☎ **01495-711816** Fax **01495-726630**
Open all year A 🚐 🚐

Parc Bryn Bach is ideally situated to explore South Wales and the Brecon Beacons National Park. The park presents panoramic views in an attractive setting.

Size 32 touring pitches, 20 with electric hookup, 32 level pitches, 6 ⚲, 7 WCs, 1 CWP
£ car/tent £3.50, car/caravan £6-£7.50, motorhome £6-£7.50, motorbike/tent £3.50
🗶¼ ✗ 🖃 🗶 🅰 ♿ 🍴
Last arrival time: 9:00
➤ From A465 (Heads of Valley Road) run onto A4048 towards Tredegar. After garage on right turn towards Tafaunabach and site is ½ mile of left.

Woodlands Holiday Park

Bryncrug, Tywyn LL36 9UH
☎ 01654-710471 Fax 01654-710100
Open Easter-end September ⊕ ⇶

Within the Snowdonia National Park and now offering the latest hookup services including electric, water, TV and sewage disposal. On site country club.

Size 25 acres, 20 touring pitches, 20 with electric hookup, 20 level pitches, 122 static caravans, 2 ⌂, 4 WCs, 1 CWP
£ car/caravan £6-£7.50
Rental ⊕ Chalet. £90-£235 p.w.
✗ ➴ 🅵 📞 ⑤ GR 📞 TV ⚠ ⚑ Calor 🐕
➡ At Bryncrug, 18 miles S of Dolgellau and 2 miles N of Tywyn, turn E on B4405 for 1 mile to site on left.
Advert: Quarter Page

Camping & Caravanning Club Site

c/o the Racecourse, Bangor-Is-Y-Coed, Wrexham LL13 0DA
☎ 01978-781009
Open April-October ▲ ⊕ ⇶
Size 6 acres, 100 touring pitches, 29 with electric hookup, 3 ⌂, 10 WCs, 1 CWP
£ car/tent £4.60-£6.80, car/caravan £4.60-£6.80, motorhome £4.60-£6.80, motorbike/tent £4.60-£6.80, children £1.40
✗ MasterCard Visa
➴ 🅵 📞 ⅃ 🐕
Last arrival time: 11:00

James Caravan Park

Ruabon, Wrexham LL14 6DW
☎ 01978-820148 Fax 01978-820148
Open all year ▲ ⊕ ⇶
Size 8 acres, 40 touring pitches, 60 with electric hookup, 25 level pitches, 6 ⌂, 6 WCs, 1 CWP
£ car/tent £6.50-£7.50, car/caravan £6.50-£7.50, motorhome £6.40-£7.50
➴¼ ✗¼ ➴¼ 📞 Calor Gaz ⅃ 🐕
Last arrival time: 10:30
➡ Situated on A539 Llangollen-Whitchurch road on W side of junction with A483 at Ruabon.

Plassey Touring Caravan & Leisure Park

Eyton, Wrexham LL13 0SP
☎ 01978-780277 Fax 01978-780019
Open March-November ▲ ⊕ ⇶

Set in beautiful countryside with level, grassy pitches and many amenities on site. Ideal for walking, fishing, golfing and touring North Wales.

Size 9 acres, 120 touring pitches, 80 with electric hookup, 120 level pitches, 10 ⌂, 20 WCs, 8 CWPs
£ car/tent £7-£9, car/caravan £7-£9, motorhome £7-£9, motorbike/tent £7-£9
CC MasterCard Visa
🐟 ✗ ➴ 🅵 📞 ☕ ⑤ 🎱 📲 📞 🅁 ⅃ GR 📞 TV ⚠ ⚑ Calor Gaz ⅃ 🐕 WS
Last arrival time: 9:00
➡ Take A483 S of Wrexham. Follow brown and cream signs to Plassey at exit to B5426. Site 2½ miles on left

Free yourself

RAC Hotel Reservations will find you a room in the UK or Ireland and if you're an RAC Member, the service is absolutely free.
Phone 0870 603 9109.

If you're travelling in Europe, RAC Motoring Assistance provides rapid help in the event of breakdown, fire, accident, theft or illness.
In addition, our **Personal Travel Insurance** covers you for lost luggage, theft of personal belongings, personal injury or cancellation.
Call us on 0800 550 055.

RƎC

www.rac.co.uk

Northern Ireland & Republic of Ireland

Top: Maghery Caravan Park, Maghery

Right: Seals Caves Caravan Park, Dugort

Below: Tain Holiday Village, Omeath

Castlerock Holiday Park
24 Sea Road, Castlerock
☎ 01265-848381
Open Easter-October
Size 12 acres, 36 with electric hookup, 36 level pitches, 230 static caravans, 4 ⚲, 14 WCs, 2 CWPs
⚲¼ ✕¼ ⚑ ⚑¼ ⚙ GR TV ⚠ Calor Gaz WS
Last arrival time: 10:00
➜ 5 miles NW of Coleraine on B1119. Turn right at Thatched Cottage.

Maghery Caravan Park
Maghery
☎ 01762-322205 **Fax** 01762-347438
Open April-September ⚑ ⚑ ⚑

Situated on the southern shore of Lough Neagh, in the heart of Northern Ireland, the tranquil park offers wonderful views of Coney Island and Lough Neagh.

Size 30 acres, 9 touring pitches, 9 with electric hookup, 4 ⚲, 7 WCs, 1 CWP
£ car/tent £5, car/caravan £6, motorhome £6
⚲¼ ✕ ⚙ ⚑ ⚿ ⚞
Last arrival time: 5:00
➜ From M1 (junction 12) take B196 to Maghery and follow signs.

Jordanstown Loughshore Park
Shore Road, Newtownabbey BT37 0ST
☎ 01232-868751 **Fax** 01232-365407
Open all year ⚑ ⚑ ⚑
Size ½ acre, 6 touring pitches, 6 with electric hookup, 6 level pitches, 2 ⚲, 2 WCs, 1 CWP
£ car/tent £6.50, car/caravan £6.50, motorhome £6.50, motorbike/tent £6.50
⚲¼ ✕¼ ⚑¼ ⚙ ⚠ ⚿ ⚞
Last arrival time: 3:00
➜ 5 miles N of Belfast on Shore Road, A2 (Belfast to Carrickfergus road). Signposted on right between Whiteabbey village and University of Ulster.

Republic of Ireland

When calling the Republic of Ireland dial 00 353 followed by the site number omiting the initial zero

ACHILL ISLAND Co. Mayo   16A3

Keel Sandybanks Caravan & Camping Park

Keel, Achill Island

☎ 094-32054 Fax 094-32351

Open 23 May-5 September ▲ ⛺ 🚐

Size 14 acres, 40 touring pitches, 40 with electric hookup, 40 level pitches, 17 static caravans, 7 🚿, 15 WCs, 1 CWP

£ car/tent £5-£6.50, car/caravan £6-£8, motorhome £6-£8, motorbike/tent £5-£6.50

Rental ⛺ Chalet. £180-£260

🛁¼ ✗¼ 🚿¼ 🗑 🔌 🍴 📺 🏔 🔥 🐕

Last arrival time: 10:30

➜ Castlebar to Newport to Mulranny to Achill Sound then R319 from Achill Sound. At western end of Sandybanks beside Keel Village and immediately adjacent to Keel Beach. Visable from road.

ATHLONE Co. Westmeath   16C4

Hodson Bay Caravan and Camping Park

Hodson Bay, Kiltoom, Athlone

☎ 0902-92448

Open 9 May-15 September ▲ ⛺ 🚐

Size 2 acres, 34 touring pitches, 20 with electric hookup, 30 level pitches, 6 🚿, 9 WCs, 1 CWP

£ car/tent £7.50, car/caravan £8, motorhome £8, motorbike/tent £7, children £1

🛁¼ ✗¼ 🚿¼ 🗑 🔌 🍴 📻 📺 🏔 Calor Gaz ⚓

Last arrival time: 10:30

➜ From N6 take N61 for 2½ miles. Turn right and follow signs.

BANDON Co. Cork   18C4

Murrays Caravan & Camping Park

Kilbrogan Farm., Bandon

☎ 023-41232

Open 1 April-30 September ▲ ⛺ 🚐

Size 2 acres, 19 touring pitches, 10 with electric hookup, 19 level pitches, 2 🚿, 6 WCs, 1 CWP

£ car/tent £5, car/caravan £5, motorhome £5, motorbike/tent £5, children £1

🗑 Calor Gaz ⚓ 🐕

➜ Follow official signs from town.

BANTRY Co. Cork   18B4

Eagle Point Caravan & Camping Site

Ballylickey, Bantry

☎ 027-50630

Open 24 April-30 September ▲ ⛺ 🚐

Located on a peninsula with direct access to safe pebble beaches suitable for all forms of water activities. Top standard amenities and central for touring.

Size 20 acres, 200 touring pitches, 150 with electric hookup, 200 level pitches, 18 🚿, 33 WCs, 2 CWPs

£ car/tent £9.50-£10, car/caravan £9.50-£10, motorhome £9.50-£10, motorbike/tent £8

🛁¼ ✗¼ 🚿¼ 🗑 🔌 🍴 📺 🏔 🔥

Last arrival time: 10:00

➜ Site is 4 miles N of Bantry on N71.

BENNETTSBRIDGE Co. Kilkenny   19E2

Nore Valley Park

Bennettsbridge

☎ 056-27229 Fax 056-27748

Open 1 March-31 October ▲ ⛺ 🚐

Situated on a working and visitor farm overlooking the scenic River Nore valley. Home baked bread, scones and pies available. Irish breakfast June - August inclusive.

Size 3 acres, 70 touring pitches, 40 with electric hookup, 40 level pitches, 4 static caravans, 5 🚿, 10 WCs, 2 CWPs

£ car/tent £6-£9, car/caravan £9-£10, motorhome £8-£9, motorbike/tent £5, children £0.50

🛁 ✗ 🚿 🗑 🔌 🍴 📺 🏔 Calor Gaz ⚓ 🐕 WS

Last arrival time: 10:00

➜ From Kilkenny take T20 (R700) to Bennettsbridge. Just before bridge turn right at sign to park.

BUNRATTY CASTLE & FOLK PARK
Bunratty, Co. Clare

Bunratty Castle is one of the most complete examples of mediaeval castles surviving in Ireland today. Built in 1425, it is wholly intact and houses an exceptional collection of late mediaeval European furniture and tapestries. The domestic theme at Bunratty is carried into the Folk Park which contains typical nineteenth century rural and urban dwellings.

Bunratty Castle & Folk Park open daily, year round: 9.30 a.m. – 5.30 p.m. (Open until 7 p.m. June – Aug.)

CENTRAL RESERVATIONS AT BUNRATTY CASTLE & FOLK PARK
061-361511

BOYLE Co. Roscommon   16C3

Lough Key Caravan & Camping Park
Boyle
📞 044-48761 Fax 01-676 8598
Open April-September

A well landscaped site in a 350 hectare forest park on the Shannon river system. Accessible by cruiser.
Size 13 acres, 72 touring pitches, 52 with electric hookup, 52 level pitches, 4 🚿, 12 WCs, 1 CWP
£ car/tent £7-£8, car/caravan £7.50-£8.50, motorbike/tent £3
⚡¼ 🚐 🚐¼ 🔲 🔳 📺 🅰 ♿ ✈
Last arrival time: 9:00
➔ 10 km W of Carrick-on-Shannon, 6 km E of Boyle on N4.

CAHERDANIEL Co. Kerry   18A4

Wave Crest Caravan & Camping Park
Caherdaniel
📞 066-75188 Fax 066-75188
Open March-October 🅰 🚐 🚐
Size 4½ acres, 45 touring pitches, 45 with electric hookup, 30 level pitches, 4 static caravans, 10 🚿, 11 WCs, 1 CWP
£ car/tent £8.50, car/caravan £8.50-£10.50, motorhome £8.50, motorbike/tent £7, children £0.50
⚡ ✕¼ 🔲 🔳 🔳 GR 🔲 📺 🅰 Calor Gaz ♿ ✈ WS
Last arrival time: 11:00
➔ From Kenmare take N70 SW for 30 miles. Site is on left just before Caherdaniel village.

CASTLEBAR Co. Mayo   16B3

Carra Caravan & Camping Park
Castlebar, Belcarra
📞 094-32054 Fax 094-32351
Open 6 June-5 September 🅰 🚐 🚐
Size 1 acre, 20 touring pitches, 10 with electric hookup, 20 level pitches, 2 🚿, 4 WCs, 1 CWP
£ car/tent £4-£5, car/caravan £5, motorhome £5, motorbike/tent £4
Rental 🚐 £125-£180 weekly.
⚡¼ ✕¼ 🚐¼ 🔲 🔳 🔳 📥 Calor ♿ ✈ WS
Last arrival time: 9:00
➔ 8 km S of Castlebar, close to village centre at Belcarra.

CLOGHEEN Co. Tipperary — 19D3

Parsons Green Caravan & Camping Park
Clogheen
📞 052-65290 Fax 052-65504
Open all year A 🚐 🚍

Small, family run park with excellent on-site facilities. Centrally situated for touring the whole south of Ireland.

Size 20 touring pitches, 20 with electric hookup, 20 level pitches, 6 🚿, 9 WCs, 1 CWP
£ car/tent £5-£7, car/caravan £8, motorhome £8, motorbike/tent £5-£7
Rental Chalet.
🛁¼ ✕ 👝 🖻 🔧 🖯 ▸ 🔲 ✍ 🔳 GR 🔲 TV ⚠ ✕ 🔊 ♞
➡ Nearest town Clogheen: take R668 from Cahir and Lismore or take R665 from Clonmel and Mitchels Town.

CLONAKILTY Co. Cork — 18C4

Desert House Caravan & Camping Park
Ring Road, Clonakilty
📞 023-33331 Fax 023-33048
Open Easter/May-October A 🚐 🚍
Size 5 acres, 36 touring pitches, 14 level pitches, 5 🚿, 6 WCs, 1 CWP
£ car/tent £6, car/caravan £7, motorhome £8, motorbike/tent £6
✕ MasterCard Visa
🖻 🔧 🖯 TV ⚠ ♞
Last arrival time: 11:30
➡ 1 mile SE of Clonakilty, off N71 Cork-Bandon-Clonakilty road, on road to Ring village.

COURTOWN Co. Wexford — 19F2

Parklands Holiday Park
Ardamine, Courtown Gorey, Courtown
📞 055-25202 Fax 055-25202
Open May-September
Size 13 acres, 76 touring pitches, 16 with electric hookup, 170 static caravans, 14 🚿, 13 WCs, 2 CWPs
✕ Visa
🛁 ✕ 👝 🔲 Gaz 🔊 WS
2 miles S of Courtown, on R742 coast road.

DINGLE Co. Kerry — 18A3

Ballintaggart House
Dingle
📞 066-51454

Ballintaggart House, fully serviced caravan and camping site. Situated near Dingle town on the beautiful Dingle Peninsula. IRB approved, restaurant, free hot showers, kitchen and eating area. Pets and families welcome. Electricity and running water.

DONARD Co. Wicklow — 19F1

Moat Farm
Donard
📞 045-404727 Fax 045-404727
Open all year A 🚐 🚍

Select family run park. Secluded rural setting yet only a one minute walk from the village. Fully serviced. Ideal for relaxing or a base for touring, hill walking, mountain climbing. One hour from Dublin, 1½ hrs from Rosslare.

Size 3 acres, 20 touring pitches, 20 with electric hookup, 20 level pitches, 7 🚿, 7 WCs, 1 CWP
£ car/tent £10, car/caravan £10, motorhome £10, motorbike/tent £7, children £0.50
🛁 ✕¼ 👝 🖻 🔧 🖯 TV ⚠ Gaz 🔊 ♞ WS
Last arrival time: 12:00
➡ From Dun Laoghaire follow signs marked N4 and N7 then onto N81. 15 kms S of Blessington turn left at The Old Toll House pub. Park 2 kms from here.

DUBLIN Co. Dublin	19F1

Camac Valley Tourist Caravan & Camping

Naas Road, Clondalkin, Dublin 22
📞 01-464 0644 Fax 01-464 0643
Open all year A 🚐 🚏

*Excellent facilities coupled with pleasant parkland
surroundings make Camac Valley the ideal choice for
families and backpackers alike. Phone for a brochure.*

Size 15 acres, 163 touring pitches, 163 level pitches,
12 ☊, 20 WCs, 2 CWPs
£ car/tent £8-£10, car/caravan £7-£10, motorhome £7-
£9, motorbike/tent £7
🛁 🖫 📞 🖭 📺 ⚠ Calor Gaz も ⊁
➔ From Cork or Limerick on N7 pass by turns for
Rathcoole and Saggart, then 5 km further on go under
Citywest bridge. The park is 2 km further on N7
clearly signposted on left. From Dublin take N7.
When you reach Newlands Cross signposts clearly
indicate route to take. Go to Citywest Business Park

on N7 and cross bridge following signs for Camac
Valley. Coming from either direction on M50
motorway (jn 9) take N7 S to Cork. Once on N7
follow signs as above.

Shankill Caravan & Camping Park

Sherrington Park., Shankill
📞 01-2820011
Open all year A 🚐 🚏

*Caravan park and camp site with lovely view of the
Dublin mountains. Nearest caravan park to Stena
Line and HSS fast ferry. 8 km from Dun Laoghaire car
ferry terminal. 16 km south of Dublin city centre. 3
km from Bray and the sea.*

Size 7 acres, 70 with electric hookup, 50 level
pitches, 15 ☊, 20 WCs, 2 CWPs
£ car/tent £7-£8, car/caravan £7-£8, motorhome £7-
£8, motorbike/tent £7-£8, children £0.50
Rental 🚐 Mobile homes £190 high season pw
🛁 ✕¼ 🖤¼ 🖫 📞 🖫 Gaz も ⊁
➔ East of N11 Dublin/Wicklow road. Direct bus from
Dublin city centre and Dun Laoghaire car ferry
terminal. Fast electric train service (DART) from
Shankill station serving Dublin, Dun Laoghaire and
Bray.

DUGORT Co. Mayo	16A3

Seal Caves Caravan Park

The Strand, Achill Island, Dugort
📞 098-43262
Open 1 April-30 September A 🚐 🚏

Set in sheltered and scenic area beside safe bathing beach. Place of interest near by, deserted village colony settlement.

Size 1½ acres, 30 touring pitches, 30 with electric hookup, 30 level pitches, 10 ♠, 16 WCs, 2 CWPs
£ car/tent £6-£6.50, car/caravan £6-£6.50, motorhome £6-£6.50, motorbike/tent £6-£6.50, children £0.50
⚏ ▣ 📞 🖧 TV ⚠ Gaz ⚰
Last arrival time: 10:30
➡ R319 from Achill Sound to Bunacurry junction, turn right, onto valley crossroads, turn left, drive 3 miles to park.

DUNGARVAN Co. Waterford   19D3

Casey's Caravan Park
Clonea, Dungarvan
📞 0044-58-41919 **Fax** 0044-58-41919
Open 2 May-7 September 𝐀 ⚏ ⚏

Family run park adjacent to beaches and a hotel with a leisure centre. Many scenic drives are nearby.

Size 20 acres, 118 touring pitches, 83 with electric hookup, 284 level pitches, 166 static caravans, 18 ♠, 36 WCs, 2 CWPs
£ car/tent £9.50-£10, car/caravan £9.50-£10, motorhome £9.50-£10, motorbike/tent £7.50
⚏¼ ✗¼ ⚏¼ ▣ 📞 🖧 GR Q TV ⚠ Calor Gaz ♿ ⚰ WS
Last arrival time: 10:00
➡ 2½ miles off N25. ½ mile off R675.

GALLURUS-DINGLE Co. Kerry   18A3

Campail Theach An Aragail
Gallarus Dingle
📞 066-55143
Open 1 May-25 September 𝐀 ⚏ ⚏
Size 2 acres, 36 touring pitches, 12 with electric hookup, 36 level pitches, 6 ♠, 9 WCs, 1 CWP
⚏ ✗ ⚏ 📞 🖧 ⚠ Calor
Last arrival time: 9:00
➡ 5 miles W of Dingle. Follow Gallarus Oratory signs.

Prices shown are in £IR

GLENGARRIFF Co. Cork   18B4

O'Shea's Camping Site
Inchantaggart, Glengarriff
📞 027-63140
Open March-October 𝐀 ⚏
Size 4 acres, 15 touring pitches, 15 with electric hookup, 4 ♠, 5 WCs, 1 CWP
£ car/tent £7, car/caravan £7, motorhome £7, motorbike/tent £7
⚏¼ ✗¼ ⚏¼ ▣ 📞 🖧 ⚰
Last arrival time: 12:00
➡ 2 km W of Glengarriff on Castletown Bay road.

KENMARE Co. Kerry   18B3

Ring Of Kerry Caravan & Camping Park
Kenmare
📞 064-41648 **Fax** 064-41631
Open all year 𝐀 ⚏ ⚏
Size 4 acres, 30 touring pitches, 20 with electric hookup, 30 level pitches, 6 ♠, 10 WCs, 1 CWP
£ car/tent £11, car/caravan £11, motorhome £11, motorbike/tent £11, children £0.75
⚏ ▣ 📞 🖧 🖧 ⚠ Gaz ⚰
Last arrival time: 11:00
➡ 4 miles W of Kenmare on N70 Ring of Kerry road.

KILKENNY Co. Kilkenny   19E2

Tree Grove Caravan & Camping Park
Danville House, Kilkenny
📞 056-70302
𝐀 ⚏ ⚏

Ideal site for touring Kilkenny and the South East. Excellent hygiene standards. Personally supervised. Camping equipment on site. Route planning and advice given for tourers by owners.

Size 2½ acres, 30 touring pitches, 12 with electric hookup, 30 level pitches, 4 ♠, 6 WCs, 1 CWP
£ car/tent £7, car/caravan £8, motorhome £8, motorbike/tent £6
Rental 𝐀 Chalet. chalets £150, tents £12.
⚏¼ ⚏¼ ▣ 📞 🖧 GR TV ⚠ Calor Gaz ♿ ⚰ WS
➡ 2 km from city centre past Kilkenny Castle on R700 after roundabout, in direction of New Ross.

KILLARNEY Co. Kerry   18B3

Flesk Camping & Caravan Park
Muckross Road, Killarney
📞 064-31704 Fax 064-34681
Open 12 March-31 October ▲ 🚐 🚙
Size 7 acres, 75 touring pitches, 21 with electric
hookup, 30 level pitches, 5 static caravans, 10 🚿, 16
WCs, 1 CWP
£ car/tent £8.50-£9, car/caravan £9-£9.50, motorhome
£9-£9.50, motorbike/tent £8-£8.50, children £0.75
CC MasterCard Visa
🐕 ✕ 🍴 🍔 📞 🚻 Calor Gaz &
Last arrival time: 11:00
➡ On N71 to Kenmare, 1½ km S of Killarney town
centre. Follow signs for Killarney National Park and
Lakes.

White Villa Farm Caravan & Camping Site
Cork Road, Killarney
📞 064-32456
Open Easter-31 October ▲ 🚐 🚙
Size 4 acres, 24 touring pitches, 24 with electric
hookup, 24 level pitches, 5 🚿, 6 WCs, 2 CWPs
£ car/tent £7-£8, car/caravan £7-£8, motorhome £7-
£8, motorbike/tent £7-£8, children £0.75
Rental 🚐 Chalet from £120 for two people.
🍔 📞 🚻 🏧 📺 🏍 & 🛒
Last arrival time: 9:00
➡ 3 km E of Killarney on N22 Cork road. Park
entrance is 300 yards E of N72 Mallow junction.
Follow signposts.

KILLORGLIN Co. Kerry   18B3

West's Holiday Park
Killarney Road, Ring of Kerry, Killorglin
📞 066-61240 Fax 066-61833
Open May-September ▲ 🚐 🚙

*Family run site, where relaxing comes as naturally as
the surrounding beauty. Wonderful central location.
Luxury, mobile homes for hire. Ferry inclusive prices
available.*

Size 5 acres, 20 touring pitches, 12 with electric
hookup, 20 level pitches, 60 static caravans, 4 🚿, 5
WCs,

£ car/tent £8, car/caravan £8, motorhome £8,
motorbike/tent £7, children £0.50
Rental 🚐 from £99
CC MasterCard Visa
🍔 📞 🚻 📺 🏍 Calor Gaz & 🛒 WS
➡ On Ring of Kerry. At Killorglin bridge take Killarney
road R562. Park is 1½ km from town on right.

KILMUCKRIDGE Co. Wexford   19F2

Morriscastle Strand Caravan Park
Kilmuckridge
📞 01-453 5355 Fax 01-454 5916
Open 4 May-29 September ▲ 🚐 🚙

*This site nestles at the end of a country road
overlooking the longest stretch of sandy beach in
Ireland. Ideal for families with small children. Village
within two miles.*

Size 16 acres, 100 touring pitches, 60 with electric
hookup, 105 level pitches, 145 static caravans, 11 🚿,
10 WCs, 2 CWPs
£ car/tent £8-£10, car/caravan £8-£10, motorhome £7-
£9, motorbike/tent £4.50-£5.50
🐕 📞 🚻 📺 Calor Gaz & 🛒
Last arrival time: 11:00
➡ From Wexford take R742 to Kilmuckridge and
follow signposts. Site is at very end of public road.

KILRUSH Co. Clare   18B2

Aylevarroo Caravan Park
Kilrush
📞 065-51102 Fax 065-51102
Open 15 May-11 September
Size 7½ acres, 38 touring pitches, 24 with electric
hookup, 36 level pitches, 6 static caravans, 6 🚿, 11
WCs, 1 CWP
📞 🚻 📺 🏍 Calor Gaz
Last arrival time: 10:00
➡ Site signposted off N67 Kilrush to Killimer Road. 1½
miles from Kilrush, 4 miles from Killimer.

Prices shown are in £IR

LAHINCH Co. Clare 18B1

Lahinch Camping & Caravan Park

Lahinch

☎ 065-81424 Fax 065-81194

Open 1 May-30 September ▲ ⊕ ⊞

Located just south of Lahinch village, with a sandy beach. Ideal for visits to the Cliffs of Moher, the Burren and the Aran Islands or for lovely scenic walks.

Size 7 acres, 62 touring pitches, 36 with electric hookup, 62 level pitches, 30 static caravans, 11 ℞, 24 WCs, 2 CWPs

£ car/tent £8-£10, car/caravan £9-£10, motorhome £8-£10, motorbike/tent £8, children £1

⚑¼ ✗¼ ☛¼ ⊡ ☎ ⊟ GR ☒ TV /Λ Calor ☛ WS

Last arrival time: 12:00

➔ 200 yards S of village coast road.

LAURAGH VILLAGE Co. Kerry 18A4

Creveen Lodge

Healy Pass, Lauragh Village

☎ 064-83131

Open Easter-31 October ▲ ⊕ ⊞

This small family run park, set in the heart of the beautiful scenery of south Kerry, provides a high standard of personal supervision and is fully serviced with excellent amenities.

Size 4 acres, 20 touring pitches, 7 with electric hookup, 15 level pitches, 2 ℞, 5 WCs, 1 CWP

£ car/tent £8, car/caravan £8, motorhome £8, motorbike/tent £7, children £0.50

Rental Chalet.

✗ ⊡ ☛ ⊟ TV /Λ Gaz ☛ WS

Last arrival time: 12:00

➔ From Kenmare turn right at Sound Bridge onto R571. Follow signs at Lauragh for site. Site is on Healy Pass road (R574).

MIDLETON Co. Cork 18C3

Burkes Caravan & Camping Park

Shanagarry, Midleton

☎ 021-646796

Open 1 May-1 October ▲ ⊕ ⊞

Size 4 acres, 10 touring pitches, 8 with electric hookup, 8 level pitches, 39 static caravans, 2 ℞, 4 WCs

£ car/tent £7-£8, car/caravan £7-£8, motorhome £7-£8, motorbike/tent £7-£8

Rental ⊕ mobile homes £130-£250

⚑ ✗¼ ☛¼ ⊡ GR Calor ☛

Last arrival time: 10:30

➔ Turn off N25 at Castlemartyr for Ladysbridge, Garryvoe. At Garryvoe hotel turn right for Shanagarry/Ballycotton, 1 mile from Garryvoe.

Trabolgan Holiday Village

Midleton
☏ 021-661551
Open March-November

Situated on the breath-taking Atlantic coastline, amid rolling meadows and majestic woodland, Trabolgan is the ideal family holiday location. Facilities include sub-tropical swimming paradise, indoor and outdoor adventure playgrounds, 18 hole par 3 golf course and sports centre.

Size 140 acres, 23 touring pitches
🛊 ✕ 🍴 ⑤
➨ R630 from Midleton to Whitegate, turn S on to unclassified road, site signed.

MULLINGAR Co. Westmeath   17D4

Lough Ennel Caravan & Camping

Tudenham, Mullingar
☏ 044-48101 Fax 044-48101
Open 1 April-end September ⚑ ⊡ 🚐

On the shore of Lough Ennel. Children's play area. Windsurfing equipment and tuition. Some gas available. Caravans for hire.

Size 50 touring pitches, 50 with electric hookup, 50 static caravans, 8 🚿, 20 WCs, 1 CWP
£ car/tent £8, car/caravan £8, motorhome £8, motorbike/tent £8
🛊 ✕ 🍴 ⊡ ☏ TV ⚟ Calor 🐾 WS
Last arrival time: 11:00
➨ N52 from Mullingar to Kilbeggan for 5 miles, right at Lough Ennel-Tudenham to site.

OMEATH Co. Louth   17E3

Tain Holiday Village

Ballyvoonan, Omeath
☏ 042-75385 Fax 042-75417
Open 14 March-1 November ⚑ ⊡ 🚐
Size 10 acres, 90 touring pitches, 87 with electric hookup, 90 level pitches, 9 static caravans, 16 🚿, 16 WCs,
£ car/tent £14.50-£16.50, car/caravan £16.50-£18.50, motorhome £16.50-£18.50, motorbike/tent £14.50-£16.50, children £3-£3.50
Rental ⊡
℃ MasterCard
🛊 ✕ 🍴 ⊡ ☏ ⑤ ⊞ ⚟ ⊠ ⊞ GR ⊚ TV ⚟ ⊞   Calor 🔥
🐾
Last arrival time: 9:30
➨ 10km from Newry, just off main Belfast to Dublin road, on coastal road from Newry to Dundalk. Go through Omeath village 1 mile. Camp site is on left as you drive towards Carlingford village.

REDCROSS Co. Wicklow   19F2

Johnson's Caravan & Camping Park

Ballintim, Redcross
☏ 0404-48133
Open 14 March-28 September ⚑ ⊡ 🚐
Size 8 acres, 18 touring pitches, 18 with electric hookup, 18 level pitches, 43 static caravans, 6 🚿, 11 WCs, 1 CWP

£ car/tent £7-£9, car/caravan £7-£9, motorhome £7-£9, motorbike/tent £5-£7, children £1

⚡ 🔌 📞 🔲 🚿 🛒 📡 🔋 📺 ⛰ Calor Gaz WS

Last arrival time: 11:00

➜ From Dublin follow N11 and travel S via Ashford, turn right in Rathnew and then left onto Wexford/Wicklow road (under railway bridge). Drive for 11 km and turn right at Lil Doyles pub. Park is 1 mile on right.

ROSBEG Co. Donegal   16C2

Tramore Beach Caravan Park

Rosbeg

📞 075-51491 Fax 075-51492

Open Easter-September

Size 20 touring pitches

➜ From Donegal take N56, then R261.

ROSSES POINT Co. Sligo   16C3

Greenlands Caravan & Camping Park

Rosses Point

📞 071-77113 Fax 071-45618

Open May-September ⛺ 🚐 🚍

Size 4 acres, 78 touring pitches, 78 with electric hookup, 78 level pitches, 12 static caravans, 8 🚿, 15 WCs, 1 CWP

£ car/tent £7.50-£8.50, car/caravan £7.50-£8.50, motorhome £7.50-£8.50, motorbike/tent £7.50-£8.50, children £0.50

Rental 🚐 £100-£300

⚡¼ ✗¼ 🔌¼ 🔲 📞 🚿 ▶ 📡 📺 Calor Gaz ♿ ↟

Last arrival time: 10:00

➜ From Sligo city, 8 km W to Rosses Point. Site is beside golf club.

ROSSLARE Co. Wexford   19F3

Burrow Caravan & Camping Park

Rosslare

📞 053-32190

Open 15 March-10 November ⛺ 🚐 🚍

Size 14 acres, 100 touring pitches, 100 with electric hookup, 100 level pitches, 150 static caravans, 6 🚿, 10 WCs, 1 CWP

£ car/tent £7-£14, car/caravan £7-£14, motorhome £7-£14, motorbike/tent £5-£12

₡₡ Visa

⚡ ✗¼ 🔌 🔲 📞 🚿 🛒 📡 🔋 📺 ⛰ Calor Gaz ♿ ↟

Last arrival time: 10:00

➜ N25 W from Rosslare Harbour to Kilrane, then turn N onto R736. Site ¾ mile N of Rosslare village.

ROSSNOWLAGH Co. Donegal   16C2

Manor House Camping Park

Rossnowlagh

📞 072-51477

Open Easter/15 June-September

Size 5½ acres, 30 touring pitches, 9 with electric hookup, 60 level pitches, 30 static caravans, 6 🚿, 7 WCs, 1 CWP

£ car/tent £8, car/caravan £8, motorhome £8, motorbike/tent £5

⚡ 🔌 📞 📺 🔋 Calor ♿

Last arrival time: 9:00

➜ Take R231 coast road N from Ballyshannon, pass the Rossnowlagh turning and take next left, then first right to site on shore.

ROUNDWOOD Co. Wicklow   19F1

Roundwood Camping & Caravanning Park

Roundwood

📞 01-281 8163

Open April-September ⛺ 🚐 🚍

Size 7 acres, 30 touring pitches, 30 with electric hookup, 55 level pitches, 6 🚿, 10 WCs, 1 CWP

£ car/tent £9-£10, car/caravan £9-£10, motorhome £9-£10, motorbike/tent £8-£9, children £1

⚡ ✗¼ 🔌¼ 🔲 📞 🚿 🔋 📺 ⛰ Calor Gaz ↟ WS

Last arrival time: 11:00

➜ From Dublin & Dun Laoghaire take N11. Turn right at Kilmacanogue, follow signs for Glendalough. From Rosslare take N11, turn left at Ashford village.

SLIGO Co. Sligo   16C3

New Gateway Camping & Caravan Park

Ballinode, Sligo

📞 071-45618 Fax 071-45618

Open all year ⛺ 🚐 🚍

Size 24 touring pitches, 24 with electric hookup, 5 🚿, 7 WCs, 1 CWP

£ car/tent £7.50-£8.50, car/caravan £7.50-£8.50, motorbike/tent £5

➜ ¾ mile town centre on N16 Sligo/Belfast road at Ballinode traffic lights.

STRANDHILL Co. Sligo   16C3

Strandhill Caravan & Camping

Strandhill

📞 071-68120

Open mid May-mid September ⛺ 🚐 🚍

Size 15 acres, 48 touring pitches, 32 with electric hookup, 48 level pitches, 15 static caravans, 8 🚿, 12 WCs, 1 CWP

£ car/tent £6.50-£7.50, car/caravan £6.50-£7.50, motorhome £6.50-£7.50, motorbike/tent £6.50-£7.50, children £0.50

Rental 🚐 £120-£225

⚡¼ ✗¼ 🔌¼ 🔲 📞 🚿 📡 📺 ♿ ↟

Last arrival time: 10:00

➜ From Sligo 6km W. Site at Strandhill on Airport Road.

TRAMORE Co. Waterford   19E3

Fitzmaurice's Caravan Park

Riverstown, Tremore

📞 051-81968

Open 1 April-30 September A ⊞ ⌁

Size 5½ acres, 20 touring pitches, 20 with electric hookup, 4 📷, 23 WCs, 1 CWP

£ car/tent £9-£10, car/caravan £9-£10, motorhome £9-£10, motorbike/tent £9-£10

Rental ⊞

⚗ 🔳 🔲 🔳 GR TV 🐾

➡ 7 miles from Waterford city on main Waterford to Tramore road. Site situated in Tramore 500 yards from beach.

WATERVILLE Co. Kerry   18A3

Waterville Caravan & Camping Park

Waterville

📞 066-74191 Fax 066-74538

Open 17 April-21 September A ⊞ ⌁

Size 5 acres, 58 touring pitches, 58 with electric hookup, 58 level pitches, 23 static caravans, 12 📷, 15 WCs, 2 CWPs

£ car/tent £8.50-£9, car/caravan £9.50-£10, motorhome £9.50-£10, motorbike/tent £7.50-£8.50, children £0.50

Rental ⊞ £137-£352

⚗ ✕¼ 🔳 🔳 🔳 🔳 🔳 GR TV 🔳 Gaz 👤 🐾

Last arrival time: 10:00

➡ ½ mile N of Waterville, just off N70 'Ring of Kerry' road.

Prices shown are in £IR

WEXFORD Co. Wexford   19F3

Carne Beach Caravan & Camping Park

Wexford

📞 053-31131 Fax 053-31131

Open May-September A ⊞ ⌁

Beach site with swimming, angling and riding available. Close to Rosslare ferry.

Size 30 acres, 50 touring pitches, 50 with electric hookup, 50 level pitches, 300 static caravans, 16 📷, 30 WCs, 2 CWPs

⚗ ✕ 🔳 🔳 🔳 🔳 🔳 🔳 GR TV 🔳 👤 Calor Gaz WS

Last arrival time: 11:00

➡ From Rosslare Harbour take N25 W to Kilrane, then due S to coast.

Ferrybank Caravan Park

Ferrybank, Wexford

📞 053-44378/42611

Open Easter-October A ⊞ ⌁

Size 5 acer's 53 touring pitches, 29 with electric hookup, 14 📷, 39 WCs, 1 CWP

£ car/tent £7-£10, car/caravan £9-£10, motorbike/tent £7-£10

Last arrival time: 24:00

➡ Situated on seafront overlooking Wexford town and harbour on R741..

Channel Islands & Isle of Man

*Top: Grandstand Campsite
Douglas*

*Right: Peel Camping Park,
Peel*

*Below: Gorey
Jersey*

DOUGLAS   10A4

Grandstand Campsite, Nobles Park

c/o Douglas Corporation Parks Dept., Ballaughton
Nurseries, Douglas IM2 1JJ
☎ 01624-621132 Fax 01624-662792
Open mid June-mid August **А** ⛺

*Situated next to Nobles Park, an ideal base for touring
the island, or enjoying the park amenities and visiting
Douglas.*
Size 2 acres, 30 touring pitches, 20 with electric
hookup, 8 ⓡ, 16 WCs, 1 CWP
£ car/tent £5.50, motorhome £5.50, motorbike/tent
£5.50
⚑¼ ✗¼ ◻ ☎ ⓕ ▨ ⚠ ♿ ⚓
➡ From ferry terminal travel along promenade to first
set of traffic lights, turn left, then right at next traffic
lights. The campsite is behind the TT Grandstand, a
further 500 yards on right

PEEL   10A4

Peel Camping Park

Derby Road, Peel
☎ 01624-842341 Fax 01624-844010
Open mid May-late September **А** ⛺

*Situated on the edge of the town in a rural setting, just
three miles from the TT course. A level site with
facilities for the disabled.*
Size 4 acres, 100 touring pitches, 12 with electric
hookup, 100 level pitches, 8 ⓡ, 10 WCs, 1 CWP
£ car/tent £7, motorhome £9, motorbike/tent £77,
children £1.75
⚑¼ ✗¼ ◻¼ ◻ ☎ TV ♿
➡ A1 from Douglas and turn right at first crossroads
entering Peel. Follow signs to site on A20 on edge of
town, adjacent to primary school.

GUERNSEY   2A2

La Bailloterie Camping

Vale GY3 5HA
☎ 01481-43636 Fax 01481-43225
Open 15 May-15 September **А**
Size 8 acres, 120 touring pitches, 4 with electric
hookup, 120 level pitches, 12 ⓡ, 12 WCs, 1 CWP
£ car/tent £6-£7.50, , motorbike/tent £6-£7.50,
children £1.50-£1.95
Rental А £50-£195
⚑ ⚑¼ ✗¼ ◗ ◗¼ ◻ ☎ ⏚ GR TV ⚠ Calor Gaz ⚓
➡ Leave St Peter Port to the N. Bear left at Half Way
Plantation following signs for Pembroke and
L'Ancrosse. At second set of traffic lights turn right,
then take first left. Follow signpost.

Le Vaugrat Campsite

Route de Vaugrat, St Sampsons GY2 4TA
☎ 01481-57468 Fax 01481-51841
Open 21 May-16 September **А**
Size 5 acres, 150 touring pitches, 130 level pitches, 8
ⓡ, 13 WCs, 1 CWP
Rental А £10-£11.50 per night
ℂℂ MasterCard Visa
⚑ ✗¼ ◗ ◗¼ ◻ ☎ ⏚ TV ⚠ Calor Gaz ♿

JERSEY   2A2

Beuvelande Camp Site

Beuvelande, St Martins JE3 6EZ
☎ 01534-853575 Fax 01534-857788
Open May-mid September **А** ⛺
Size 6 acres, 60 touring pitches, 20 with electric
hookup, 60 level pitches, 30 ⓡ, 20 WCs, 1 CWP
£ car/tent £8-£12, , motorbike/tent £8-£12, children
£3
Rental А
ℂℂ Visa
⚑ ⚑¼ ✗ ✗¼ ◻ ☎ ⏚ ⏏ GR ▣ TV ⚠ ⏛ Calor Gaz ♿ ⚓
➡ A6 from St Helier to St Martin's church, then follow
signs.

Key to Maps

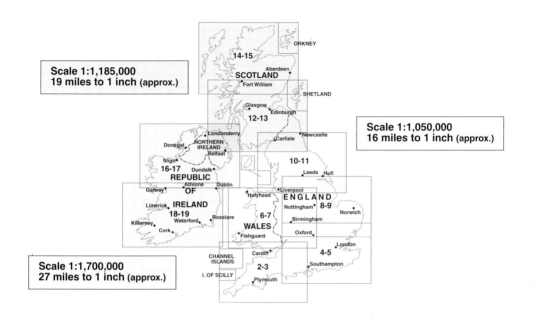

Scale 1:1,185,000
19 miles to 1 inch (approx.)

Scale 1:1,050,000
16 miles to 1 inch (approx.)

Scale 1:1,700,000
27 miles to 1 inch (approx.)

ORKNEY

14-15

Aberdeen
SCOTLAND
Fort William

SHETLAND

Glasgow
Edinburgh
12-13

Londonderry
Carlisle • Newcastle
NORTHERN
Donegal IRELAND
Belfast
Sligo
Dundalk
16-17
REPUBLIC
10-11
Leeds Hull
Galway
OF
Athlone Dublin
Liverpool
Holyhead
Limerick
IRELAND
Nottingham • 8-9
18-19
Norwich
Killarney
Waterford Rosslare
Birmingham
Cork
WALES
Oxford
Fishguard
London
CHANNEL
Cardiff
4-5
ISLANDS
2-3
Southampton
I. OF SCILLY
Plymouth
6-7
E N G L A N D

Legend

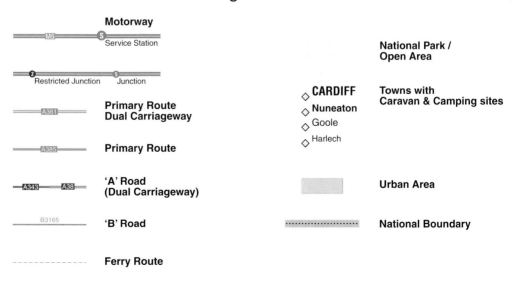

Motorway
Service Station

Restricted Junction   Junction

Primary Route
Dual Carriageway

Primary Route

'A' Road
(Dual Carriageway)

'B' Road

Ferry Route

◇ **CARDIFF**
◇ **Nuneaton**
◇ Goole
◇ Harlech

National Park /
Open Area

Towns with
Caravan & Camping sites

Urban Area

National Boundary

Ramsey Island

St. Bride's Bay

Skomer Island

Skokholm Island

St. Ann's Head

To Rosslare

A Milford Haven

Haverfordwest

Whitland

Carmarthen

Llan

Llan

Am

Narberth

Laugharne

Pembroke Dock

B Saundersfoot

Bur

Tenby

Carmarthen Bay

Burry Port

Kidwelly

C

S

Llanelli

M4

S

Pembroke

Manorbier

Caldey Island

SWANSEA

A4

Linney Head

St. Govan's Head

Rhossili

Worms Head

Penmaen

Langland Bay

Mur

Port Eynon

To Cork (summer only)

To Plymouth, Weymouth & Poole

St Anne

Alderney

Channel Islands

Lundy

Combe Martin

Ilfracombe

Lyn

Guernsey

L'Ancresse

Castel

St Martin

St Sampson

Herm

St Peter Port

Sark

Lee Bay

Woolacombe

Croyde

Saunton

Braunton

Barnsta

Barnstaple or Bideford Bay

Instow

Westward Ho

Bishop Tawton

Jersey

Hartland Point

Clovelly

Bideford

Umberleigh

St Ouen

St Lawrence

St Brelade's Bay

St Aubin's Bay

St Helier

St Clements

Gorey

Hartland

Parkham

Great Torrington

Torrington

Beaford

Bu

Eggesfo

Bude

Stratton

Holsworthy

Hatherleig

Crackington Haven

Okehampton

Isles of Scilly

Tresco

St. Martin's

Hugh Town

St. Mary's

St. Agnes

Boscastle

Tintagel

Port Isaac

Polzeath

Pendoggett

Padstow

Rock

Trevose Head

Constantine Bay

Wadebridge

Bodmin

Mawgan Porth

St Columb Major

Newquay

Liskeard

Hallworthy

Launceston

Lifton

Lydford

DARTMOOR

Two Bridges

BODMIN MOOR

Tavistock

Callington

Yelverton

Buckfa

South B

Torpoint

PLYMOUTH

Modbur

Kingston

Crantock

Rejerrah

Perranporth

St. Agnes

Porthtowan

Portreath

Goonhavern

Truro

Par

Lostwithiel

Pelynt

Fowey

Looe

Polperro

St. Austell

Mevagissey Bay

Mevagissey

Gorran

St. Ives

Carbis Bay

Hayle

Camborne

Redruth

Marazion

Portscatho

Veryan

Penzance

Sennen

Land's End

Porthleven

Marazion

Falmouth

Helston

St. Mawes

Falmouth Bay

St Keverne

Bigbury-on-sea

Thurleston

Hope Cov

Sa

B

Mount's Bay

Mullion

Kennack Sands

Lizard

To Isles of Scilly

Lizard Point

To Santander

To Roscoff

A

B

C

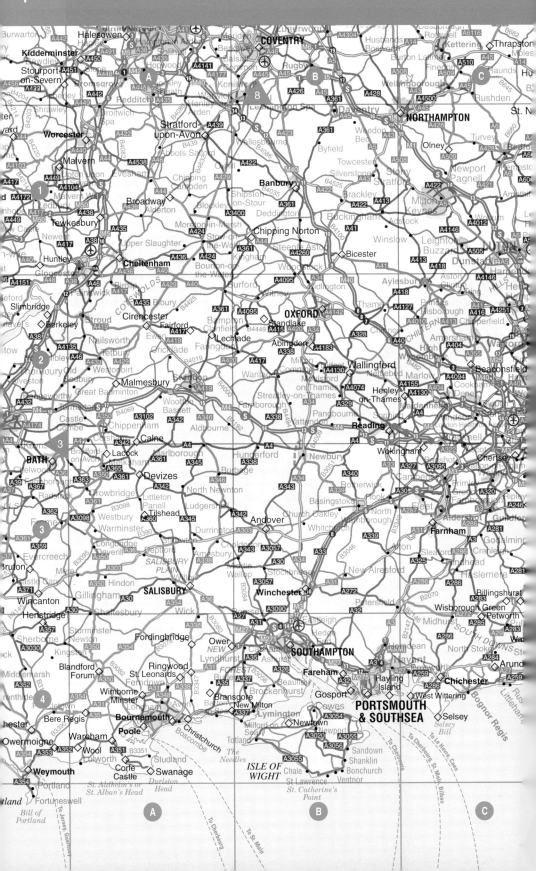

A   B   C

To Dublin
To Dun Laoghaire

0   10   20 Miles
0   10   20 Kilometres

1

Carmel Head
Cemaes
A5025
Amlwch
Lligwy Bay
Brynteg
Benllech Bay
Abergele
Great Ormes Head
Llandudno
Holyhead
Llanerchymedd
ANGLESEY
Deganwy
Colwyn Bay
Holy Island
Llanbedgoch
Pentraeth
Beaumaris
Penmaenmawr
Conwy
Abergele
Trearddur Bay
Llangefni
A545
Betws-yn-Rhos
Llanfairpwll
Menai Bridge
Bangor
A55
Llanfairfechan
A548
Bodorgan
A4080
Brynsiencyn
Bethesda
A544
Caernarfon
Llanberis
Llanrwst
A5
Capel Curig
A543
Caernarfon Bay
A4085
A4086
Rhyd-Ddu
Betws-y-coed
A498
Clynnog-Fawr
Beddgelert
Blaenau Ffestiniog
A5

2

Morfa Nefyn
A499
A487
A4085
A496
Ffestiniog
Criccieth
Porthmadog
A497
A4212
Bala
A497
Portmeirion
Talsarnau
Pwllheli
Tremadog Bay
Harlech
A470
Llanbedrog
Llanbedr
Ganllwyd
Aberdaron
Abersoch
A494
Bardsey Island
A496
Bontddu
Dolgellau
Dyffryn Ardudwy
Barmouth
A493
Tal-y-llyn
A487
Abergynolwyn
A489
Tywyn
A493
Machynlleth

3

Cardigan Bay
Aberdyfi
Borth
A487
Tal-y-bont
Llanidloes
Aberystwyth
A4159
Llandrind
A4120
Ponterwyd
A44
WALES
A44
Llanrhystud
A485
Pontrhydfendigaid
To Rosslare
Aberaeron
Cross Inn
Tregaron
Builth
New Quay
A482
Cemaes Head
Aberporth
B4333
Llanwrtyd Wells
Dinas Head
A486
Drefach
Lampeter
A482
Strumble Head
Cardigan
Newcastle Emlyn
A475
Llandysul
A483
Goodwick
A487
A484
Llansawel
Fishguard
Newport
Boncath
A485
Llandovery
MYNYDD PRESELI
A478
Mynachlogddu
Cynwyl Elfed
Llangadog
A40
4
St. David's
Whitland
A4069
Llandeilo
Ramsey Island
A487
Solva
A40
Carmarthen
A4067
St. Bride's Bay
Haverfordwest
Narberth
A48
A4068
Abercraf
Skomer Island
A4076
A4075
Laugharne
A4066
A474
A4221
Milford Haven
A477
A484
Kidwelly
A4109
A465
Skokholm Island
A4138
M4
A406
St. Ann's Head
Pembroke Dock
A4319
B4318
Tenby
2
Carmarthen Bay
Burry Port
Llanelli
A4127
A4063
C
To Rosslare
Manorbier
A
B
SWANSEA
Linney Head
Caldey Island
Rhossili
Penmaen
A4067
Port Talbot
A4064
St. Govan's Head
Worms Head
A4118
Port
Langland
Mumbles

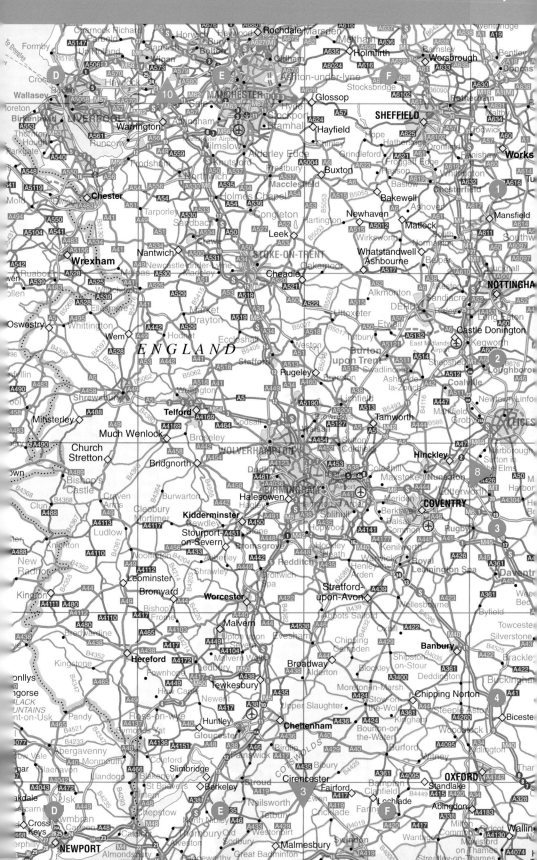

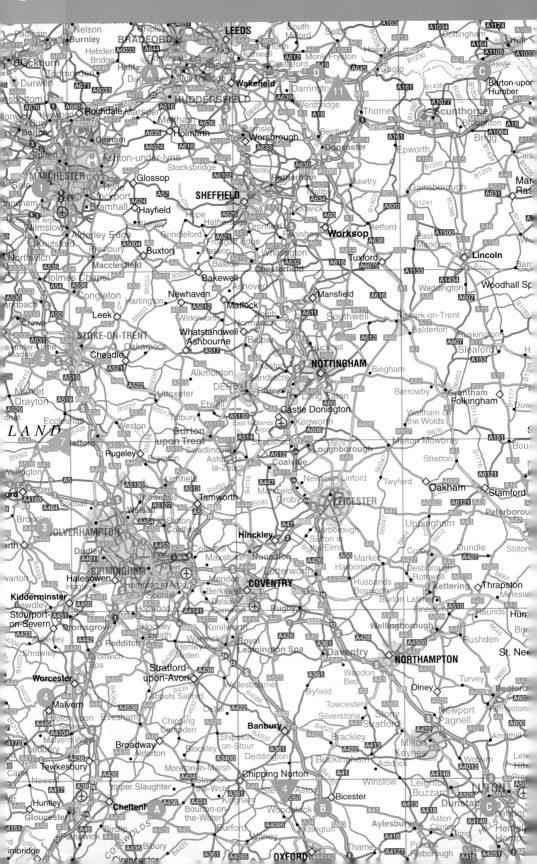

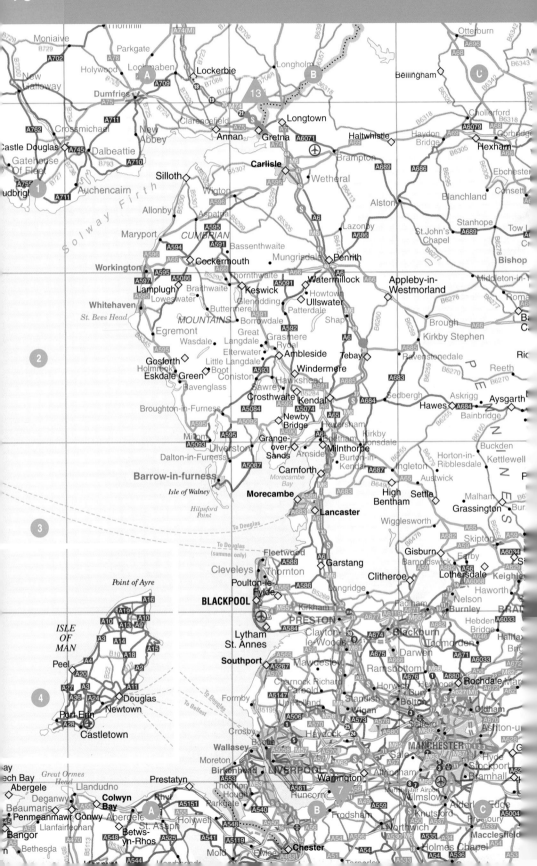

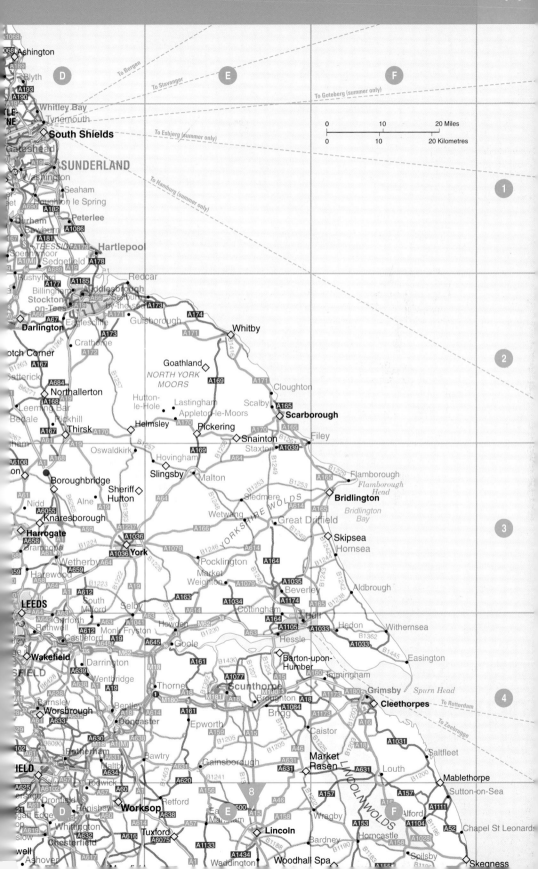

Fort William
Strontian
Onich
A861
A861
Ballachulish
Glencoe
Rannoch
Kinloch
Rannoch
Coll
Tobermory
Coll-Tobermory
Tiree
Tiree-Tobermory-Oban
A848
A884
Fortingall
A849
MULL
A827
Ulva
Oban
Connel
Clifton
Taynuilt
Tyndrum
St. Fillan
Iona
A849
Kilchrenan
A85
Crianlarich
Lochearnhead
Con
Colonsay-Oban
A816
A819
A84
Callar
Arduaine
Inveraray
Strachur
A82
Scarba
Colonsay
A816
Lochgilphead
A815
Luss
Aberfoyle
A821
A873
Stir
Oronsay
JURA
A886
A83
Rhu
Drymen
Dunb
Port Askaig
Kilfinan
B800
Helensburgh
Balloch
A811
A809
A875
Killearn
A891
Cumb
Colonsay-Port Askaig (summer only)
Port Askaig
Dunoon
A770
Dumbarton
Milngavie
ISLAY
A846
A847
A846
Tarbert
A886
Innellan
Ardbeg
Skelmorlie
Greenock
Langbank
Erskine
GLASG
Gigha
Rothesay
Howwood
Paisley
Bothwell
Mull of Oa
BUTE
A844
Largs
East Kilbride
A72
KINTYRE
Dalry
A735
Stewarton
Strathaven
Carradale
A841
Ardrossan
A719
Kilwinning
Rathlin
Island
Blackwaterfoot
Isle of
Arran
Holy Island
Irvine
Kilmarnock
Whiting Bay
Troon
A78
A76
Campbeltown
B842
Kilmory
Prestwick
A70
Cumnoc
Sanda
Ailsa Craig
Ayr
A719
New Cu
Mull of
Kintyre
Turnberry
Maybole
Dalmellington
Mon
Girvan
B741
allintrae
A2
Bushmills
Ballycastle
Ballantrae
A714
New
Galloway
Crossmichael
A762
Coleraine
B67
Cushendall
Garron Point
Milleur
Point
Bargrennan
A712
ghadowey
ANTRIM
A26
A43
Carnlough
A718
Newton
Stewart
Gatehouse
of Fleet
A54
A42
A2
Stranraer
A714
Wigtown
Ballymena
Larne
Magheramorne
Glenluce
Kirkcudbright
RN IRELAND
Ballyclare
Carrickfergus
Portpatrick
A77
Sandhead
A747
Wigtown
Bay
Antrim
M2
B90
Dunadry
Newtownabbey
Bangor
A716
Luce
Bay
Port
William
Lough
Neagh
Holywood
BELFAST
Crawfordsburn
Newtownards
Drummore
Burrow
Head
17
Lisb
Mull of Galloway
adown
Lurgan
Hillsborough
Dromore
Ballynahinch
Portaferry
ISLE OF
Point of Ayre

Shetland Islands

F

HERMA NESS

UNST

FETLAR

YELL

OUT SKERRIES

WHALSAY

MUCKLE ROE

PAPA STOURR

BRESSAY

MAINLAND

Brae

Lerwick

West & East Burra

Mousa

0   10 Miles
0   15 Kilometres

Sunburgh Head

To Torshavn, Seydisfjordur, Bergen (Summer only)

To Aberdeen

To Stromness

Atholl
Pitlochry
feldy
Blairgowrie
nkeld
Perth
Stanley
Auchtermuchty
Kinross
Rosyth
EDINBURGH
Laurencekirk
Edzell
St Cyrus
Montrose
Forfar
Colliston
Arbroath
Carnoustie
DUNDEE
Inchture
Newport-on-Tay
Tayport
Cupar
St. Andrews
Fife Ness
Falkland
Glenrothes
Leven
Crail
Anstruther
Earlsferry
Isle of May
Kirkcaldy
Kinghorn
Aberdour
North Berwick
Longniddry
Aberlady
Dunbar
Prestonpans
Musselburgh
Haddington
Dalkeith
Bonnyrigg
Humbie
Lauder
Peebles
Galashiels
Melrose
Selkirk
Kelso
St. Boswells
Berwick-upon-tweed
Holy Island
Cornhill-on-Tweed
Belford
Bamburgh
Seahouses
Beadnall
Farne Islands
Wooler
Jedburgh
Hawick
Ettrick
Huntford
Alnwick
Alnmouth
Warkworth
Amble
Moffat
Rothbury
Lockerbie
Alwinton
Morpeth
Ashington
Bellingham
Otterburn
Bedlington
Blyth
Annan
Longtown
Gretna
Haydon Bridge
Corbridge-on-Tyne
Hexham
NEWCASTLE-UPON-TYNE
Whitley Bay
Tynemouth
South Shields
Gateshead
SUNDERLAND
Carlisle
Brampton
Wetheral
Ebchester
Stanley
Washington
Seaham
Silloth
Wigton
Alston
Blanchland
Consett
Chester-le-Street
Houghton-le-Hole
Durham
Peterlee
Bassenthwaite
Penrith
Tow Law
Crook
Bowburn
Hartlepool
Mungrisdale
Thornthwaite
Watermillock
Middleton-in-Teesdale
Bishop Auckland
Witton-le-Wear
Shildon
Newton Aycliffe
Billingham
Sedgefield
Redcar
Braithwaite
Keswick
Appleby-in-Westmorland
Romaldkirk
Stockton-on-Tees
Middlesbrough
Buttermere
Glenridding
Patterdale
Shap
Barnard Castle
Darlington
Eaglescliffe
Guisbrough
Borrowdale
Grasmere
Brough
Kirkby Stephen
Richmond
Scotch Corner
Crathorne
Rydal
Ambleside
Ravenstonedale

CHEVIOT HILLS

UPLANDS

Tweedsmuir

Crawford

CUMBRIAN MOUNTAINS

15

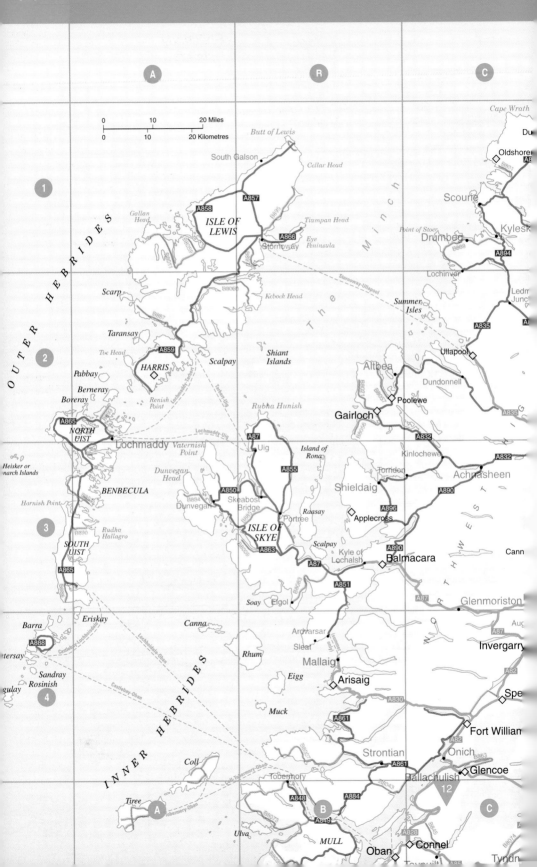

Cape Wrath

A

R

C

Butt of Lewis

0   10   20 Miles
0   10   20 Kilometres

South Galson

Cellar Head

Oldshore

1

A857

Scourie

A858

Point of Stoer

Drumbeg

Kylesk

ISLE OF
LEWIS

Tiumpan Head

A894

A866

Eye
Peninsula

Stornoway

Lochinver

Ledm
Junc

Gallan
Head

The

Minch

Scarp

Kebock Head

Stornoway-Ullapool

Summer
Isles

A835

Taransay

Toe Head

Scalpay

Shiant
Islands

Ullapool

HARRIS

Altbea

Dundonnell

A859

Pabbay

2

OUTER   HEBRIDES

Berneray

Renish
Point

Rubha Hunish

Poolewe

Boreray

A865

Lochmaddy-Uig

Gairloch

A832

NORTH
UIST

Uig

A87

Island of
Rona

Kinlochewe

A832

Lochmaddy

Vaternish
Point

A855

Torridon

Achnasheen

Heisker or
Monach Islands

Dunvegan
Head

A850

Skeabost
Bridge

Shieldaig

A890

BENBECULA

Dunvegan

Raasay

A896

Applecross

Portree

3

Hornish Point

ISLE OF
SKYE

A890

Cann

Rudha
Hallagro

Scalpay

SOUTH
UIST

A863

Kyle of
Lochalsh

Balmacara

A87

A865

A87

A851

Glenmoriston

Barra

Eriskay

Canna

Soay   Elgol

Ardvarsar

A888

Sleat

Aug

A87

Rhum

Invergarry

Sandray
Rosinish

Mallaig

A82

4

gulay

Eigg

Arisaig

Spe

INNER   HEBRIDES

Muck

A861

A830

Fort Willian

Coll

A82

Onich

Strontian

A861

Glencoe

Tobermory

Ballachulish

12

Tiree

A

B

C

A848

A884

Ulva

A849

Connel

MULL

A828

Oban

Tyndr

Orkney Islands

Mull Head
Papa Westray
North Ronaldsay
Start Point
WESTRAY
SANDAY
ROUSAY
EDAY
STRONSAY
Auskerry
MAINLAND
SHAPINSAY
Mull Head
Rorh Head
HOY
Flotta
Burray
SOUTH RONALDSAY
To Lerwick
To Aberdeen
Brough Ness

Strathy Point
Dunnet Head
Isle of Stroma
John o'groats
Duncansby Head
Mey
Dunnet
A9
Thurso
A836
Noss Head
Halkirk
A882
Wick
A897
Forsinard
A895
Altnaharra
Dunbeath
Lybster
Tongue
B871
Ord of Caithness
Helmsdale
A9

Dunnet Head
Island of Stroma
Duncansby Head

0 — 10 Miles
0 — 15 Kilometres

Lairg
A839
Rogart
Brora
Bonar Bridge
Golspie
A949
Dornoch
Tarbat Ness
Tain
A9
Alness
Moray Firth
Invergordon
Lossiemouth
Kinnairds Head
ngwall
A832
Forres
A941
Elgin
Buckie
Banff
Macduff
Fraserburgh
Fortrose
Nairn
Fochabers
A98
A981
A90
Rattray Head
Inverness
A940
A939
Keith
Turriff
A947
A950
Peterhead
A862
A95
A97
A952
Craigellachie
A920
A948
Huntly
A96
A947
A975
Grantown-on-Spey
A941
Elon
A920
Carrbridge
A938
Dulnain Bridge
Inverurie
A947
A90
Nethy Bridge
A97
Kildrummy
Aviemore
Boat of Garten
A944
A980
A944
ABERDEEN
Kingussie
MOUNTAINS
A939
A97
Kincardine O'Neil
Girdle Ness
A86
Aboyne
A889
Ballater
Banchory
A9
SCOTLAND
Braemar
A957
A93
Stonehaven
A92
Laurencekirk
Edzell
Blair Atholl
St Cyrus
A924
Kirkmichael
A937
Montrose
Pitlochry
A935
13
Bridge of Cally
A934
Aberfeldy
A926
Forfar
A932
A933
A92
Lunan Bay
Blairgowrie
Glamis
Colliston
A827
A923
A984
A928
Arbroath
A826
A93
A923
Carnoustie
Dunkeld
A94
A90
A930
DUNDEE
Inchture
Stanley

ATLANTIC

OCEAN

Tor

Bloody Foreland
Falcarragh
Bunbeg
Aran
Burtonpoint
Gweedore
DERRYVE
R257
R259
Dunglow
R254
R250
Rosbeg
Glenties
Ardara
R262
Rossan Point
R263
N56
Glencolumbkille
Killybegs
Donegal Bay
Ross
Ballyshannon
Bundoran
Erris
Head
Downpatrick
Head
N15
R250
R252
Rosses
Point
Ballycastle
R314
Eacky
N16
R280
R297
Strandhill
Sligo
Belmullet
R314
R315
N59
Ballysadare
Blac
Bangor
SLIEVE GAMPH. MTS.
SLIGO
Collooney
Drunk
Ballina
R287
R312
N58
R294
N17
Riverstown
Blacksod Bay
Lough
Conn
Charlestown
R294
Drumshar
Dugort
Keel
N57
Gorteen
N4
Boyle
Achill Head
Mallaranny
R310
MAYO
N5
Ballaghaderreen
N5
Frenchpark
N61
Ca
*Achill
Island*
Newport
Castlebar
Kiltimagh
ROSCOMMON
Rooskey
Shan
Clare
Clew Bay
Westport
N17
Castlerea
Elphin
Louisburgh
R335
Claremorris
R367
Tulsk
Strokes
Inishturk
N59
R327
Long
Irishbofin
Renvyle
*Lough
Mask*
Ballinrobe
Cashel
N60
N63
Leenaun
N84
Roscommon
Lough
Ree
Clifden
CONNEMARA
Cong
N83
R328
Tuam
N63
R362
O
Slyne Head
Recess
N59
Oughterard
R347
Roundstone
R340
*Lough
Corrib*
GALWAY
R335
18
Galway
Athenry
R360
Ballina
Gorumna Islands
R33
Salthill
Oranmore
R33
Galway Bay
Fanore
Kilreekill
Loughrea
R356
Aran
Kinvara
N66
IRELA

B L I C

WESTMEATH

Lough
Ree

D

R390

R446

N4

Castlepollard

Kells

Mullingar

N51

Slane

Delvin

Athboy

Navan

N153

Balbriggan

E

R156

N3

Dunshaughlin

F

N1

Skerries

◇Athlone

Clara

Kinnegad

Tyrrellspass

R402

Innfield

Maynooth

Leixlip

17

Malahide

Portmarnock

DUBLIN

Howth

To L
& H

F

O F F A L Y

N62

N351

Tullamore

R357

R420

Daingean

Edenderry

Straffan

Celbridge

DUBLIN

Dublin Bay

To H

A N D

R52

N80

Droichead Nua

KILDARE

Prosperous

Naas

Dun Laoghaire

1

Birr

R421

Mountmellick

Portarlington

Kildare

R445

Blessington

Enniskerry

Bray

N11

Greystones

Delgany

R501

L A O I S

R427

R430

N9

Dunlavin

Donard

WICKLOW

Roundwood

Glendalough

Wicklow

I R I S H

Roscrea

N7

Portlaoise

Athy

N81

Laragh

Rathdrum

Wicklow
Head

S E A

N62

Abbeyleix

R433

Baltinglass

WICKLOW MOUNTAINS

Aughrim

Redcross

lemore

R503

R502

N78

Carlow

Arklow

Thurles

N77

Castlecomer

Freshford

R693

Ballon

CARLOW

Carnew

Gorey

N8

Kilkenny

N9

Bennettsbridge

Bunclody

N11

Courtown

Killenaule

Callan

KILKENNY

R702

Ferns

N80

Cahore Point

Cashel

N76

R703

Thomastown

Graiguenamanagh

WEXFORD

Kilmuckridge

Fethard

R701

Enniscorthy

N79

Carrick-on-Suir

N24

Clonmel

New Ross

Wexford
Bay

Clogheen

Ballymacarbry

N25

Wexford

WATERFORD

Waterford

Rosslare

Cappoquin

Kilmacthomas

R675

Kilmore
Quay

Rosslare Harbour

3

To Fishguard

N72

Cappagh

Tramore

Carnsore
Point

Dungarvan

Hook
Head

N25

Ardmore

Youghal

Knockadoon
Head

St George's Channel

To Swansea

4

D

E

F